# Colonial Exploitation and Economic Development

Whereas the Indonesian economy progressed rapidly during the last three decades of the twentieth century and Indonesia became a self-reliant and assertive world power, the Congo regressed into a state of political chaos and endemic violence which continues until the present. To what extent do the different legacies of Dutch and Belgian colonial rule in Indonesia and the Congo explain these different development trajectories? The Netherlands Indies and the Belgian Congo rank among the most "exploited" cases of modern European imperialism. The atrocities committed under the forced cultivation system in Java and Leopold's wild rubber scheme in the Congo have become synonymous with unscrupulous European greed. Can two systems of extractive institutions produce a distinctively different long-term legacy?

This book discusses the comparative legacy of colonial rule in the Netherlands Indies and the Belgian Congo during the nineteenth and twentieth centuries from a wide range of social, political, economic, and institutional perspectives. The authors reveal notable contrasts in the development of the rural subsistence sector, the plantation economy (rubber), and the industrial sector. The book also discusses differences in labour relations, land tenure policies, and varying features of colonial state formation, such as the development of the fiscal system, the education system, and the direction of post-independence economic policies pursued under Suharto and Mobutu, two of the most callous dictators of the twentieth century.

The comparative approach contributes to a deeper understanding of the role of colonial institutional legacies in long-run patterns of economic divergence. It adds the thought-provoking cases of Dutch and Belgian rule to the existing literature comparing the evolution of the British, French, Spanish and Portuguese empires and complements the literature that seeks to understand the notable Africa–Asia divergence in the post-independence era.

**Ewout Frankema** is Full Professor and Chair of Rural and Environmental History at Wageningen University, the Netherlands.

**Frans Buelens** is a researcher at the Faculty of Applied Economics, University of Antwerp, Belgium.

## Routledge explorations in economic history
Edited by Lars Magnusson
*Uppsala University, Sweden*

# Colonial Exploitation and Economic Development

The Belgian Congo and the Netherlands Indies compared

**Edited by Ewout Frankema and Frans Buelens**

Routledge
Taylor & Francis Group

LONDON AND NEW YORK

First published 2013
by Routledge
2 Park Square, Milton Park, Abingdon, Oxfordshire OX14 4RN

Simultaneously published in the USA and Canada
by Routledge
711 Third Avenue, New York, NY 10017

First issued in paperback 2014

*Routledge is an imprint of the Taylor and Francis Group, an informa business*

*British Library Cataloguing in Publication Data*
A catalogue record for this book is available from the British Library

*Library of Congress Cataloging in Publication Data*
A catalog record has been requested for this book

ISBN 978-0-415-52174-1 (hbk)
ISBN 978-1-138-90229-9 (pbk)
ISBN 978-0-203-55940-6 (ebk)

Typeset in Times New Roman
by Wearset Ltd, Boldon, Tyne and Wear

# Contents

## 10 Manufacturing and foreign investment in colonial Indonesia 211

J. THOMAS LINDBLAD

## 11 The industrialization of the Belgian Congo 229

FRANS BUELENS AND DANNY CASSIMON

## 12 Mobutu, Suharto, and the challenges of nation-building and economic development, 1965–97 251

JAN-FREDERIK ABBELOOS

## Conclusion 274

EWOUT FRANKEMA AND FRANS BUELENS

# Figures

# Tables

# Contributors

**Jan-Frederik Abbeloos**, Ghent University

**Anne Booth**, SOAS, University of London

**Frans Buelens**, University of Antwerp

**Danny Cassimon**, University of Antwerp

**William G. Clarence-Smith**, SOAS, University of London

**Piet Clement**, PhD in history, freelance researcher

**Andreas Exenberger**, University of Innsbruck

**Ewout Frankema**, Wageningen University and Utrecht University

**Leigh Gardner**, London School of Economics

**Simon Hartmann**, Austrian Research Foundation for International Development, Vienna

**Vincent Houben**, Humboldt University of Berlin

**Thee Kian Wie**, Indonesian Institute of Sciences (P2E-LIPI), Jakarta

**J. Thomas Lindblad**, Leiden University

**Julia Seibert**, American University, Cairo

**Abdul Wahid**, Utrecht University

# Preface

The conception of this book can be traced back to the late afternoon of Monday August 3, 2009. In a session on African business history at the World Economic History Congress 2009 in Utrecht, Frans Buelens presented a paper on the equity development of Union Minière, Belgium's largest mining company active in the Belgian Congo from 1906. Ewout Frankema was in the audience. In the aftermath of that session we engaged in a lively discussion about why the Dutch and the Belgians know so little about each other's colonial history. Apparently, states and nations, like people, have their own ways of digesting the past and are typically not keen to share the most shameful aspects with outsiders. In fact, until today even a frank national debate about the colonial legacy has been continuously frustrated by politicians and lobby groups in the Netherlands and Belgium. However, when nations cannot come to terms with the black pages of their history, they will find it impossible to take genuine responsibility for the consequences of their deeds.

That afternoon we decided to try to organize a meeting where some leading Belgian and Dutch scholars could exchange their views on colonial exploitation and also explicitly address the question of how this legacy may have affected the long-term development of the subject peoples in the Congo and Indonesia. The project grew bigger than we originally envisaged when we obtained a grant from the Vlaams–Nederlandse Comité voor Nederlandse Taal en Cultuur, enabling us to organize two workshops, one in Utrecht (December 2010) and one in Antwerp (October 2011), and to invite a number of international scholars to join the exchange. The proceedings of these workshops have eventually resulted in this book.

We are grateful for the generous support of the Dutch and Flemish Science foundations. We also thank the N.W. Posthumus Institute (the research school for economic and social history in the Netherlands and Flanders) for financial support. We thank Utrecht University and the University of Antwerp for hosting our workshops. We are grateful to Simon Holt and Emily Kindleysides of Routledge for guiding us smoothly through the logistical details of the publication process. A final word of thanks goes to our former colleague Daan Marks, who was a co-initiator of this project until he took up his current job at the Ministry of Foreign Affairs.

Things are changing. In the spring of 2010 David van Reybrouck's *Congo. Een geschiedenis* (De Bezige Bij) started to conquer the Belgian and Dutch market. This book about Belgium's colonial past won two major literary prizes in the Netherlands, the AKO-Literatuurprijs and the Libris Geschiedenis Prijs, testifying to a huge hidden interest in the topic. It is our hope that our book can further contribute to the struggle against the great amnesia.

# Introduction

*Ewout Frankema and Frans Buelens*

## 0.1 Colonial exploitation and economic development

During the first half of the twentieth century approximately one-third of the total world population lived under some form of European colonial rule. Since many of what are now the poorest countries in the world were part of European empires in the not so distant past, there is a strong belief that colonial policies and institutions have shaped the long-run development of their economies for the worse. Ample historical literature has shown that particular practices of colonial exploitation have caused widespread impoverishment, not only because colonial powers prioritized their own economic, political, and military interests at the expense of the majority of subject peoples, but also because they bequeathed to their overseas possessions distorted institutions which have undermined political stability and the growth of prosperity in the post-colonial era (Mamdani 1996; Rodney 1972).

Scholars who stress the "developmental" features of colonialism tend to argue that the tightening of global connections within the imperial framework has facilitated the transfer of capital, technology, knowledge, and ideas, and that these transfers have enhanced the productive capacity of former colonial economies. The diffusion of capitalist modes of production has enhanced market exchange, structural change and labor productivity growth. Corresponding investments in "modern" systems of education, health care, transport and communications, whether by private (missionary) or government initiative, have improved living standards in former European colonies by measurable degrees (Ferguson 2002; Warren 1980). This position is also supported by studies arguing that colonies held for a longer period of time, or those which were governed in a direct manner, performed significantly better after independence than regions where the colonial connection remained rather superficial (Grier 1999; Lange 2009).

The stifling ideological blanket that has covered the colonial legacy debate for so long has gradually been pulled away, especially since the end of the Cold War. However, scholarly opinions on the root causes of poverty in former colonies have hardly converged.[1] Contrasting performance characteristics between the so-called neo-European settler economies and an undifferentiated "rest" have been neatly cast in global comparative and quantitative studies, but whether these should be ascribed to differences in colonial institutions or differences in local (pre-colonial) geographical and institutional characteristics is hotly debated (Acemoglu *et al.* 2002; Diamond 1997; Gallup *et al.* 1999; Putterman and Weil 2010). What makes this research question so challenging is that among the undifferentiated "rest" the colonial experiences have varied so widely that varying "truths" at the disaggregated level can easily be taken to support any particular perspective.

When defining "colonial extraction" exclusively in terms of outcome, namely as *a net transfer of economically valuable resources from indigenous to metropolitan societies*, and "colonial exploitation" as *the practices and procedures facilitating the extraction of resources without adequate compensation to indigenous peoples and their natural environment*, it is easy to see that there is a wide range of transmission channels with varying effects on local socio-economic and political structures: land alienation, labor corvée, forced cultivation, trade monopolies, excessive taxation (of various kinds), forced army service, and so on and so forth. Indeed, the varieties of exploitation in colonial settings contain answers to many of the unresolved questions of long-term development, but to arrive at them we need to disentangle the historical practices and institutions of colonial extraction by digging deeper into the myriad relationships between colonial extraction and long-term development. This book offers such an in-depth analysis of the comparative cases of the Belgian Congo and the Netherlands Indies, two of the most exploited colonies in world history. The point of departure of this book is a shared belief among the authors that colonial legacies have been shaped by the specific interaction between metropolitan policy principles, local policy practices and indigenous institutional responses. How did these interactions evolve? What specific sets of conditions did these interactions create? Does this help to understand better the phenomenon of post-colonial economic divergence?

Exploring the links between colonial extraction and long-term economic development poses at least three major challenges to historical research. First, virtually every aspect of extraction involves combined elements of coercion, destruction, and production: exploitation presupposes productive investments, and the creation of economic growth is not necessarily impeded by the creation of economic rent. As studies of colonial taxation and state formation show, it is not clear whether high tax rates, on balance, create positive or negative conditions for future economic development, but a weak fiscal system almost certainly inhibits long-term economic progress (Frankema 2010, 2011). However, the balance between creation and destruction has varied enormously both across and within colonial realms. Second, the institutions imposed by colonial administrations, whether directly or indirectly via co-opted local representatives, have been subject to *change* – change as a result of colonial policy reforms as well as changing responses by different groups in indigenous societies. This is the main reason why casting "extractive colonial institutions" into a time-invariant indicator of "risk of expropriation" in standard cross-space regression analyses is extremely problematic. Third, short-term economic consequences of colonial extraction may differ substantially from long-term consequences, but the latter are notoriously hard to isolate as the number of "control variables" grows as time goes on.

The added value of a comparative historical approach, as developed in this book, lies in its genuine attempt to combine two key aspects: a *systematic analysis* of practices and institutions of colonial extraction, enforced by the adoption of a comparative perspective, intertwined with a *dynamic view* of the evolution of extractive institutions, local responses, and long-term developmental consequences, a view in which the notion of *historical change* is at the heart of the explanatory framework.

## 0.2 Comparing the Belgian Congo and the Netherlands Indies

The colonial history of Belgium and the Netherlands in the modern era (since *c.*1820) differs from the colonial history of France, England and early-modern Spain and Portugal in at least two fundamental respects. First, the Dutch and Belgians both had access to one "big" colony, while the other European powers were in charge of multi-polarized empires, with a number of territories scattered across various continents. Second, there exists absolutely no doubt that the colonial profits the Dutch and the Belgians managed to extract from their overseas territories outweighed the profits from alternative investment opportunities during considerable periods of time (Booth 1998; Buelens 2007). Indeed, the Belgian Congo and the Netherlands Indies rank among the most effectively exploited colonies of the modern era.[2] Yet the British academic debate about the costs and benefits of empire is still largely unsettled (Davis and Huttenback 1988; Gann and Duignan 1967; O'Brien 1988; Offer 1993). In French historiography this discussion has recently flared up again, but still leans to the view that empire was a burden rather than a boon (Huillery 2010; Lefeuvre 2006; Marseille 1984).

Part of the intrinsic similarities between Dutch and Belgian practices of colonial extraction flowed from a direct historical connection: the Belgian King Leopold II (1835–1909) admired the Dutch for the effective organization of forced tropical cultivation programs in Indonesia (*Cultuurstelsel, c.1830–70*). Leopold's desire to replicate the Cultivation System underpinned his relentless attempts to obtain a personal fiefdom in the tropics (Stengers 1977). The Congo project, as it unfolded after the major powers had agreed on the general framework of a free trade zone at the Berlin conference (1884–5), fitted seamlessly into Leopold's vision of Belgium as a modern, industrial, and self-conscious nation-state (Pakenham 1992). Large parts of the money earned from rubber in the Congo Free State (CFS) were turned into prestigious construction projects at home. These projects gave Leopold the nickname of the Builder King (*le Roi-Bâtisseur*). Leopold shared this outspoken entrepreneurial attitude with his Dutch predecessor, King William I (1772–1843), the Trader King (*Koning-Koopman*), who founded the Dutch Trading Company (Nederlandsche

Handel-Maatschappij, NHM) which was responsible for the transport of East Indian commodities to, and sale in, Europe.

The potential for colonial extraction in the Congo revealed striking similarities with Indonesia. Figures 0.1–0.3 show that both countries are located in the heart of the tropics. The sheer size of the land, the distances, the climate, and the ecological diversity were simply incomparable to the relative compactness of the two neighboring river delta countries in Northwestern Europe. Their soils offered excellent conditions for the cultivation of rubber, cotton, palm oil, tea, coffee, sugar, and cocoa, none of which would grow in Belgium or the Netherlands. Both countries possess vast mineral wealth, such as copper, tin, petroleum, and a dozen other valuable mineral ores in the Congo. The emerging mining economy in the Congo raised demands for infrastructure, transport equipment, food supplies, and utilities, thus creating favorable conditions for the development of an industrial complex, one that in terms of size and diversity was unique in colonial Africa. In Indonesia lucrative mining activities in oil and tin were started under Dutch rule as well.

At its high tide in the 1850s the net profits of the forced cultivation of tropical commodities in the Indies such as sugar, tea, indigo, and especially coffee contributed up to 52 percent of Dutch central state tax revenue and constituted almost 4 percent of total Dutch GDP (van Zanden and van Riel 2000: 223). The forced cultivation programs, which were initially introduced in Java but later extended to other islands as well, were targeted to create a net surplus (*batig slot*) on the Indonesian balance of payments, a surplus which was directly remitted to the Dutch treasury. The Dutch used these profits to service their extraordinarily high state

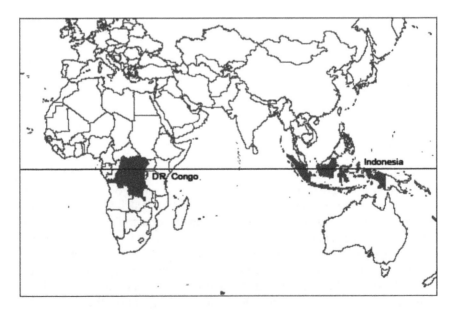

*Figure 0.1* The equatorial location of the Congo (DRC) and Indonesia.

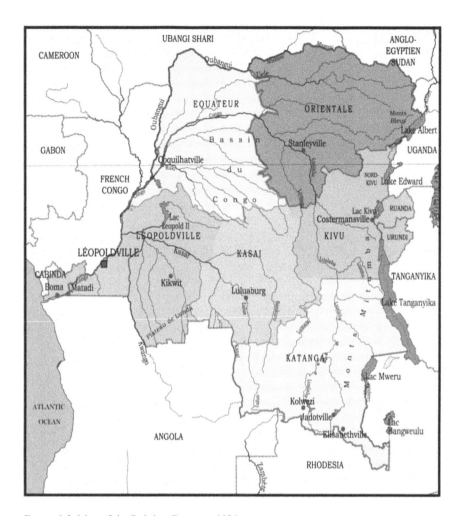

*Figure 0.2* Map of the Belgian Congo, *c.*1920.

debt, to reduce the tax burden on Dutch citizens, to finance domestic infrastructural investment programs, and to subsidize the exploitation of Dutch colonies in the West Indies. Indeed, the net flows from Indonesia during the 1830s to 1870s helped the Dutch economy to overcome a long period of stagnation and to embark on a path of modern economic growth from the 1860s onwards.

In Belgium the profits made in the Congo were mediated in a different way, but the gains were not less substantial. Belgian companies such as the Abir (1892), the Société Anversoise de Commerce au Congo (1892), or the Compagnie du Kasai (1901) were granted exclusive concessions by King Leopold II to exploit the rubber, copal, and ivory potential of the Congo area. These companies were given a virtually free hand to coerce local labor in order to enforce

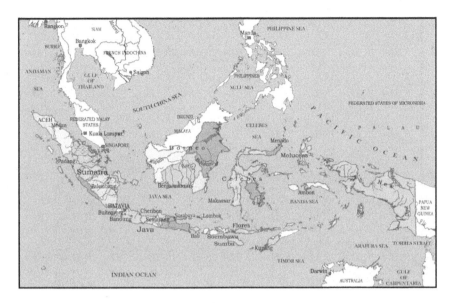

*Figure 0.3* Map of the Netherlands Indies, *c.*1920.

extraction. As the world demand for rubber boomed in the 1890s the vast economic potential of the Congo basin was put on the map once and for all. In 1897 King Leopold II was able to finance a huge building program for the world exhibition in Brussels based on the proceeds from Congolese rubber. The splendor of the Avenue de Tervueren and the Royal Museum of Central Africa bear silent testimony to the new wealth that was pouring into Belgium. Yet the glory days of resource extraction still lay ahead: during 1920–55 the rate of return on colonial company shares rose to an incredible annual average of 7.2 percent, 2.5 times more than the return paid on Belgian stocks (2.8 percent) (Buelens and Marysse 2009).

Contrary to the direct remittances from the Indies to the Netherlands, the government accounts of the Congo and Belgium remained strictly separate, as the Belgian government took care to protect the interests of Belgian taxpayers against reckless royal colonial adventures. But even though direct transfers from and to the Belgian treasury remained negligible during the entire period of colonial rule, there is no doubt that the Belgian treasury benefited indirectly. The mushrooming colonial companies were paying taxes in Belgium. Belgian manufacturing industries received cheap access to raw materials from the Congo such as rubber, cotton, copper, tin, and gold. The Congo connection also gave an enormous impulse to transport movements and jobs in Antwerp harbor, and investments in the extractive activities of colonial companies in the Congo acted as a magnet for rapid accumulation of Belgian industrial savings capital.

The Dutch cultivation system and Leopold's red rubber campaign became symbols of excessively immoral practices of colonial extraction, both in their own time and in later academic studies and public literature. Multatuli's *Max Havelaar* ([1860], 2010), discussing the practices of forced coffee cultivation in the Netherlands Indies, was one of the first public indictments of the cultivation system and has gradually acquired the status of being one of the most important works in Dutch literature. The invention of the term Ethical Policy (*Ethische Politiek*) for the policy reform program introduced in 1901 by Queen Wilhelmina was an explicit recognition of the atrocities committed by the Dutch colonial regime in the past.

The media campaign against Leopold's rule in the Congo, started by the British journalist Edmund Morel and the British consul in Boma (the capital city until 1926, lower Congo) Roger Casement, raised the international pressure on Belgium to intervene in what was formally a private undertaking. Joseph Conrad's novel *Heart of Darkness* (1899), which was partly based on his voyage as a vice-commander on a Congo river steamer in 1890, offered a symbolic critique of the dark side of European colonization (Hawkins 1981–2). In 1905 Mark Twain's satiric pamphlet *King Leopold's Soliloquy* offered a devastating personal critique on Leopold that spread all over the world. In 1908 the Belgian government could no longer neglect the damage to its reputation and decided to take over the colonial administration and put a direct end to the terror campaigns of the rubber companies. A century later the alleged lack of responsibility demonstrated by the Belgian state is still a thorny issue and the related debate about the size and causes of the Congolese population collapse between 1890 and 1920 is far from settled (Hochschild 1999; van Reybrouck 2010; Vansina 2010).[3]

## 0.3 Post-colonial economic divergence

It is impossible to deny the divergence in economic performance between the two former colonies after 1970. As illustrated in Figure 0.4, per capita GDP in what had become Zaïre was still some 20 percent higher than in Indonesia in the late 1960s. By 2009, per capita GDP in what had become the Democratic Republic of the Congo (DRC) had collapsed to only 22 percent of its 1970 level. Indonesia had forged ahead, to the point where per capita GDP in 2009 was well over six times its 1960 figure, and 17 times larger than in the DRC. It is probably true that the post-1980 data exaggerate the extent of the economic decline in the DRC because of the huge growth in the unrecorded economy. But a divergence of the magnitude shown in Figure 0.4 cannot be explained away simply in terms of statistical discrepancies.[4] Clearly economic performance has been superior in Indonesia than in the DRC since the 1970s. What explains the divergence? Did varieties of exploitation in colonial settings play a role?

To some degree these divergent economic development trajectories reflect a wider Africa–Asia disjuncture in post-independent performance. Many African economies collapsed in the period 1973–95. The case of the Congo is quite special, however, because it has shown so little signs of progress even since

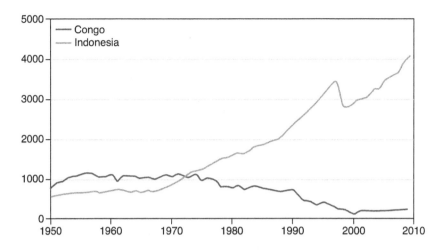

*Figure 0.4* GDP per capita of Indonesia and the Congo (DRC), 1950–2010 (source: GDP per capita series taken from the Penn World Tables, version 7.0, see Heston *et al.* (May 2011); for Indonesia the 1950–9 years were extrapolated using Maddison (2010)).

1995. The Congo was among the richer countries, such as Ghana, in the 1960s, but the twin collapse of the state and the economy puts it more on a level with Somalia or Sudan than with any of the rapidly growing West African countries of today.

Indonesia's post-colonial economic performance may be described as "fair." Its post-colonial economic development was less impressive than that of neighboring Malaysia or Thailand, let alone Taiwan or South Korea. On the other hand, it escaped this long-term stagnation of countries such as Burma, Cambodia, or Bangladesh. The Indonesian economy stagnated during the Sukarno years (1945–67), but never reached a situation of complete institutional breakdown as witnessed in the Congo. After the mid-1960s, and supported by the windfall gains of the oil crises in the early 1970s, the Indonesian economy under Suharto entered a period of sustained growth combined with deep structural transformation. Interestingly, the three decades of the Suharto regime (1967–98) ran virtually parallel in time to the Mobutu regime (1965–97) in the Congo. Mobutu and Suharto are often mentioned in one breath as examples of dictatorial brutality and perverse self-enrichment, but a comparison of economic policies under both rulers reveals enormous contrasts in effectiveness.

## 0.4   Differences in the evolution of colonial connections

Apart from a number of striking similarities in the nature of colonial extraction, there were of course also various critical differences in the way the colonial connection developed. We will briefly highlight two of these differences, because they turn up in almost every chapter of the book. The first factor concerns the different length of colonial rule and the timing of colonial administrative expansion. The second factor concerns the very different demographic response to the intensification of the colonial connection.

Although one can recognize similar evolutionary stages in many colonial connections, especially a reconfiguration of a rather one-sided model of metropolitan profit maximization through colonial labor and resource extraction toward a more development-oriented approach, these transitions occurred in a markedly briefer period of time in the Congo than in Indonesia. This had perhaps less to do with the fact that the Dutch East India Company (Vereenigde Oost Indische Compagnie, VOC) had already established a stronghold at Java in the early seventeenth century (Batavia was founded in 1619) than one may think. After all, Portuguese explorers, traders, and missionaries had penetrated the Congo area already in the late fifteenth century. The difference is rather that Dutch attempts to extend their control over the entire archipelago and the different strata of indigenous societies started much earlier. After the brief British interlude (1811–16) during the French occupation of the Netherlands, the Dutch acted decidedly for the establishment of full-scale political hegemony. They allocated significant amounts of resources to military campaigns, starting with the Java war (1825–30) and ending with the extremely brutal Aceh war (1873–1913). The pacification wars were followed by the consolidation of colonial rule. The number of recorded Europeans in the Netherlands Indies rose from 8935 in 1820 to 27,499 in 1870 and 62,477 in 1900 (Boomgaard and van Zanden 1990: 124. 133).

A comparable expansion of the physical presence of Belgians in the Congo occurred almost a full century later, after World War I, when the number of Belgians rose from c.3000 to 90,000 in 1960, the eve of Congolese independence. Hence, whereas the Dutch introduced the Ethical Policy in 1901 as a departure from the central nineteenth-century ideology that *the colony is there to serve the mother country*, the Governor-General of the Congo Pierre Ryckmans (1934–46) defended a similar change in conception of the grand purpose of the colonial connection in a manifesto entitled *Dominer pour servir* in 1931. As will be argued throughout this book, the difference in the timing and length of the colonial state formation process impacted upon the design and functionality of vital public institutions and investments concerning, for instance, the education system, the fiscal system, the transportation system, rural development programs, and the banking sector. In view of the distinct timing and pace of colonial institutional development, it is also easier to understand that the nature and timing of indigenous responses to colonial rule and institutional reforms differed. The emancipation process, and especially the political organization of independence movements, gained momentum at a later stage in the Congo (basically the late 1950s) and was, on the whole, far less intensive than it was during the interwar years in Indonesia. Whereas World War II and the Japanese occupation acted as a catalyst toward full independence in Indonesia (Ricklefs 2008), the whole idea of Congolese independence was still deemed irrelevant in the 1940s. For sure, the war invoked significant colonial reforms in the Congo, but these were all pursued in a widely shared belief that the Belgian presence in the area would last for centuries to come (Neudt 2002; van Bilsen 1993).

Perhaps the most distinctive feature of the colonial connection in both countries is the impressive rate of population growth in Indonesia since, at least, the start of the nineteenth century and the equally impressive collapse of the Congolese population shortly after the erection of the Congo Free State. According to recent guesstimates of the decline of the Kuba population in the Congo, it is possible that the collapse was about 30 percent between 1890 and 1920 (Vansina 2010: 127–49; Huybrechts 2010: 25). When we take ten million as a proxy for the total Congolese population in 1920, based on extrapolating from post-1950 estimates, it may have been around 15 million before the onset of colonial rule. The causes of the population collapse are heavily debated (Gewalt 2006; Hochschild 1999), but Vansina attributes the largest share to the disastrous effects of European diseases (smallpox), outbursts of tropical epidemics (sleeping sickness, dysentery), and the spread of venereal diseases such as syphilis and gonorrhea, which negatively affect female fertility. The population decline was further compounded by the sharp increase in emigration of various peoples out of the Congo territory, as well as the effects of the Arab war (1892–4, c.70,000 deaths) in the eastern part of the Congo, succeeded by an ethnic cleansing of "Arab elements" (Marechal 1992).

In contrast, the Indonesian population increased fivefold between 1820 and 1940, with annual average growth rates hovering around 1 percent during the nineteenth century (Maddison 2010). Part of this growth can be attributed to the early introduction of malaria eradication programs and inoculation campaigns against smallpox, which may have been responsible for a significant decrease in infant mortality rates (Marks and van Zanden 2012: 113–14). The attention paid to the establishment of a rudimentary health care system in Indonesia was a direct consequence of the deliberate intentions of the Dutch to consolidate their power and tackle the problem of labor shortages in order to raise the profitability of the colony. Table 0.1 shows how these different demographic developments, while using a very rough proxy for the Congo in 1890, impacted on comparative population densities in the Congo, Indonesia, and Java.

These densities have shaped colonial and pre-colonial institutions in ways that are, to some extent, illustrative of a wider Africa–Asia distinction. With a few exceptions, Asian societies have sustained greater populations per unit of cultivable land than African societies throughout most of human history. Herbst (2000) made a compelling argument that European conceptions of state boundaries and private land property were alien to virtually all pre-colonial African societies because of exceptionally high land–labor ratios. This was no less true for the Congo when Leopold II launched his land alienation program, stipulating that all "unoccupied" land would fall to the Congo Free State.

The different densities of population in Indonesia, and its particular concentration on the smaller island of Java, posed different challenges to the colonial authorities. Java contained more than 60 percent of the total population in the

*Table 0.1* Estimated and guesstimated population densities in the Congo, Indonesia and Java, 1890, 1920, and 1950

|  | Congo | | Indonesia | | Java | |
|---|---|---|---|---|---|---|
|  | Population (millions) | Density (no./km²) | Population (millions) | Density (no./km²) | Population (millions) | Density (no./km²) |
| 1890 | 14.0 | 6.0 | 40.5 | 21.1 | 23.90 | 171.9 |
| 1920 | 10.0 | 4.3 | 54.9 | 28.6 | 34.80 | 250.4 |
| 1950 | 13.5 | 5.8 | 82.6 | 43.0 | 49.56 | 356.5 |

Source: The population figures for the Congo in 1890 and 1920 are guesstimates based on (Vansina 2010: 144–9); Indonesian population (Maddison 2010); Javanese population (Boomgaard and van Zanden 1990).

Note
Land surface for the Congo has been estimated at 2,345,000 square kilometers, for Indonesia at 1,919,000 square kilometers and for Java 139,000 square kilometers.

archipelago and this was one of the reasons why it became the center of the Dutch colonial state. The Congo lacked a densely populated center. Of course, all the trade flows from the hinterland converged in the Congo delta, the confined coastal strip around Boma. However, after the discovery of the Katangese copper treasure, the centers of colonial economic and political activity could hardly have been farther apart.

Despite the fact that the cultivation system on Java was partly introduced as a solution to a labor shortage problem (especially a shortage of sedentary peasants), the labor problem in the Congo was clearly of a different order of magnitude and, more importantly, did not decline over time. To push the distinction further, while Java was one of the most densely populated areas in the Netherlands Indies, Katanga was one of the most underpopulated areas in the Congo. Hence, whereas the Dutch at some point in the late nineteenth century start worrying about dangerous levels of population pressure on Java and develop plans to support migration to the Outer Islands (and the West Indies), the Belgians, throughout the entire period of colonial rule, struggled with the problem of how to recruit sufficient skilled and unskilled laborers from extremely scarce supplies and how to make them settle on a permanent basis in places where they were so badly needed (mines and plantations). When Belgium acquired control of the far more densely populated highland areas of Ruanda–Urundi after World War I, Union Minière, the major Belgian mining company, almost immediately started to recruit new laborers there and after World War II it even started a permanent air connection to "transplant" laborers to the Katanga mines (Brion and Moreau 2006: 118).

In sum, the histories of colonial exploitation in the Belgian Congo and the Netherlands Indies provide a striking combination of similarities in terms of extractive *potential*, but there also were tangible differences in the way extractive policies were designed, reformed, and eventually abolished. The authors of this book all focus on the question of the comparative colonial legacy through this particular lens. We believe that colonial legacies have been shaped by the specific interaction between metropolitan policy principles, local policy practices, and indigenous institutional responses. How did these interactions evolve? What specific sets of conditions did these interactions create? Does this help us to understand the post-colonial economic divergence between the Congo and Indonesia?

## 0.5 Organization

This book contains twelve chapters. The first three chapters offer a broad comparative overview of the history of colonial exploitation in the Congo and Indonesia. Chapter 1 by Andreas Exenberger and Simon Hartmann discusses the long-term development of extractive institutions in the Congo basin, during the pre-colonial, colonial, and post-colonial eras. This chapter focuses on the path-dependent nature of political and economic developments and their impact on (effective) checks and balances, arguing that multiple phases of severe deterioration of checks and balances on political and economic power created conditions for economic extraction and authoritarian rule in the post-independence era.

Chapter 2 by Thee Kian Wie offers an historical overview of the changing nature, organization, and scale of colonial exploitation over the course of approximately three and a half centuries of Dutch presence in the Indonesian archipelago (c. 1600–1950). Thee's main argument is that the increasing Dutch interference in the structure of the indigenous economy from the early nineteenth century critically shaped the different way in which extractive institutions were implemented, reformed, and eventually abandoned in the Netherlands Indies, in contrast to the different timing (later and shorter) of Belgian rule in the Congo.

In Chapter 3 Anne Booth ties both long-term perspectives together in a comparison of the two systems of colonial exploitation. This chapter examines the extent to which the legacies of Dutch and Belgian colonialism can help to explain the post-independence divergence of the two economies and discusses the extent to which economic policies in the two colonies were exploitative rather than developmental. Booth's key point is that, in contrast to Belgian colonial policies, the Dutch policies implemented after 1900 did leave a positive legacy which the Suharto government built on, especially in the agricultural sector, and that this difference can explain part of the post-colonial divergence in economic development.

The following chapters focus on more specific aspects of the colonial state and the colonial economy. Chapter 4 by Piet Clement discusses the land tenure system in the Belgian Congo. Clement argues that because of the Congo's initial free trade status, the colonizer had a strong incentive to expropriate indigenous land as a source of wealth extraction. This system of land tenure and legislation directly affected rural development as it formed the basis both for the creation of a "modern" agricultural sector (plantations) and for the belated attempt to revolutionize subsistence farming through the unsuccessful *indigenous peasantry* scheme. Key characteristics of the colonial land tenure system have survived in the post-colonial period and continue to shape rural development in today's Congo.

Chapters 5 and 6 explore the development of the colonial fiscal system in, respectively, the Netherlands Indies and the Belgian Congo (including the CFS). In Chapter 5 Abdul Wahid analyses the reintroduction, expansion, and demise of the colonial tax farm system in Java and Madura during the nineteenth century. He shows how the Dutch managed to diversify their revenue basis at the expense of the Javanese and discusses the long-term implications of colonial fiscal policy. Tax farming had existed in Java since the pre-colonial era, but the Dutch extended and institutionalized this practice during the nineteenth century to finance its territorial expansion and accommodate problems in the administration and collection of colonial taxes. Wahid argues that the use of Chinese middlemen to run this institution had serious short- and long-term consequences, which were partly beneficial and partly harmful to the cohesiveness of the colonial and post-colonial state. In Chapter 6 Leigh Gardner places the fiscal system of the Belgian Congo in a British African perspective and shows that the early process of colonial state formation during the CFS era was an anomaly, and that the reforms after 1908 brought the Belgian colony more into line with fiscal practices elsewhere in Africa. Gardner's comparative analysis suggests that the Belgian Congo was not only behind the Netherlands Indies in terms of state-building, as argued elsewhere in the book, but also struggled to keep up with other African countries.

The previous two chapters are intimately related to Ewout Frankema's Chapter 7, in which he compares the differential development of the state-based education system in the Netherlands Indies with the mission-based system in Belgian Congo. This chapter addresses the question of how these different approaches to indigenous education have shaped the conditions for post-colonial governance. Frankema argues that the opportunities, albeit limited, for Indonesian children to attain primary, secondary, and tertiary education featuring a full Western curriculum played an important role in the development of national leadership during the decolonization of Indonesia, whereas the racial segregation in the administration of the state and major companies prevented the development of a similar class of educated and experienced leaders in the Belgian Congo. This condition shaped part of the broader socio-political context in which the state and economy of the Congo (Zaïre) imploded during the post-colonial era.

Chapter 8 by Vincent Houben and Julia Seibert compares the different systems of labor relations and the various solutions adopted by the Belgian and Dutch administrations to cope with problems of chronic labor shortages in the tropical cash crop sector and the mining industries. This chapter shows that the alternation between so-called free and more coercive systems of labor exploitation was different in the two colonies, depending on political context, geography, labor supply, and world market demand for particular products. Houben and Seibert's analysis underpins the thesis of Booth in Chapter 3 that labor mobilization was, on the whole, less disruptive to indigenous farming in Java than it was in significant parts of the Congo.

Chapter 9 by William Gervase Clarence-Smith discusses the divergent development of the rubber industries in the two countries, focusing on the development of the plantation sector as well as the smallholder rubber sector. Given the key role of wild rubber extraction in the Congo under Leopoldian rule, this chapter unravels a direct causal connection between colonial extractive policies and the long-term development of a key export sector. Clarence-Smith shows that despite the prevalence of comparable factor endowments for rubber cultivation, the Congo's output was marginal in the 1930s, whereas Indonesia became the largest producer in the world. He argues that the key reason for this difference was that the authorities in Indonesia gave rubber smallholders a relatively free hand, whereas the Belgians applied counterproductive forms of coercion.

Chapters 10 and 11 discuss the specific patterns of industrialization in the colonial economies of, respectively, Indonesia and the Congo. In Chapter 10 Thomas Lindblad focuses on the twin issues of industrialization and foreign direct investment in Indonesia under Dutch colonial rule. This chapter emphasizes the contradiction between massive inflows of foreign investment capital under the protection of colonialism on the one hand and the very limited progress achieved in terms of industrialization on the other. A supplementary case study of Unilever, a foreign-owned manufacturing firm, illustrates that there was an unutilized potential in colonial Indonesia for an earlier industrialization using foreign capital. In Chapter 11 Frans Buelens and Danny Cassimon explore the emergence, expansion, and eventual collapse of a, from an Indonesian point of view, impressive industrial complex in the Congo. Buelens and Cassimon describe in detail how the development of manufacturing industries was intertwined with the rapid expansion of the Congolese mining industry, especially in Katanga. This chapter shows that even under colonial conditions some development toward industrialization was possible, but it also shows how quickly a country can implode into the conditions of a failed state when the economic transition is not backed up by a balanced policy of political, economic, and social development.

Finally, in Chapter 12, Jan Frederik Abbeloos offers a direct comparison of the economic policies of two of the most infamous dictators of the post-war era: Suharto and Mobutu. Both dictators were known for their merciless display of power and their extreme kleptocracy, and this makes the sharp distinction between the success and failure of their macro-economic policies all the more interesting. Abbeloos addresses the question of how far this difference can be ascribed to the lottery of global commodity prices (oil versus copper), to personalities, or to deeper structures in the two post-colonial societies with their different legacies of colonial exploitation and development. He develops the thesis that, upon seizing power, Suharto primarily had to fix economic turmoil, while Mobutu faced political chaos above all. Consequently, Suharto prioritized economic capacity-building, while Mobutu prioritized political unification. These differences in policy orientation better prepared the Indonesian economy for exogenous shocks on the volatile natural resource markets from the 1970s, even diversifying its production and export mix, while the Congolese economy collapsed. By placing the agency of post-independence political leaders in the center of his analysis, Abbeloos offers some nuances to the explicit focus on the long-term economic consequences of colonial exploitation.

## Notes

1 Fieldhouse (1999) summarized the two positions under the labels of "optimists" and "pessimists" and provides a good survey of the most important arguments in the debate.
2 During 1885–1908 the Congo area was under the private rule of the Belgian King Leopold II and was formally known as the Congo Free State. In 1908 the colony was annexed by the Belgian government as a result of international pressure to end the atrocities of Leopold's rubber policies. For conciseness we have chosen to use the term Belgian Congo in the title of the book as well as in this Introduction for the entire period of colonial rule in the Congo starting in 1885 and ending with formal independence on June 30, 1960.
3 In the Netherlands the debate about the *eereschuld* (debt of honour) had taken place in the nineteenth century, but Dutch governments kept on struggling with later atrocities during the *politionele acties* (military offensives). One example is the long-standing discussion about financial compensation for the survivors of the mass slaughter in the village of Rawagedeh in 1947. Only in December 2011 did the Dutch government, under pressure from a Dutch court ruling, officially apologize and announce a compensation schedule, to which only ten surviving relatives were eligible, as the rest had died in the meantime.
4 The Maddison estimates give Indonesia a slight edge in the period 1950–70. These differences are the result of different estimation techniques which are not that relevant here. It is the contrast in post-colonial performance that evokes the question on colonial legacies.

## References

Acemoglu, D., Johnson, S., and Robinson, J.A. (2002) "Reversal of Fortune: Geography and Institutions in the Making of the Modern World Income Distribution," *Quarterly Journal of Economics*, 117: 1231–94.

Boomgaard, P. and van Zanden, J.L. (1990) *Changing Economy in Indonesia XI. Population Trends, 1795–1942*, Amsterdam: Royal Tropical Institute.

Booth, A. (1998) *Indonesian Economic Development in the Nineteenth and Twentieth Centuries: A History of Missed Opportunities*, London: Macmillan.

Brion, R. and Moreau, J.L. (2006) *van mijnbouw tot Mars. De ontstaansgeschiedenis van Umicore*, Tielt: Lannoo.

Buelens, F. (2007) *Congo 1885–1960: Een financieel-economische geschiedenis*, Berchem: EPO.

Buelens, F. and Marysse, S. (2009) "Returns on investments during the colonial era: the Case of the Belgian Congo," *Economic History Review*, 62: 135–66.

Davis, L.E. and Huttenback, R.A. (1988) *Mammon and the Pursuit of Empire. The Economics of British Imperialism*, Cambridge, Mass.: Cambridge University Press

Diamond, J. (1997) *Guns, Germs and Steel. The Fates of Human Societies*, New York: W.W. Norton.

Ferguson, N. (2002) *Empire: The Rise and Demise of the British World Order and the Lessons for Global Power*, New York: Basic Books.

Fieldhouse, D.K. (1999) *The West and the Third World: Trade, Colonialism, Dependence, and Development*, Malden, Mass.: Blackwell.

Frankema, E.H.P. (2010) "Raising Revenue in the British Empire, 1870–1940: How 'Extractive' Were Colonial Taxes?," *Journal of Global History*, 5: 447–77.

Frankema, E.H.P. (2011) "Colonial Taxation and Government Spending in British Africa, 1880–1940: Maximizing Revenue or Minimizing Effort?," *Explorations in Economic History*, 48: 136–49.

Gallup, J.L., Sachs, J. D., and Mellinger, A.D. (1999) "Geography and Economic Development," *International Regional Science Review*, 22: 179–232.

Gann, L.H. and Duignan, P. (1967) *Burden of Empire. An Appraisal of Western Colonialism in Africa South of the Sahara*, Stanford University, Stanford, Calif.: Hoover Institution Press.

Gewalt, J.B. (2006) "More Than Red Rubber and Figures Alone," *International Journal of African Historical Studies*, 39: 471–86.

Grier, R.M. (1999) "Colonial Legacies and Economic Growth," *Public Choice*, 98: 317–35.

Hawkins, H. (1981–2) "Joseph Conrad, Roger Casement, and the Congo Reform Movement," *Journal of Modern Literature*, 9: 65–80.

Herbst, J. (2000) *States and Power in Africa. Comparative Lessons in Authority and Control*, Princeton, NJ: Princeton University Press.

Heston, A., Summers, R., and Aten, B. (2011) *Penn World Table Version 7.0*, Center for International Comparisons of Production, Income and Prices at the University of Pennsylvania.

Hochschild, A. (1999) *King Leopold's Ghost. A Story of Greed, Terror, and Heroism in Colonial Africa*, Boston, Mass: Mariner Books.

Huillery, E. (2010) "The Black Man's Burden. The Cost of Colonization of French West Africa," Working paper, Paris School of Economics.

Huybrechts, A. (2010) *Bilan économique du Congo 1908–1960*, Paris: L'Harmattan.

Lange, M.K. (2009) *Lineages of Despotism and Development. British Colonialism and State Power*, Chicago: The University of Chicago Press.

Lefeuvre, D. (2006) *Pour en finir avec la repentance coloniale*, Paris: Flammarion.

Maddison, A. (2010) Historical Statistics: www.ggdc.net/maddison/.

Mamdani, M. (1996) *Citizen and Subject. Contemporary Africa and the Legacy of Late Colonialism*, Princeton, NJ: Princeton University Press.

Marechal, P. (1992) *De "Arabische" Campagne in het Maniéma-gebied (1892–1894). Situering binnen het kolonisatieproces in de Onafhankelijke Kongostaat*, Tervuren: Koninklijk Museum voor Midden-Afrika.

Marks, D. and van Zanden, J.L. (2012) *An Economic History of Indonesia, 1800–2010*, London: Routledge.

Marseille, J. (1984) *Empire colonial et capitalisme français. Histoire d'un divorce*, Paris: Albin Michel.

Multatuli [1860] (2010) *Max Havelaar. Of Die Koffieveilingun Van De Nederlandse Handelmaatschappij*, ed. G. van Es, Amsterdam: Nieuw Amsterdam.

Neudt, D. (2002) ",Wij hebben een taak in Kongo.' De verbeelding van Afrika bij Jef van Bilsen," Thesis, Ghent University.

O'Brien, P.K. (1988) "The costs and benefits of British Imperialism, 1846–1914," *Past and Present*, 120: 163–200.

Offer, A. (1993) "The British Empire, 1870–1914: A Waste of Money?," *Economic History Review*, 46: 215–38.

Pakenham, T. (1992) *The Scramble for Africa. The White Man's Conquest of the Dark Continent from 1876–1912*, New York: Avon Books.

Putterman, L. and Weil, D.N. (2010) "Post-1500 Population Flows and the Long Run Determinants of Economic Growth and Inequality," *Quarterly Journal of Economics*, 125: 1627–82.

Ricklefs, M.C. (2008) *A History of Modern Indonesia since c. 1200*, Basingstoke: Palgrave Macmillan.

Rodney, W. (1972) *How Europe Underdeveloped Africa*, London: Bogle-L'Ouverture Publications.

Stengers, J. (1977) "La Genèse d'une pensée coloniale. Léopold II et le modèle hollandais," *Tijdschrift voor Geschiedenis*, 90: 46–71.

van Bilsen, J. (1993) *Kongo, 1945–1965. Het einde van een kolonie*, Leuven: Davidsfonds.

van Reybrouck, D. (2010) *Congo. Een Geschiedenis*, Amsterdam: De Bezige Bij.

van Zanden, J.L. and van Riel, A. (2000) *Nederland, 1780–1914. Staat, Instituties en Economische Ontwikkeling*, Amsterdam: Balans.

Vansina, J. (2010) *Being Colonized. The Kuba Experience in Rural Congo, 1880–1960*, Madison: The University of Wisconsin Press.

Warren, B. (1980) *Imperialism: Pioneer of Capitalism*, London: New Left Books.

# 1 Extractive institutions in the Congo

## Checks and balances in the *longue durée*

*Andreas Exenberger and Simon Hartmann*

## 1.1 Introduction

The Congo provides an excellent example when studying extractive institutions in the *longue durée*.[1] It is a place full of astonishing contradictions: the Congo assembles an impressive volume and variety of resources, but it is also a place of endangered human survival due to a lack of capabilities to cover basic needs and to massive violence. Statehood has existed for centuries, but political fragmentation has also occurred and continued well into the post-colonial period. World market integration became increasingly influential from the sixteenth century on, bringing additional revenues for kings and traders, but often at the expense of large parts of the population (Exenberger and Hartmann 2008). Later, the Congo became the center-piece of the colonial empire of a small European power, and also a place where the misfortunes of civilizing missions and resource curses were taken to extremes. Finally, the Democratic Republic of the Congo (DRC) emerged as one of the largest and most diverse countries of post-colonial Africa, particularly known for authoritarian rule and instability to the point of civil war, state failure, and economic collapse.

In this chapter, we organize our narrative on long-run institutional development in the Congo. Furthermore, we use the concept of path-dependence (North 1994) along with the categories "pre-colonial," "colonial," and "post-colonial." Path-dependence means tracing present and future constraints as imposed by the way human interaction and institutions have played out in the past and evolved over time. Events and decisions in the past limit the scope of present and future choices. This concept is helpful for uncovering historical parallels, repetition of events and developments (albeit in different clothes), similarities in structures, or even continuities. Hence, we agree with Jacques Depelchin:

> Economists who treat the colonial period as if it began with the Berlin Conference and had nothing to do with the preceding slave trade create an abstract, artificial historical framework.... The matter under discussion is a historical process that has transformed African societies, and that transformation did not start with the Berlin Conference.
>
> (1992: 35)

However, colonization was a serious disruption. Jan Vansina (1990) even calls it the "death of tradition," consisting of two main drivers: first, the "invention of new structures" by colonial rulers and, second, the experience of everyday life which made people "doubt their own legacies" and "adopt portions of the foreign heritage," both also influencing post-colonial developments (Vansina 1990: 246–8).

Finally, we focus on mechanisms of checks and balances embedded in political and economic institutions. Greatly simplifying, we refer to three groups: rulers ("the elite"), ruled ("the rest"), and "intermediaries." By checks and balances we mean institutions limiting the power and constraining the actions of elites and intermediaries, in the form of credible commitments by the elites to the rest or by elite support of perpetually lived organizations (North *et al.* 2009). They provide incentives for the elite to address the needs of the rest in the form of public goods rather than seeking private rents only. If they are strong, they tend to make life more predictable for the rest and the abuse of power for private interest of the elite and intermediaries more difficult. But if weak, they bias political and economic competition and cooperation by establishing elite monopolies. The position of intermediaries varies, not least with the degree of difference between the elite and the rest (most pronounced maybe in the case of external colonial elites). Consequently, unchecked and unbalanced power is related to extractive institutions (Acemoglu and Robinson 2012; Bueno de Mesquita *et al.* 2003). A long-run view makes particularly good sense in the case of the Congo because pre-colonial checks and balances already existed, usually based on clan, lineage, or property. We argue that late pre-colonial political fragmentation resulted in a weakening of checks and balances and therefore elites and intermediaries (especially at the local level) were barely restrained from bringing tyranny and disorder to the rest; this also eased the transition to colonial extraction and more recently to warlordism.

The chapter is divided into three chronological parts: a pre-colonial history of African trading networks prior to the Stanley expedition, a colonial history encompassing the reign of King Leopold II and subsequently the Belgian state, and a post-colonial history of civil wars and autocracy in the aftermath of 1960. The conclusion stresses paths and parallels in all these periods.[2] A final note of clarification: in this chapter, we usually treat the Congo as if it was a rather homogenous place, which it certainly was not, either in time or in space. We deliberately understate these differences to reveal general trends, otherwise probably obscured by the unavoidable conclusion that everything was at least to some degree different in any two places taken into comparison. This holds not only for pre-colonial times when the territory of today's DRC was shared between many fluid political entities and hence differences are most obvious, but also in colonial times when the degree of penetration and practices of administration differed, and in post-colonial times when the east and the west of the country were often hardly connected.

## 1.2 Pre-colonial history: traditional checks and balances

In the nineteenth century West-Central Africa was a multifaceted world with overlapping (social) entities of varying and fluid shape and varying degrees of hierarchy. The most significant of these entities were the Kingdom of Kongo, the Kuba Kingdom, the Luba Empire, the Lunda Commonwealth, and the Tio Kingdom. But there were also other clusters of people and larger social groups (Ngombe, Mongo, Mamvu-Lese, Maniema brotherhoods, and "forest people"). There was a great diversity of institutions among them (centralized or decentralized, broader or smaller power base, etc.). Some adopted institutions inspired by other kingdoms or peoples with whom they exchanged commodities or maintained contacts; for example the Luba state model was adopted by the Lunda. Some did not. The Lele, for example, did not copy the neighboring Bushong

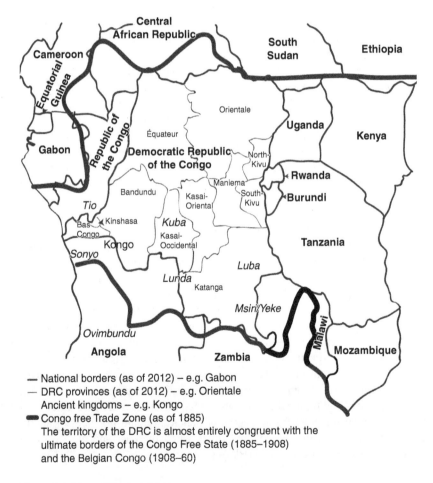

*Figure 1.1* Map of Central Africa.

(Vansina 1966, 1990; Douglas 1963). Additionally, external actors such as Europeans (from the west) and Arabs (from the north-east and east) had already been present for some time although external penetration of the hinterland remained occasional and weak.

In this environment, slavery (already practised for several centuries) and the ivory trade were economically and politically significant, while subsistence agriculture dominated the economy. Trade in rural surplus production occurred regularly and interacted in diverse ways with long-distance trade all over the region, further deepening in the nineteenth century (Gordon 2009; Vansina 1962). In the Lower Congo (Ekholm-Friedman 1991), archil, copal, gum, ivory, palm oil, and precious woods were traded whereas along the whole river system it was agricultural products, fish, salt, and copper. There was also iron smelting, weaponry and tool production, boat construction, and the production of ceramics, copper rods, pottery, palm and sugar wine, beer, camwood, and cloths (Harms 1981: 46–70; Vansina 1990: 212–13). Copper production, manufacturing, and trade had a long tradition in Katanga, but also in the Lower Congo, because copper was widely appreciated and valuable in art, as currency and prestige good (Herbert 1984: 185–276). Generally, economic links intensified and it was even claimed that the Congo basin was the leading trading zone in nineteenth-century Southern Africa (Zeleza 1993: 421).

In the historical Kingdom of Kongo, the best-known pre-colonial political entity in the region (its heyday was in the sixteenth but it existed until the nineteenth century), a related pattern of power distribution emerged. While rule was generally executed by local kings who were controlled by councils, resulting in "a strong egalitarian component" (Broadhead 1979: 627), the state was nevertheless quite strong. The state played a major role in "the division of land revenue, and no individual, institution or family could establish permanent rights to income through possessing title to rent-bearing land" (Thornton 1984: 160). Instead, income was distributed either by the right to collect the king's revenue from specified areas or by direct grants from the king. Furthermore, we observe important shifts in political order already in the late sixteenth century, including the strengthening of patrilineal descent categories, not least related to Christianity (Hilton 1983; Thornton 1984). Thus, contact with Europeans (starting with Diogo Cão in 1482) had an impact from the beginning via the demand for slave labor from the Americas from the sixteenth century onwards, but also with respect to culture. Coastland actors and societies profited at the expense of the hinterland and some formerly mighty kingdoms became fragile and lost power and population, finally resulting in disintegration (Ekholm 1972; Hilton 1987).

The emerging Atlantic slave trade (Klein 1999; Thornton 1998) had a more significant influence on creating that divergence than intra-African trade, precisely because of the related access to prestige goods. As transactions between Africans and Europeans intensified the area witnessed (see Figure 1.2) more slave raids (increasingly destabilizing hinterland societies through greater violence), a serious disturbance of African labor relations (domestic societies were deprived of a significant part of their productive potential), an inflow of prestigious trade

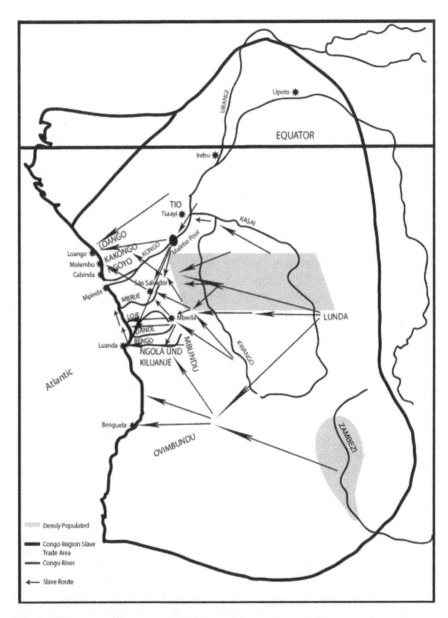

*Figure 1.2* Regional slave trade networks in the Congo Region, 1600s–1800s

Note
Map drawn by Simon Hartmann, data from Miller (1976: 80), Harms (1981: xii, 26), Miller (1988: 10, 210, 216, 1998: 80).

goods exchanged for slaves (considerably influencing domestic power relation-ships) and of iron tools fostering development (at least in societies with access to foreign markets). In addition to the slave trade's inherently violent character, the demographic losses threatened the existence of kinship groups and entire king-doms, whose political, social, and economic structures sometimes virtually disap-peared (Klein 1999: 125–9). Moreover, slave and slave-holder identities became more fluid on an individual level and slavery-related warfare presented a hazard to security on a societal level. Political power was weakened, challenges intensi-fied, and fragmentation took place including ethnic fractionalization and social alienation (Whatley and Gillezeau 2011). Additionally, this replaced and destroyed legal institutions in Africa, a basis for today's "poor legal environment" (Nunn and Wantchekon 2011). This process of social deterioration gathered pace until well into the nineteenth century as the Atlantic overseas slave trade met with the Arab inland slave trade coming from the north-east (Alpers 1967; Lovejoy 2012); it only came to a halt late in that century when it was finally crowded out by colonial rule.

In the long term, all this had a very negative impact on development. Further-more, militarization led to a continuation, if not intensification, of violence in the West-Central African hinterland. This increasingly included food raids, as shown by the destruction of the Lunda Commonwealth by the Lovale and Chokwe aggression in the late nineteenth century (Gann and Duignan 1979: 49) or the decline of the Luba Kingdom, unable to repel armed traders, after 1870 (Wilson 1972: 585–8).

By that time, other "commodities" had already gained importance, especially ivory (Rempel 1998). When global demand for this product expanded, ivory hunters, again including Arabs from the north-east and east, followed the retreat-ing herds to the Central and Eastern African hinterlands (Wilson 1972: 585–6; Vansina 1990: 240–5). In the new business, old trading relations and networks were used (Beachey 1967: 289–90; Gann and Duignan 1979: 117). Like the slave trade, it was "extractive" by definition. The consequence for power pat-terns was clear: "the definition of chieftaincy revolved around the ability to impose claims for tribute in ivory" (Gordon 2009: 932). Hence, a rising number of guns militarized the hinterlands (Reid 2010). The influence of foreign trade on the allocation of power in the Kingdom of Kongo, for example, is summa-rized by Susan Broadhead:

> Control of foreign trade and the circulation of prestige goods associated with it were at the heart of political power. Possibilities for profit, both eco-nomic and political, arose in several areas: control over the movement of caravans in a territory, charges for transit, customs duties and tolls; monop-oly rights over products such as slaves, guns, or ivory; privileged access to the market system including information about market conditions; exclusive access to foreign traders; alliances with foreign merchants; and direct partic-ipation in trading ventures.

(1979: 637)

Traditionally, societies in the region were based on a distribution of power by vertical hierarchies as well as horizontally integrated groups like lineages, secret societies, cults, or age grades (McIntosh 1999: 4). Therefore, rulers were usually experienced in the use of checks and balances. In the Kingdom of Kongo, committees of local rulers (the "chiefly office") openly chose and controlled the "councils" (Broadhead 1979: 621). Luba power was balanced not only between landowners and rulers but between the *balopwe* patrilineages and *vidie* organizations that had a say in the succession of the rulers (Wilson 1972: 585). Again the Luba as well as the Songye were political entities where secret societies held power shaping political life (de Maret 1999; Reefe 1981: 205). Because of the influence of external trade, violent political rule combined with capital accumulation became increasingly significant (Gordon 2009). Fueled by prestige goods, power shifts occurred allowing for the emergence of a new class of warlords in the Kingdom of Kongo (Ekholm 1972), and Luba and Lunda warlords gained strength long into the nineteenth century (Lovejoy 2012: 127). The resulting political fragmentation facilitated European conquest (Austin 2010). Mahmood Mamdani (1996: 40), while describing the late nineteenth century in Africa as a "time of turmoil" and "unfreedom" for an increasing number of Africans, also emphasized that there were "diverse and contradictory" dynamics in place: "state power was built not only as a consequence of processes of internal differentiation, but also as the direct result of conquest." Traditional checks and balances eroded or changed their character. While new elites profited from this, the region as a whole became more vulnerable to external influence.

## 1.3  Colonial history: unchecked power

Belgium was a colonial latecomer and would probably never have become a colonial power without the ambitions of Leopold II (king of the Belgians 1865–1909). While the extraction of slaves and ivory took place without effective territorial occupation, this changed in 1878 when Leopold commissioned Henry Morton Stanley to "explore" the Congolese hinterland and to arrange "treaties" with the locals. Colonialism had reached the shores of the Congo river, and Leopold managed to convince other powers of the idea of a Conge Free Trade Zone and an independent Congo Free State (CFS). This "state" was advertised as an area of free trade and humanitarianism. It turned out in fact to be a private venture of the king, shaped by monopoly capitalism and brutal violence. However, due to the heritage of slavery and the ivory trade, these means of organizing a society were not alien to the Congolese. The transformation of leadership continued during colonialism, explained by Kajsa Ekholm-Friedman in her study of the Lower Congo:

> The colonialization of the Lower Congo led to serious disturbances in the authority structure. Political hierarchies collapsed, chiefs lost their power, religious authority was undermined. In that situation the process of cultural creativity shattered the frozen pattern of traditional order.... In the

confrontation with western capitalism, however, all they did was in vain. Their sophisticated fetishism and their hyperintegrated clan/tribe system did not help. The immediate outcome of the encounter was, after all, dependent on the control of sources of power, on who had the most numerous soldiers, the most effective weapons and the most efficient organization.

(1991: 255)

The involvement in overseas trade and the rise of colonialism created a new elite in the Congo, and its members later became functionaries in the colony (Alpers 1975: 266). Until 1906 more than 400 new indigenous leaders ("new chiefs"), assisted by African mercenary troops, were granted an investiture in the CFS, while traditional leaders lost their influence (Slade 1962: 172–3). Although some escaped replacement by installing straw men (Gann and Duignan 1979: 206), this "liberated administrative chiefs from all institutionalized constraints, of peers or people, and laid the basis of a decentralized despotism" (Mamdani 1996: 43).[3] Hence, the already fragile political order deteriorated further. Wyatt MacGaffey (1970: 51–2, 103) described this kind of control for the Lower Congo, and Kajsa Ekholm-Friedman (1991: 253) provides examples of "disturbances in the authority structure" in the same region, notable among which were the spread and increasing arbitrariness of witchcraft accusations. But the pattern was more general (Vansina 2010: 86–126): after the conquest, the King of the Kuba, for example, "became the enforcer of the companies," while control by councils gradually faded away.

The transformation of traditional checks and balances into direct and indirect colonial rule in the sphere of politics and concessionary enterprises in the sphere of the economy formed the basis of the Leopoldian system, a system of force and "perverse incentives" (Hartmann 2011). Of course, the administration, also accompanied by Catholic and Protestant missions, failed to establish full control over the huge territory. But Leopold had both his hands in the revenues of the CFS. He secured property rights for the state by issuing decrees of expropriation of the indigenous population in 1885 (enforced in 1891 and 1892). Furthermore, he possessed property, held large shares in the concessionary companies, and taxed trade. Now, the possession of land became critical, and the decrees divided vast lands declared "vacant"[4] (Leclercq 1965: 103; Young 1994: 77) into a *domaine privé* (property of the state) and a *domaine de la couronne* (private property of the king). The *domaine privé* was partly distributed among concessionary companies, but large parts (notably including Katanga) remained mostly untouched.

Associated with the appropriation of the land were claims on its produce including valuable natural resources, at that time most notably ivory and rubber. The state also forbade the population to trade these goods on their own account (Emerson 1979: 152–3; Stengers 1969: 265). This system of acquisition was completed by the introduction of a tax, the *impôt indigène*, usually to be paid in rubber, occasionally also in ivory and food, which became a considerable source of revenue for the CFS. The system included escalating production requirements and labor for public projects (like railways), resulting in non-paid work for about 24 days a month (Emerson 1979: 147–8; Edgerton 2002: 63). Others had to provide foodstuffs for the administration and (coerced) laborers.

While the business was not fully royal and private capital played a role, the king remained in charge of granting concessions and hence controlled the colony. Jean Stengers (1969: 265) even claimed that his regime "had the effect of hindering private enterprise by an impassable barrier of state monopoly." The legal instrument of exploitation was a *carte blanche* (Morel 2005 [1906]: 37; Slade 1962: 181), which allowed colonial officers to act without restraint in their realms, while the Congolese were subject to arbitrariness and "customary law" and hence were also legally inferior to Europeans. Incentives to increase the output of the colony were provided by a bonus system, which allowed for a multiplication of the salary of colonial officers (Morel 2005 [1906]: 31). Moreover, a domestic army was built up, the *Force Publique*, run by coerced labor and consisting of roughly 19,000 African soldiers in the early twentieth century. Generally, a system of threat emerged: threats of punishment for intermediaries who failed to collect the requested amount of taxes (Morel 2005 [1906]: 47–8) as well as threats of brutal maltreatment for the rest by intermediaries equipped with arms and impunity (Slade 1962: 172–3). It resulted in a large number of direct and indirect casualties[5] and a significant drop in birth rates.

The terror embodied in this system was publicized internationally by Edmund D. Morel's Congo Reform Association in the early twentieth century. Leopold came under increasing pressure when the financial situation of the colony deteriorated with natural rubber production dramatically declining after 1905. As a result, the king handed "his" colony over to the Belgian state in 1908. Apart from the very last years, Leopold's rule in the Congo had been largely unchecked and unbalanced either by any kind of African authority or by the Belgian government and parliament – unlike the British and the French who both faced "at least modest constraints in what European colonists could and did do" (Bueno de Mesquita 2007: 215).

The new administration reorganized and modernized its practices but also faced economic change when the profits from rubber virtually disappeared. At the time of World War I, the cash crop business, for example cotton in northern Katanga (Likaka 1997) and palm oil in the Kwango district (Marchal 2008), and the detection of large reserves of valuable minerals (most notably copper in Katanga, but also diamonds and gold), provided opportunities for the economic reorientation of the Belgian Congo. This also shifted the geographical focus of exploitation to Katanga and Kilo-Moto, in particular to the mining districts of the Forminière, the Union Minière du Haut Katanga (UMHK) and the Compagnie du Chemin de Fer du Bas-Congo au Katanga (BCK). Hence from the 1920s onwards, industrial capital became dominant over commercial capital (Jewsiewicki 1980: 47–8), including investments in Katanga railways. Already during World War I the value of mineral exports outpaced that of agriculture (Jewsiewicki 1972: 233), and the Congo became one of the largest copper producers worldwide. Although the colonial state played an important role in the economy, concessions to Belgian companies ensured that three-quarters of colonial business was dominated by only five holdings (Edgerton 2002: 169; Hillman 1997). Crawford Young summarizes the character of the Belgian administration as a

> remarkable colonial system ... unparalleled in the depth of its penetration into the African societies upon which it was superimposed and in the breadth of its control of nearly the whole spectrum of human activity. The bureaucracy numbered among its successes nearly complete exemption from serious accountability to metropolitan society. There was no effective gadfly element on the left fringes of public opinion, nor was close surveillance imposed by Belgian Parliament. The advisory organs operating within the system itself were not devoid of significance, but the restraints they constituted were in the main either paternal admonition to better colonial behaviour or pressures from European interest groups in the Congo. African opinion was virtually unarticulated until 1956.
>
> (1965: 32)

The Belgian Congo was now established as a more humane, more civilizing, and more bureaucratic enterprise, but one still based on rent extraction and weak checks and balances. Methods shifted from compulsory labor to indirect methods of coercion in the form of taxes. The *impôt indigène* became a monetary tax in 1914, forcing many Congolese to work for cash, while surplus was transferred to Belgium and the colony left depleted of resources for domestic investment (Higginson 1989: 209). But the old labor system was partially reestablished in 1910 when people still had to "furnish labor" for works of "public utility" under long-term contracts (Morel 1912: 42). At that time, the production of cash crops in plantations (palm oil and cotton among others) also became a significant economic factor. However, during the 1920s the main exports consisted of copper, gold, diamonds, and tin. While this allowed high profits in times of boom, such as the world wars (Edgerton 2002: 168–73), it also made revenues vulnerable to busts. In that context, coerced labor remained necessary and peasants were recruited according to the needs of companies and plantations (Higginson 1989: 102; Jewsiewicki 1980: 48–9).

Hence, the character of rule changed in terms of violence and also to a large extent in terms of formalization, but only marginally as far as hierarchy as such is concerned. Cultural transfers intensified, but strictly in a top-down sense, the Belgian variant of the "civilizing mission." The decisions of colonial administrators may have become more concerned with the development of the colony and its people (this was often repeated by former colonial officials), but these decisions were made exclusively by Europeans. Indirect forms of subjugation were widespread, and included positive incentives like the spread of (mission) schooling (Edgerton 2002: 174–7) and access to European consumer goods of high prestige value (Derksen 1983: 53). In general, the interplay of state, church, and companies proved to be ambiguous at best for the Congolese, and was described as "triple alliance" (Young 1965: 10), establishing a "claustrophobic kind of social control, in which advancement for Africans was very difficult" (Clarence-Smith 1983: 9). David M. Gordon (2009: 938) summarizes the change, with reference to the Belgian Congo, as follows:

> European colonial states quickly came to rely on a less overtly violent form of chiefly despotism, especially in efforts to mobilize labor. In the colonial period, chiefs remained the principal African agents who transformed dependent subjects into the labor required for the production of commodities, now copper instead of ivory, destined for international markets.[6]

The Congo was still a land surplus economy, but particularly during the copper boom in the 1920s food became short in some regions. As a result of the monetization of the economy and of the status associated with occupation in the mines (despite unstable real wages), people migrated on a large scale. Regular employment spread, particularly in the mines (Higginson 1989: 178), resulting in 1.1 million wage laborers in 1955, the second largest number in colonial Africa (Young and Turner 1985: 85). But force was still necessary to meet demand in times of production booms. At least in the 1910s and 1920s production of supplies for wage laborers was considered economically more attractive by the local populations (Jewsiewicki 1972: 220) than particularly, plantation work. The result was that women, the elderly, and children were left behind in the villages (Marchal 2008: 126; Young 1965: 12), which meant that production remained low and food supply vulnerable. Summing up, the Belgian administration chose not so much terror but more indirect ways to mobilize the workforce. While taxes decreased from 50 percent of the overall revenue of the colony in 1900 to less than 5 percent in 1958 (Leclercq 1965: 112), the individual burden rose, putting pressure on the Congolese to earn wages. Furthermore, coerced labor remained an option for infrastructure construction and other essentials, its quality being improved by the almost ubiquitous expansion of basic schooling, while Congolese were almost totally excluded from even secondary education (see Frankema, Chapter 7 below and Houben and Seibert, Chapter 8 below).

Certainly, the population had agency in this process although it was strictly constrained. Major acts of opposition, such as the 1941 strike movement and the 1944 rebellion at the UMHK, were suppressed, not least because "[w]ithout the right to express their political and social opinions freely, the African workers had no means for adequately counterposing their own power to the economic might and political access of the Union Minière" (Higginson 1989: 214–15). There was basically no freedom of association and cultural organizations were only permitted when ethnically homogeneous, prohibiting "trans-ethnic political parties" (Schatzberg 1997: 72). However, at least after World War II, a class of *évolués* emerged, mostly secondary-educated employees such as teachers, nurses, or civil servants, who aspired to recognition by Europeans and demanded rights for the Congolese (Anstey 1970: 200–1). They were successful at least for themselves and acquired a *carte mérite civique* granting access to courts and the right to purchase land (Anstey 1970: 205).

Hence, the responsiveness of the administration increased. However, despite all reforms and some improvements, the wealth and power distribution between the colonizers and the colonized remained extremely unequal, as exemplary (but representative) data from 1958 show (see Table 1.1).

Generally, the measures taken by the Belgian administration continued to dissolve the traditional political order in the Congo and in the long run produced an alienated leadership instead of legitimate patterns of governance. On the one hand, the Belgian administration did not solve conflicts inherited from precolonial times, as in the case of the Lunda and the Chokwe (Bustin 1975; Gordon 2001). On the other hand, the state formally integrated and transformed "chieftaincy" as a subdivision of the administration (Young and Turner 1985: 35–6) and managed to increase the number of loyal Congolese leaders to 6000 by 1919 (Gann and Duignan 1979: 206–7). A colonial legacy of constrained rights, coercive institutions (especially in labor recruitment), and selective access to education was a real burden. In the words of Crawford Young (1994: 242), the "corrosive personality of Bula Matari" was the "silent revenge of the colonial state" for having to grant independence. When the Congo was rashly decolonized in 1960, it was ill-equipped for independence and democracy. Hence, the elected Lumumba government remained short-lived, while the country experienced the Katanga (1960–3) and South Kasai (1960–1) secessions, the Simba rebellion (1964), and the Mobutu coups (1960 and 1965).

## 1.4  Post-colonial history: the unbalanced failing state

Decolonization in 1960 resulted in the so-called "Congo Crisis," a mixture of civil, secessionist, and proxy war. Democratization (including elections of a two-chamber parliament and a president controlling the prime minister) was probably aspired to by the *loi fondamentale* of 1960, but failed almost instantaneously. A college of commissioners seized power, resulting in Mobutu Sese Seko introducing an autocratic single-party state in 1965 and favoring private interest over the provision of public goods. He developed a system of rent-seeking, leading to an extraordinary discrepancy in wealth and power between the elites and the rest

*Table 1.1*  Inequality between Europeans and Africans in the Belgian Congo, 1958

|  | *Europeans (%)* | *Africans (%)* |
| --- | --- | --- |
| Population | 1 | 99 |
| Wage laborers | 2 | 98 |
| Wages | 45 | 55 |
| Farmed land | 15 | 85 |
| Agricultural output | 58 | 42 |
| Number of enterprises | 82 | 18 |
| Material output | 70 | 30 |
| Capital assets | 95 | 5 |

Source: Peemans (1968: 386).

(Lemarchand 2003: 32–8; MacGaffey 1991). Hence, the basis and methods of extraction and rule did not change fundamentally, and pre-colonial and colonial patterns continued into the post-colonial period, serving the purpose of regime stabilization. The state was well controlled but weak: "however weak the state has become in certain respects, it retains the ability to prevent the active organization of resistance" (Young and Turner 1985: 405). But economically, there was also reason for optimism. While in the 1960s minerals remained by far the most important export item and source of government revenue (Akitoby and Cinyabuguma 2004: 9; Dunning 2005: 465), resource abundance combined with high world market prices ensured a solid economic performance (Akitoby and Cinyabuguma 2004: 6). The terms of trade also improved between 1964 and the early 1970s (Bézy *et al.* 1981: 105) (see also Abbeloos, Chapter 12 below).

Politically, Mobutu relied not only on the cronies he enriched but also on the army he controlled by his military authority as well as by utilizing conflicts within the upper ranks. Arthur House (quoted in Young and Turner 1985: 262) regarded this as his most important "political strength." Mobutu acted as the central figure in the army and made it the "strongest single organized group in the First Republic," amounting – at least on paper – to more than 50,000 men. In the east he also relied on mercenaries and police forces, an estimated 30,000 men. The use of violence was "less instrumental" than in colonial times, but it became "more capricious and random." (Young and Turner 1985: 261–71).

The colonial heritage of primary extraction, unfavorable policies (Young and Turner 1985: 323–4), and bad luck in the commodity price lottery brought the Congo an almost unparalleled decline in terms of economic development from the early 1970s onwards (Akitoby and Cinyabuguma 2004: 7) (see Figure 1.3). As well as kleptocracy and cronyism, "Zaïrianization," promulgated as a nationalization program, substantially contributed to the decline (Emizet 1998: 103–4; Lemarchand 2003: 31; Reno 1999: 154). Besides renaming the country Zaïre in 1971, the program consisted of widespread expropriation of foreign enterprises (particularly light industries and plantations) and their redistribution to Mobutu himself and his cronies, including "undeveloped" land. Publicized as "radical economic nationalism," it turned out to be a "rally for assets" benefiting only a small group while destroying the basis of the economy and causing supply shortages already in 1974, even in basic goods (Young and Turner 1985: 341–50).

The most serious problems were directly related to the insufficiently diversified extractive economy, concentrated on rent-seeking. The economic downturn in the early 1970s resulted in a collapse of several world commodity prices and a dramatic deterioration of the Congolese terms of trade (Bézy *et al.* 1981: 105). The regime was hit particularly hard because it depended heavily on the revenues of the biggest mining company, the Générale des Carrières et Mines (GECAMINES), a follow-up of the UMHK. Predatory structures intensified. Mobutu even actively promoted further de-diversification of the economy, which trapped the country in an "inefficient, 'no-investment' equilibrium" (Dunning 2005: 467). At the same time, megalomaniac infrastructure projects (for example the Inga–Shaba high-tension power line) were badly implemented and their main

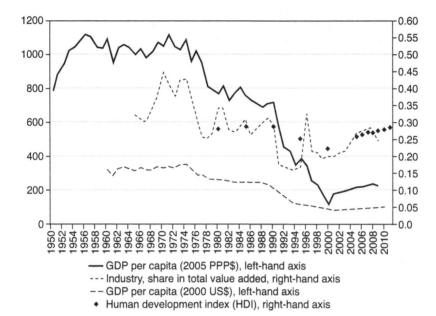

*Figure 1.3* Economic deterioration in the Congo, 1950–2010 (source: Ndikumana and Emizet (2005: 73), based on Penn World Tables (GDP, using chain rule) and World Bank Data Base (value added)).

effect was to increase public indebtedness (Schatzberg 1997: 74). Mobutu was especially anxious to avoid developing any technology or infrastructure which could be used to challenge his power: "Mobutu believed that investments in economic infrastructure, including those as simple as maintaining the network of roads left by the Belgian colonials, would pose a threat to his hold on political power by facilitating collective mobilization against his regime" (Dunning 2005: 465). In the words of William Reno (1997: 44). "This state retreat from citizens reflected the extent to which Mobutu relied on his extensive personal networks rather than effective institutions for regime survival."

Police and army were no longer paid regularly, but Mobutu offered them some kind of "tacit *carte blanche*" (Bustin 1999: 87) to take what they needed from civilians (Lemarchand 2003: 32–8). Based on Banque du Zaïre data, William Reno (1999: 154) estimated that an ever-increasing share of up to 95 percent of all government expenditure was exclusively reserved for the president. This also shows how the price of rewarding cronies had escalated over the years in the Congo, while the economy suffered. From 1960 to 1980, real wages in the private and the public sector had fallen to 4 and 47 percent respectively (Bézy *et al.* 1981: 227). Consequently, most people escaped into a "second economy," in which unofficial activities, particularly smuggling, by far outperformed official ones (De Herdt and Marysse 1996; MacGaffey 1991). The mining enterprises also suffered financial depletion, hence unofficial labor-intensive artisanal mining evolved (Nest 2011). It was a "post-colonial tragedy"[7] due to exploitation, alienation, abandonment, and curse, as – by downplaying African agency – Benjamin Rubbers (2009: 281–2) puts it:

> With regard to history, discourses relating to exploitation and alienation place the post-colonial tragedy within the continuity of colonial terror and of the slave trade, showing ruptures in the course of time as only indicating changes in the way external powers subjugate Africans.

At least from the early 1990s onwards, the Mobutu regime increasingly lost control over the territory and also the economy to the point of "de facto regional autonomy" (Schatzberg 1997: 82). With the state already dramatically weakened, the turmoil following the Rwandan genocide in 1994 acted as a catalyst for state collapse by setting the stage for "Africa's World War" (Prunier 2008), in which various Congolese "rebel" groups as well as several foreign armies (particularly from Uganda and Rwanda) were involved. Contributing to conflict was a policy of ethnicity which aggravated tensions. While Mobutu granted citizenship rights (including the right to own land) to Congolese of Rwandan descent in 1972, essentially Banyamulenge and Banyarwanda communities, he at least partially stripped them of that right in the 1990s (Nest 2011: 71–2). Because of related insecurity and impoverishment, many people welcomed foreign intervention although this also implied the import of the Hutu–Tutsi atrocities.

In 1997 Mobutu was finally overthrown by Laurent Kabila and his allies, partly because his cronies withdrew their loyalty from their old and ill patron (Mobutu died later that year; Kabila himself was murdered in 2001, his son Joseph succeeded him). As a consequence, war intensified, stability deteriorated further, and Kinshasa's claim to leadership was heavily challenged on various fronts after Kabila banned political parties and asked foreign troops to leave the country. Revenue was inadequate to sustain overall leadership and the rent-seeking kleptocratic economy fragmented into a prize-seeking war economy.

During the post-colonial period, the Congo moved backward in terms of its extractive pattern. From having a mining business connected to industrialization, it moved back to extractive artisanal business related to luxuries and low-tech alluvial production. Diamonds and gold, as well as copper, cobalt, and coltan (UN 2001: 41), became more and more important as the major "prize" (Olsson 2006), fueling and perpetuating the intensifying civil war in the 1990s and early 2000s (Samset 2002). Most of these resources can be extracted by limited military control over resource-rich enclaves and hence countries like Rwanda (diamonds) and Uganda (gold, diamonds, tropical woods) were officially exporting goods not to be found on their territories (UN 2001: 19–26). Even foreign aid contributed to looting (Reid 2006: 82–4), also involving companies from Germany, Belgium, and other Western countries (UN 2002: 46–7). The Congolese (particularly in the east) hardly profited from extraction. In the case of coltan, their revenue share, even during the price boom in 2000, was only about

12 percent, of which only a small portion remained in the hands of the diggers (Nest 2011: 59; Jackson 2003: 25–6). Furthermore, after giving up agriculture because of insecurity and better revenues in mining, many Congolese became highly dependent on selling resources but vulnerable to food shortages (Jackson 2005; Richens 2009). All this resulted in informal and illegal networks of plunder spreading over inter- and intra-continental borders (Taylor 2003). While Belgium, France, and the US remained the most influential international actors in the Congo (McNulty 1999), neighboring African and former Soviet countries joined in (UN 2001). A notable recent extension is the establishment of economic ties between China and the DRC in the 2000s, embodied in large-scale investments in Katanga (Brautigam 2009).

The downward trend may have been stopped recently although at an extraordinarily low level. At last, the war formally ended in 2003 when a transitional government was installed. But large parts of the country are devastated, no public security is assured, not even full control over the territory by government forces, and also economic prospects (in the sense of fulfilling survival needs) are doubtful. While Joseph Kabila has managed to remain in power since 2001 and was elected president twice in 2006 and 2011, the procedures and results of these elections were far from unquestioned. Hence whether today's Congo is expecting a new phase in its long-term history or a simple rearrangement of power relations perpetuating the post-colonial pattern is at best an open question.

## 1.5 Conclusions

Dealing with poverty and violence in the Congo can easily be interpreted as facing "the tunnel at the end of the light," as put by René Lemarchand (2002). From a historical perspective, this is far from surprising. Besides personal errors, recurrent failure is certainly also the result of a long-lasting heritage which is partly post-colonial (the Mobutu system), partly colonial (be it Belgian or Leopoldian), and partly even pre-colonial. It was the result of a combination of internal and external factors and subject to historical path-dependence although never deterministic or simply imposed. Political checks and balances were considerably challenged and significantly eroded from time to time. Consequently, the use of violence became normal. It is far less an anomaly disturbing the function of institutions than it is the very result of the proper functioning of distinct extractive institutions, increasingly perverted by counter-productive incentives and power abuse.

Already in pre-colonial history the political institutional pattern established and sustained to serve the slave and ivory trade as well as colonization contributed to the erosion of established accountability and sanction mechanisms and thus to increased fragility of the political order. Rule became more violent, life increasingly unpredictable, checks and balances were lastingly weakened. Colonization harnessed fragility, continued to undermine traditional authority, and finally established alienated leadership. And while rule was relatively stable in the Belgian colonial phase, the kind of rule established also left the country ill-equipped for independence. Consequently, the idea of democracy, in the form of traditional checks and balances in a conciliatory government, even if rooted in indigenous pre-colonial structures (although eroded already), was alien to the elites in the new state, which were socialized in a system much more similar to a command economy.

Hence, in the light of path-dependent similarities the seminal changes in the history of the Congo become less significant. This holds even for the two breaks organizing this chapter, the moves to and from colonial rule. There are also notable similarities before and after 1908. In the words of Ingrid Samset (2002: 467), "While King Leopold II set a precedent for conflict promoting activities through large-scale looting, the Belgian state brought exploitation into more regulated forms." In the colonial period, checks and balances between Europeans and Africans especially remained fundamentally the same, that is, practically non-existent, be it in the form of reorganizing chieftaincy, direct or indirect coercion, or grants for concessionary companies. Certainly, the resource base and the geographical focus changed, profits became more "Belgian" and "development" became an issue. Formalized education served the purpose of holding the balance between the colonial state's need to have able people at its disposal but at the same time avoid the evolution of a critical mass of people displeased by colonial rule. When this rule could no longer be maintained, the new state inherited this framework and – after settling the initial chaotic situation – Mobutu adapted it to the needs of regime stabilization. However, due to his economic policy failures and the depletion of revenues, he failed to sustain the balance between enabling and controlling people in the long run and finally faced a "mass" of competitors "critical" enough to overthrow his regime – but hardly to establish a stable new order so far.

In conclusion, we identify two traces particularly worth investigating in the case of the Congo. The first one is about path-dependence, which is a story not about determination but about long-term persistence and influence over time. The Congo did not necessarily have to evolve into a collapsing autocratic regime. But this was likely, given the decisions people made at "critical junctures" in the past, especially those connected to resource extraction. The second one is the issue this volume is dedicated to: What can the Congo tell us in a comparative sense and how applicable are insights from this case study to others? While this chapter has provided a broader historical context linking (post-)colonial development to the pre-colonial period, the rest of this volume will look at many of the issues only touched on here in much more detail and hence aim to answer these and more questions.

## Notes

1  When we use the term "Congo," we refer to the Belgian Congo, post-colonial Zaïre and the DRC, as well as to a broader region not fully congruent with today's boundaries in the pre-colonial period. "Congolese" has to be understood as a summary term for the indigenous population living in the region concerned. The concept of *longue durée* refers to Fernand Braudel (1958). For two recent examples of excellent

narratives about the Congo's history (although not directly applying the concept), see van Reybrouck (2010) for the long view and Prunier (2008) for the crisis of the last two decades.

2 What we will not do, even if it is difficult to avoid, is intervene in the political debate about the evaluation of Belgian colonial history, a debate closely related to several issues of national identity. In an informed analysis, which is itself part of the surveyed debate, Geert Castryck (2007) provides an overview, directly referring to the controversies related to Adam Hochschild (1998) and the screening of the TV documentary *White King, Red Rubber, Black Death* by Peter Bate in 2003 and also briefly surveying earlier Belgian historical writings on the Congo (though these are often denounced as non-Belgian and non-historical in this debate), particularly the works of Jean Stengers, Jules Marchal, and Jan Vansina.

3 There were only a few administrators at the beginning, but the number increased and was large compared to other colonies. The administrative manpower amounted to around 430 in 1889 (Hochschild 1998: 140); in the Belgian Congo the number rose to 2480 in 1914 (Gann and Duignan 1979: 184), and reached around 10,000 in 1960 (Young 1965: 11).

4 All land not actually used for housing and permanent agriculture, and hence almost all land in the colony (most was used for shifting cultivation, transhumance, and collection of forest products), was declared "vacant" by the administration.

5 Most often cited is the number of 10 million (or 50 percent of population), popularized by Adam Hochschild (1998). But estimates range from "well below 100,000" (quoted in Castryck 2007: 74) to about 22 million (*Encyclopaedia Britannica* 1995), both completely implausible. The contemporary Casement Report (1904) estimated three million until 1904 alone, which is in line with the Royal Museum for Central Africa in Belgium today, accepting a depopulation of 20 percent. Most people died of famine, exhaustion, diseases and crude violence (including the large-scale cutting off of hands), some were executed or slaughtered, and some simply fled. Anyway, Jean Stengers is certainly right when emphasizing that "any attempt to translate the phenomenon of depopulation into precise or even approximate figures, is an almost impossible task" (Louis and Stengers 1968: 252).

6 While revenues generally expanded in the colonial period, only in the 1950s did those from domestic activities surpass those related to export (Lacroix 1965: 158).

7 Overall casualties between 1960 and 1997 are estimated at around 400,000 (Ndikumana and Emizet 2005), which may considerably underestimate the losses during the military campaigns of the Congo Crisis.

# References

Acemoglu, D. and Robinson, J. (2012) *Why Nations Fail. The Origins of Power, Prosperity, and Poverty*, New York: Crown Publishers.

Akitoby, B. and Cinyabuguma, M. (2004) "Sources of Growth in the Democratic Republic of the Congo: A Cointegration Approach," *IMF Working Paper*, 04 (114).

Alpers, E. A. (1967) *The East African Slave Trade*, Berkeley, Calif.: East African Publishers.

Alpers, E. A. (1975) *Ivory and Slaves: Changing Pattern of International Trade in East Central Africa*, Berkeley: University of California Press.

Anstey, R. (1970) "Belgian Rule in the Congo and the Aspirations of the Évolué Class," in L. H. Gann and P. Duignan (eds.), *Colonialism in Africa 1870–1960*, Vol. 2, Cambridge: Cambridge University Press.

Austin, G. (2010) "African Economic Development and Colonial Legacies," *International Development Policy Series*, 1: 11–32.

Beachey, R. W. (1967) "The East African Ivory Trade in the Nineteenth Century," *The Journal of African History*, 8: 269–90.

Bézy, F., Peemans, J.-P. and Wautelet, J.-M. (1981) *Accumulation et sous-développement au Zaïre, 1960–1980*, Louvain-la-Neuve: Presses Universitaires de Louvain.

Braudel, F. (1958) "Histoire et sciences sociales: la longue durée," *Annales*, 13: 725–53.

Brautigam, D. (2009) *The Dragon's Gift. The Real Story of China in Africa*, Oxford: Oxford University Press.

Broadhead, S. H. (1979) "Beyond Decline: The Kingdom of the Kongo in the Eighteenth and Nineteenth Centuries," *The International Journal of African Historical Studies*, 12: 615–50.

Bueno de Mesquita, B. (2007) "Leopold II and the Selectorate: An Account in Contrast to a Racial Explanation," *Historical Social Research*, 32: 203–21.

Bueno de Mesquita, B., Smith, A., Siverson, R. M., and Morrow, J. D. (2003) *The Logic of Political Survival*, Cambridge, Mass.: MIT Press.

Bustin, E. (1975) *Lunda under Belgian Rule: The Politics of Ethnicity*, Cambridge, Mass.: Harvard University Press.

Bustin, E. (1999) "The Collapse of 'Congo/Zaire' and its Regional Impact," in D. C. Bach, *Regionalisation in Africa. Integration and Disintegration*, Oxford: James Currey.

Casement, R. (1904) *Report of the British Consul Roger Casement, on the Administration of the Congo Free State*, Parliamentary Papers, LXII, c.1933.

Castryck, G. (2007) "Whose History is History? Singularities and Dualities of the Public Debate on Belgian Colonialism," in L. Csaba (ed.), *Europe and the World in European Historiography*, Pisa: Pisa University Press.

Clarence-Smith, W. (1983) "Business Empires in Equatorial Africa," *African Economic History*, 12: 3–11.

De Herdt, T. and Marysse, S. (1996) *L'Economie informelle au Zaïre: (Sur)vie et pauvreté dans la période de transition*, Paris: L'Harmattan.

de Maret, P. (1999) "The Power of Symbols and the Symbols of Power through Time: Probing the Luba Past," in S. K. McIntosh (ed.), *Beyond Chiefdoms: Pathways to Complexity in Africa*, Cambridge: Cambridge University Press.

Depelchin, J. (1992) *From the Congo Free State to Zaire: How Belgium Privatized the Economy – A History of Belgian Stock Companies in Congo-Zaire from 1885 to 1974*, London: CODESRIA.

Derksen, R. (1983) "Forminière in the Kasai, 1906–1939," *African Economic History*, 12: 49–65.

Douglas, M. (1963) *The Lele of the Kasai*, London: Oxford University Press.

Dunning, T. (2005) "Resource Dependence, Economic Performance, and Political Stability," *Journal of Conflict Resolution*, 49: 451–82.

Edgerton, R. B. (2002) *The Troubled Heart of Africa: A History of the Congo*, New York: St. Martin's Press.

Ekholm, K. (1972) *Power and Prestige: The Rise and Fall of the Kongo Kingdom*, Uppsala: Skriv Service AB.

Ekholm-Friedman, K. (1991) *Catastrophe and Creation: The Transformation of an African Culture*, Chur: Harwood Academic Publishers.

Emerson, B. (1979) *Leopold II of the Belgians – King of Colonialism*, London: Weidenfeld and Nicolson.

Emizet, K. N. F. (1998) "Confronting Leader at the Apex of the State: The Growth of the Unofficial Economy in Congo," *African Studies Review*, 41: 99–137.

*Encyclopaedia Britannica* (1995) *The New Encyclopaedia Britannica,* Chicago: Encyclopaedia Britannica.

Exenberger, A. and Hartmann, S. (2008) "The Congo and World Market Integration: A Dark History of Recurring Exploitation," in H. Marques, E. Soukiazis, and P. Cerqueira (eds.), *Perspectives on Integration and Globalisation,* Münster: Lit.

Gann, L. H. and Duignan, P. (1979) *The Rulers of Belgian Africa 1884–1914,* Princeton, NJ: Princeton University Press.

Gordon, D. M. (2001) "Owners of the Land and Lunda Lords: Colonial Chiefs in the Borderlands of Northern Rhodesia and the Belgian Congo," *International Journal of African Historical Studies,* 34: 315–37.

Gordon, D. M. (2009) "The Abolition of the Slave Trade and the Transformation of the South-Central African Interior during the Nineteenth Century," *The William & Mary Quarterly,* 66: 915–38.

Harms, R. W. (1981) *River of Wealth, River of Sorrow – The Central Zaire Basin in the Era of the Slave and Ivory Trade, 1500–1891,* London: Yale University Press.

Hartmann, S. (2011) "Die Institutionen des Leopoldianischen Systems: Wie pervertierte Anreize zu extremer Gewalt im Kongo beitrugen," in A. Exenberger (ed.), *Afrika – Kontinent der Extreme,* Innsbruck: Innsbruck University Press.

Herbert, E. W. (1984) *Red Gold of Africa. Copper in Precolonial History and Culture,* Madison: The University of Wisconsin Press.

Higginson, J. (1989) *A Working Class in the Making: Belgian Colonial Labor Policy, Private Enterprise, and the African Mineworker, 1907–1951,* London: University of Wisconsin Press.

Hillman, J. (1997) "Chartered Companies and the Development of the Tin Industry in Belgian Africa, 1900–1939," *African Economic History,* 25: 149–73.

Hilton, A. (1983) "Family and Kinship among the Kongo South of the Zaïre River from the Sixteenth to the Nineteenth Centuries," *The Journal of African History,* 24: 189–206.

Hilton, A. (1987) *The Kingdom of Kongo,* Oxford: Clarendon Press.

Hochschild, A. (1998) *King Leopold's Ghost: A Story of Greed, Terror and Heroism in Colonial Africa,* Boston: Houghton Mifflin.

Jackson, S. (2003) "Fortunes of War: The Coltan Trade in the Kivus," in S. Collinson (ed.), *Power, Livelihoods and Conflicts: Case Studies in Political Economy Analysis of Humanitarian Action,* London: Overseas Development Institute.

Jackson, S. (2005) "Protecting Livelihoods in Violent Economies," in K. Ballentine and H. Nitzschke (eds.), *Profiting from Peace – Managing the Resource Dimension of Civil War,* Boulder, Colo.: Lynne Rienner.

Jewsiewicki, B. (1972) "Notes sur l'histoire socio-économique du Congo (1880–1960)," *Etudes d'Histoire Africaine,* 3: 209–41.

Jewsiewicki, B. (1980) "African Peasants in the Totalitarian Colonial Society of the Belgian Congo," in M. A. Klein (ed.), *Peasants in Africa: Historical and Contemporary Perspectives,* London: Sage Publications.

Klein, H. S. (1999) *The Atlantic Slave Trade,* Cambridge: Cambridge University Press.

Lacroix, J.-L. (1965) "Le concept d'import substitution dans la théorie du développement économique," Université Lovanium, Institut de Recherches Economiques et Sociaux, *Cahiers Economiques et Sociaux,* III (2): 141–76.

Leclercq, H. (1965) "Un mode de mobilisation des ressources: le système fiscal. Le cas du Congo pendant la période coloniale, contribution à l'histoire économique du Congo, II," Université Lovanium, Institut de Recherches Economiques et Sociaux, *Cahiers Economiques et Sociaux,* III (2): 95–141.

Lemarchand, R. (2002) "The Tunnel at the End of the Light," *Review of African Political Economy*, 29: 389–98.

Lemarchand, R. (2003) "The Democratic Republic of Congo: From Failure to Potential Reconstruction," in R. I. Rotberg (ed.), *State Failure and State Weakness in a Time of Terror*, Washington, DC: Brookings Institution Press.

Likaka, O. (1997) *Rural Society and Cotton in Colonial Zaire*, Madison: The University of Wisconsin Press.

Louis, W. R. and Stengers, J. (1968) *E. D. Morel's History of the Congo Reform Movement*, Oxford: Clarendon Press.

Lovejoy, P. E. (2012) *Transformations in Slavery: A History of Slavery in Africa*, 3rd edn, Cambridge: Cambridge University Press.

MacGaffey, J. (1991) *The Real Economy of Zaire – The Contribution of Smuggling & Other Unofficial Activities to National Wealth*, Philadelphia: University of Pennsylvania Press.

MacGaffey, W. (1970) *Custom and Government in the Lower Congo*, Berkeley: University of California Press.

McIntosh, K. S. (1999) "Pathways to Complexity: An African Perspective," in S. K. McIntosh (ed.), *Beyond Chiefdoms: Pathways to Complexity in Africa*, Cambridge: Cambridge University Press.

McNulty, M. (1999) "The Collapse of Zaïre: Implosion, Revolution or External Sabotage?," *The Journal of Modern African Studies*, 37: 53–82.

Mamdani, M. (1996) *Citizen and Subject. Contemporary Africa and the Legacy of Late Colonialism*, Princeton, NJ: Princeton University Press.

Marchal, J. (2008) *Lord Leverhulme's Ghost. Colonial Exploitation in the Congo*, New York: Verso.

Miller, J. C. (1976) "The Slave Trade in Congo and Angola," in M. L. Kilson and R. I. Rotberg (eds.), *The African Diaspora – Interpretive Essays*, Cambridge, Mass.: Harvard University Press.

Miller, J. C. (1988) *Way of Death – Merchant Capitalism and the Angolan Slave Trade, 1730–1830*, London: University of Wisconsin Press.

Miller, J. C. (1998) "The Numbers, Origins, and Destinations of Slaves in the Eighteenth-Century Angolan Slave Trade," in J. E. Inikori (ed.), *The Atlantic Slave Trade – Effects on Economies, Societies, and Peoples in Africa, the Americas, and Europe*, Durham, NC: Duke University Press.

Morel, E. D. (1912) *The Present State of the Congo Question, Official Correspondence between the Foreign Office and the Congo Reform Association*, London: Edward & Hughes.

Morel, E. D. (2005 [1906]) *Red Rubber – The Story of the Rubber Slave Trade Flourishing on the Congo on the Year of Grace 1906*, reprint, Hawaii: University Press of the Pacific.

Ndikumana, L. and Emizet, K. N. F. (2005) "The Economics of Civil War: The Case of the Democratic Republic of Congo," in P. Collier and N. Sambanis (eds.), *Understanding Civil War – Evidence and Analysis, Vol. 1: Africa*, Washington, DC: The World Bank.

Nest, M. (2011) *Coltan*, Cambridge: Polity Press.

North, D. C. (1994) "Economic Performance through Time," *American Economic Review*, 84: 359–68.

North, D. C., Wallis, J. J., and Weingast, B. R. (2009) *Violence and Social Orders. A Conceptual Framework for Interpreting Recorded Human History*, Cambridge: Cambridge University Press.

Nunn, N. and Wantchekon, L. (2011) "The Slave Trade and the Origins of Mistrust in Africa," *American Economic Review*, 101: 3221–52.

Olsson, O. (2006) "Diamonds are a Rebel's Best Friend," *The World Economy*, 29: 1133–50.

Peemans, J.-P. (1968) *Diffusion du progrès économique et convergence des prix. Le cas Congo-Belgique, 1900–1960*, Louvain: Editions Nauwelaerts.

Prunier, G. (2008) *Africa's World War: Congo, the Rwandan Genocide and the Making of a Continental Catastrophe*, Oxford: Oxford University Press.

Reefe, T. Q. (1981) *The Rainbow and the Kings: A History of the Luba Empire to 1891*, Berkeley: University of California Press.

Reid, R. (2010) "The Fragile Revolution: War; Polity and Development in Africa over la Longue Durée," Paper Presented at "Understanding African Poverty over the Longue Durée," Accra, July 15–17, 2010.

Reid, T. B. (2006) "Killing Them Softly: Has Foreign Aid to Rwanda and Uganda Contributed to the Humanitarian Tragedy in the DRC?," *African Policy Journal*, 1: 74–94.

Rempel, R. (1998) "Trade and Transformation: Participation in the Ivory Trade in Late Nineteenth-Century East and Central Africa," *Canadian Journal of Development Studies*, 19: 529–52.

Reno, W. (1997) "Sovereignty and Personal Rule in Zaire," *African Studies Quarterly*, 1: 39–64.

Reno, W. (1999) *Warlord Politics and African States*, London: Lynne Rienner.

Richens, B. (2009) "The Economic Legacies of the 'Thin White Line': Indirect Rule and the Comparative Development of Sub-Saharan Africa," Working Paper 131/09, Economic History Department, London School of Economics.

Rubbers, B. (2009) "The Story of a Tragedy: How People in Haut-Katanga Interpret the Post-colonial History of Congo," *Journal of Modern African Studies*, 47: 267–89.

Samset, I. (2002) "Conflict of Interests or Interests in Conflict? Diamonds and War in the DRC," *Review of African Political Economy*, 29: 463–80.

Schatzberg, M. G. (1997) "Beyond Mobutu: Kabila and the Congo," *Journal of Democracy*, 8: 70–84.

Slade, R. (1962) *King Leopold's Congo: Aspects of the Development of Race Relations in the Congo Independent State*, London: Oxford University Press.

Stengers, J, (1969) "The Congo Free State and the Belgian Congo before 1914," in L. H. Gann and P. Duignan (eds.), *Colonialism in Africa 1870–1960, Vol. 1: The History and Politics of Colonialism 1870–1914*, Cambridge: Cambridge University Press.

Taylor, I. (2003) "Conflict in Central Africa: Clandestine Networks and Regional/Global Configurations," *Review of African Political Economy*, 30: 45–55.

Thornton, J. (1984) "The Development of an African Catholic Church in the Kingdom of Kongo, 1491–1750," *The Journal of African History*, 25: 147–67.

Thornton, J. (1998) *Africa and Africans in the Making of the Atlantic World, 1400–1800*, Cambridge: Cambridge University Press.

UN (2001) *Report of the Panel of Experts on the Illegal Exploitation of Natural Resources and Other Forms of Wealth of the Democratic Republic of the Congo* (S/2001/357), April 12, 2001.

UN (2002) *Final Report of the Panel of Experts on the Illegal Exploitation of Natural Resources and Other Forms of Wealth of the Democratic Republic of the Congo* (S/2002/1146), October 16, 2002.

van Reybrouck, D. (2010) *Congo. Een geschiedenis*, Amsterdam: De Bezige Bij.

Vansina, J. (1962) "Long-Distance Trade-Routes in Central Africa," *The Journal of African History*, 3: 375–90.

Vansina, J. (1966) *Kingdoms of the Savanna*, Madison: The University of Wisconsin Press.

Vansina, J. (1990) *Paths in the Rainforests. Toward a History of Political Tradition in Equatorial Africa*, London: James Currey.

Vansina, J. (2010) *Being Colonized. The Kuba Experience in Rural Congo, 1880–1960*, Madison: The University of Wisconsin Press.

Whatley, W. and Gillezeau, R. (2011) "The Impact of the Transatlantic Slave Trade on Ethnic Stratification in Africa," *American Economic Review*, 101: 571–6.

Wilson, A. (1972) "Long Distance Trade and the Luba Lomami Empire," *The Journal of African History*, 13: 575–89.

Young, C. (1965) *Politics in the Congo. Decolonization and Independence*, Princeton, NJ: Princeton University Press.

Young, C. (1994) *The African Colonial State in Comparative Perspective*, Michigan: Yale University Press.

Young, C. and Turner, T. (1985) *The Rise and Decline of the Zairian State*, Madison: The University of Wisconsin Press.

Zeleza, T.-P. (1993) *A Modern Economic History of Africa: The Nineteenth Century*, Dakar: CODESRIA.

# 2 Colonial extraction in the Indonesian archipelago

## A long historical view

*Thee Kian Wie*

## 2.1 Introduction[1]

This chapter assesses the history of Dutch colonial extraction in the Indonesian archipelago in a long-term perspective. The gradually increasing intensity of Dutch involvement in the indigenous economies and polities since the late sixteenth century highlights one of the key distinctions from the extension of Belgian domination over the Congo, which evolved in a much shorter period of time. The chapter starts with a discussion of the bilateral monopoly that the Dutch East India Company (Vereenigde Oost-indische Compagnie, henceforth VOC) obtained on the spice trade in the Moluccas in the early seventeenth century. The VOC's control of the spice trade took the form of a monopsony on the purchase of spices cultivated by the local population and a monopoly on the sale of these spices in the Dutch Republic. The chapter then addresses the change in extractive institutions during the expansion of state rule under the Netherlands Indies government after the Napoleonic wars, focusing on the development of the infamous Cultivation System (*Cultuurstelsel*, CS) in Java (1830–70) and the debate concerning the welfare effects of the CS.

The chapter then goes on to discuss the abolition of the CS and the liberal reforms introduced in the 1870s, highlighting the emergence of alternative means of colonial extraction in the form of a penal sanction (a specific form of later coercion) imposed on the indentured workers recruited by the plantations in East Sumatra in the second half of the nineteenth century. The Ethical Policy launched by the Netherlands Indies government in the first decade of the twentieth century can be considered as a first attempt to use public policy instruments to raise the welfare of broad layers of the Indonesian population, but it will be argued that this shift in the approach of the Dutch was partial and not sustained. Finally, the chapter briefly delves into the extractive policies imposed by the Japanese military authorities to support Japan's war effort during its occupation of the Netherlands Indies (March 1942 to mid-August 1945), namely forcibly acquiring food and manpower from the Indonesian population.

## 2.2 The Dutch East India Company (VOC), 1602–1799

Unlike the Spanish and the Portuguese, who came to the Indonesian archipelago not only as traders but also as crusaders to spread the Christian gospel among the local population, the first voyages by the Dutch in the late sixteenth century were exclusively motivated by the wish to find trade opportunities in the archipelago. Dutch trading companies were particularly attracted by the spices cultivated on the Moluccan islands, such as nutmeg (on the Banda islands), peppers, and cloves. These spices were extremely profitable because of their scarcity and the rapidly rising demand in Europe (Burger 1975: 22). During the early years of the seventeenth century, one *baer* (about 600 pounds) of nutmegs could be purchased for approximately 120 guilders and sold for approximately 1200 guilders in Europe, an enormous profit margin (Gonggrijp 1949: 28).

In 1602, the VOC was founded to represent the combined interests of several Dutch trading companies. Cooperation between the trading companies proved more efficient given the long distance between the Netherlands and the Moluccas. A unified company was also easier to protect while the Dutch Republic was engaged in its prolonged struggle for independence from Habsburg Spain during the Eighty Years War, 1568–1648 (Burger 1975: 22). To avoid competition from other European trading companies – initially, the Portuguese and Spanish, and later, the English (Ricklefs 1994: 28) – the VOC enforced a bilateral monopoly on the spice trade in the Moluccas: a monopsony on the purchase of the spices in the Moluccas combined with a monopoly on the sale of these spices in the Dutch Republic. This monopsony on spice purchases was not self-evident as Moluccan cultivators preferred to establish sales monopolies themselves (Burger 1975: 22).

Evidence suggests that the local population in the Moluccas suffered badly from the brutal methods with which the VOC enforced its control over the spice trade. By the end of the eighteenth century, the Moluccan population had declined to approximately 100,000 people, two-thirds of the estimated total population at the beginning of the seventeenth century (Gonggrijp 1949: 35). The local population also likely suffered from European diseases. The VOC's clove monopoly in the Moluccas was sustained for almost two centuries. By the late eighteenth century, two French expeditions managed to capture clove plants from the Moluccas, introduced the clove in Mauritius, and soon expanded cultivation to other French colonies. By that time, the VOC had long stopped making profits; the company's financial position was undermined by all the wars it had waged against the Indonesian population and its European rivals. The company also suffered from endemic corruption among its officials. The VOC was disbanded in 1799, four years after the French occupation of the Dutch Republic.

The VOC established monopsonies on tropical commodities and introduced measures to enforce the cultivation of particular crops in various other parts of the archipelago. The most well-known example is the forced cultivation of coffee in the Prianger regencies in the mountain areas south of Batavia. The forced supply of locally produced coffee to the VOC rose from a trickle in the 1720s to approximately 12,000 tons in the 1790s (Breman 2010: 83). To support and maintain the system of exclusive rights on indigenous produce, the VOC tried to control flows of in- and out-migration, eliminate market competition and tie farm labor to the soil as much as possible. Indeed, the introduction of the CS in Java in 1830 was historically rooted in the mercantilist policies pursued by the VOC in the seventeenth and eighteenth centuries.

## 2.3 The transformation of colonial rule, 1799–1830

The Netherlands had been under French domination since 1795. In 1806, in the interests of greater centralization of France's power, Napoleon Bonaparte appointed his younger brother Louis Napoleon as king of the Netherlands. Two years later, Louis Napoleon sent Marshal Daendels, a supporter of Napoleonic reforms in the Netherlands, to Java as the new governor general with the prime task of defending Java against a possible attack by the British. To this end, Daendels ordered the construction of a major highway (*Grote Postweg*) of around 1000 kilometers connecting Anyer at the western end of Java to Panarukan on the eastern end (see Figure 2.1). This mega-project was a first step to bringing larger parts of the Indonesian archipelago under Dutch political-military control.

Because Daendels faced an empty treasury when he arrived in Java, the construction of this highway was executed on the basis of traditional labor *corvée* services (*heerendiensten*). The project was completed in just one year. The extremely hard physical work and the iron discipline of the surveyors resulted in the death of thousands of unpaid peasant workers. The construction of this highway never made a great contribution to the defense of Java and could not prevent a British takeover in 1811, but it did contribute to a more efficient organization of transport on the island (Gonggrijp 1949: 70). The British considered Java to be the most important of the Dutch possessions in Asia (Ricklefs 1994: 112) and counted the conquest as a strategic victory against French attempts to isolate Britain.

The British Interregnum lasted until 1816. The British appointed Raffles as lieutenant governor of Java. In this capacity, Raffles continued Daendels' reform agenda by transforming the corrupt and factionalized colonial administration

*Figure 2.1* The Great Post Road (*De Grote Postweg*) from Anyer to Panarukan built by governor general Willem Daendels in 1808 (source: Map produced by Gunkarta Gunawan Kartapranata, provided under a Creative Commons License: http://commons.wikimedia.org/wiki/File:Java_Great_Post_Road.svg).

inherited from the VOC into a more rational and reliable bureaucracy. Daendels and Raffles were thus the main architects of the new Dutch colonial state that emerged in the nineteenth century (Houben 2002: 58–9). Raffles introduced a land rent (land tax) system and restored free trade principles. He obliged the peasants to pay rent for the possession of their land equivalent to two-fifths of the value of the annual harvest; rent could be either in kind or, preferably, in cash. The system was inspired by the tax system of British-occupied Bengal, but proved difficult to transplant to Java because little accurate information existed concerning the size and fertility of arable lands. The district heads (the regents) who acted as the main intermediaries in the system of indirect rule established by the VOC siphoned off a considerable portion of the tax revenue. The sharp increase in the tax burden during this period drove many peasants into the arms of Chinese moneylenders, particularly in years with crop failures that made it impossible for them to pay their land rent on time (Houben 2002: 64).

After the Napoleonic wars ended in 1815, the Dutch were allowed to resume authority in Java. The Dutch government subsequently established the General Commissioners, who received the instruction that the Javanese peasants could, with a few exceptions, freely dispose of their land and of the crops they culti-vated.[2] The most acute problem of the new administration was the restoration of an effective fiscal system because the administration of the land tax had become chaotic. To solve this problem, the General Commissioners introduced a village tax. The amount of this tax was based on bargaining between government offi-cials and the villagers (Gonggrijp 1949: 76–7). The restoration and expansion of the colonial fiscal system were especially important in view of the Dutch ambi-tion to expand their territorial control across the archipelago.

The subsequent process of conquest and (fiscal) consolidation initially focused on Java. The Java War lasted for five years (1825–30) and established the political status quo for more than a century to come; the Java War was the last significant war to be fought between the Javanese and the Dutch until the war of independence in the late 1940s. The "pacification" of Java freed the way for the conquest of other major islands, such as Sumatra, Celebes, and Borneo, but it also created sufficiently stable conditions for the reintroduction of pro-grams of forced cultivation. The leader of the Javanese forces, Prince Dipone-goro, was the son of Sultan Hamengkubuwono III of Yogyakarta. After the initial victories of Diponegoro's forces, by 1827 the Dutch learned how best to use their army and adopted the fortress system (*benteng stelsel*): small mobile columns operated independently of an ever-growing network of strategic forti-fied posts that permanently policed the local population. Diponegoro's forces lost ground and by 1828 the Dutch had clearly gained the upper hand. When Diponegoro was arrested by the Dutch in March of 1830, the war had been more or less decided (Ricklefs 1994: 117). Over 200,000 Javanese peasants and sol-diers and an estimated 8000 Dutch soldiers lost their lives in the Java War. The financial burden of the war almost bankrupted the treasury of the Dutch govern-ment (Brown 2003: 77).

## 2.4 The Cultivation System (CS), 1830–70

Throughout the first half of the nineteenth century, Dutch state finances were in dire straits because of the adverse impact of the Napoleonic Wars, the loss of a substantial part of its foreign trade (and corresponding trade tax revenues) to the British, and the large expenditures it had incurred during the Java War (Boomgaard 1989: 34) and the Belgian revolt in 1830–1 (Houben 2002: 64). After the secession of Belgium in September 1830, the Dutch government was on the verge of state bankruptcy. Yet the Dutch King Willem I refused to accept the reality of his "amputated" kingdom and kept the Dutch army in the field for nine consecutive years until 1839 (Fasseur 1992: 24). The government finances in the Netherlands Indies were also in poor shape in 1830 with a debt burden of almost 40 million guilders (van den Doel 1996: 48–50). Because of this large debt, the Dutch government had to lend almost 40 million guilders – an enormous amount of money in those days – to the Indies government, despite the generally held idea that colonies exist for the mother country, not the mother country for its colonies. Indeed, the Dutch government was compelled to explore new sources of revenue at home and abroad without delay.

In 1830 Johannes van den Bosch, a former military officer with the Dutch colonial army, was appointed as the new governor general of the Netherlands Indies. van den Bosch persuaded King Willem I that forced cultivation of export crops for the European market would offer the most effective remedy against structural deficits. His first argument was that Dutch private entrepreneurs with the necessary capital and entrepreneurial spirit were lacking, therefore government involvement in the cultivation process would be necessary in order to expand the revenue basis (Fasseur 1992: 24–5). His second argument was that Javanese peasants were, by their very nature, unresponsive to profit incentives from export opportunities. Therefore, they had to be persuaded, if not forced, to allocate one-fifth of their land, or one-fifth of their labor, to the cultivation of export crops (van den Doel 1996: 50). The introduction of the CS in Java proved to be "a stroke of fiscal genius" (Geertz 1963: 52–3) and the proceeds were directly remitted to the Dutch treasury (Booth 1998: 138).

True to his philanthropic inclinations, van den Bosch initially devised a plan to reduce labor costs while raising the real income of peasant workers and extending their educational opportunities. Whereas the Javanese peasants were required to surrender two-fifth of their rice harvest under Raffles' land rent system, under the CS the Javanese peasants were required to set aside only one-fifth of their land for the cultivation of export crops, for which they would receive a fixed price in return. However, government officials determined the type and quantity of export crops each village was to deliver (van Baardewijk 1993: 12), which in practice often far exceeded one-fifth of the total production value. The CS was introduced over a period of five years after 1830, and by 1840 it was in full operation. However, little was left of the idealistic intentions that had characterized the early period (van Baardewijk 1993: 12). The land rent tax introduced by Raffles during the British Interregnum was eventually maintained, and closer supervision and regulation of the compulsory cultivation and *corvée* services greatly reduced the opportunities for peasants to escape the increased tax burden (Boomgaard 1989: 35). The expansion of education, despite the increase of missionary schooling activities, was postponed until the early twentieth century (see Frankema, Chapter 7 below).

With only minor modifications, the CS remained in operation until 1870, despite the provisions made in the Constitutional Regulations of 1854 to terminate the system. In 1870, the system was formally abolished, but only gradually dismantled in practice. Part of the reason for its success was the long-term rise in the terms of trade between Southeast Asia and Europe, a rise that lasted from the late eighteenth to the late nineteenth century. The improvement of the terms of trade was much greater in Southeast Asia, namely 1.4 percent per annum in real terms, than for instance in Latin America (0.7 percent per annum). Moreover, within Southeast Asia, the terms of trade in Indonesia grew faster, at 3.3 percent per annum, than anywhere else, especially when compared to 0.7 percent in the Philippines and 0.4 percent in Siam (Williamson 2008: 8).

The profitability of the system also depended on the successful selection of export crops. Sugar and indigo were the leading crops in the early years of the CS. In 1833, more than 37,000 *bau* were planted with sugar cane, and more than 23,000 *bau* were planted with indigo.[3] The cultivation of other tropical crops such as tea, tobacco, and cotton remained insignificant (Burger 1975: 106). Coffee was also initially disfavored by the government, but this changed quickly after 1832–3, when the economic prospects of the crop were reassessed. The data in Table 2.1 show the average output and export of coffee and sugar from Java and Madura from 1833 to 1869.

*Table 2.1* Production and exports of Java and Madura during the Cultivation System (1833–69) (yearly averages)

|  | 1833–9 | 1840–9 | 1850–9 | 1860–9 |
|---|---|---|---|---|
| *Coffee production (in tonnes)* | | | | |
| Deliveries to government | 34.1 | 50.5 | 57.2 | 53.3 |
| Private production | 2.0 | 4.3 | 6.8 | 7.9 |
| Total | 36.1 | 54.9 | 64 | 61.1 |
| *Sugar production (in tonnes)** | | | | |
| Total | 34.6 | 62.2 | 91.5 | 114.3 |
| *Exports (millions of Dutch guilders)* | | | | |
| Principal crops (coffee, sugar) | 22.9 | 38.6 | 54.4 | 73.2 |
| Other crops | | 9.1 | 10.2 | 8.5 |
| Total agricultural commodities | | 47.7 | 64.7 | 81.7 |
| Total exports | 33.3 | 53.8 | 72.0 | 92.4 |

Source: Creutzberg (1975: Table C, 20).

Note
* from 1836 onwards.

The boom in commodity exports caused the production of rice and cash crops for the local market to stagnate and, in some places, even decline (Boomgaard 1989: 36). This decline was primarily caused not by the increasing pressure on land – after all, there was still an open land frontier – but rather by the greatly reduced freedom of peasant households to decide on the allocation of their family labor. The forced supply of labor was not only due to obligatory cultivation services, but also due to an increasing reliance on the traditional *corvée* services for the improvement of Java's infrastructure, irrigation systems, and other public works. Another outcome of the CS was deeper state penetration into Javanese society and the strengthening of the economic position of the village head (*lurah*) because he received a share of the proceeds from export crops (*cultuur procenten*) (Boomgaard 1989: 36).

From 1847 onwards, a variant of the compulsory CS was introduced in West Sumatra, focusing on the forced delivery of coffee to the Indies government at a fixed low price. A profitable, indigenous, and private cultivation of and trade in coffee already existed in this region. The introduction of the CS was facilitated by the fact that Dutch monopolies on the sale of cloth and salt served as an effective means to persuade the West Sumatran peasants to purchase these products in return for coffee (Elson 1997: 37–8).

Thus, the CS became both a classic example of colonial exploitation, with the aim of forcibly increasing the productive capacities of Java's agriculture for the benefit of the Dutch treasury, and an outstanding success, generating progressively greater amounts of revenues for the Dutch treasury (Elson 1997: 26). Table 2.2 shows the financial contribution from the Netherlands Indies to the Dutch treasury during the third decade of the CS. During the period 1832–67, the Dutch treasury received 497 million guilders and in the following 10 years, 187 million guilders (Burger 1975: 120).

The policy of obtaining a surplus on the colonial budget due to the proceeds from the CS was called the *batig slot*. Even a rather conservative Dutch economic historian such as Gonggrijp characterized this policy as one of the

*Table 2.2* Contributions from the Netherlands Indies to the Dutch treasury, 1851–61 (in current thousands of Dutch guilders)

| Year | Normal revenues | Contributions from the Netherlands Indies | General government expenditures | Interest on National Debt | Amortization of National Debt |
|------|------|------|------|------|------|
| 1851 | 59,013 | 16,383 | 31,940 | 35,839 | 7667 |
| 1855 | 63,319 | 24,348 | 38,809 | 33,696 | 12,392 |
| 1860 | 62,402 | 32,359 | 41,279 | 29,645 | 13,206 |
| 1861 | 63,261 | 32,995 | 43,026 | 29,382 | 14,306 |

Source: Fasseur (1992: Table 8.1, 150).

Note
Contributions from the Netherlands Indies include interest on the Netherlands Indies debt and exclude the sums paid for the West Indies and Guinea from the Indies finances.

most shameful pages in Dutch colonial history (1949: 101). The profits from the Netherlands Indies accounted for, on average, almost one-fifth (19 percent) of total annual Dutch public revenue before 1850. During the period 1851–60 (Table 2.2), profits from the Netherlands Indies accounted for almost one-third (31.5 percent), while in some years the revenues exceeded one-half of total national revenues. Indeed, the profits from the Netherlands Indies were indispensable for servicing the high Dutch national debt and for maintaining balance in the state budget (Fasseur 1992: 149–50).

Clearly, the excessive degree of labor coercion had adverse effects on Java's population. The focus on the cultivation of tropical export commodities drew resources away from domestic food production. Failures in rice harvests led to famines in Demak in 1848 and in Grobogan in 1849–50. According to some estimates, the population in Demak declined from 336,000 to 120,000 because of excess mortality and an exodus of refugees, while the population in Grobogan, where the famine was much worse, declined from 89,500 to 9000 (Gonggrijp 1949: 128). Elson estimated a total of 83,000 famine-related deaths in the years 1848–9, which constituted almost one-fifth of the pre-1848 population (Elson 1985: 56) in these regions.

However, despite the generally held view that the CS greatly impoverished the Javanese population, Elson also advanced three limitations of this view. First, contemporary impressions in official sources (although probably biased) indicated improvements in the material living conditions of the peasantry in various parts of Java under the CS. Many of these sources refer to the eastern half of East Java, an area subject to intensive forced cultivation. This assessment is consistent with the observed rates of population growth under the CS (Elson 1994: 307). Second, although statistical evidence in nineteenth-century Java must have been very imprecise, the available statistics from the so-called Cultivation Reports (*Kultuur Verslagen*) between 1838 and 1852 reveal that the sugar revenues of peasants were always greater than the total land rent due from the peasants concerned (Elson 1994: 310–11). Third, the CS facilitated and enforced radical changes in the organization of the rural economy, which probably improved the peasantry's abilities and skills to respond to new arrangements and commercial opportunities in the long run (Elson 1994: 317).

Therefore, Elson concluded that the argument for the impoverishment of the Javanese peasants is seriously deficient. The CS was certainly harsh and oppressive, and its aims and methods morally indefensible, but in the final analysis the CS seemed to have provided, both directly and indirectly, opportunities for a more secure management of domestic economic life and possibilities for economic growth in a peasant society whose options, up to that time, had been severely limited (Elson 1994: 324).

## 2.5 The liberal reforms, 1870–1900

Although the publication in 1860 of Multatuli's famous novel *Max Havelaar*, which described the abuses of Javanese regents (district heads) perpetrated on the Javanese peasants, greatly shocked the Dutch public, this book did not actually redirect the political debates in the Netherlands concerning the virtues and vices of the CS (Houben 2002: 65–6). The abolition of the CS was primarily an economic decision. Private entrepreneurs were anxious to invest in the colony and expressed their criticism of the CS via the Liberal Party, which was steadily gaining ground in the Dutch political arena. The proportion of export crops cultivated by private Dutch planters had risen steadily from 1850. Only in 1870, however, under increasing pressure from Dutch commercial businesses, was private capital allowed to enter the colony freely (Houben 2002: 66). These reforms heralded the end of the CS and the beginning of a new "Liberal Era" in the economic history of the Netherlands Indies (Marks and van Zanden 2012).

The colonial government withdrew from the forced cultivation of export crops, albeit at a varying pace depending on the particular type of crop (Prince 1989: 205–6). The emerging class of private Dutch entrepreneurs demanded freedom to invest and operate in the Netherlands Indies. This required releasing the rural population from its traditional feudal and communal ties. The CS had shown how profitable the cultivation of export crops was, and the transport and communications revolution of the second half of the nineteenth century had greatly increased opportunities for private investors to set up businesses at the other end of the globe. The right areas in Java had now been identified for the cultivation of sugar cane, for instance, while the techniques of cane cultivation were improved, enabling a considerable increase in the output per hectare. Private entrepreneurs began recruiting "free" workers on a larger scale, workers who would work for wages stipulated in a voluntary agreement (Burger 1975: 121).

The Netherlands Indies' government enlarged the opportunities for private enterprise – particularly Dutch private enterprise – but also promoted indigenous entrepreneurs to respond actively to the stimuli provided by free market forces. As a result, private initiative indeed became increasingly important in the economic life of the Indonesian peasantry. Indigenous smallholders began producing sugar and rubber for the international market (see Clarence-Smith, Chapter 9 below). Private enterprises initially focused on setting up plantations, mines, and road companies. After 1880, private investments increased rapidly, as they were facilitated by an increasing number of private banks acting as creditors. Rural credit facilities for the indigenous peasants also emerged under the auspices of Dutch banks. After the abolition of the consignment system, which had granted the Netherlands Trading Company (Nederlandsche Handel-Maatschappij, NHM) a monopoly on the transport of colonial commodities within the archipelago and between Indonesia and the Netherlands, the NHM also engaged in the provision of credits to diversify its business portfolio (Prince 1989: 206).

With the gradual expansion of the *Pax Neerlandica* across the Indonesian archipelago, Dutch private entrepreneurs also ventured to regions outside of Java. The most notable development in the so-called Outer Islands began with the establishment of tobacco plantation agriculture by Jacob Nienhuys in Deli, East Sumatra, in 1863 (Thee 1977). The rise of the tobacco plantation sector in this region offered a classic example of the evolution of a large-scale colonial plantation economy (Steinberg 1971: 219). Nienhuys, a Dutch tobacco planter, first visited Deli to explore the possibility of purchasing tobacco cultivated by local farmers. He soon found out that the small scale of local production limited a profitable trade in tobacco. Because the climate and soil appeared eminently suitable, Nienhuys decided to start growing tobacco himself, after he acquired a land concession from the Sultan of Deli (Pelzer 1978: 34). Yet Nienhuys was unsuccessful in recruiting the local Malays and Bataks to work on his plantation. East Sumatra at the time was sparsely populated and land was abundantly available, which meant that the labor-intensive tobacco plantations were in a difficult bargaining position.

Within a period of five decades, tobacco cultivation in Deli (a relatively small region, about 150 miles long and 50 miles wide) experienced such an impressive expansion and transformation that the island was referred to as the "America of the Indies" (*Indisch Amerika*) (Encyclopaedisch Bureau 1919: 127). Nienhuys solved the labor problem by importing workers from other, more densely populated areas, particularly southern China and, to a much lesser extent, India and later Java. Table 2.3 shows the number of Chinese, Javanese, and Indian workers in East Sumatra during the period 1883–1930.

The data in Table 2.3 show that after 1914 many Chinese workers were replaced by Javanese coolies.[4] The rate of increase of Javanese coolies was also considerably higher than the overall rate of increase in the coolie population (Lindblad 1999: 52). All these workers were recruited as indentured workers. In view of the high costs and difficulties in bringing the prospective workers to East Sumatra, the plantations needed certainty that the workers would stay for at least a number of years. On the other hand, the workers too demanded protection as they were traveling to work in a foreign country (Thee 1977: 36).

To ensure that the indentured workers would not leave the plantations before their official contract period ended the Netherlands Indies government introduced the penal sanction (*poenale sanctie*). In 1880, the government issued the first so-called Coolie Ordinance (*Koelie Ordonnantie*). This ordinance was initially only applied in East Sumatra, but later it was implemented in other regions

*Table 2.3* Number of Chinese, Javanese, and Indian workers in East Sumatra, 1883–1930

| Year | Chinese workers | Javanese workers | Indian workers |
|------|-----------------|------------------|----------------|
| 1883 | 21,136 | 1711 | 1528 |
| 1893 | 41,700 | 18,000 | 2009 |
| 1898 | 50,846 | 22,256 | 3360 |
| 1906 | 53,105 | 33,802 | 5260 |
| 1913 | 55,617 | 118,517 | 4172 |
| 1920 | 27,715 | 209,459 | 2010 |
| 1930 | 26,037 | 234,554 | 1021 |

Source: Pelzer (1935: 105).

in the Outer Islands. The ordinance gave the employers – that is, the plantation owners – the right to contract workers for a pre-specified period, but also protected the workers against abuses from their employers. To enforce the proper implementation of the ordinance, violations by both employers and workers were to be penalized. Those who ran away from the plantations could be arrested by the police and forcibly returned to the plantations to serve out their contract.

The first Coolie Ordinance was followed by new ordinances in 1884 and 1893, which gave the employers effective legal control over their indentured workers (Thee 1977: 36–7). Clearly, these Coolie Ordinances, specifically the provision regarding the penal sanction, were biased against the indentured workers and supported the process of colonial extraction. Around the turn of the century, controversy began to rise around the penal sanction, which did not subside until the early 1930s when it was finally abolished. The publication of a pamphlet "The Millions of Deli" (*De Millioenen van Deli*) by van den Brand (1902), a Dutch lawyer in Medan, disclosed the brutal treatment of the indentured workers by their European supervisors to the Dutch public. The consternation aroused by the pamphlet in the Netherlands forced the colonial government to improve the labor conditions in East Sumatra, amongst other measures by establishing a labor inspectorate (*Arbeidsinspectie*) tasked with supervising the correct implementation of the labor contract by both parties (Encyclopedisch Bureau 1919: 194).

Over time, the planters began to realize that providing better working and living conditions for their workers was more effective in keeping them than adopting coercive measures. However, the political controversy surrounding the penal sanction was only finally resolved when the Netherlands Indies government decided to abolish the penal sanction in 1934. The adoption of the Blaine Amendment in the US Congress in 1929, along with the modification of US tariff law, sped up the abolition of the penal sanction. This amendment called for a ban on the import into America of goods produced by forced labor, including workers under a penal sanction system (Thee 1977: 40–1).

A final key feature of Dutch extractive policies in the Indies during the latter part of the nineteenth century was the increased use of ethnic minorities, and in particular the Chinese, to administer economic and political affairs (see Wahid, Chapter 5 below). Under the aegis of the Netherlands Indies government, the resident Chinese became important middlemen in the tax farm system (*Pachtstelsel*). This system involved the lease through auction of the monopoly right to conduct a particular service, such as collecting taxes from the local population or to engage in a particular profit-yielding activity, in return for an agreed, fixed price routinely paid to the colonial state. Unusually heavy levies by the Chinese, who controlled tax farms, made serious inroads into peasants' cash incomes from the sale of their produce, and thus their ability to service land rent commitments (Elson 1985: 60).

The tax farm system also provided a substantial contribution to the revenues of the Netherlands Indies government, especially due to the lucrative opium farm (*opiumpacht*). The *pacht* term usually lasted from one to three years. One of the adverse long-term consequences of the tax farm system was the strong anti-Chinese sentiment among the Javanese population which has persisted to the present day. Although this system was one of the oldest tax collecting systems in Java, dating back to the ninth and tenth centuries according to some sources, it was only institutionalized under the Dutch. The tax farm system was yet another effective instrument to solve the manpower shortage and dispense with the high cost of tax administration by high-salaried Dutch officials.

Altogether, the liberal reforms were quite successful in supporting the expansion of the colonial economy; GDP per capita estimates revealed a 50 percent rise in the four decades prior to World War I (Marks and van Zanden 2012: 117). However, there is little evidence that the liberal reforms led to a significant improvement in the welfare of the population. Real wages remained at subsistence levels and average real incomes of the majority of Indonesians rose only by an estimated 8 percent. Neither do studies of height development reveal a substantial improvement in the biological standard of living (Burger 1975: 146; Marks and van Zanden 2012: 113–25; Földvari *et al.* 2010). The explanation is that the increasing economic surpluses were mainly pocketed by Europeans and foreign Asiatics (Chinese mainly) and, to some extent, also usurped by the rapid growth of the indigenous population. Moreover, although the economic expansion progressed with increasing investments in transport and communications infrastructure, the sectoral structure of the economy did not change significantly. Indonesia remained, by and large, a rural economy with a growing service sector dominated by profit-seeking foreign entrepreneurs.

## 2.6  The Ethical Policy, 1900s–1920s

By the dawn of the twentieth century, Dutch colonial policy in the Netherlands Indies was undergoing its most fundamental change. The exploitation of the Indies began to recede as the main justification of Dutch rule and was replaced by a greater concern for the welfare of the indigenous population. The Ethical Policy (*Ethische Politiek*), as it was euphemistically called, emerged after 1900 out of the Dutch colonial authorities' concern with the general level of prosperity in the country, particularly Java, and had the explicit aim of raising this level. Although this greater concern was not focused on reversing the fundamental fact of socio-economic and political inequality, it did lead to a more structural approach in improving the safety, health, and education of Indonesians (Ricklefs 1994: 151; see also Frankema, Chapter 7 below). Therefore, the Ethical Policy has often been referred to as an embryonic form of "development policy." The Dutch colonial officials stressed that the Ethical Policy was meant to facilitate the process of economic change, not to accelerate the pace of change. Direct government intervention in the economy did not become an issue until the 1930s (van der Eng 1993: 16) when the country was hit hard by the world economic depression.

The Dutch Queen Wilhelmina officially announced the Ethical Policy in her speech from the throne in 1901. The original philosophy had two essential components: bringing Christian ethics into practice and the obligation of the Netherlands to take responsibility for the welfare of the Indonesian people to compensate for excessive exploitation in former periods. The origins of this philosophy can be traced back to a public discussion in the Netherlands in the late 1890s that was triggered by the Dutch parliamentarian van Deventer who argued that the Netherlands, having obtained such large financial benefits from the CS, had incurred a "debt of honor" (*ereschuld*) toward the Indonesian people, and therefore had to give something back in return, especially at a time when the colony had to borrow from the mother country to cover recurrent deficits in the colonial budget (Lindblad 2002: 117).

The Ethical Policy also promoted a more scholarly approach to colonial affairs, which resulted in an intensification of existing programs to train civil servants for their jobs in the Indies. From the mid-nineteenth century, civil servants destined for service in the government bureaucracy of the Netherlands Indies received training in the customs (*adat*), languages, and social structures of Indonesia. Civil servants arrived in Indonesia with a special degree in Indonesian studies, spoke the Indonesian (Malay) language, and were well versed in Indonesian history and culture (Higgins 1968: 689–90). The first training in what came to be known as Indology (*Indologie*) was provided at the Indies Institute in Delft in 1843 and later at Leiden University and Utrecht University (Fasseur 1993: 13). Many Indologists developed an interest in serving in the Netherlands Indies after reading Multatuli's *Max Havelaar*. The curriculum in Indology studies in turn stimulated scientific interest in Indonesia (Fasseur 1993).

Many of the Dutch civil servants working in the Netherlands Indies after 1900 were not only highly trained for their jobs in the Indies, but were also genuinely devoted to the cause of improving the welfare of the Indonesian people. Among them was Boeke, who became famous for developing his theory of socio-cultural and economic dualism (Higgins 1968: 690). In Boeke's writings, social dualism was defined as the clashing of two fundamentally different social systems. In a colonial context, the imported social system is usually high capitalism, although it could also be socialism or communism. Boeke argued that the appearance of capitalism in pre-capitalistic societies is bound to result in social disintegration (Boeke 1930; Higgins 1968: 227–8).

However, a basic contradiction existed between the practices of colonial policy, which was primarily aimed at private initiative, and the official welfare ideology of the Ethical Policy. Some scholars have argued that policy programs introduced to promote the expansion of agriculture, irrigation works, credit services, and the establishment of rural cooperatives reached only a small group of already relatively well-to-do peasants. In fact, it was often stated explicitly that all reforms should begin with the better-off peasants (Boomgaard 1986: 78–9). Because development efforts under the Ethical Policy remained modest, they hardly raised productivity in the traditional sectors of the economy. Thus, the Ethical Policy has also been referred to as the "Doctrine of the Little Push" (Higgins 1968: 689–91).

The limited success of the Ethical Policy was also apparent after three decades of educational investments. According to the population census of 1930, the literacy rate of adult Indonesians in the entire Netherlands Indies was only 7.4 percent, and only 6 percent in Java, 13 percent in Sumatra, and 4 percent in Bali and Lombok. Moreover, much of this literacy was due to education given by the indigenous Indonesian educational institutions, such as the Taman Siswa schools and the Islamic schools (see Frankema, Chapter 7 below). The overall literacy rate in the Dutch language among Indonesians was only 0.32 percent, although it rose to 50 percent in the Christian areas of the South Moluccas (Ricklefs 1994: 160).

By the late 1920s, in spite of the substantial growth in government expenditure on irrigation, the per hectare yields of *padi sawah* remained stagnant. The total *padi* area could hardly increase further, while population was growing fast.[5] As a result, rice production per capita declined and rice imports were rising, but were on aggregate inadequate to make up the difference. Hence, the consumption of inferior foods, such as maize and cassava, increased (Booth 1989: 115). The colonial government did little to dismantle this ticking time-bomb. Institutional reform and budgetary expansion for the Ethical Policy came to a halt in the early 1920s when the post-war recession of 1920–3 led to a cut in government expenditures. Moreover, the political will to implement the Ethical Policy declined when the colonial government became increasingly repressive in response to rising Indonesian nationalism. By the early 1920s, the Ethical Policy had been virtually abandoned (Lindblad 2002: 119) – if not officially, then at least in practice.

## 2.7  The Great Depression, the Japanese occupation, and Indonesia's independence, 1929–45

The world economic depression of the 1930s hit the Netherlands Indies hard, particularly the large estates whose exports contracted severely. In response to the crisis, in May 1934 the governments of Britain, the Netherlands, France, British India, and Thailand signed the International Rubber Regulation Agreement (IRRA) to regulate the production and export of rubber from the rubber-producing areas under their control (Allen and Donnithorne 1957: 125). While plantation rubber exports from the Netherlands Indies were regulated by individual export licenses allocated to the plantations according to basic production quotas, peasant rubber exports were regulated by a special export tax. This tax lowered the internal price in order to keep peasant rubber exports as a constant fraction of total rubber exports. The ratio was fixed in favor of the plantations, since the output capacity of peasant rubber had expanded rapidly as a result of new rubber plantings during the boom period of 1925–6. These young rubber trees had not yet reached maturity by 1929, the year on which the ratio was based. Because peasant rubber exports proved to be highly price-elastic, a variable export tax generated the desired degree of restriction.

The export tax was not intended to cause any hardship to the peasant rubber smallholders because the proceeds were solely reserved for projects benefiting the population in the rubber-producing areas. However, devising concrete projects on which the tax revenues could be spent for the benefit of the population proved to be quite difficult (McFadyean 1944: 96).

The Indies government also responded to the economic crisis by raising domestic self-sufficiency in rice and other food crops, and by embarking on a policy of protectionist, import-substituting industrialization that drew on Java's abundant supplies of cheap labor (Dick 2002: 153). Yet the economic recovery that occurred after the mid-1930s came to a halt when Japanese troops occupied the Indies in early March 1942. The Japanese occupation was catastrophic for the Indonesian population, as the export-oriented economy was immediately transformed into a war economy to support the Japanese war effort. To assure the acquisition of rice, the Japanese introduced a program of forced delivery of paddy, stipulating that the peasants should sell a certain quantity of their output to the military authorities at a fixed price which was much lower than the market price (Kurosawa-Inomata 1997: 112).

In spite of a determined campaign to increase rice production, a dramatic fall in production ensued during the Japanese occupation. This decline could be attributed to various problems, including black marketing, corruption, and deliberate hoarding for speculation. The shortage was exacerbated by the excessive control imposed by the Japanese and the uneven distribution of rice due to malfunctioning transportation systems. Japanese statistics from the Central Hospital in Semarang, Central Java showed that during the six months between February 1943 and September 1943, 832 persons were treated for starvation, while 366 died in the hospital from undernourishment-related diseases (Kurosawa-Inomata 1997: 111).

From October 1943 onwards, the Japanese military authorities also began drafting so-called *romusha* (or economic soldiers) in Java (van den Doel 1996: 262). These *romusha* were forced to work on physical infrastructure projects such as railroads, including the construction of the so-called Pekanbaru railroad to connect the town of Pekanbaru with the town of Muara, the endpoint of the railroad to the city of Padang. As elsewhere, these *romusha* were harshly treated by the Japanese soldiers, often with fatal results. Between 165,000 and 200,000 Javanese *romusha* were sent overseas, mostly to Thailand, to work on the construction of railroads alongside prisoners-of-war from the Allied countries (van den Doel 1996: 262).

The Japanese occupation of Indonesia ended following Japan's unconditional surrender to the Allied forces on August 15, 1945. With the end of the Pacific War, Sukarno and Hatta, Indonesia's two foremost nationalist leaders, proclaimed Indonesia's independence on August 17, 1945. The declaration of independence was not recognized by the Netherlands. Only after a bloody armed struggle, which was ended by the intervention of the United Nations, did Netherlands give up and transfer its sovereignty over the Netherlands Indies to Indonesia on December 27, 1949. In Indonesia's historiography, this date is referred to as the official Dutch recognition of Indonesia's independence.

In the Financial and Economic Agreement (Financiele en Economische Overeenkomst, Finec) reached at the Round Table Conference in the autumn of

1949, the Indonesian delegation agreed to a clause that Dutch business in independent Indonesia could continue to operate unhindered, just as if had under colonial rule. The Finec also included a clause stating that nationalization of the Dutch enterprises would only be permitted if it was in Indonesia's national interest and if compensation was paid (Meijer 1994: 46–7). Yet the achievement of political independence without economic independence posed a serious problem for the Indonesian government. The inability to exert control over important segments of the Indonesian economy restricted the scope of action for the Indonesian government, which gave rise to the widely held notion that the economic phase of decolonization had not yet been completed (Thee 2009: 22).

This problem was finally resolved with the Indonesian nationalization of Dutch enterprises after the complete breakdown in Indonesia–Dutch relations in 1957. The festering dispute regarding the status of West Irian (presently the provinces of West Papua and Papua), which Indonesia claimed as an integral part of Indonesia, but the Dutch resisted giving up, convinced the Sukarno government that confronting the former colonial power was better than cooperating. Consequently, in late 1957 the regime allowed militant trade unions to take over all Dutch enterprises in the country. This action was followed by the official nationalization of all Dutch enterprises in early 1959. With this drastic action, the basis on which some semblance of colonial extraction could be retained in independent Indonesia evaporated completely.

## 2.8  Conclusion

More than 50 years later, evaluating the long-term consequences of such a long period of colonial domination remains extremely difficult. A few factors may be highlighted in conclusion. On the positive side are the investments in public goods and services, investments that resulted from the relatively strong commitment of Dutch administrators, private entrepreneurs, and missionaries to consolidate power, generate profits, and spread the gospel. To achieve their aims, the Dutch built a vast network of physical infrastructure (roads, railroads, bridges, and a telecommunications network) as well as large estates, mines, factories, and banks. A considerable part of this infrastructure remains in operation today. During the late colonial period, particularly from the early 1910s, the Netherlands Indies government began investing in primary and secondary schools as well as in various institutions of higher learning, including the School of Engineering (Technische Hogeschool, TH) in Bandung, the Medical School (Geneeskundige Hogeschool, GH), the Law School (Rechtshogeschool, RH) in Jakarta, and the School of Agriculture (Landbouwhogeschool) in Bogor. Upon independence, these institutions of higher learning formed the nucleus of Indonesian academia and a breeding ground for new political leadership. Although the Dutch have often been accused of investing too sparsely in the Indonesian education system (Furnivall 1943; Booth 1998), the rudimentary system that was left behind was certainly better developed than in the Congo, and most other African colonies for that matter (see Frankema, Chapter 7 below). Similar commitments to improve public health formed one of the reasons for the impressive population growth rates in Indonesia from the early nineteenth century onwards.

On the negative side stands the fairly explosive socio-ethnic design of Indonesian society, partly created by Dutch policies favoring the position of the ethnic Chinese as intermediate traders and moneylenders to the farmers in the countryside. Their preferential treatment gave rise to strong anti-Chinese feelings, both during the late colonial era and in the post-independence period. Moreover, institutions and practices of extraction, leading to regressive distribution of assets, income, and wealth, have been sustained during the post-colonial era. During the late Suharto era in particular, the government introduced a range of new monopolies, such as the citrus monopoly held by the second son of Suharto and the infamous clove monopoly held by the youngest son of Suharto. The abuse of public resources by rent-seeking elites has been a constant factor in Indonesian history and Dutch colonial rule set the example in its most extreme form.

One of the key differences from the Congo, however, is that the development of a well-functioning state bureaucracy, albeit a bureaucracy focused on effective exploitation and taxation, was initiated in the early nineteenth century. At the dawn of the twentieth century it was an advanced and experienced bureaucracy in many respects. At that time, the mere concept of a colonial state was still something entirely unknown in the Congo.

## Notes

1  I am grateful to Ewout Frankema, Frans Buelens, Pierre van der Eng, and Jeffrey Williamson for their valuable comments on an earlier draft of this chapter. Naturally, I alone am responsible for any errors and shortcomings in this contribution.
2  The General Commissioners consisted of a group of three political leaders *(het triumviraat)*. In the first term (1816–19), these were Elout, Buyskes, and van der Capellen.
3  A *bau* is an Indonesian unit of land measurement equivalent to 0.71 hectares.
4  The term "coolie" refers to an Asian slave or manual worker. The term became more widely used in the Dutch language (*koelie*) during the second half of the nineteenth century to refer to colonial contract workers from various parts of the Indian subcontinent, China, and Southeast Asia.
5  *Padi sawah* is rice grown on irrigated rice fields.

## References

Allen, G.C. and Donnithorne, A.G. (1957) *Western Enterprise in Indonesia and Malaya*, New York: Macmillan.
Boeke, J.H. (1930) "Dualistische economie," Inauguration speech at the University of Leiden.
Boomgaard, P. (1986) "The welfare services in Indonesia," *Itinerario*, 10: 57–81.
Boomgaard, P. (1989) *Children of the Colonial State. Population Growth and Economic Development in Java, 1795–1880*, CASA Monographs 1, Amsterdam: Free University Press.
Booth, A. (1989) "The state and economic development in Indonesia: the ethical and New Order eras compared," in R.J. May and W.J. O'Malley (eds.) *Observing Change in Indonesia. Essays in Honour of J.A.C. Mackie*, Bathurst: Crawford House Press.

Booth, A. (1998) *The Indonesian Economy in the Nineteenth and Twentieth Centuries. A History of Missed Opportunities*, London: Macmillan Press.

Breman, J. (2010) *Koloniaal profijt van onvrije arbeid*, Amsterdam: Amsterdam University Press.

Brown, C. (2003) *A Short History of Indonesia. The Unlikely Nation*, Crows Nest, NSW: Allen & Unwin.

Burger, D.H. (1975) *Sociologisch-Economische Geschiedenis van Indonesië, Deel 1. Indonesia voor de 20e eeuw*, Amsterdam: Koninklijk Instituut voor de Tropen.

Creutzberg, P. (1975) *Changing Economy in Indonesia I: Indonesia's Export Crops, 1816–1940*, The Hague: Martinus Nijhoff.

Dick, H. (2002) "Formation of the nation state, 1930s–1966," in H. Dick, V.J.H. Houben, J.T. Lindblad, and Thee K.W. (eds.) *The Emergence of a National Economy. An Economic History of Indonesia, 1800–2000*, Crows Nest, NSW: Allen & Unwin.

Elson, R.E. (1985) "The famine in Demak and Grobogan in 1849–1850: its causes and circumstances," *Review of Indonesian and Malayan Affairs*, 19: 39–85.

Elson, R.E. (1994) *Village Java under the Cultivation System, 1830–1870*, Sydney: Allen & Unwin.

Elson, R.E. (1997) *The End of Peasantry in Southeast Asia. A Social and Economic History of Peasant Livelihood, 1800–1990s*, London: Macmillan Press.

Encyclopaedisch Bureau (1919) *De Buitenbezittingen: De Oostkust van Sumatra*, Vol. II, no. 3, Weltevreden.

Fasseur, C. (1975) *Kultuurstelsel en Koloniale Baten. De Nederlandse Exploitatie van Java, 1840–1860*, Leiden: Universitaire Pers.

Fasseur, C. (1992) *The Politics of Colonial Exploitation. Java, the Dutch and the Cultivation System*, Studies on Southeast Asia, Ithaca, NY: Cornell University Press.

Fasseur, C. (1993) *De Indologen. Ambtenaren voor de Oost*, Amsterdam: Uitgeverij Bert Bakker.

Földvari, P., Gall, J., Marks D., and van Leeuwen, B. (2010) "Indonesia's regional welfare development, 1900–1990: new anthropometric evidence," Paper presented at the Asian Historical Economics Congress, Beijing, May 2010.

Furnivall, J.S. (1943) *Educational Progress in Southeast Asia*, New York: Institute of Pacific Relations.

Geertz, C. (1963) *Agricultural Involution. The Process of Ecological Change in Indonesia*, Berkeley: University of California Press.

Gonggrijp, G. (1949) *Schets Ener Economische Geschiedenis van Nederlands-Indië*, Haarlem: De Erven F. Bohn, N.V.

Higgins, B. (1968) *Economic Development. Problems, Principles, and Policies*, rev. edn, New York: W.W. Norton.

Houben, V. (2002) "Java in the nineteenth century: consolidation of a territorial state," in H. Dick H, V.J.H. Houben, J.T. Lindblad, and K.W. Thee (eds.) *The Emergence of a National Economy. An Economic History of Indonesia, 1800–2000*, Crow's Nest, NSW: Allen & Unwin.

Houben, V., Lindblad, J.T. and others (1999) *Coolie Labor in Colonial Indonesia: A Study of Labor Relations in the Outer Islands, c. 1900–1940*, Wiesbaden: Harrasowitz Verlag.

Kurosawa-Inomata, A. (1997) "Rice shortage and transportation," in P. Post and E. Touwen-Bouwsma (eds.) *Japan, Indonesia and the War: Myths and Realities*, Leiden: KITLV Press.

Lindblad, J.T. (1999) "Coolies in Deli: labor conditions in Western enterprises in East

Sumatra, 1910–1938," in V. Houben et al., *Coolie Labor in Colonial Indonesia. A Study of Labor Relations in the Outer Islands, c.1900–1940*, Wiesbaden: Harrasowitz Verlag.

Lindblad, J.T. (2002) "The late colonial state and economic expansion, 1900–1930s," H. Dick V.J.H. Houben, J.T. Lindblad and K.W. Thee (eds.) *The Emergence of a National Economy. An Economic History of Indonesia, 1800–2000*, Crows Nest, NSW: Allen & Unwin.

McFadyean, A. (1944) *The History of Rubber Regulation, 1914–1943*, London: Allen & Unwin.

Marks, D. and van Zanden, J.L. (2012) *An Economic History of Indonesia, 1800–2010*, London: Routledge.

Meijer, J.F. (1994) *Den Haag–Djakarta: De Nederlands–Indonesische betrekkingen 1950–1962*, Utrecht: Aula.

Multatuli [1860] (2010) *Max Havelaar. Of Die Koffieveilingun Van De Nederlandse Handelmaatschappij*, ed. G. van Es, Amsterdam: Nieuw Amsterdam.

Pelzer, K.J. (1935) *Die Arbeiterwanderungen in Südostasien. Eine wirtschafts- und Bevoelkerungsgeografische Untersuchung*, Hamburg: Friederichsen, de Gruyter, and Co.

Pelzer, K.J. (1978) *Planter and Peasant: Colonial Policy and the Colonial Struggle in East Sumatra, 1863–1942*, The Hague: Martinus Nijhoff.

Post, P. and Touwen-Bosma, E. (eds.) (1997) *Japan, Indonesia, and the War*, Leiden: KITLV Press.

Prince, G. (1989) "Dutch economic policy in Indonesia, 1870–1942," in A. Maddison and G. Prince (eds.) *Economic Growth in Indonesia, 1820–1940*, Dordrecht: Foris Publications.

Ricklefs, M.C. (1994) *A History of Modern Indonesia Since c.1300*, 2nd edn, London: Macmillan Press.

Steinberg, D.J. (ed.) (1971) *In Search of Southeast Asia: A Modern History*, New York: Praeger.

Thee, K.W. (1977) *Plantation Agriculture and Export Growth: An Economic History of East Sumatra, 1863–1942*, Jakarta: LEKNAS-LIPI.

Thee, K.W. (2009) "Indonesianization. Economic aspects of decolonization in Indonesia in the 1950s," in J.T. Lindblad and P. Post (eds. *Indonesian Economic Decolonization in Regional and International Perspective*, Leiden: KITLV Press.

van Baardewijk, F. (1993) *Changing Economy in Indonesia XIV: The Cultivation System, Java, 1834–1880*, Amsterdam: Royal Tropical Institute.

van den Brand, J. (1902) *De millioenen van Deli*, Amsterdam: Höveker & Wormser.

van den Doel, H.W. (1996) *Het Rijk van Insulinde. Opkomst en Ondergang van Nederlandse Kolonie*, Amsterdam: Prometheus.

van der Eng, P. (1993) *Agricultural Growth in Indonesia since 1880. Productivity Change and the Impact of Government Policy*, Groningen: University of Groningen Press.

Williamson, J.G. (2008) "Globalization and the great divergence: terms of trade booms, volatility and the poor periphery," revised version of the Hicks Lecture given at All Souls College, Oxford University, May 27, 2008.

# 3 Varieties of exploitation in colonial settings

## Dutch and Belgian policies in Indonesia and the Congo and their legacies

*Anne Booth*

### 3.1 Colonial exploitation: some definitions

Before examining the record of both colonial and post-colonial governments in these two countries, it is important to clarify terminology. Let us start with colonial exploitation. In recent decades, predatory, exploitative or "grabbing hand" theories of the state have attracted a wide range of adherents from across the ideological spectrum. Most of these theories view the state essentially as controlled by ruling cliques or classes. Its main function is thus to maximize the incomes accruing to the rulers, almost regardless of the impact on the rest of the citizenry.[1] Such theories have been propounded by both Marxist and neo-classical economists, and by other scholars who do not fit comfortably into either of these camps but who wish to explain the failure of particular countries or empires to achieve self-sustaining economic growth.

To many historians, not least those from former colonies, it might seem that theories of the predatory state could serve quite well to explain the growth of Western colonial control over large parts of Africa and Asia. As the countries of Northern Europe developed industrially, they acquired both the need for new markets for their rapidly growing output and the superior military and transport technologies which made large colonial empires strategically and administratively feasible.[2] By the end of the nineteenth century, radical critics of Western colonialism attributed it at least partly to the need of industrial capitalism for raw materials, and for ever larger markets for manufactured products, although in fact only some industries (especially the cotton textile industries in Britain, France, and to a lesser extent the Netherlands) were dependent on colonial markets for a substantial share of their sales.[3]

In addition, during the nineteenth century, profits from the sale of colonial produce made a substantial contribution to the Dutch budget, a point to which I return below. In terms of balance of payments accounting, exports from Java greatly exceeded imports of both goods and services, so that there was a large surplus on the current account, which in turn was used to finance the colonial contributions to the Dutch budget. After 1870, when the payments to the Dutch budget largely ceased, the balance of payments was often in deficit until the end of the century, but surpluses increased again after 1900, as a result of remittances of profits by companies operating in the colony and also because of pension and other payments (Booth 1998: 210–14). To many nationalist leaders in Indonesia, these surpluses were in themselves proof of colonial exploitation by Dutch and other capitalists.

Thus "colonial exploitation" could be defined in general terms as any policy pursued by a colonial power which was designed to benefit the metropolitan economy, particularly through remittance of capital on either government or private account, or through securing raw materials and new markets for goods produced in the home economy. But other definitions have also been suggested in the literature. In a paper published 50 years ago, Landes (1961) suggested that a useful definition would link colonial exploitation to coercion, which leads to the employment of labor at lower wages than would prevail in a free market, or the purchase of products at lower prices than would obtain in free markets. More generally, according to Landes, colonial exploitation must imply non-market constraint. This is a definition which has in fact been widely used in the literature in the decades since Landes suggested it; its relevance to both the Netherlands Indies and the Belgian Congo will be discussed further below.[4]

A further definition of colonial exploitation concerns the burden of taxation. In fact, some defenders of European colonialism in Asia have argued that it brought about a rationalization and lowering of tax burdens on the local populations, and thus curtailed the predatory nature of the pre-colonial state. But others have argued that colonialism simply replaced one form of fiscal predation with another. The imposition of cash taxes was frequently used as a means of forcing indigenous cultivators into the wage labor market or into producing crops for sale. Following Landes, it has been argued that when workers were forced into wage labor to pay taxes, the wage rates were manipulated to benefit the main employers of labor, often large corporations domiciled in the colonial metropole. If they grew crops for sale, prices were often depressed below world market levels by export taxes or state marketing boards.

Heavy taxation of indigenous populations could be justified if colonial governments used the revenues from taxes and other sources to provide infrastructure, education, health care, and other modern services which pre-colonial governments had neglected or been unaware of. Many studies in both Asia and Africa have stressed that colonial governments spent few resources in any of these areas. Infrastructure spending, when it took place, was usually skewed toward roads, railways, and ports required by foreign enterprises in order to export agricultural and mineral products. For a range of reasons, little was done to provide either education or modern health services to indigenous populations; schools, hospitals, and clinics where they existed were frequently provided by missions. The issue of fiscal exploitation will be assessed in this chapter in the context of both the Belgian Congo and the Netherlands Indies.

## 3.2 Explaining the divergence in GDP growth after 1970

Given that colonial exploitation can be defined in several ways, to what extent did colonial exploitation differ between the Belgian Congo and Netherlands

Indonesia? To the extent that there were differences, how did they influence the post-independence growth outcomes discussed in the introduction? Those who support the view that all colonial regimes were, to a greater or lesser extent, predatory could argue that, while the colonial systems of the Dutch and the Belgians may have varied in some details, they were essentially the same, and in both countries resulted in mass impoverishment. According to this argument, the very low per capita GDP figures found in both the DRC and Indonesia in 1960 are surely proof enough of the exploitative nature of both the Dutch and the Belgian colonial regimes. In 1960 per capita GDP in the DRC was only 19 percent of that in Belgium, and in Indonesia it was a meager 9 percent of that in the Netherlands. These differentials (which widened between the DRC and Belgium after 1960, and narrowed only slowly between Indonesia and the Netherlands) must, according to the critics, have been the result of colonial policies. Therefore the post-1960 divergence must reflect the different approaches of the post-independence leadership, combined with external factors such as aid, and the provision of modern industrial technology through foreign investment.

This chapter does not downplay the role of post-independence leadership or accidents of geography which caused Indonesian policy-makers after 1970 to be influenced by the powerful models of post-1945 Japan, South Korea, Taiwan, and Singapore. But I also argue that, while a case can be made for many colonial regimes being predatory, including those of the Dutch and the Belgians, important differences emerged, especially after 1900. In Indonesia, policies were adopted which could be termed, in at least some respects, developmental rather than predatory. After 1900, there were innovations in Dutch colonial thinking, which were themselves partly due to the advent of new colonial powers in Asia. Both the Japanese in Taiwan and the Americans in the Philippines began to implement policies which were more overtly "developmental" in their aims than the rather crude stereotype of the colonial extractive state seems to allow for. In particular, there was a growing recognition in most parts of Asia that governments had a responsibility to improve living standards of the indigenous populations, by improving agricultural productivity and public health facilities and by increasing access to education. I now examine these policy changes in Indonesia in the next section, before comparing and contrasting Belgian policies in the Congo.

## 3.3  Indonesia, 1830–1942: a better class of exploitation?

### Forced cultivation

Virtually all discussions of Dutch policy in Indonesia in the nineteenth century focus on the system of forced cultivation of export crops which was known in Dutch as the *cultuurstelsel*, and is usually translated into English as the Cultivation System (CS). As Thee points out in Chapter 2 above, the Dutch Governor-General who presided over the introduction of the system had humanitarian motivations and believed that his system would lead to an improvement in native welfare. But the reality was rather different. From its inception the CS was controversial. It was introduced by the Dutch government after the rather disappointing results of their attempts in the years from 1815 to 1830 to persuade private individuals to produce crops for export (van Niel 1992: 137ff.; see also Emmer 1998: 167). At its height in 1840, around 57 percent of the total population of Java, excluding the residency of Batavia and the self-governing states of Java, worked for the system although the proportion had declined to 46 percent by 1850 (Fasseur 1992: 239). The system was also extended to some regions outside Java, especially the modern provinces of North Sulawesi and West Sumatra.

While debates continue about the ultimate impact of the CS, both in Java and in other parts of the archipelago, there is no doubt that in its first decade the growth in exports from Java accelerated rapidly. Over the decade as a whole export growth was around 13 percent per annum (Booth 1998: 18; see also Thee, Chapter 2 above). The development of the CS had important implications for the Dutch economy. van Zanden and van Riel (2004: 143) have described the growth of a "colonial complex" in which industries such as shipbuilding, sugar refining, and textiles in the Netherlands benefited from the growth in trade between the Netherlands and Indonesia. In the case of textiles, the Dutch limited exports from Britain into Java in order to protect the market for Dutch products (Booth 1998: 138). The budget of the Netherlands also benefited from the *batig slot*, which was the term used for the remittances on government account to the home budget. van Zanden and van Riel (2004: Table 5.1) estimate that in the 1830s, the remittances already accounted for around 32 percent of tax income in the Netherlands, rising to 53 percent by the 1850s and almost 4 percent of Dutch GDP.

Given the obvious benefits which the metropolitan government derived from the CS, not least in terms of a substantial contribution to the home budget, it might seem surprising that by the 1860s pressure was mounting in the Netherlands for a reform of the system. While moral outrage at the exploitation of native labor may have been one reason for this pressure, another was the realization that a system based on coercion was expensive to maintain, especially as, with growing population, free wage labor was becoming more abundant.[5] By 1850, the population was estimated to be 14 million, compared with only 7.5 million in 1800 (Boomgaard and Gooszen 1991: 82). Part of this growth was due to higher birth rates and part to public health measures, especially vaccination against smallpox, which reduced death rates. Some historians have also argued that the higher birth rates were the direct result of intensified labor demands made on rural households although the evidence for this is contentious.[6]

The CS was formally terminated, at least in Java, with the liberal reforms of the 1870s but the legacy lasted well into the twentieth century. As Furnivall (1944: 174–5) argued, the idea that the colony was a business concern, *(bedrif)* became entrenched in the minds of Dutch politicians, and the post-1870 reforms were significant mainly in that they admitted more shareholders. While the remittances from the colony to the Dutch budget had dwindled to nothing by

1900, private enterprise and private individuals continued to remit profits until the end of Dutch colonial rule. It was the expectation of the liberal reformers that free markets for land and labor, as well as goods, would replace coercion, but in fact the indigenous populations of both Java and other parts of the country remained subject to coercion until well into the twentieth century.

Some Dutch historians have been harsh in their evaluation of the impact of the CS, both on the colonial economy and in the Netherlands. Emmer (1998: 169) argued that "the cultivation system retarded the introduction of a modern market economy in Java and it also retarded the adaptation of the Dutch economy to the competitive capitalism of the nineteenth century." These views, which have also been echoed by other writers, conflict with the much more optimistic assessment of Elson (1994: 305) that the CS "promoted a previously unknown level of general prosperity among the peasantry." This argument is based on an assertion that living standards in many parts of Java were very low before the CS began, which is not easy to prove or to disprove. The national income data assembled by van Zanden (2002) indicate that per capita GDP grew only quite slowly between 1830 and 1870, and that household consumption expenditures probably fell in per capita terms. This does not suggest that living standards on average improved significantly as a result of the CS, even if they were very low before the system began. There were gainers and losers, but the net impact on incomes and living standards of the majority could hardly have been very positive.

### The liberal and ethical eras: 1870–1920

The liberal reforms enacted in the 1870s were intended to allow market forces a stronger role in the economy, although the agrarian legislation in fact imposed controls on the sale of land owned by indigenous cultivators to other parties, including Chinese. The legislation was also intended to facilitate the long-term leasing of land to estate companies. As discussed in Chapter 2 above (Thee), one of the most important consequences of the liberal reforms was the growth of large estates in both Java and Sumatra, especially in the area of northern Sumatra around the town of Medan. But after more than two decades of liberal policies, there were increasing concerns about the direction of colonial policy. By 1900, influential commentators in both Indonesia and the Netherlands were concerned over evidence that, far from benefiting the indigenous population of Java, the liberal reforms had actually led to declining living standards. Falling per capita availability of rice was a particular worry. The population of Java had continued to grow, and by 1900 was estimated to be around 30 million. The fear was that, with finite supplies of arable land, it would not be possible to accommodate more people in agriculture in Java, or indeed in some of the more densely settled regions outside Java.

The Calvinist–Catholic coalition which came to power in The Hague in 1901 announced a new approach to colonial management which became known as the Ethical Policy (Penders 1977: 61). The Ethical Policy was motivated mainly by a concern over living standards in Java, and Dutch policy emphasized agricultural intensification through improved irrigation which would lead to more double cropping. There was also a recognition that educational opportunities for the indigenous populations would have to be increased. Departments of Public Works, Health, and Education were created or expanded, and both expatriate and indigenous officials were recruited to staff them.[7] But some officials worried that such policies would not by themselves be enough to stave off the threat of a Malthusian catastrophe in Java. Even if new land could be brought under cultivation, and existing land cultivated more intensively, it was still unlikely that a continually growing population could be accommodated in agriculture in Java.

The obvious solution, especially at a period when large numbers of Europe's surplus populations were moving across the Atlantic to settle in parts of North and South America, was to encourage more Javanese to settle in those parts of the archipelago where the agricultural potential was being held back by small populations and a lack of agricultural labor. Javanese had in fact been moving to Lampung at the southern tip of Sumatra for many decades. The Dutch plan was to accelerate movement to new agricultural settlements in both Sumatra and Sulawesi through ambitious land development schemes. In addition, many Javanese were persuaded to move to northern Sumatra to meet the demand for wage labor on the agricultural estates. This movement was particularly encouraged because after 1900 the Dutch had imposed controls on in-migration from other parts of Asia, especially China. While the out-migration of Javanese was supposedly voluntary, there was considerable controversy about the movement of indentured workers from Java to Sumatra; Chapter 2 above discusses these debates, and government responses.

## *The rise of nationalism*

As pointed out in Chapter 2, some observers have tended to belittle the achievements of the Ethical Policy as too little, too late. But there were important achievements, especially in the first two decades of the twentieth century. There was a marked increase in government expenditures, particularly in public works (Booth 1998: 144–8). There was also a jump in public debt, which by the early 1920s had increased to around 94 percent of export earnings. The increase led to some alarm in policy circles, and the 1920s saw increasing pressures for fiscal reform. If spending on infrastructure, health, education, and land settlement projects outside Java was to be sustained, more revenues would have to be raised from taxation. But a report published in 1921 found that the indigenous population was already being "taxed to the utmost limit" (Penders 1977: 96). There appeared to be no alternative to cutting budgetary expenditures.

Population movements continued, and the impact of the population movement was clear in the results of the 1930 population census. More than 31 percent of the population of the northeast coast of Sumatra was born in Java, and over one-quarter of the population of Lampung (Pelzer 1945: 260). This ethnic mixing caused some problems, both before and after independence, but it did serve to help create the idea of Indonesia as a single national entity. The lingua franca, Malay, became more widely used, especially after its adoption as the language of the independence movement in 1928. The independence movement itself consisted of people from various parts of the archipelago, with Sumatrans as well as Javanese playing a prominent role. Although Dutch policy was to encourage the use of local vernaculars in the expanding education system, the increasing use of a common language was an important factor in spreading the "idea of Indonesia" among increasing numbers of people (Elson 2008: 64–5).

An important reason for the growth of nationalism in the early decades of the twentieth century was a widespread conviction among many indigenous Indonesians that neither the liberal reforms of the last part of the nineteenth century nor the ethical policies after 1901 had brought them much benefit. Although the years from 1901 to 1914 saw some improvement in food availability in Java, the post-1918 period brought worrying developments. Inflation accelerated, leading to sharp increases in the prices of food and non-food staples. Another development which attracted adverse attention was the persistent current account surplus on the balance of payments. This had fallen after the termination of the CS, partly because of the growth of military expenditures in the colony. But the surplus began to grow again after 1900 (Booth 1998: 212–13). For much of the period from 1900 to 1930, it amounted to between 2 and 5 percent of GDP. The surplus financed outflows of capital on the private rather than public account. They were the result of higher levels of private savings, both personal and corporate, part of which were remitted abroad.

Defenders of Dutch policy over these years claim that, on average, private firms in Indonesia were not earning unusually large profits and that even if profits were remitted abroad, the colonial economy still benefited from the development of private enterprise whether in agricultural estates, mining, manufacturing, transport, or banking and financial services. These enterprises paid taxes into the colonial budget, and employed local workers. Debates over the costs and benefits of foreign investment were to continue after independence.[8] It has also been argued that after 1900 the Dutch share of imports to and exports from Indonesia steadily declined (van der Eng 1998: Table 1). Certainly the Netherlands was not using its colonies as captive markets for high-cost home producers of manufactures to the same extent as the French were doing after 1918.[9] It suited the interests of many Dutch and other investors in Indonesia that their workers could purchase low-cost wage goods. After 1920 that increasingly meant imported manufactures from Japan, especially cotton textiles, garments, and household goods. The increase in Japanese imports into colonial Indonesia was also assisted by the Dutch decision to stay on the gold standard after 1930, which caused a substantial real appreciation of the guilder relative to the yen. In 1934, the Dutch authorities, worried more by the political than the economic ramifications of Japan's growing penetration of the colonial market, began to impose quotas on Japanese imports, although Indonesia remained an important market for Japanese textiles until 1942 (Booth 1998: 219–20).

By the mid-1930s the Dutch had managed to stifle the nationalist movement by incarcerating most of the leadership. But by then the idea of Indonesia as a unified nation, and by implication a unified economy, had gained widespread support among educated elites both in Java and elsewhere. The Malay language was also being used more widely across the archipelago and after independence became the official language for government and increasingly in legal and commercial transactions, and in the media. Last but by no means least, the great majority of Indonesians shared a common religion in Islam, even if there was considerable variation in the degree of commitment to Islamic values and practices.

A common language, a common religion, and a shared commitment among most of the political elite to making Indonesia work as a modern state were important components in the glue which held the country together through the difficulties of the post-independence era. But the various political parties which emerged after 1950 had very different views on appropriate policies to improve living standards for the majority of Indonesia's still impoverished people, while the army increasingly viewed itself as the bastion of secular nationalism against the divisive strategies of the political parties, whether religious, nationalistic, or communist. Tensions built up which were only resolved in the bloody massacres of 1965–6.

### A colonial balance sheet

Drawing up a balance sheet for the colonial era in Indonesia is no easier than for many other former colonies, and debates continue to rage over the costs and benefits of Dutch policies. On the benefit side, the Dutch provided infrastructure both in Java and in some parts of the Outer Islands. In Java, infrastructure development, including roads, railways, and irrigation, proceeded further than in most other parts of colonial Asia with the exception of Taiwan.[10] Administrative structures reached deep into indigenous society, especially in Java, and these structures survived largely intact after independence. Among the indigenous population, there was considerable diversification of employment away from agriculture; in Java one-third of the indigenous labor force was employed outside agriculture in 1930 (Booth 2007: 121). By the end of the 1930s, many millions of Indonesians, both in Java and elsewhere, were working in the monetized economy, either as producers of agricultural products and manufactures for sale, or as wage workers or as traders.

Although some influential Dutch officials were disappointed with the results of the Ethical Policy, the policies adopted after 1900 did lead to increased food production and to the cultivation of new cash crops.[11] Smallholder production of rubber grew rapidly after 1920, especially in Sumatra and Kalimantan, and marketing networks developed to get the crops to coastal ports, to the Singapore entrepot, and ultimately to destinations in the USA and Europe. Although these networks were often dominated by Chinese, indigenous Indonesians were also involved in large numbers. After 1950, smallholders dominated in the production of most export commodities including rubber and coffee. Smallholder production of export crops has continued to flourish in many parts of Indonesia down to the present.

But to set against these achievements, there were serious failings in Dutch policy. Although the Ethical Policy did emphasize education, the achievements of the Dutch were modest, especially when compared with the Americans in the Philippines. As late as 1940, very few indigenous Indonesian children were able to progress beyond a few years in a rural school teaching a limited number of subjects in a vernacular language. Although the policy changes of the 1870s were intended to end coercion and usher in an era of free markets, the reality was rather different. Indentured labor policies were often brutal, and in Java smallholders had little option but to rent their rice land to the sugar estates, whether or not they had more profitable alternative uses. While taxation in labor and kind did end in some parts of the country, it was still in use in parts of the Outer Islands until well into the twentieth century. In Java a range of cash taxes fell on the indigenous population, which pushed them either into the wage labor market or into other cash-earning activities. And there was the vexed issue of private sector remittances, which in the eyes of many nationalists resulted from the fact that foreign companies were exploiting Indonesia's resources and remitting the profits, with little benefit accruing to the indigenous populations.

## 3.4  The evolution of the Congo Colonial State: comparisons with Indonesia

### The evolution of the Belgian Congo until 1940

Even before he ascended the Belgian throne, Leopold II had already become involved in various unsuccessful colonial projects, including an attempt to purchase Sarawak. Influenced by the success of the Cultivation System in boosting revenues accruing to the budget of the Netherlands, Leopold turned his attention to Central Africa, and in 1885 established the Congo Free State, of which he was king in his personal capacity (Anstey 1966: 1–2). From the outset, Leopold's system consisted of two key policies: control of land and mobilization of labor. As eager for profits from the colony as the Dutch king had been 50 years earlier, Leopold through his administration enacted a decree in 1885 which "established the right of the state to dispose of all lands that were not effectively occupied by African tribes" (Peemans 1975a: 169). Some officials may have been aware that indigenous agriculture was based on shifting cultivation and hunting; both of these activities required large amounts of land which would not necessarily have appeared "occupied." But the 1885 decree gave the state legal sanction to take over these lands (see Clement, Chapter 4 below).

As in Java in the 1830s, Leopold's plans for accelerating export growth in the Congo depended crucially on mobilization of labor. An important aim of Leopold's system was to create a legal framework which "allowed the state to mobilize the potential labor force by authoritarian means" (Peemans 1975a:

170). In the Lower Congo, trading activities were already well established, based on palm oil and kernels; traders bought the merchandise from African cultivators and state revenues from these products were derived from export taxes. This system was broadly similar to that implemented in Indonesia, and in parts of West Africa. But in the newly occupied lands beyond Leopoldville, the government's sights were set on increasing production of three valuable products, rubber, ivory, and copal. There was no expectation that Africans could produce and sell these products in the desired quantities through the market mechanism alone. Instead official policy was to coerce Africans into producing rubber through taxes in labor and kind, combined with force where necessary (Peemans 1975a: 170–4).

Rubber exports increased from zero in 1887 to over 5000 tons in 1902, which was more than Indonesia was exporting at that time.[12] But after 1903 a press campaign was launched in Belgium and England which exposed the abuses of the system of forced cultivation. In addition it was argued that, given the labor constraints, it was pointless trying to wring more output from what was in many regions still a hunter-gatherer economy. These pressures led to the demise of the Congo Free State, and Belgium assuming direct responsibility as a colonial power. But policies did not undergo a dramatic change after the termination of the Free State. Coercive labor recruitment continued both for cultivation of crops and for public works projects. The Ordinance of February 20, 1917 imposed 60 days annually of obligatory cultivation of the crops decreed by government agricultural services (Young 1994: 253). Penal sanctions were applied if the crops were not cultivated as ordered. Vansina (2010: 215) describes the impact of compulsory cultivation on rural people in the district of Kasai. According to his estimates, by the 1950s almost all the male population in this district had spent some time in jail because of noncompliance with the ordinance.

The growth of the copper mining industry in Katanga posed particular problems because this was a region which was very lightly populated, even compared with other parts of the colony. Merlier (1962: 133–5) has described the means by which male workers were mobilized to work in the mining sector which by 1939 employed 231,000 men out of an estimated wage labor force of 530,000. This was estimated to be around 21 percent of all adult males in the Congo. The growth in the wage labor force meant that over time more and more Africans were living outside the traditional economy, many in urban areas or mining camps. Traditional agriculture lost large numbers of young adult males, who moved in search of wage work. After mining, the largest labor force was in estate agriculture, whose growth was facilitated by large-scale land alienation. Between 1885 and 1944, 12.1 million hectares of land was legally alienated to private companies, missions, and settlers (Peemans 1975a: Table 31). This amounted to around 5 percent of the total land area of the Belgian Congo. Land alienation occurred on a larger scale than in most parts of Indonesia, where in 1940 around 1 percent of the total geographic area was planted by agricultural estates. Only in densely settled Java was the percentage of land leased to

Western enterprises (7.4 percent) greater than the figure in the Belgian Congo (Central Bureau of Statistics 1947: 36).[13]

The Belgian policies shared some similarities with Dutch policies under the CS. Both colonial regimes were responding to the challenge of inducing small populations to exploit land more intensively in order to produce crops and minerals in high demand on world markets. But whereas in Java the CS was accompanied by growing population, the reverse was the case in the Congo, at least before 1920. Although there is debate about the magnitude, most historians agree that the Congo experienced a significant population decline between 1880 and 1920 (de St. Moulin 1990: 300–3). The main reason was the spread of diseases such as sleeping sickness, smallpox, and influenza, against which the indigenous populations had little immunity. In addition, venereal disease, which was also spread by migrants from Europe and the Middle East, reduced fertility in many parts of the Congo. According to de St. Moulin, population only began to increase after 1920, and then at a very slow rate. By 1939, the population was put at 10.6 million.[14]

Stagnating or declining populations also posed problems for the collection of taxes, which performed two crucial roles in the colonial state (Nelson 1994: 19). On the one hand they provided revenues for the colonial budget, while on the other hand the money taxes levied on the African population forced them into the wage economy. As mineral exports surged ahead of agricultural exports after 1920, mines became important employers of labor. Peemans (1975a: 176) argued that the tax system played a crucial role in creating a labor market characterized by migration and high turnover. He estimated that before 1940, poll taxes absorbed between 20 and 60 percent of the annual cash incomes of the African population.[15] He does not give an estimate of cash incomes as a proportion of total income. One assumes this must have varied considerably across the Belgian Congo. But most scholars agree that the burden was often heavy and was the main reason why young men left the villages to seek work in mines and plantations.

By the late 1930s, the fiscal system in the Belgian Congo had developed to a point where both revenues and expenditures in per capita terms were roughly similar to French West Africa and the Sudan (controlled by the British) but lower than in other parts of Africa and lower than in Indonesia (Table 3.1). The revenue system had become more diversified, although trade taxes still accounted for around 30 percent of total budgetary revenues (Table 3.2). Earlier in the 1930s, the world depression affected tax receipts and the Belgian government was forced to grant a "metropolitan subsidy" to the colonial government which in 1934 and 1935 amounted to more than 30 percent of total budgetary revenues, although this was reduced as the economy recovered toward the end of the decade (Naval Intelligence Division 1944: 438–9). A further innovation at this time was the introduction of the "colonial lottery," which after 1934 contributed almost as much to the colonial budget as the metropolitan subsidies, and remained an important source of revenue until 1940 (Stengers 1957: 110–14). Reliance on customs and excise duties also remained high, at around 30 percent of total revenues (Table 3.2).

*Table 3.1* Budgetary revenues and expenditures per capita, *c.*1938, African colonies and Indonesia (pounds)

| Country | Revenues | Expenditures |
|---|---|---|
| Kenya | 1.12 | 1.15 |
| Northern Rhodesia | 1.16 | 1.03 |
| Gold Coast | 0.98 | 0.88 |
| Netherlands Indies | 0.76 | 0.85 |
| Angola | 0.67 | 0.67 |
| Uganda | 0.50 | 0.54 |
| Belgian Congo | 0.48 | 0.51 |
| Sudan | 0.43 | 0.40 |
| Nigeria | 0.34 | 0.34 |

Sources: Naval Intelligence Division (1944: 448); Indonesia: Creutzberg (1976: Table 4); Gold Coast: Kay and Hymer (1972: Table 23); Nigeria: Helleiner (1966: 429, 557).

The incidence of these duties would have fallen largely on Europeans and Africans consuming imported commodities, but the native poll tax fell on the great majority of African households, who paid either in cash or in kind. This amounted to around 15 percent of budgetary revenues in 1937 (Moeller 1938: 117). There was also an income tax, which fell on both Europeans and Africans earning more than an income threshold, which was set higher for Europeans than for others. A range of license and permit fees fell on small traders, most of whom were African (Naval Intelligence Division 1944: 436–9). Revenues from taxes and other fees together with the metropolitan subsidy covered ordinary (mainly administrative) expenditures but in addition government borrowing accelerated after 1908. Some of this borrowing was in effect investment by

*Table 3.2* Budgetary and trade indicators compared: Netherlands Indies and the Belgian Congo, 1937

| Indicator | Belgian Congo | Netherlands Indies |
|---|---|---|
| Exports per capita (pounds) | 1.66 | 1.61 |
| Budget expenditures per capita (pounds) | 0.48 | 0.82 |
| Budget revenues per capita (pounds) | 0.35 | 0.76 |
| Trades taxes as % of exports and imports | 4.40 | 5.30 |
| Trade taxes as % of total revenues | 30.30 | 17.10 |
| Debt service as % of total expenditures | 33.80 | 16.10 |
| Debt service as % of total exports | 9.70 | 8.10 |
| Total debt as a ratio of budget expenditures | 9.30 | 2.80 |
| Exports as a ratio of imports in 1929 | 0.74 | 1.35 |
| Exports as a ratio of imports in 1937 | 2.19 | 1.89 |

Sources: Belgian Congo: Naval Intelligence Division (1944: 249, 414, 436), Moeller (1938: 117, 137); Indonesia: Creutzberg (1976: Tables 1 and 4); Korthals Altes (1991: Tables 1B, 2B); Central Bureau of Statistics (1947).

government in private companies in the colony which were charged with developing both infrastructure and directly productive enterprises.

After 1920, government expenditures on capital works, particularly transport infrastructure, accelerated. Louis Franck, then the Minister of Colonies had bold ideas for infrastructure development, for which he envisaged borrowings amounting to hundreds of millions of francs (Stengers 1957: 87–95). The actual amounts borrowed between 1921 and 1925 were much lower. Railway development was largely in private hands, with government guarantees about minimum returns on investment; the government was responsible for road and river development.[16] But progress in developing the transport network was considerable. The rail network expanded more than fourfold to 4600 kilometers by 1938; the road network grew more than ten-fold, and by 1938 had reached 140,000 kilometers. By 1937, the total debt outstanding was estimated at 6.65 billion francs (around £45 million sterling). Most of this was "extraordinary debt" for major projects, including interest guarantees to utility companies (Moeller 1938: 137). Debt service payments amounted to around one-third of total budgetary expenditures in 1937, which was twice the percentage in Indonesia (Table 3.2).

By the late 1930s, road densities were about the same as in Indonesia, although rail densities were lower (Table 3.3). In addition there were over 11,000 kilometers of navigable rivers. While it was true that large tracts of the Belgian Congo had seen very little infrastructure development before 1940 that was equally the case in many parts of Indonesia outside Java. Critics such as Peemans pointed out that the policy of building up an integrated transport network within the colony was expensive, and it would have been cheaper to have integrated the eastern part of the Belgian Congo into the transport networks to the Indian Ocean through British territories. But the Belgian colonial authorities regarded the lower transport costs of the other colonial networks as a danger rather than an opportunity (Peemans 1975a: 207). A similar attitude encouraged the Dutch to disrupt the traditional trading links between Singapore and Sumatra, Kalimantan and other parts of the Outer Islands, and redirect them to Java, although this policy was at best only partially successful.[17]

*Table 3.3* Road and rail densities: Indonesia and the Congo, 1938–9 and 1958–9

|  | *Congo* | *Indonesia* |
| --- | --- | --- |
| *1938–9* |  |  |
| Road densities | 29.0 | 27.7 |
| Rail densities | 2.0 | 3.8 |
| *1958–9* |  |  |
| Road densities | 59.7 | 41.7 |
| Rail densities | 2.1 | 3.5 |

Sources: Peemans (1975a; 203); Central Bureau of Statistics (1959: 166–9).

Note
Road and rail densities refer to kilometers per thousand square kilometers of geographic area.

Many students of Belgian colonialism in the decades from the 1880s to the 1940s would agree that

> the prime motive and most consistent defining characteristic of the Belgian enterprise in the Congo was the pursuit of profits for the benefit of Europeans. From the late 1880s to 1940, colonial officials implemented numerous strategies designed to minimize expenses, while maximizing receipts. Indeed, the profit motive is revealed in nearly all aspects of the colonial endeavor. It fundamentally shaped the relationship between Belgium and its colony: the Congo was established as a distinct financial entity, generating no liabilities but only profits for the mother country.
>
> (Nelson 1994: 195)

If this was indeed the case, it would be expected that both the budget and the balance of payments would have been in surplus, and remittances on both public and private accounts very large, as was the case in Indonesia for much of the century from 1830 to 1930. But the available evidence from the Belgian Congo suggests that different mechanisms were at work. Budget deficits were common after 1920, necessitating metropolitan grants which in the 1930s did not have to be repaid, and after 1934 the introduction of the lottery. Outward remittances on government account, if they occurred at all, appear to have been small; certainly their importance was nowhere near as great as the *batig slot* was to the Dutch budget at the height of the CS. Belgian companies operating in the Congo certainly made large profits, and remittances of profits were substantial, as Buelens and Marysse (2009) have shown. But these remittances did not result in sustained balance of payments surpluses, at least in the years from 1920 to 1939. In these two decades the balance of payments was in deficit for 11 years; the surpluses only amounted to 25 percent or more of commodity imports in the latter part of the 1930s (Vandewalle 1966: 77).

### The final phase of Belgian colonialism: 1945–60

The years from 1945 to 1960 have been described as golden years by Peemans, especially for wage workers who experienced a doubling in real wages (Peemans 1975b: 152). Real industrial output more than trebled between 1949 and 1958 (Vandewalle 1966: 118). Both agricultural and mineral exports grew in real terms. Per capita GDP grew quite rapidly in real terms between 1950 and 1960. Investment expenditures also grew; estimates by Vandewalle (1966: 144) show that they more than doubled between 1948 and 1956, and were well over 30 percent of GDP in the early and mid-1950s. There was a considerable expansion of the road network and by the late 1950s road densities were higher than in Indonesia. They were much higher than in the islands outside Java, where, with the partial exception of Sumatra, the development of transport infrastructure was very limited until the end of the colonial era and into the 1950s (Tables 3.3 and 3.4).

*Table 3.4* Population densities and road and rail densities: Zaïre and the Outer Islands of Indonesia, *c.*1960

|  | *Population* | *Rail densities* | *Road densities* |
|---|---|---|---|
| Belgian Congo | 7.2 | 2.1 | 59.7 |
| Sumatra | 32.7 | 4.1 | 57.8 |
| Other Islands* | 14.1 | 0 | 17.4 |
| Other Islands** | 19.2 | 0 | 24.7 |

Sources: Peemans (1975a: 203); Central Bureau of Statistics (1963a: 1); Central Bureau of Statistics (1963b: 186–8).

Notes
* refers to Kalimantan, Sulawesi, Maluku, Bali, West and East Nusatenggara and West Irian.
** excludes West Irian, now Papua and Papua Barat.
Population densities refer to people per square kilometer; road and rail densities refer to kilometers per thousand square kilometers of area. Data for the Belgian Congo refer to 1958–9; for Indonesia to 1962.

Several reasons have been put forward for the changes in colonial policies after 1950, which in some respects have much in common with the first two decades of the Ethical Policy in Indonesia (1900–20). Vansina (2010: 172) points out that the traditionally anti-colonialist Socialist Party participated in several post-1945 coalition governments in Belgium, and pushed for reforms, although the party was later to become a defender of Belgian colonial policy. The bitter experience of German occupation also changed the mindset of younger Belgian officials who saw their mission as one of improving the skill levels of the Congolese so that they could eventually govern themselves. Air travel made it possible for Belgian parliamentarians, journalists, and other opinion leaders to visit the colony to see problems for themselves. By the early 1950s, when most Asian colonies had been granted independence or a large measure of self-government, it was increasingly clear to the British, if not to other colonial powers in Africa, that their African colonies would in time achieve full independence.

The strong growth through the 1950s in the Belgian Congo contrasted with the mounting problems in Indonesia, where independence had not brought a dramatic improvement in indigenous living standards. In spite of some growth after 1950, real per capita GDP in 1960 was still below pre-independence levels. Successive governments in the young republic struggled to increase budgetary revenues in order to finance recurrent expenditures and carry out much needed infrastructure rehabilitation. In the mid-1950s the real value of central government revenues per capita was still below the level of the late 1930s, and the five-year plan launched in 1956 was only partially implemented.[18] The Belgian authorities had launched an ambitious ten-year development plan in 1950, with the plan expenditures largely financed from loans. Most of the plan projects were implemented (Vansina 2010: 173). Government revenues from all sources increased rapidly after 1950 and by 1956 revenues per capita in dollar terms were more than ten times what had been achieved in 1939

*Table 3.5* Budgetary revenues and expenditures per capita, Belgian Congo/Zaïre: 1939–70 ($ per capita)

|  | *Revenues* | *Expenditures* |
|---|---|---|
| 1939 | 2.57 | 2.45 |
| 1945 | 4.69 | 6.67 |
| 1950 | 15.21 | 19.15 |
| 1956 | 28.37 | 28.11 |
| 1970 | 59.12 | 76.31 |

Sources: Revenues and expenditures: 1939–56; Belgian Congo (1960: 54), 1970: World Bank (1980: 59–70); population data: St. Moulin (1990: 307); exchange rates: Vandewalle (1966: 228), Depelchin (1992: 33).

(Table 3.5). Government borrowing increased rapidly to fund plan projects, with the result that the current account of the balance of payments was in deficit from 1952 to 1958 (Vandewalle 1966: 155).[19]

But the apparently robust performance of the Belgian Congo in the final decade of colonial rule masked some worrying trends. Modernization of indigenous agriculture was given high priority in the ten-year plan; a new class of yeoman farmers was supposed to arise (Vansina 2010: 173–4). The attempts at agricultural extension were aimed at men, ignoring the fact that women did most of the farming, and often the advice amounted to coercion based on a poor understanding of the agro-climatic conditions in local areas (Vansina 2010: 219–21). Indigenous agricultural production of both food and non-food crops did increase but, with the exception of cotton, much of the growth in agricultural exports came from European companies. Apart from the failure on the part of the government to grant secure land rights, officials were slow to grasp the significance of more rapid population growth on demand for food. Over the 1950s, population growth accelerated to over 2 percent per annum, a sharp contrast with the rate prior to 1940 (de St. Moulin 1990: 307).

Most of the increase in food crop output was in the smallholder sector, which experienced little or no productivity growth in terms of output per hectare. Although there was a considerable growth in area under cultivation of food crops between 1929 and 1956, only in the case of manioc was there any growth in output per hectare. For most other crops, output per hectare fell, which suggests that the growing population was forced on to less fertile land (Peemans 1997: 52–4). Peemans (1997: 52–3) contrasted the performance of agriculture in Zaïre with that of Taiwan under Japanese rule, when a "green revolution" in rice agriculture based on high-yielding rice varieties developed in Japan was successfully transferred to Taiwan. In Indonesia, the Dutch were not as successful as the Japanese in increasing output per hectare in food crop agriculture, although investment in irrigation did lead to growth in double-cropping. There appears to have been little irrigation development in the Congo.

After 1950, the Belgian government did try to encourage, or coerce, the growth of smallholder cultivation of cash crops, though with mixed success.

Chapter 9 below (Clarence-Smith) analyzes the reasons for the poor perform-ance of the smallholder rubber sector; by 1958, the area under smallholder rubber production was only around 10,000 hectares compared with an estimated 1.3 million hectares in Indonesia (Table 3.6). By far the largest smallholder crop in terms of area was cotton, although cotton cultivation was often unpopular with local populations because it exhausted the soil; where they were given a choice farmers in some locations preferred rubber (Vansina 2010: 169). The other crops where smallholders accounted for a considerable share of total planted area in the Belgian Congo in 1958 were palm oil and coffee; the area planted by both estates and smallholders with palm oil and palm nuts was almost 80 percent higher than in Indonesia (Table 3.6). The area planted to coffee by smallholders was much larger in Indonesia, while the coffee area planted by estates was larger in the Congo.

Turning to food crops, in 1958 per capita harvested area of root crops (mainly cassava and sweet potatoes) was higher in the Belgian Congo than in Java, or in Indonesia as a whole (Table 3.7). Harvested area per capita of cereals (mainly corn and rice) was slightly higher in Indonesia. But higher yields per hectare of

*Table 3.6* Area under main cash crops, 1958 ('000 hectares)

|                               | Smallholder | Estate  |
| ----------------------------- | ----------- | ------- |
| *Belgian Congo*               |             |         |
| Sugar                         | 0.90        | 4.80    |
| Palm oil                      | 59.20       | 119.70  |
| Sesame                        | 17.00       | n.a.    |
| Cotton                        | 339.40      | 0.10    |
| Urena and punga               | 9.80        | n.a.    |
| Coffee                        | 18.80       | 76.80   |
| Rubber                        | 10.00       | 48.00   |
| Cocoa                         | 0.10        | 15.40   |
| Total per capita (hectares)   | 0.03        | 0.01    |
| *Indonesia*                   |             |         |
| Sugar                         | 43.30       | 52.10   |
| Palm Oil                      | n.a.        | 104.50  |
| Tea                           | 60.10       | 74.30   |
| Coffee                        | 198.90      | 47.10   |
| Rubber                        | 1301.50*    | 498.20  |
| Cloves/Nutmeg                 | 33.40       | n.a.    |
| Pepper                        | 33.40       | n.a.    |
| Coconut/Areca                 | 1706.70     | n.a.    |
| Kapok                         | 220.10      | 9.50    |
| Tobacco                       | 178.30      | 7.60    |
| Total per capita (hectares)   | 0.04        | 0.01    |

Sources: Belgian Congo (1960: 90–1); Central Bureau of Statistics (1963b: 74–83).

Note
* Estimated hectarage.

*Table 3.7* Hectares of food crops per thousand people, 1958

|                | Belgian Congo | Java  | Indonesia |
|----------------|---------------|-------|-----------|
| Cassava        | 45.1          | 18.1  | 14.7      |
| Sweet potatoes | 3.5           | 5.1   | 4.9       |
| All root crops | 48.9          | 27.5  | n.a.      |
| Corn           | 25.2          | 35.5  | 29.7      |
| Rice           | 11.6          | 74.0  | 76.7      |
| Other cereals  | 59.2          | n.a.  | n.a.      |
| All cereals    | 96.0          | 109.6 | 106.4     |
| Fruit          | 16.5          | n.a   | n.a       |
| Peanuts        | 19.6          | 4.8   | 3.6       |
| Other beans    | 8.5           | n.a.  | n.a.      |
| Soybeans       | n.a.          | 9.0   | 6.5       |
| All nuts       | 28.1          | 19.5  | n.a       |

Sources: Belgian Congo (1960: 90–1); Central Bureau of Statistics (1963b: 68–9).

cereals meant that production per capita in Indonesia was considerably higher than in the Congo, although root crop production per capita was much higher in the Congo (Table 3.8). It is striking that, in spite of the low population densities in much of the Belgian Congo, by 1958 cultivated area per agricultural worker was lower than in densely settled Java (Table 3.9). The difference was due to the much higher cultivation ratios in Java. By the early 1960s around 63 percent of the geographic area of the island was under smallholder cultivation and a further 5 percent under estate crops (Central Bureau of Statistics 1963b: 66, 80). In the Belgian Congo only about 1 percent of the geographic area was under small-holder cultivation, while around 5 percent of the land was alienated to private companies, missions, and settlers.

*Table 3.8* Production of food crops, 1958 (kg per capita)

|                   | Belgian Congo | Java   | Indonesia |
|-------------------|---------------|--------|-----------|
| Paddy rice        | 13.6          | 161.0* | 168.4*    |
| Corn              | 24.9          | 33.9   | 28.9      |
| Other cereals     | 4.5           | n.a.   | n.a.      |
| Fresh cassava     | 590.7         | 136.6  | 123.8     |
| Other tubers**    | 26.1          | 29.5   | 34.1      |
| Peanuts           | 13.2          | 3.2    | 2.5       |
| Other peas/beans  | 5.4           | n.a.   | n.a.      |
| Soybeans          | n.a.          | 6.4    | 4.6       |
| Bananas           | 141.9         | n.a.   | n.a.      |

Sources: Belgian Congo (1960: 90–1); Central Bureau of Statistics (1963b: 70–1).

Notes
* Dry stalk paddy.
** Belgian Congo includes sweet potatoes and potatoes; for Java and Indonesia, sweet potatoes.

*Table 3.9* Area cultivated by peasant households per agricultural worker, 1934 and 1958 (hectares)

|  | Belgian Congo | Java |
|---|---|---|
| **1934** | | |
| Cultivated area per male worker | 0.76 | 1.09 |
| Cultivated area per worker | 0.35 | 0.83 |
| **1958** | | |
| Cultivated area per male worker | 1.17 | 0.86 |
| Cultivated area per worker | 0.43 | 0.65 |

Sources: Peemans (1997: 168); Central Bureau of Statistics (1947: Tables 54, 1963a: 33–5, 1963b: 67).

Note
Data for Java refer to 1930 and 1961; area cultivated refers to harvested area of all crops grown by smallholders.

Were there biophysical, legal, or other constraints which prevented further extension of the cultivation frontier in the Congo? Did the Belgian authorities actively deter smallholders from cultivating more land, even where suitable land was available? It would appear that, even during the 1950s when Belgian policies became more developmental, agricultural policies were still biased in favor of encouraging large European-owned estates producing export crops such as palm oil, coffee, and rubber. There was little or no research into ways of increasing productivity among smallholder food crop farmers who went on replicating existing technologies, as indeed they continued to do after independence.

### Post-1960 developments

By 1956, open discussion had begun in both Belgium and the colony over a process of decolonization. The Belgian government envisaged a slow transfer of some government functions but in 1959 a wave of civil disobedience forced the Belgian king to promise a much more rapid handover of power (Young 1994: 256–9). On June 30, 1960, Lumumba became prime minister; his first speech implied that a continuing Belgian administrative presence was essential in order to preserve the Congolese state. But events began to spiral out of his control, and as his rhetoric became increasingly anti-Western, the USA and Belgium began to plot his downfall. After his brutal assassination, and the ensuing political turmoil, most observers expected the economic progress of the 1950s to be reversed.

Economic performance was poor until 1967, when a package of reform measures was implemented including a devaluation of the currency and fiscal reforms. From 1967 to 1970 the economy grew at around 10 percent per annum (World Bank 1980: 4). All sectors except agriculture grew rapidly over these years. Copper exports boomed on the back of favorable world prices. In 1970 the dollar value of both government revenues and expenditures was more than twice the level achieved in 1956 (Table 3.5). Growth slowed after 1970, and until 1973 averaged around 5 percent per annum. If Zaïre had been able to maintain this growth momentum until the end of the Mobutu era, the country today would be unrecognizable. But when copper prices fell in the mid-1970s, the government proved unable to cope. Several reform packages were implemented, but did not succeed in curbing the growing budget deficit or in controlling inflation. By 1980, per capita GDP had fallen back to 1950 levels.

In principle, what became Zaïre after Mobutu seized power could have diversified its export base away from dependence on copper after 1975. In particular, the scope for increased exports from the smallholder agricultural sector should have been considerable. What held this sector back? Most accounts of economic development after 1965 stress the continuing failure of the state to support smallholder agriculture. Admittedly the problems were formidable, given the huge area of the country and the light population densities in most parts. But even during the years of rapid growth from 1967 to 1973, the agricultural sector performed poorly. The bulk of investment went to mining and manufacturing and to the urban service sector. Chronic underinvestment and inadequate incentives were blamed for agriculture's poor performance (World Bank 1980: 5). Although the central importance of agriculture was well recognized in official circles, and agriculture was a central plank in the "Mobutu Plan" launched in November 1977, the rhetoric was not translated into reality. The government commitment resulted in neither "the practical allocation of state resources nor ... policies offering inducements to villagers" (Young and Turner 1985: 310).

Young and Turner point out that the share of budgetary outlays going to agriculture had dropped to only 1 to 2 percent in 1973–4, compared to 4 to 5 percent in the late colonial era, itself hardly a high percentage.[20] And the impact of even these modest resources was doubtful. An agricultural credit scheme was established, but the criteria were strict and the procedures very bureaucratic. Few of those who got access to credit were actually farmers. The delivery of agricultural support services was hampered by poor maintenance of the rural road network. Government pricing policy also operated as a substantial tax on farmers; the government was still focused on providing urban consumers with cheap food to avoid social and political unrest, and also as a means of holding down urban wages.

Arguably, the neglect of smallholder agriculture had its roots in the colonial era, but the Mobutu regime made little effort to repair this neglect. If anything, the urban bias of government policy became more pronounced in the 1970s and after. Young and Turner (1985: 312–14) examine the case of coffee, where world prices increased rapidly after a frost devastated the Brazilian crop in 1975. The government imposed an export tax, and this combined with various illicit taxes meant that the farmers were getting less in real terms for their beans than before the world price increase. State pricing policy had a similar negative impact on palm oil producers. Peemans (1997: 274) gives a breakdown of the public investment program for the 1980s. Agriculture accounted for 4 percent of total investment in 1981–3, rising to 8 percent in 1983–5 and 13 percent in

1987–9. How much of this was actually implemented is unclear. In Indonesia, agriculture received far more government support. The implementation report of the first five-year plan of the Suharto era (1969–74) reported that 22 percent of plan expenditures had gone on projects in agriculture and irrigation (Department of Information 1974: 167). Although subsequent five-year plans gave less prominence to agriculture, rural infrastructure continued to be given priority, especially outside Java.

A particular success under Suharto was achieved in the rice sector. The Indonesian government transferred the new seed-fertilizer technology developed at the International Rice Research Institute in the Philippines to rice farmers in Java, and in some parts of the Outer Islands, especially Sumatra and Sulawesi. The irrigation networks developed by the Dutch were rehabilitated and extended, and fertilizers, particularly urea, were sold at subsidized prices. There was also considerable success in improving yields of corn, which was an important food staple in Java and in many parts of eastern Indonesia. By the mid-1980s, Indonesia could boast that rice consumption per capita was higher than at any time in the previous century, and that it had eliminated reliance on imports.

## 3.5  Looking again at the post-1970 divergence

It is time to return to the questions posed at the beginning of this chapter. To what extent is the divergence in per capita GDP after 1970 the result of post-independence policies, rather than colonial legacies? And to what extent did colonial policies influence post-independence decisions? In the DRC, as in other parts of Africa, many post-colonial scholars have been inclined to blame economic failures on an unfavorable colonial legacy, and in the case of the DRC it is not difficult to make a strong argument along these lines. Apart from the neglect of smallholder agriculture, at least until the 1950s, the Belgian administration left education almost entirely to the missions, and made little attempt to recruit Congolese into the administration. As is discussed further in Chapter 7 below (Frankema), tertiary and technical education was almost completely neglected, so that when independence was granted in 1960 there were hardly any Congolese with qualifications in law, medicine, agriculture, economics, or public administration.

In addition, taxes on the indigenous population in money and kind were often heavy and forced many young men into the wage labor sector. Faced with slow or even negative population growth, at least until the 1930s, the government and the large European enterprises appeared to believe that there was no alternative to coercion to get Congolese into the wage labor force, where wages were low and conditions often harsh. Not only did the government fail to encourage smallholder export agriculture but it seems to have prevented small farmers from taking on more land, even where it was available. Although the drain through the balance of payments was not as large, or as sustained, as in the Netherlands Indies, there can be little doubt that Belgian policy favored large enterprises from the metropolitan country as the main drivers of growth in the colonial economy.

It is not difficult to detect similarities in colonial policies between Java under the CS and the Belgian Congo, at least until the 1930s. Both the CS in Java and Leopold's policies in the Congo Free State can be seen as strategies employed by two of Europe's small colonial powers to extract profits from colonial territories which appeared to have abundant potential for producing both agricultural and mineral exports in high demand in the rapidly industrializing countries of Europe and North America. In both cases the key constraint was perceived to be shortage of labor. In Java this problem solved itself through the natural increase of population. After 1900, Dutch policy was to utilize what was seen as the "surplus population" in Java to develop the agricultural potential of the huge areas outside Java. A land settlement program was launched, which has continued, with varying degrees of government and donor support, down to the present day.

The view that the colony was a *bedrif*, a commercial enterprise to be developed for the profit of the metropolitan economy, motivated policy in both colonies, although in Java after 1900 policies became directed more to improving living standards among the indigenous populations. While ethical considerations were important in the post-1900 policy changes in Indonesia, it was also acknowledged that a poverty-stricken colonial population would not be an asset to the mother country and could become a serious liability. If, as Furnivall (1944: 174–5) claimed, Dutch policy changed after the CS only to the extent that it admitted more shareholders, by the early twentieth century at least some segments of the Dutch colonial establishment realized that indigenous Indonesians would have to become shareholders as well. The Ethical Policy did lead to changes in budgetary policies in Indonesia, both on the expenditure and the revenue side. Expenditures on infrastructure and land settlement projects grew rapidly until 1920, while tax policies became more broadly based.

Although there were changes in policy in the Congo after it became a formal responsibility of the Belgian state, the attitude that the colony was a *bedrif* seems to have continued much longer, with fewer concessions to a more developmental colonial policy. There was certainly progress in infrastructure development which was, in part at least, the result of the rapid growth in the mining sector, and in ancillary services. But taxes bore heavily on the indigenous population in the Belgian Congo, although after 1920 poll and hut taxes fell as a proportion of total revenues. A British observer, writing in 1924, pointed out that the European community in the Congo, both official and private, was determined to maintain wages at a low level, and did not seem to appreciate that a more prosperous labor force would mean higher taxes for the government and greater demand for manufactured imports (Ledger 1924). To be fair, such attitudes were widely held by colonial officials in many parts of Africa and Asia, including the British. But they often led to policies which inhibited economic progress among indigenous populations.

There were obvious similarities between Mobutu and Suharto, especially in their early years in power. Both had learnt bitter lessons from the secessionist movements which broke out in Indonesia and Zaïre in the early post-independence years. Both were authoritarian rulers, impatient with political parties and anxious to centralize power in their own hands. Both seemed willing to tolerate corruption among their close associates as the price for staying in power. But increasingly Mobutu came to resemble Sukarno rather than Suharto, particularly in macro-economic management. Young and Turner (1985: 306) speak of a tidal wave of disaster which hit Zaïre in 1974–5, triggered by the collapse in world copper prices. The Mobutu regime appeared unable or unwilling to deal with the problems which hit them at this time, and the economy went into a downward spiral from which it has not yet recovered.

Faced with similar problems in the early 1980s (falling oil rather than copper prices) Suharto and his ministers were able to act more decisively. In addition, Suharto, after initial reluctance, grasped the importance of birth control in the Indonesian context. A successful national family planning program was launched soon after he came to power, and fertility declined sharply, especially in Java and Bali. In stressing the importance of both rural infrastructure and agricultural development, as well as land settlement outside Java, Suharto was building on key elements of the Ethical Policy. But he was able to pursue these policies more successfully, while at the same time greatly expanding the school system and improving access to health facilities. Literacy rates improved greatly, while infant and child mortality declined. A recent analysis has placed Indonesia in the top ten "improving" nations between 1970 and 2010, both in terms of income growth and in terms of non-monetary indicators of human development such as literacy and life expectancy. The DRC by contrast was one of a very small number of countries where human development indicators deteriorated (UNDP 2010: 29–30).

Some writers on Zaïre during the Mobutu era and beyond blame class factors for the failure of economic reforms, especially from the early 1970s onwards when per capita GDP began its decline. Peemans (1975b: 163–5) drew attention to the emergence of a "State bourgeoisie"; this class benefited from the enlargement of the state sector and the take-over of foreign trade and service enterprises. There were clear parallels with the Guided Democracy period in Indonesia, and the oil boom era of the 1970s also saw an enrichment of a bureaucratic class in Indonesia who profited through access to government revenues.[21] But that class was not powerful enough to prevent the reforms of the 1980s, which were widely seen as benefiting the private sector, and especially the economically powerful Chinese business class. Suharto demonstrated considerable skill in balancing the competing demands of the state and private sectors in implementing reforms, although by the early 1990s private interests had gained the upper hand. The last decade of Suharto's period in power was marked by the growing power of large conglomerates, several of them controlled by members of Suharto's family and their business associates. But however predatory their behavior might have seemed to many Indonesians, the impact on economic growth was hardly as destructive as in Zaïre.

From the vantage point of the early twenty-first century, it seems clear that the divergence between the DRC and Indonesia in the decades after 1970 was the result of policy decisions driven by two powerful and autocratic leaders, who shared a number of similar characteristics but who in the final analysis acted very differently when it came to implementing policy reforms. Both were influenced by their experiences in the last phase of the colonial eras in their two countries, and in the sometimes chaotic post-independence years. But Suharto seems to have been able to draw on positive aspects of the Dutch colonial legacy to a greater extent than Mobutu. This probably reflected the policy advice which he received from key ministers, and his own background in rural Java. But it also reflected the fact that the Dutch themselves had, at least for the last four decades of their rule, been concerned with improving living standards in their vast Southeast Asian colony.

Such concern does not seem to have been shared to the same extent by Belgian officials in the Congo, even during the years from 1945 to 1960. While the Dutch educational legacy was meager, some Indonesians did get access to professional training in law, medicine and engineering in the final phase of colonial rule and significant numbers were recruited into government service. They were given more responsible posts during the Japanese occupation and in the immediate post-independence years. By the time Suharto came to power, there were enough trained people in the civil service to formulate and implement development projects. This was not the case in the Belgian Congo at the time of independence, although it is questionable whether Mobutu would have been willing to use such people even if they had been available.

## Notes

1 Evans (1989: 562) argues that a predatory state is one where "those who control the state apparatus seem to plunder without any more regard for the welfare of the citizenry than a predator has for the welfare of its prey." He contrasts this definition with the revenue-maximizing definition used by writers in the neo-classical tradition such as North. Shleifer and Vishny (1998: Chapter 1) in their discussion of the "grabbing hand" model would seem to be in close agreement with Evans' definition; they emphasize that "at the root of the grabbing hand analysis are models of political behavior that argue that politicians do not maximize social welfare and instead pursue their own selfish objectives" (Shleifer and Vishny 1998: 4).

2 Kuznets stresses this implication of the industrial revolution in his Nobel lecture (Kuznets 1971: 168). See also Landes (1961) for further elaboration of this point.

3 It should be noted that net exports of manufactures from Britain to the empire grew rapidly after 1860, while net exports to the rest of the world stagnated, and in fact declined from 1870 to 1904. See Cain and Hopkins (1993: Table 5.4). For a robust denial of the argument that colonial outlets were essential for industrialization in the West, see Bairoch (1993: Chapter 6). Bairoch (1993: Chapter 5) and Lewis (1978: 30) also deny that raw materials from colonial possessions were crucial for industrialization in Western Europe.

4 See Darwin (2008: 23) who argues that European imperialism was based on expropriation of both land and labor to create agricultural estates and mining ventures.

5 van Zanden and van Riel (2004: 181–2) argue that one consequence of the growth of exports from Java after 1830 was that a rising merchant class became more influential; by the 1860s they were confident that they could manage export agriculture more efficiently, and at less cost to the budget, with free wage labor than with the increasingly discredited system of forced labor.

6  For a review of the literature see Alexander and Alexander (1979).
7  See Boomgaard (1986) for a discussion of the evolution of what were termed the welfare services in Indonesia between 1900 and 1942.
8  The substantial remittances back to the Netherlands gave rise to the conviction that the loss of the Indies would be a catastrophe for the Dutch economy. The Derksen–Tinbergen memorandum, written during the German occupation of the Netherlands and published in 1945, used a rather crude multiplier model to argue that the Dutch economy, already weakened after the German occupation, would be severely affected if Indonesian independence was accompanied by a diminution in trade and investment ties. A brief analysis of the findings of Derksen and Tinbergen is given by van der Eng (1998: 315–16).
9  A good discussion of the economic aspects of French colonial policy can be found in Thomas (2005: 98–118).
10  Road networks (in terms of kilometers of road per 1000 square kilometers of territory) were more developed in Java than anywhere else in colonial Asia, although rail networks and electricity capacity were lower than in Taiwan (Booth 2007: 80).
11  For a pessimistic evaluation of the Ethical Policy, see Boeke (1927). He stressed that the population of Java had reacted to the welfare policies by "growing in size like a flash flood."
12  In 1905 exports of rubber from Indonesia amounted to only 25 tons (Creutzberg 1975: 93). Production in British Malaya was already 57,000 tons in 1905 and almost doubled over the next five years (Barlow 1978: 442).
13  The total land leased to Western enterprises in Indonesia included both planted area and land held in reserve. Planted area in both Java and the Outer Islands amounted to 1.2 million hectares in 1940, but the total area controlled by estates was higher. See Central Bureau of Statistics (1947: 36–9).
14  A detailed analysis of the population data for a district in the Congo is given in Vansina (2010: Chapter 5). He concludes that in many cases, erroneous conclusions were reached about demographic decline on the basis of very fragmentary evidence.
15  Another source states that one-quarter to one-third of cash incomes were used to pay head or hut taxes in the 1930s. See Office of Strategic Services (1945: 10).
16  These guarantees led to substantial payments to private companies in 1935; see Naval Intelligence Division (1944: 441).
17  Lindblad (2002: 101) argues that at the end of the nineteenth century, the Outer Islands of Indonesia were still highly integrated with mainland Southeast Asia, especially the Straits ports. This changed only slowly after 1900.
18  The reasons for Indonesia's poor post-independence revenue performance are discussed in Booth (2011). Other former colonies in Asia, including the Philippines, also had problems maintaining the real value of per capita government revenues after independence.
19  The total public debt grew rapidly after the commencement of the plan. In 1949 it amounted to 3.7 billion francs; by 1958 it had grown to 42.5 billion francs (Belgian Congo 1960: 56). Stengers (1957: 359–60) claims that there was no contribution from the Belgian government to the financing of the plan, although it is not clear whether the Belgian government guaranteed the loans. Revenues from borrowing after 1950 together with the surpluses from the ordinary budget covered all the plan expenditures, although there were also extraordinary expenses outside the plan projects. These must have been financed by non-loan extraordinary revenues and drawing down reserves (Belgian Congo 1960: 54).
20  Gran (1976: 12) cites figures from an IMF report which confirm the estimates of Young and Turner.
21  The Guided Democracy period began with the appointment of an extra-parliamentary business cabinet, headed by Juanda, in April 1957, and continued until the effective removal of President Sukarno from power in March 1966. For a discussion of the

early years of the Guided Democracy era see Feith (1962: 578–608). An analysis of trends in income distribution in Indonesia over the 1970s is given in Booth and Sundrum (1981).

## References

Alexander, J. and Alexander, P. (1979) "Labor Demands and the 'Involution' of Javanese Agriculture," *Social Analysis*, 3: 22–44.

Anstey, R. (1966) *King Leopold's Legacy: The Congo under Belgian Rule 1908–1960*, London: Oxford University Press.

Bairoch, P. (1993) *Economics and World History: Myths and Paradoxes*, Chicago: University of Chicago Press.

Barlow, C. (1978) *The Natural Rubber Industry*, Kuala Lumpur: Oxford University Press.

Belgian Congo (1960) *Belgian Congo, Volume II*, Brussels: Belgian Congo and Ruanda-Urundi Information and Public Relations Office.

Boeke, J.H. (1927) "Objective and Personal Elements in Colonial Welfare Policy," as translated and reprinted in W.F. Wertheim *et al.* (eds.) (2nd edn 1966) *Indonesian Economics: The Concept of Dualism in Theory and Practice*, The Hague: van Hoeve.

Boomgaard, P. (1986) "The Welfare Services in Indonesia, 1900–1942," *Itinerario*, X(1): 57–81.

Boomgaard, P. and Gooszen, A.J. (1991) *Changing Economy in Indonesia, Volume 11: Population Trends, 1795–1942*, Amsterdam: Royal Tropical Institute.

Booth, A. (1998) *The Indonesian Economy in the Nineteenth and Twentieth Centuries*, Basingstoke: Macmillan Press.

Booth, A. (2007) *Colonial Legacies: Economic and Social Development in East and Southeast Asia*, Honolulu: University of Hawaii Press.

Booth, A. (2011) "Colonial Revenue Policies and the Transition to Independence in Southeast Asia." Paper prepared for the workshop *State and Economy in Indonesia's Transition to Sovereignty: A Comparative Perspective*, Leiden University, October 13–14.

Booth, A. and Sundrum, R.M. (1981), "Income Distribution," in Anne Booth and Peter McCawley (eds.), *The Indonesian Economy during the Soeharto Era*, Kuala Lumpur: Oxford University Press.

Buelens, F. and Marysse, S. (2009) "Returns on Investments during the Colonial Era: The Case of the Belgian Congo," *Economic History Review*, 62(S1): 135–66.

Cain, P.J. and Hopkins, A.G. (1993) *British Imperialism: Innovation and Expansion, 1688–1914*, London: Longman.

Central Bureau of Statistics (1947) *Statistical Pocketbook of Indonesia 1941*, Jakarta: Central Bureau of Statistics.

Central Bureau of Statistics (1959) *Statistical Pocketbook of Indonesia 1959*, Jakarta: Central Bureau of Statistics.

Central Bureau of Statistics (1963a) *Sensus Penduduk 1961 (Population Census 1961), Series SP II*, Jakarta: Central Bureau of Statistics.

Central Bureau of Statistics (1963b) *Statistical Pocketbook of Indonesia 1963*, Jakarta: Central Bureau of Statistics.

Creutzberg, P. (ed.) (1975) *Changing Economy in Indonesia, Volume 1: Indonesia's Export Crops 1860–1940*, The Hague: M. Nijhoff.

Creutzberg, P. (ed.) (1976) *Changing Economy in Indonesia, Volume 2: Public Finance, 1816–1939*, The Hague: M. Nijhoff.

Darwin, J. (2008) *After Tamerlane: The Rise and Fall of Global Empires, 1400–2000*, London: Penguin Books.

Department of Information (1974) *Pidato Kenegaraan Presiden R.I. Didepan Sidang Pleno DPR Tgl 15 August 1974*, Jakarta: Department of Information.

Depelchin, J. (1992) *From the Congo Free State to Zaire: How Belgium Privatized the Economy*, Dakar: Codesria Book Series.

de St. Moulin, L. (1990) "What is Known of the Demographic History of Zaire Since 1885?," in B. Fetter (ed.), *Demography from Scanty Evidence: Central Africa in the Colonial Era*, Boulder: Lynne Rienner.

Elson, R.E. (1994) *Village Java under the Cultivation System: 1830–1870*, Sydney: Allen and Unwin.

Elson, R.E. (2008) *The Idea of Indonesia: A History*, Cambridge: Cambridge University Press.

Emmer, P.C. (1998) "The Economic Impact of the Dutch Expansion Overseas, 1570–1870," *Revista de Historia Economica*, XVI(1): 157–75.

Evans, P. (1989) "Predatory, Developmental, and Other Apparatuses: A Comparative Political Economy Perspective on the Third World State," *Sociological Forum*, 4(4): 561–87.

Fasseur, C. (1992) *The Politics of Colonial Exploitation: Java, the Dutch and the Cultivation System*, Ithaca, NY: Southeast Asia Program, Cornell University.

Feith, H. (1962) *The Decline of Constitutional Democracy in Indonesia*, Ithaca, NY: Cornell University Press.

Furnivall, J.S. (1944) *Netherlands India: A Study of Plural Economy*, Cambridge: Cambridge University Press.

Gran, G. (1976) "An Introduction to Zaire's Permanent Development Crisis," in G. Gran (ed.), *Zaire: The Political Economy of Underdevelopment*, New York: Praeger.

Helleiner, G.K. (1966) *Peasant Agriculture, Government and Economic Growth in Nigeria*, Homewood: Richard D. Irwin.

Kay, G.B. and Hymer, S. (1972) *The Political Economy of Colonialism in Ghana: A Collection of Documents and Statistics, 1900–1960*, Cambridge: Cambridge University Press.

Korthals Altes, W.L. (1991) *Changing Economy in Indonesia, Volume 12a: General Trade Statistics 1822–1940*, Amsterdam: Royal Tropical Institute.

Kuznets, S. (1971) "Modern Economic Growth: Findings and Reflections," Nobel Memorial Lecture, as reprinted in S. Kuznets, *Population, Capital and Growth: Selected Essays*, London: Heinemann Educational Books.

Landes, D.S. (1961) "Some Thoughts on the Nature of Economic Imperialism," *Journal of Economic History*, XXI(4): 496–512.

Ledger, C.K. (1924) *Report on the Economic Situation in the Belgian Congo*, London: Her Majesty's Stationery Office for the Department of Overseas Trade.

Lewis, W.A. (1978) *Growth and Fluctuations, 1870–1913*, London: George Allen and Unwin.

Lindblad, J.T. (2002) "The Outer Islands in the 19th Century: Contest for the Periphery," in H. Dick, V.J. Houben, J.T. Lindblad and K.W. Thee, *The Emergence of a National Economy: An Economic History of Indonesia, 1800–2000*, Sydney: Allen and Unwin.

Merlier, M. (1962) *Le Congo de la colonisation belge à l'indépendance*, Paris: François Maspero.

Moeller, A. (1938) "Les finances publiques du Congo belge et du Ruanda-Urundi," in *Les Novelles, Corpus Juris Belgici, Droit Colonial, Tome III*, Brussels: Maison F. Larcier.

Naval Intelligence Division (1944) *Geographical Handbook Series: The Belgian Congo*, London: Naval Intelligence Division.

Nelson, S.H. (1994) *Colonialism in the Congo Basin, 1880–1940*, Athens: Ohio University Monographs in International Studies, Africa Series, No. 64.

Office of Strategic Services (1945) *Trade Policies in the Congo Basin*, Washington: Office of Strategic Services, Research and Analysis Branch.

Peemans, J.P. (1975a) "Capital Accumulation in the Congo under Colonialism: The Role of the State," in P. Duignan and L.H. Gann (eds.), *Colonialism in Africa, 1870–1960, Volume 4: The Economics of Colonialism*, Cambridge: Cambridge University Press.

Peemans, J.P. (1975b) "The Social and Economic Development of Zaire since Independence: An Historical Outline," *African Affairs*, 74(295): 148–79.

Peemans, J.P. (1997) *Le Congo-Zaïre au gré du XXe Siècle: Etat, économie 1880–1990*, Paris: L'Harmattan.

Pelzer, K. (1945) *Pioneer Settlement in the Asiatic Tropics*, New York: American Geographical Society.

Penders, C.L.M. (1977) *Indonesia: Selected Documents on Colonialism and Nationalism 1830–1942*, St. Lucia: University of Queensland Press.

Shleifer, A. and Vishny, R. (1998) *The Grabbing Hand: Government Pathologies and Their Cures*, Cambridge, Mass.: Harvard University Press.

Stengers, J. (1957) *Combien le Congo a-t-il couté à la Belgique?*, Brussels: Académie Royale des Sciences Coloniales.

Thomas, M. (2005) *The French Empire between the Wars: Imperialism, Politics and Society*, Manchester: Manchester University Press.

UNDP (2010) *Human Development Report 2010: The Real Wealth of Nations*, Basingstoke: Palgrave Macmillan for the United Nations Development Programme.

Vandewalle, G. (1966) *De Conjuncturele Evolutie in Kongo en Ruanda-Urundi van 1920 tot 1939 en van 1949 tot 1958*, Ghent: University of Ghent.

van der Eng, P. (1998) "Exploring Exploitation: The Netherlands and Colonial Indonesia, 1870–1940," *Revista de Historia Economica*, XVI(1): 291–321.

van Niel, R. (1992) *Java under the Cultivation System*, Leiden: KITLV Press.

Vansina, J. (2010) *Being Colonized: The Kuba Experience in Rural Congo, 1880–1960*, Madison: University of Wisconsin Press.

van Zanden, J.L. (2002) "Economic Growth in Java, 1815–1939: The Reconstruction of the Historical National Accounts of a Colonial Economy," *Working Memorandum IISG*. Online. Available at www.iisg.nl/research/jvz-reconstruction.pdf (accessed October 30, 2010).

van Zanden, J.L. and van Riel, A. (2004) *The Structures of Inheritance: The Dutch Economy in the Nineteenth Century*, Princeton, NJ, and Oxford: Princeton University Press.

World Bank (1980) *Zaire: Current Economic Situation and Constraints: A World Bank Country Study*, Washington, DC: International Bank for Reconstruction and Development.

Young, C. (1994) "Zaire: The Shattered Illusion of the Integral State," *Journal of Modern African Studies*, 32(2): 247–63.

Young, C. and Turner, T. (1985) *The Rise and Decline of the Zairian State*, Madison: University of Wisconsin Press.

# 4 The land tenure system in the Congo, 1885–1960

## Actors, motivations, and consequences

*Piet Clement*

## 4.1 Introduction

The Congo Free State, with the Belgian King Leopold II as its sovereign, officially came into being on July 1, 1885.[1] The very first legislative act of the new state, promulgated the same day, concerned the question of land ownership (EIC, *Bulletin Officiel* 1885). It is easy to see why this was vital to the newly founded colonial state. First of all, the state had to assert its monopoly on treating land questions in order to prevent an uncontrolled scramble for land, in which private adventurers might seek to obtain land claims directly from indigenous chiefs – at gunpoint or otherwise. Second, the nascent state had to satisfy its own requirements, not only in terms of direct land occupation to accommodate state services (military posts), infrastructure (roads, later railroads), and non-indigenous settlements (trading stations), but also in terms of securing the natural and mineral riches of the state. Third, from the outset the colonial state was keenly aware that its claim to possession of the Congo needed to be backed up by effective occupation – a condition imposed by the 1885 Berlin Conference. To achieve this, land was the foremost asset at its disposal. The Congo was not only vast but, for European settlers, also remote and insalubrious. To help occupy and open up the land for modern development, European companies and settlers had to be lured by the offer of large land concessions at a very cheap price or even for free, with the prospect of an unencumbered and highly profitable exploitation.

In order to achieve these goals, colonial land legislation sought to reconcile the requirements of Western-style private property rights with the reality of customary land occupation and utilization, and to create a coherent legal framework to settle land ownership issues. This was, to say the least, a very ambitious undertaking. Placed in an historical context, it is clear that land ownership questions are not just about economic opportunity, but also about social status and power relationships (politics), about culture ("the politics of belonging"), and about religion and beliefs (earth shrines, burial grounds of forebears) – and hence go straight to the heart of the pre-colonial society's intricate organization (Lentz 2006: 1–34). The way in which a land tenure system is devised and imposed tells us a lot about the power structures and institutional arrangements within a given society, and its capacity to change or adapt to new circumstances.

Moreover, land policies and land ownership rights directly affect the conditions and direction of agricultural development, and therefore potentially have a long-term impact on economic development and living standards more generally.[2]

This chapter focuses on the political economy story of land legislation and land policies in the Belgian Congo, primarily on the basis of colonial archives and contemporary literature.[3] How did this legislation and these policies take shape between 1885 and 1960? What explains their evolution? What role did pre-colonial African traditions play? How did colonial and African interests and agency interact? And how were these policies implemented and enforced on the ground? A better understanding of land ownership issues in the Congo, placed in an evolving historical context, can help answer important related questions: how did land legislation affect land utilization, and thereby food production and nutritional standards? How did colonial land legislation and policies interact with other key policies (also discussed elsewhere in this book), particularly labor and fiscal policies, and agricultural development policies? And, finally, what has been the post-colonial legacy of colonial land tenure and rural development policies?

## 4.2  Staking a claim: land ownership status in the Congo Free State, 1885–1908

Formally, the land legislation enacted from 1885 onward recognized "customary" land rights and thus protected the land already occupied by the indigenous population from alienation.[4] In reality, colonial interests took precedence. First of all, customary land rights were complex, variable, and not well understood by the colonizers, who in fact redefined or even reinvented these customary rights to suit their own aims (Heyse 1934).[5] Moreover, customary land occupation was far from static, but evolved in time and space. Many communities were semi-nomadic and entire villages were known to move and occupy new lands at irregular intervals. By "protecting" the indigenous land rights as they existed in 1885, the law theoretically enshrined a status quo where there was none. Most importantly, however, the law became the foundation for the state's hold over the largest part of the vast territory. In practice, indigenous land rights were defined very restrictively, usually limited to the Congolese villages and the surrounding fields effectively tilled by the villagers. All remaining land was declared "vacant" and as a result automatically fell under the control of the colonial state (as *domanial land*). Thus, with one stroke of the pen, the vast majority of Congolese land was expropriated. This stark distinction between land effectively occupied by the indigenous population and so-called vacant lands was at the very core of colonial land legislation and would determine its further development until the end of the colonial period. It did not take long before a growing body of researchers, ethnologists, and lawyers argued that it rested on a legal fiction: in pre-colonial Congolese societies, it was held, no such thing as "vacant" lands existed (Vinck 2011: 3–9). Even the most remote expanse of forest or swamp was usually held to "belong," in one way or another, to a specific ethnic group, clan, village, or chief.

As a result of the 1885 decree, the state held vast tracts of land in its own hands (domanial land), and was at liberty to give hundreds of thousands of hectares of land in concession to a handful of commercial companies and to the missions. This proved a decisive factor in luring these companies and missionary societies to the Congo. But there was another reason why the colonial state was so keen to lay claim to Congolese land. The 1885 Berlin Conference had imposed a free trade regime on the Congo basin, and Leopold II could therefore not rely on customs duties as a source of revenue. Land ownership provided an alternative source of wealth extraction to help fund colonization. The resulting land expropriations on behalf of the colonial state set the Congo Free State apart from many other colonies – including the Netherlands Indies.

In the early 1890s, at a time when the Congo Free State was facing financial bankruptcy, the colonial administration went one step further. By virtue of the 1885 decree on land, the state and the concessionary companies may have enjoyed nominal ownership of vast expanses of Congolese land, but these did not generate revenue unless they were effectively exploited. To help kick-start profitable (i.e., low-cost) exploitation it was argued that any natural produce derived from the domanial lands fell exclusively to its lawful owners. Thus, anything the villagers gathered or hunted on vacant lands, as they were wont to do, suddenly belonged no longer to them but to the state or the concession holder. The principle that the colonial state had the exclusive right to the produce of the domanial lands – particularly rubber, ivory, and copal – was enshrined in a number of decrees promulgated in 1891–3. The consequences were devastating. The Congo Free State's land legislation was directly at the basis of the "red rubber" tragedy that was played out over the 1890s–1900s (Boelaert 1956). The local population was forced, under appalling conditions, to collect ever-increasing quantities of wild rubber in the forests of the Congo basin, for the sole benefit of the state and the concessionary companies. The rubber campaign allowed Leopold II to turn the losses he had initially suffered in his colonial enterprise into huge profits, but it also led to an international outcry over the humanitarian tragedy taking place in the Congo Free State.[6] Eventually, Leopold II was forced to allow an international commission of inquiry access to the Congo. In its report (1905), this commission singled out the land legislation, and the way in which it had been put into practice, as one of the main causes of the abuses and as a continuing threat to the livelihood and future development of the indigenous communities (EIC, *Bulletin Officiel* 1905: 152).

## 4.3  From the Congo Free State to the Belgian Congo: hesitant reform

In response to the commission of inquiry's report, the colonial government issued a new decree on indigenous land rights on June 3, 1906. While the original land decree of July 1, 1885 had made only a very crude distinction between land occupied by the indigenous people and vacant lands, the 1906 decree defined "land occupied by the indigenous people" more precisely and more

broadly as "the land on which they live as well as all the lands which they cultivate or exploit in whichever way in conformity with customs and local practices" (EIC, *Bulletin Officiel* 1906: 226).[7] In 1909–10, after the Congo Free State
had ceased to exist and had been taken over formally by Belgium as the Belgian
Congo, further land decrees introduced the important notion that the local communities enjoyed certain customary rights on domanial lands too – particularly
the right to gather firewood or natural products and the right to hunt (also called
accessory rights or rights *sui generis*). Accordingly, for any land to be declared
well and truly vacant, so that it could be given into cession or concession by the
colonial state, the customary rights resting on it had to be established and the
holders of such rights had to be compensated for surrendering them. An important effect of the 1906 and 1909–10 decrees was to bury once and for all the
notion that the produce of vacant lands belonged exclusively to the state or to the
concessionary companies. This put an end to the worst abuses of the system
inaugurated in 1885. But it did not fundamentally alter the underlying power
balance in land questions.

The legislation enacted in 1906 and 1909–10 prescribed a proper investigation
into the indigenous rights resting on a particular tract of land before it could be
declared vacant and given into concession. However, no model or detailed procedure for how this was to be achieved in practice was provided. The application of
the land legislation was largely left to the local authorities. This proved to be problematic. Many colonial administrators considered the obligations resulting from
the land decrees to be overly cumbersome and impractical. On the ground they
were clearly not applied very rigorously, if at all. Local administrators – the so-
called territorial service (*Service Territorial*) – often complained that drawing up a
systematic inventory of indigenous land rights – a laborious and time-consuming
process at the best of times – was simply beyond the limited means at their disposal. When the Belgian Minister of the Colonies Jules Renkin visited the Congo
in 1909, he was told by the head of the Land Registry Office in the capital Boma
that the implementation of the decree of June 3, 1906 faced major difficulties.[8] Just
a handful of surveyors were available to demarcate indigenous versus vacant land.
Through lack of manpower and funds, surveyors were usually sent out into the
bush on their own and ill-equipped. Many in the service became demotivated as
their work, difficult as it was, was met with indifference or even scorn from the
territorial administrators who were themselves overstretched and felt they had
better things to do. Over a decade later, in 1923, there were still just 78 surveyors
employed by the colony, the majority of them active in Leopoldville and Katanga
province, with the remainder spread out extremely thinly over the vast 2.3 million
km[2] territory.[9] Moreover, after the end of World War I, the demand to perform
such demarcations of vacant lands increased steadily. The Belgian Congo was
going through a period of rapid economic development and witnessed a fresh
influx of European immigrants. The total number of Belgian citizens residing in
the colony increased from barely 3600 in 1920 to over 17,000 in 1930.

Soon, a revolt from below against the dispositions of the 1906 decree took
shape. Local administrations, e.g., in the northwestern Equateur province and in

the Lac Léopold II district (Mai Ndombe), complained bitterly that it was nearly impossible to implement the 1906 decree. The lack of resources was not the only reason. On the ground, attempts to demarcate land were often challenged, openly or surreptitiously, by the Congolese villagers.[10] Boundaries drawn were simply ignored and boundary posts mysteriously disappeared shortly after the surveyor had put them up. Even more frustrating from the administration's perspective was the habit of many communities of migrating from time to time: indigenous lands that had just been demarcated were abandoned only months later. On the occasion of return visits to recently surveyed areas, surveyors and administrators had to acknowledge that entire villages seemed to have vanished into thin air. Often the village names used in the surveyors' reports did not match those figuring in the territorial administration's register, adding further to the confusion. It was repeatedly suggested that, rather than going through the laborious and futile exercise of demarcating the land on the ground, it would be far easier to allocate for exclusive indigenous use a fixed surface area of land (two or three hectares) per head of the village population and then to consider all other land as vacant and thus as domanial land.[11]

As a result of these persistent difficulties and complaints, the Council of the Government General, advising the Governor-General resident in the then capital of the Belgian Congo, Boma, debated the issue of the demarcation of indigenous lands on three consecutive occasions over the years 1918 to 1920. It invariably concluded that, in spite of the difficulties encountered, the regime introduced in 1906 had to be maintained, as the alternatives were bound to create even more problems. In order to encourage a more consistent application of the 1906 land decree, an enabling ordinance of September 30, 1922 prescribed a formal procedure for the cession of indigenous land, but its effect seems to have been limited.

An even more fundamental and sustained challenge was raised by the authorities of the southeastern Katanga province. The rapid development of the mining industry there put an enormous strain on the indigenous workforce, while at the same time leading to a strong influx of Europeans. Against this background, the local colonial administration wanted a free hand to award the best arable land to European colonists in order to create a modern farming and livestock industry capable of supplying the copperbelt mining communities. The situation in Katanga was further complicated by the fact that sovereignty over the province was not only exercised by the colonial government itself, represented by the Vice-Governor-General in Elisabethville, but was shared with a semi-private concessionary company (of which the colonial state was a shareholder), the Comité Spécial du Katanga (CSK), also operating out of Elisabethville. By its charter, the CSK enjoyed large privileges in terms of land and mining concessions all over Katanga province. Its primary interest was in "opening up" Katanga for modern economic development (primarily copper mining).

In 1921, the CSK, in agreement with the provincial government, had ordered an assessment of vacant lands in the Elisabethville hinterland. The purpose was not only to free up and demarcate land that could be given in concession to European farmers, but also to fix (and limit) once and for all the land that would remain at the disposal of the indigenous communities. Katanga province was vast and very sparsely populated, but the colonial authorities considered the fact that the indigenous people lived in small villages dispersed over a wide area and had a tendency to move around at irregular intervals a real nuisance and a potential hindrance to the future settlement of white colonists. In practice, the solution adopted came down to the creation of indigenous reservations. In order to free up land for white colonization, entire ethnic groups were "invited" to regroup in designated areas, thereby surrendering their customary rights to the land they had occupied before.[12]

In less than five years, between 1921 and 1925, the Katanga authorities signed conventions with at least ten local chiefdoms for the creation of indigenous reservations. Some were in the immediate vicinity of Elisabethville (then a rapidly expanding city of some 20,000 inhabitants), others farther north, near the mining towns of Jadotville (Likasi) and Kolwezi (see Figure 4.1). The total land surface of this first bloc of indigenous reservations exceeded half a million hectares

*Figure 4.1* Railroads and navigable waterways in the Belgian Congo, *c.*1932 (source: © A. Sarlet. The thick dark lines indicate railways, the narrow dark lines navigable waterways).

(5000 km$^2$), and an estimated 17,000 Congolese villagers were directly affected.[13] Where possible, the location of the indigenous villages was not changed, but they were grouped together and a contiguous surrounding area was demarcated as a "native reservation." However, in some cases, entire villages had to move location to achieve this goal. The Governor of Katanga province, Léon Bureau, wanted to extend the system to other districts in the interior, along the Lualaba river between Bukama and Kongolo, which he held to be a very "interesting region" for the development of European colonization.[14] Martin Rutten, the Governor-General of the Belgian Congo from 1923 to 1927, was well acquainted with this practice. Before his appointment as Governor-General he had been Attorney General at the Court of Appeal in Elisabethville (Dellicour 1958). He was in favor of the "Katanga system" of native reservations, which, he argued, held considerable advantages for the Congolese too, not least because it would provide them with easier access to the missionary stations and company-sponsored medical infrastructure.

In 1926–7, Governor-General Rutten actively lobbied the administration in Brussels – i.e., the Ministry of Colonies and its main advisory body, the Colonial Council – for a revision of the 1906 decree and the generalized acceptance of the Katanga system. But the Governor-General would not have it his way. The creation of native reservations in Katanga first came under fire locally. Monseigneur Jean-Félix de Hemptinne, the influential head of the Benedictine missions in Katanga and vice-president of the local commission for the protection of the indigenous people, opposed the factual segregation that would result from a generalized reservations policy. He was in any case very skeptical about the chances of success of large-scale European farming in the Congo and wanted to give precedence to the development of Congolese agriculture instead. Soon, in Brussels too – particularly among the more progressive members of the Colonial Council – opposition to the land policies as practiced in Katanga mounted.[15]

Matters came to a head as the result of a dispute over the convention concluded on March 14, 1924 between the CSK and the chiefdoms of Panda-Guba, located west of Jadotville, which provided for the transfer of the Guba village to Muyeke land in order to vacate land earmarked for European settlers. An inquiry conducted in July 1926 on behalf of the Colonial Council established that the local chiefs concerned had agreed to the 1924 convention only because they felt they had no choice but to comply with an order given by the colonial state: "Si Bula Matari le veut, je le ferai."[16] The village chief of Guba, however, had changed his mind after he had put his fingerprint on the convention he had been unable to read. He now refused to move his village to Muyeke land because he feared his people would be absorbed by the local population there and because he desired to continue to live on the land where his father was buried. This particular case was eventually settled by offering the Guba chief another site, much closer to its original location. The officer in charge of the inquiry was careful to stress in his report that in his negotiations with the local notables he had "not used an intimidating tone at any time." The Guba affair nevertheless demonstrated the arbitrariness and barely concealed compulsion of the Katanga system.

Faced with widespread challenges to the 1906 land decree and with the application of the highly controversial Katanga system, the Colonial Council in Brussels decided to set up a special commission to look into the existing system of land concessions and its compatibility with the development of modern-style agriculture and livestock breeding. The commission met between December 1926 and March 1927. After heated debate, the reservations policy pursued by the CSK since at least 1921 and strongly favored by Governor-General Rutten was soundly rejected. Instead, the commission recommended that the 1906 decree be upheld, and that the assessment of indigenous land rights should be conducted with the utmost care, case by case, and "in such a way that the natives clearly understand the demands made on them."[17] It was recommended that as a rule of thumb, the Congolese villagers should be granted an exclusive right to an area of land equal to ten times the surface of the land they effectively occupied, in order to cover all their current and future needs. The commission also insisted that the concession holders of vacant lands should always pay a fair compensation to the local villagers for giving up the use or benefits they derived from the conceded land, i.e., the so-called accessory rights such as hunting and gathering.

## 4.4 Surveying the land: the decree of 1934 and formalized land adjudications

Thus, in 1927, the attempt to force a resolution of the land issue through the creation of indigenous reservations had been discarded. The colonial state's desire to establish a clear distinction between indigenous and vacant lands, and the problems this caused on the ground, remained nonetheless acute. An important reason was the sheer effort in time and resources it took to assess and then demarcate existing indigenous claims on land. Local administrations continued to look for ways to circumvent the strict obligations imposed by the decrees of 1906 and 1922. In 1931, the Governor of the Katanga province coolly informed the Governor-General in Leopoldville that, for the sake of efficiency, already two years earlier he had authorized his services to radically shorten the lengthy procedure for assessing indigenous land rights. The territorial administrators had been given full authority to determine the indigenous rights resting on land to be declared vacant, and to decide and pay out the required compensation for giving up these rights on the spot, without formal approval from a superior authority and without recourse to appeal. In his reply, the Vice-Governor-General condemned this practice and, once again, enjoined the provincial authorities to strictly uphold the 1906 and 1922 decrees.[18] But even in those cases where the formal procedure for establishing the vacancy of land was fully abided by, experience demonstrated that the dice were in any case heavily weighted in favor of the colonial authorities.[19] It was clear to Brussels that the procedure for assessing the vacancy of land would have to be revised if it was ever to be applied effectively and more or less fairly.

Eventually, the issue was tackled by a new commission established by the Colonial Council, which helped prepare the decree of May 31, 1934 on the procedure for assessing the vacancy of land.[20] In the words of Théodore Heyse, its principal author, the main aim of the 1934 decree was to protect indigenous land rights more effectively and at the same time to create legal certainty for the holders of ceded or conceded domanial land (Heyse 1935). In one important respect the decree further strengthened the hand of the colonial state and of the private (European) concession holders: henceforth the assessment of a piece of land and the decision at the end of the assessment procedure regarding its status as domanial or vacant land would be final and irrevocable. This was to avoid the possibility that, once a tract of land had been declared vacant and had been given into concession, new claims regarding indigenous accessory rights resting on the land could be raised; under the previous procedure, this would have required reopening the assessment. In exchange for this legal certainty, the commission of the Colonial Council insisted that indigenous rights ought to be better protected by making a formal assessment mandatory for any prospective concession in excess of two hectares, following a strictly prescribed procedure.

This procedure had to be initiated by the district commissioner, usually following a request from a prospective concession holder, and was executed by the territorial administrator.[21] It required that the land up for assessment be marked out on the ground (e.g., by chalked boundary poles) and that the territorial administrator convene the chiefs and clan heads of the affected villages to walk the land in question with him. A standardized survey was taken of all present inquiring into the customary rights possibly attached to the assessed land. Questions covered the past and current occupation of the land, its possible use for cultivation or for pasturing cattle, and its possible exploitation through hunting, gathering, logging, or fishing. The aim was also to establish precisely whether any such rights were exercised collectively or privately, systematically or occasionally, and on what scale. This was important as it determined the final status of the land as either indigenous or vacant (domanial) land. Land that was neither tilled nor pastured, but the fruits of which were systematically (e.g., by deliberately planting fruit or palm trees) and exclusively exploited by a named individual, clan, or village, would normally be considered indigenous land under the definition introduced by the 1906 decree: "land which the indigenous people cultivate or exploit in whichever way, in conformity with customs and local practices." Land that was not systematically exploited or worked but from which the local people might occasionally benefit, from use as hunting and fishing grounds or by gathering fruit and other natural produce, was considered vacant land on which certain customary rights rested. In order to completely free up such vacant land so that it could be given in cession or concession, these customary (accessory) rights had to be established very precisely so that a fair compensation for relinquishing them could be calculated. The surface area of the land being assessed and its precise location had to be indicated on an area map, and compared to the surface of arable and exploitable land that would remain at the disposal of the local population if the assessed land were to be ceded. This was to avoid too much land being declared domanial and being ceded, thereby compromising the future development of the nearby communities. Finally, the proposed compensation for giving up the customary rights resting on the assessed land was to be accepted by the chiefs and clan heads, including the way in which it was to be disbursed.

This procedure, first introduced in 1934, remained in place, with certain modifications and additions, until the end of the colonial period. Generally, it was felt to be bureaucratic and cumbersome, but it was applied quite rigorously nonetheless. To minimize arbitrariness, it involved different echelons of the colonial administration and magistrature who gave advice and official approval (all arguably representing the interests of the colonial state). The assessment conducted by the territorial administrator or his delegate had to be signed by the indigenous chiefs and the notables present. In the course of the procedure, they were repeatedly asked whether they had fully understood the questions put to them and whether they concurred with the replies as recorded. The district commissioner then gave his advice, particularly concerning the key question of whether the land could be considered domanial land and could therefore be ceded, and on what grounds and in what amount compensation had to be paid for relinquishing customary rights. Further advice had to be sought from the district magistrate (office of the public prosecutor) and from the provincial agronomic service and the provincial department for indigenous affairs (AIMO). Once the administration had agreed on the compensation to be paid and to whom, the chiefs and clan heads were convened once again. The decision was read to them and a duly signed copy of this decision was handed over to the sector chief (with additional copies being sent to the prosecutor's office and to the provincial registrar's office). The entire procedure could easily take one to two years before being completed. But as it ended in a legal act, it gave the future concession holder the legal certainty that the question of the property title had been settled once and for all. As for the indigenous population, the new – or rather refined – system introduced in 1934 curbed some of the abuses to which the weak enforcement of the 1906 decree had given rise, particularly by imposing a more rigorous assessment procedure. But it did not fundamentally alter the fact that, as before, the burden of proof rested on the local communities vis-à-vis an all-powerful colonial state.

Thus, as of 1934, a standardized process had to be followed, using standardized forms, for conducting the assessments regarding the vacancy of land. Some of such completed surveys – *enquêtes de constatation de la vacance des terres* – have been preserved in colonial archives in Belgium and the Congo. They offer interesting insights, not only into how Congolese villagers provided for their livelihood through subsistence farming, gathering, and hunting, but also into colonial power structures and into the ways in which the different actors reacted to the incentives and disincentives implicit in the assessment system. The analysis of a small sample of about a dozen such surveys, originally conducted in the 1940s–50s,[22] allows a few sociological observations, for instance regarding the prevalent illiteracy among the village notables (a majority signing documents by fingerprint) or the persistent gender and age imbalance in many villages in the Congolese interior (resulting from predominantly male migration to the booming urban and industrial centers a long distance away).

What is striking about these surveys is the level of bargaining to which they gave rise, albeit between very unequal parties. The Congolese villagers, represented by their notables and elders, usually had a very weak bargaining position. Land was over-abundant in the Congo (although easily accessible arable land less so). Not least in view of the migration away from the interior referred to above, the indigenous population grew only very slowly during most of the colonial period. As a result, the value of land was depressed in most of the country, with the exception of the booming cities and some more densely populated and highly developed regions such as the Bas-Congo and Kivu. Moreover, the power relationships between the colonizer and the colonized remained characterized by dominance and expected (or enforced) obedience right up to the end of the colonial period. When the territorial administration opened a survey to assess the possible vacancy of a given tract of land, the local communities often interpreted this as an order to vacate the land in question and, in any case, considered the outcome of the assessment a foregone conclusion: "Si Bula Matari le veut, je le ferai." The only aspect on which the indigenous communities possessed some leverage was that of the compensation to be determined for the relinquishment of their customary rights resting on the assessed land. The real difficulty for the territorial administrators was to establish whether the claimed rights were genuine, who owned or exercised them, and to whom the compensation for their relinquishment should be paid . Usually, the colonial administration relied on the village chiefs or foremen (*capitas*) – who had mostly been appointed by that same administration – to resolve these questions. As the privileged interlocutors of the administration, these notables held considerable sway in settling compensation questions, which possibly further enhanced their position within their local communities. Compensation was usually paid out in cash, sometimes to individuals, more often to the village chiefs and elders for the benefit of the collectivity. The authorities were very much aware of the potential for disputes caused by these compensation payments, and therefore decided in 1954 that henceforth these would be paid out exclusively to the treasuries of the local administrative units, which operated under the control of the territorial administrators.[23]

In many cases, the compensation seems to have been regarded by the colonial administration as a sweetener to make the de facto expropriation of land more acceptable to the local community. Normally it was calculated on the basis of the presumed loss in produce suffered through the relinquishment of traditional gathering, logging, or hunting rights. However, quite often compensation was also granted nominally "for reasons of political expediency" or "as a matter of principle." To a certain extent, the central authorities in Leopoldville and Brussels wanted to counteract the tendency of many local administrations to set compensation at derisorily low levels that were bound to be met with contempt by those entitled to it.[24] In more than one case, the amount of compensation initially requested by the local notables was drastically reduced by the local colonial administration, only to be increased again by the next higher echelon of authority.

## 4.5 Land legislation disputes and the end of colonialism

After World War II a new influx of Europeans (the total number of Belgians residing in the Congo rose from about 20,000 in 1940 to 80,000 in the late 1950s) began to put pressure on farmland adjudications in the most densely populated regions of the Congo, in particular the provinces of Bas-Congo and Kivu. This, and a gradual rise in social and political awareness among Congolese elites, turned the land question into a highly contentious issue (Louwers 1954; Sohier 1955). The Congolese considered the colonial land legislation to be extremely unfair, as in their eyes it enabled unjust expropriation on a massive scale. The notion that an indigenous community would give up its traditional rights to certain parts of the ancestral land – completely and permanently – was hard to reconcile with ingrained cultural traditions and religious beliefs. But more mundane material interests played a role, too. Increasingly, legal challenges were raised in the local courts, sometimes with the active support of European missionaries who took the plight of the Congolese population to heart. One of them, Father Edmond Boelaert (1899–1966), active in the Equateur province (Coquilhatville), in 1953 took the unprecedented initiative of organizing a comprehensive survey on customary land rights among the Congolese themselves (Vinck 2011). His close colleague, Father Gustaaf Hulstaert (1900–90), repeatedly tried to put the land question on the agenda of the Commission for the Protection of the Indigenous People, of which he had become a member in 1953, but he was met with delaying tactics. Nevertheless, in the mid-1950s, as a result of such internal pressures and in the light of events in Kenya and Algeria – where around this time bitter conflicts broke out in which land rights played a prominent role – the colonial government came round to the view that a fundamental overhaul of its land policies was unavoidable.

There was a growing feeling that the customary land rights of the Congolese should be given more weight, but that at the same time a development toward private property should be encouraged, not only in the cities – where this development was already under way – but also in the countryside. Guy Malengreau (1911–2002), one of the co-founders of the University of Lovanium near Kinshasa and an influential opinion maker, recognized the urgency of the problem. Because of its political nature he pleaded for a radical departure from the system enshrined in the decrees of 1906 and 1934. When the Minister of Colonies finally created a commission within the Colonial Council to investigate the best way forward, Malengreau was appointed special consultant. This new Commission on Indigenous Land met between December 1955 and March 1956.[25] In essence, it recommended a reversal of the existing system: henceforth the presumption would be that *all* land in the Congo was indigenous land, unless it could be proven to be truly vacant, i.e., land on which no indigenous claims or rights rested whatsoever. In consequence, even land that was only occasionally or marginally used by the local communities, e.g., for gathering, logging, or hunting, would from now on be considered indigenous land. Moreover, the authority to declare indigenous land vacant and to cede it for European colonization would be transferred fully to the indigenous communities. Instead of the colonial state assessing a plot of land and declaring it vacant, it would now be these indigenous communities themselves that would declare land vacant and cede it. However, in order to "protect" colonial interests and to avoid a sell-out of land by the villages, the colonial administration would continue to supervise land adjudications. Moreover, the status quo ante would be respected: in other words, land already declared vacant and concessions granted under the previous system would remain untouched.

This fundamental reform would not see the light of day. In the following years, the Belgian Congo was caught up in a feverish rush toward decolonization. The rapid and unexpected advent of Congolese independence in 1960 prevented the plans for a revised legislation on land from being realized.

## 4.6 Land policies and rural development

On the face of it, it might seem that land legislation and disputes did not matter that much in the Belgian Congo. As the vast colony was land-abundant and only sparsely populated, pressure on land remained subdued. This did not change fundamentally throughout the colonial period, mainly because the Belgian Congo, after an initial steep population decline, witnessed a persistent demographic stagnation until at least the 1950s. Moreover, it never fully developed into a settler colony, and therefore pressure on land from white colonists was relatively marginal. Nevertheless, this brief historical survey demonstrates that land legislation actually mattered a lot. For one thing, land expropriations impacted directly on the affected indigenous communities: they brought colonialism – quite literally – to the doorstep of the villagers. Land adjudications were often resented as they defied deeply rooted customs and beliefs (ancestral lands) and laid bare the villagers' powerlessness in the face of direct colonial intrusions in their daily lives. Second, while land may have been abundant, good arable land was in much shorter supply, as the largest part of the Congo was (and remains) covered by rain forests and savannah. European colonists, though few in number, were usually granted huge concessions of several hundreds, even thousands, of hectares of the best available land.[26] At the end of the colonial period concerns were raised that in certain regions (Bas-Congo, Kivu) the number and size of concessions granted had reached saturation level.[27] Finally, land legislation mattered as it was a key part of the much broader colonial compact. It provided the basis for other policies that directly affected not only the ownership but also the utilization of land.

The primary purpose of the colonial legislation on land ownership, as it developed between 1885 and 1960, was to provide a legal justification for the appropriation of so-called vacant lands for the benefit of the colonial state and of the European companies, missions, and colonists that settled in the Congo for a variety of reasons. The claim that this legislation went out of its way to respect customary land rights seemed to suggest that the colonizer had no intention of interfering with these or, by extension, with agriculture as it was practiced in the indigenous villages. Of course the reality was different. The confiscations of land and the concessions granted had an immediate impact on the local communities affected, if for no other reason than that they laid claim to local labor resources that were often already scarce. But there were at least three other ways in which the colonial administration interfered directly with indigenous land tenure systems and agriculture: colonial labor and fiscal policies, the forced introduction of cash crops, and the late-colonial attempt to create an indigenous class of agricultural entrepreneurs through the "indigenous peasantry" (*paysannat indigène*) scheme, discussed below. Any comprehensive study of land tenure systems and rural development in the Belgian Congo will have to deal extensively with these main issues and analyze their evolution, their close interrelation, and their continuous adaptation prompted by colonial requirements and by the African responses these elicited.

Throughout most of the colonial period, labor policies worked to the disadvantage of indigenous agriculture and rural development. In the 1920s, an acute shortage of workers in the booming mining industry led to very active, and often compulsory, labor recruitment campaigns in the villages in the interior of the colony, and this in spite of the fact that the 1908 Colonial Charter contained a clear condemnation of any form of forced labor (Clement 2007). The notion of "able adult men" (*hommes adultes valides*) was introduced and the proportion of such men who could be recruited safely within each village – i.e., without jeopardizing the village's future development – was fixed. The result was nonetheless that many villages were left with a disproportionately high number of elderly people, children, and women, and that the agricultural work increasingly fell to the women, even more than was already the case. Fiscal policies reinforced this trend, as taxation (poll tax) acted as an incentive for adult male villagers to seek remunerated employment in mining and industry, in government service or on European-owned plantations. After the crisis of the 1930s, the industrial centers and nascent cities of the Belgian Congo – foremost Leopoldville, Elisabethville, Stanleyville, and Jadotville – developed a dynamic of their own, attracting increasing numbers of young villagers seeking to escape the "customary milieu." This was the start of a process of rural migration that was a source of major concern to colonial administrators, but that they were unable to stop. These developments, partly caused by the colonial government, partly the result of endogenous social and economic processes, naturally placed the agricultural sector in a very weak labor position. Colonial administrators complained continuously that they had to contend with a true rural exodus.

These labor and tax policies and the sharp distinction that was made between a modern (European) agricultural sector on the one hand, and traditional, indigenous agriculture on the other, resulted in a relative neglect of the latter. It was not until the end of World War I, that the colonial state developed a more or less coherent agricultural policy to compensate somewhat for the primacy assigned to mining, infrastructure, and industry. The underlying development premise was the same as for the whole colonial enterprise: "valorization" (*mise en valeur*). To unlock the potential of Congolese agriculture, it had to be forced to modernize both in direction (away from subsistence farming) and in methods of cultivation (increased productivity thanks to modern farming techniques). Subsistence farming practiced on customary lands produced mainly cassava, maize, groundnuts, plantain bananas, and rice for local consumption. In the first instance, modernizing traditional agriculture was to be achieved through the introduction of cash crops – palm oil, cotton, coffee, and others – not only on large-scale concessions owned by European companies or settlers and worked by hired Congolese laborers, but also on the customary land of the villages and clans themselves, by way of "compulsory cultivation" (*cultures obligatoires*) imposed by the colonial state. The compulsory cultivation of cash crops, first introduced in 1917, was meticulously laid down and monitored closely by state agents. It was generally hated by the Congolese villagers. The theory was that it would earn the rural communities extra income and help to modernize agriculture, but, as Osumaka Likaka (1997) has shown for cotton, this was only marginally the case, while the system profoundly disturbed social and economic relations within the villages (for instance by increasing the leverage the chiefs enjoyed over their villagers, or by systematically undervaluing the role of women in the agricultural process). Fragmentary evidence suggests that the introduction of cash crops may have had a negative impact on nutritional standards, particularly through a reduction of dietary variety (Vansina 2010). It is hardly surprising, then, that the compulsory cultivation of cash crops was to a certain extent self-defeating as it became one more cause of the rapidly increasing rural exodus.

The cash crop scheme proved hugely profitable for the European concession holders and for the colonial state. However, by the mid-1930s, faced with the reality of rural emigration which threatened the long-term viability of cash crop cultivation, the colonial government had come round to the view that the living standards of the rural population needed to be improved significantly. To this end, the "indigenous peasantry" scheme was introduced. The underlying idea was that rural society could only be stabilized and further developed if and when an autonomous class of relatively well-to-do individual farmers emerged that in a distant future might even aspire to formally titled individual land ownership. At the same time, it was an occasion to do something about what many in the administration regarded as the antiquated and inefficient methods of subsistence farming practiced in the Congolese villages. A scheme was worked out to promote the creation of such an indigenous peasantry (Malengreau 1949). Basically, it consisted in regrouping farmers in model villages, where they tilled contiguous plots of land using the latest agricultural techniques (including a scientifically determined rotation of crops and fallow, measures to fight soil erosion, and the use of improved, high-yield seeds provided by the state agronomic services).[28] The land was, usually, customary land belonging to the local community or clan, but it was mostly tilled individually. The colonizer's intention that the indigenous peasantry scheme should over time lead to private ownership of land implied that eventually customary land would be privatized and, presumably, become marketable. However, this was not mentioned in the propaganda for the program, probably out of fear that raising such a prospect might further inflame the already contentious land issue. Instead, it was argued that joining the scheme was the best way for the village community to prevent customary land from being declared vacant and given into concession to "foreigners."[29]

By the mid-1950s nearly 10 percent of the Congolese rural population (some 150,000 farmers with their families) was enrolled in the *paysannat indigène* scheme. But even so, the colonial authorities had to concede that its results remained precarious at best. Bar a few localized showcase successes, short-run results in terms of output and productivity growth were disappointing. Colonial administrators blamed this on the lack of enthusiasm on the part of the Congolese farmers, and their unwillingness to adopt rational, scientific farming methods and processes; but equally on shortcomings on the part of the colonizer: lack of professional staff and resources to guide the implementation of the scheme, and insufficient training provided to the farmers.[30] The administration remained convinced that, given time and resources, such failings could be rectified. In reality, the attempt to revolutionize subsistence farming through a centrally planned and strictly implemented scheme "from above" was most likely doomed to failure in the colonial context in the Congo. The incentives the scheme purported to provide were rather abstract (private land ownership) or would only materialize in a more or less distant future, if at all (substantially higher earnings). They were in any case insufficient to convince distrustful farmers to take part in the scheme voluntarily. As a result, the scheme suffered from the start from the same flaw that characterized – and ultimately undid – so many colonial schemes, namely the need to resort to coercion – even if, at this late stage of colonialism, it was rather implicit or "soft" coercion. Most Congolese farmers who took part in the *paysannat indigène* farming scheme, did so not because they saw clear benefits in it, but because the colonial state wanted them to. Not surprisingly, the scheme was utterly disliked (Vansina 2010: 219–21). As late as 1953, a provincial commissioner in the western Katanga province reported that the local Chokwe people termed their enlistment in the indigenous peasantry scheme "kasangisa," meaning "being forced, being coerced."[31]

## 4.7 Conclusion

Looking at the evolution of land ownership legislation in the Belgian Congo, it is clear that the primary concern was to give the state and the colonial elites (European companies, missions, and colonists) the strongest possible hold on land to allow them to benefit as much as possible from the wealth extracted from it. Nevertheless, with time, in reaction to widespread abuses and because of growing resistance from the Congolese, the customary land rights of the indigenous communities were given increased consideration. African agency did play a role in bringing about this change. This was reflected in the more stringent controls on land expropriations introduced in 1934 and in the plans to make the indigenous communities responsible for land adjudications discussed at the end of the 1950s. However, land legislation was not only about ownership of land, but also about the agricultural development policies that went along with it. After a period of relative neglect, the colonial state took it upon itself to revolutionize traditional subsistence farming, first through the compulsory cultivation of cash crops and later through the introduction of the indigenous peasantry scheme. As a result, throughout the colonial period, the Congolese villagers were confronted with an increasingly intrusive colonial state, not only interfering with customary land rights, but also telling them what to plant and how to plant it. In many cases, it would seem, the potential benefits of colonial agricultural development policies – in terms of productivity and output growth and increased earnings – were not or were only incompletely realized, mainly because of the explicit and implicit coercion with which these various schemes were implemented and the natural resistance this provoked among Congolese farmers. The colonizer's intention to introduce fully titled private ownership of agricultural land did not materialize.

After independence in 1960, the colonial legacy in agricultural development policies was largely swept away. The *paysannat indigène* scheme was abandoned immediately and large-scale cash crop cultivation collapsed in many regions (cotton production in particular). With the gradual deterioration of the (transport) infrastructure, and of the economic and social fabric generally, under the Mobutu regime and subsequently during the Congolese wars of 1997–2002, the agricultural sector reverted more and more to subsistence farming, practiced mostly on small plots under a customary tenure system. This has had serious repercussions on the Congo's food safety situation, as in the recent past the country's agricultural production has consistently failed to guarantee food self-sufficiency (USAID 2010; ACE Europe 2011).

On the other hand, key features of the colonial land legislation have survived into the post-colonial era. These include the coexistence of customary land rights with a marginal system of formal land titling, and, above all, the predominance of the state in land questions (Musafiri 2009). The 1966 law on land ownership (Bakajika Law), the 1973 General Property Law and, more recently, the 2005 Constitution, have declared all Congolese land to be state property. The Congolese state has the exclusive right to grant land concessions, just as the colonial state used to have (incidentally, for the Congolese state this includes the right to expropriate land concessions granted in the colonial period). However, as in many other sub-Saharan countries, the state's monopoly on land is in reality constrained, as the majority of the arable land, although formally owned by the state, continues to be cultivated on the basis of customary tenure systems. As a result of this mixed system ("legal pluralism"), and because of failing institutional capacity, land rights in today's Congo are often ambiguous, inadequately documented and, therefore, tenuous (Ansoms and Marysse 2011: 28–31, 70–3). Moreover, this system, in which state-sponsored land adjudications and regular renewals of concessions continue to play an important role, lends itself to multiple rent-seeking opportunities. The level of leverage enjoyed by state officials and village chiefs also has its parallel in colonial practices particularly regarding the negotiation and allocation of compensation payments for renouncing customary land rights.

Whatever the merits or limitations of this mixed system, it is the basis from which any attempt at reforming land holding and agriculture in the Congo must start.[32]

## Archival sources

AAB = African Archives, Brussels, Belgian Federal Public Service for Foreign Affairs.
ARNACO = Archives Nationales du Congo, Kinshasa, Democratic Republic of the Congo.

## Notes

1 My special thanks go to Greet van Malderen, Françoise Donnay, Michel Helaers and Roger Angbongi for accompanying me on this journey.
2 There is a large body of literature that upholds enforceable, formal private property rights in land as a prerequisite for modern economic growth, mainly because they encourage long-term investments in land, render it marketable and allow it to be put up as collateral to obtain credit. This literature is indebted to such classics as: North, Douglas C. (1990) *Institutions, Institutional Change and Economic Performance*, Cambridge: Cambridge University Press; and Acemoglu, D., Johnson, S., and Robinson, J.A. (2005) "Institutions as a fundamental cause of long-term growth," in Aghion, P. and S. Durlauf (eds.), *Handbook of Economic Growth*, Elsevier. However, other research shows that in certain circumstances, such as those prevailing in much of sub-Saharan Africa, informal ("customary") systems of allocating and enforcing property rights may actually be more efficient and more fair than formal land titling systems. See: Platteau, J.-P. (2000), "Allocating and enforcing property rights in land: informal versus formal mechanisms in Subsaharan Africa," *Nordic Journal of Political Economy*, 26, 55–81; and: Angeles, L. (2011) "Institutions, Property Rights and Economic Development in Historical Perspective," Working Paper, University of Glasgow. The empirical evidence linking private property rights in land to investment growth and efficiency gains in agriculture is not always unambiguous. See: Fenske, J. (2011) "Land tenure and investment incentives: Evidence from West Africa," *Journal of Development Economics*, 95, 137–56.
3 The archives of the former Belgian Ministry of Colonies and of the colonial administration in Africa (Government-General), currently preserved in Brussels (Federal Public Service of Foreign Affairs) and Kinshasa (Archives Nationales du Congo). These sources have to be treated with caution as they often offer a one-sided or biased view. This can be compensated somewhat by making use of oral history. See for instance Likaka (2009); Vansina (2010).
4 "Nul n'a le droit d'occuper sans titre les terres vacantes, ni de déposséder les indigènes des terres qu'ils occupent. Les terres vacantes doivent être considérées comme appartenant à l'Etat" (Etat Indépendant du Congo, *Bulletin Officiel*, 1885, p. 30). ("No one has the right to occupy vacant land without legal title, nor to dispossess indigenous people from the land they occupy. All vacant lands must be considered to belong to the State.")
5 See in this context the ongoing discussion (until the very end of the colonial period) on the question of whether the concept of private land ownership was known in customary practice or not.
6 Most notoriously through the Congo Reform Association and the publications of Roger Casement and Edmund D. Morel (e.g., *King Leopold's Rule in Africa*, London: Heinemann, 1904).

7 Decree of June 3, 1906: "sont terres occupées par les indigènes ... les terres que les indigènes habitent, cultivent ou exploitent d'une manière quelconque conformément aux coutumes et usages locaux."

8 M. Drapier, "Rapport sur les délimitations des terres indigènes," November 7, 1909, AAB, RF 1439 – *Régime Foncier, dossier 13, 1: Droits des indigènes, Instructions générales.*

9 Ministère des Colonies, "Relève des ventes et locations de terres domaniales conclues au Congo pendant le 1er trimestre de 1923," January 10, 1924, AAB, RF 1428 – *Régime Foncier, dossier 5, Administration: personnel du service des terres en Afrique.*

10 M. Drapier, "Note sur les travaux de la délimitation des terres indigènes," Boma, August 29, 1909, AAB, RF 1439 – *Régime Foncier, dossier 13, 1: Droits des indigènes, Instructions générales.* "Note handed over to the Minister of Colonies during his visit in August," it reads in the margin.

11 AAB, A15 – *Affaires Indigènes, AI/II.L1 Terres indigènes,* folder 1403, dossier 3: "Conseil du Gouvernement, Délimitation des terres indigènes, 1918–20."

12 AAB, A15, dossier 1403 – Affaires Indigènes, AI/II.L1: *Terres indigènes, correspondance générale.*

13 Conseil Colonial, Séance du 18 mars 1927, AAB, GG 6.201 – *Katanga, Elisabethville: projet village industriel, 1921–30.*

14 Letter L. Bureau to Governor-General Rutten, October 6, 1926, AAB, A15, dossier 1403, 3 – Affaires Indigènes, AI/II.L1: *Terres indigènes, correspondance générale.*

15 Among them Octave Louwers (1878–1959), secretary and vice-president of the Colonial Council. See van Pottelbergh (2006).

16 "If Bula Matari wants it so, I will do it." "Rapport au sujet de l'enquête faite par le commissaire général Heenen en ce qui concerne l'exécution des conventions, en date du 14 mars 1924 conclues avec la chefferie Pande et la sous-chefferie Guba," Elisabethville, July 16, 1926, AAB, A15 – *Affaires Indigènes, AI/II.L1: Terres indigènes,* folder 1403, dossier 3: Terres indigènes: correspondance générale. Bula Matari, or "breaker of stones," in reference to Morton Stanley's use of dynamite to clear a passage through the Crystal mountains from the Congo's Atlantic coast upstream to the Leopoldville plateau, was used by the Congolese as a generic term for the colonial state, and indeed for any form of authority wielded by the whites, denoting its irresistible and compelling force.

17 "Commission pour l'étude des concessions de terres, Conclusions," AAB, PPA 3438 – *Droit publique,* No. 229: *Commission des concessions de terres destines à l'agriculture ou à l'élevage.*

18 Correspondence between Postiaux, Governor ad interim of Katanga province, and Vice-Governor-General Beernaert of September 15 and October 28, 1931, AAB, GG 12.005 – *TF Katanga: instructions divers, 1931–46.*

19 As commented by Father Le Grand at the Colonial Council meeting on March 18, 1927: "I am informed that in certain territories the officials charged with assessing indigenous land rights have been ordered in advance to declare such lands vacant in favour of the prospective concessionaries." Conseil Colonial, Séance du 18 mars 1927, AAB, GG 6.201 – *Katanga, Elisabethville: projet village industriel, 1921–30.*

20 AAB, PPA 3440, no. 245 – *Droit publique: commission vacance des terres, cession des droits des indigènes,* 1934.

21 The Belgian Congo was divided into four provinces (from 1933, six), governed by a governor; each province into a number of districts (24 for the whole Congo), led by a district commissioner; and each district into a number of territories (about 120 in all), led by a territorial administrator.

22 Examples from the Katanga, Equateur and Leopoldville provinces found in: AAB, GG 13.477 – TF AIMO Katanga: *Enquêtes de vacance terrains, dossiers individuels, 1938–56;* and: ARNACO, Série Congo belge – *titres fonciers, dossier AF 4/14.*

23  The CACI or Caisse Administrative de la Circonscription Indigène. In one recorded case, when the village notables learned that the compensation would be paid out not to them but to the local CACI, they "expressed their considerable disappointment [*vifs regrets*] at this decision, but did not oppose it as they had no means to oppose it." ARNACO, Série Congo belge – *titres fonciers, dossier AF 4/14: concession de 150 ha. à Mpambi-Bokotokiri, lac Léopold II, 1954–56.*

24  "Priver les indigènes du bénéfice de ces indemnités, c'est s'exposer à les voir refuser désormais leur acquiescement à toute cession ou concession" ("Depriving the Congolese of the benefit of these indemnities would mean increasing the risk that in future they will refuse to acquiesce in further cessions or concessions"). Draft letter of the Minister of Colonies, Brussels, to the Governor-General, Leopoldville, January 1929, AAB, A15, dossier 1403 – Affaires Indigènes, AI/II.L1: *Terres indigènes, correspondance générale.*

25  AAB, PPA 3446, no. 274 – Droit publique: *Commission des terres indigènes, 1955–56.*

26  It was estimated that in the mid-1950s, only 1.2 percent of the total land surface of the Congo was under regular cultivation (some 2.8 million hectares out of a total of 234 million hectares): two million hectares of customary lands, on which subsistence farming produced mainly cassava, maize, groundnuts, plantain bananas, and rice for local consumption; and 0.8 million hectares earmarked for cash crops, most importantly palm oil, cotton, coffee, and hevea. In the mid-1950s, these 2.8 million hectares provided a livelihood to a Congolese rural population (defined as those living in the villages, under the statute of customary law) of close to ten million out of a total population of over 13 million (a population density of about six inhabitants per km²). The European population for the whole of the Congo, at that time, counted some 80,000 (of whom 80 percent were Belgian), but only a few thousands of them were registered as settlers (*colons*). These settlers, together with a handful of commercial companies, did, however, directly occupy or control over 320,000 hectares of prime agricultural land, devoted almost entirely to cash crops. Figures taken from Inforcongo 1958: 261–90.

27  Proposal to grant the Governor-General the right to declare a halt to further land concessions in certain regions. AAB, PPA 3446, no. 274 – Droit publique: *Commission des terres indigènes, 1955–56.*

28  For that purpose the colony operated from the 1930s a network of agronomic stations and experimental fields, coordinated from the vast, state-of-the-art state agronomic center at Yangambi (INEAC – Orientale province). See: Institut National pour l'Etude agronomique du Congo (1960).

29  R. Flament, "Situation du paysannat indigène de Coquilhatville au 30 juin 1954," AAB, GG 7698 – *Equateur: paysannat indigène, rapports inspection 1950–55.*

30  F. Peigneux, "Les paysannats en milieu rural congolais," June 10, 1958; and Note "Pourquoi les nouvelles techniques préconisées par les Centres et Stations de Recherches de l'INEAC ne sont pas appliquées par les agriculteurs congolais," August 20, 1958, AAB, GG 20.722 – *Documents ayant servi préparation congrès colonial.*

31  A. Scholler, "Territoire Sandoa: situation paysannat," AAB, GG 14.590 – *Katanga divers 1948–57.*

32  See in this respect the new agricultural bill, currently being discussed by the Congolese legislature: République Démocratique du Congo, Assemblée Nationale (2011), *Projet de loi portant principes fondamentaux relatifs à l'agriculture*, Kinshasa.

# References

ACE Europe (2011) *Analyse de la gouvernance du secteur Agriculture en RD Congo, Rapport final*, Mechelen: ACE (www.ace-europe.be).

108   *P. Clement*

Ansoms, A. and S. Marysse (eds.) (2011) *Natural Resources and Local Livelihoods in the Great Lakes Region of Africa, A Political Economy Perspective*, Houndmills: Palgrave Macmillan.

Boelaert, E. (1956) *L'Etat indépendant et les terres indigènes*, Brussels: Académie Royale des Sciences Coloniales.

Clement, P. (2007) "Het bezoek van koning Albert I aan Belgisch Congo, 1928. Tussen propaganda en realiteit," *Belgisch Tijdschrift voor Nieuwste Geschiedenis – Revue belge d'histoire contemporaine*, 37, 1–2, 175–221.

Dellicour, F. (1958) "Martin Rutten," *Biographie Coloniale Belge*, 5, Brussels: Académie Royale des Sciences Coloniales, 714–22.

Etat Indépendant du Congo (EIC), *Bulletin Officiel*.

Heyse, T. (1934) *Régime de la propriété immobilière au Congo belge*, Brussels: Librairie Falk.

Heyse, T. (1935) "Le décret du 31 mai 1934 sur la constatation de la vacance des terres et la renonciation des droits indigènes," *Bulletin des Séances*, 6, 2, Brussels: Institut Royal Colonial Belge, 282–96.

Inforcongo (1958) *Le Congo belge*, part 1, Brussels.

Institut National pour l'Etude agronomique du Congo (1960) *L'INEAC au service de l'agriculture congolaise*, Brussels.

Lentz, C. (2006), "Land rights and the politics of belonging in Africa: an introduction," in R. Kuba and C. Lentz (eds.), *Land and the Politics of Belonging in West Africa*, Leiden and Boston: Brill.

Likaka, Osumaka (1997) *Rural Society and Cotton in Colonial Zaire*, Madison: The University of Wisconsin Press.

Likaka, Osumaka (2009) *Naming Colonialism, History and Collective Memory in the Congo, 1870–1960*, Madison: The University of Wisconsin Press.

Louwers, O. (1954) "Le problème des terres indigènes," *Journal des Tribunaux d'Outre-mer*, 5, 47, 65–8.

Malengreau, G. (1949) *Vers un paysannat indigène, Les lotissements agricoles au Congo belge*, Brussels: Institut Royal Colonial Belge.

Musafiri, P. Nobirabo (2009) "The dispossession of indigenous land rights in the DRC: a history and future prospects," *Land Rights and the Forest Peoples of Africa, Historical, Legal and Anthropological Perspectives*, Moreton-in-Marsh: Forest Peoples Programme.

Sohier, A. (1955) "Le problème des terres indigènes," *Journal des Tribunaux d'Outre-mer*, 6, 63, 125–8.

USAID (2010) *Country Profile: Democratic Republic of the Congo*, at www.usaid-landtenure.net (accessed August 15, 2012).

van Pottelbergh, G. (2006) "Octave Louwers, Eminence grise van het Belgisch koloniaal establishment," *Belgisch Tijdschrift voor Nieuwste Geschiedenis – Revue belge d'histoire contemporaine*, 36, 3–4, 453–94.

Vansina, J. (2010) *Being Colonized, The Kuba Experience in Rural Congo, 1880–1960*, Madison: The University of Wisconsin Press.

Vinck, H. (2011) *Conflits fonciers au Congo belge: Opinions congolaises*, Brussels: Académie Royale des Sciences d'Outre-mer, Fontes Historiae Africanae.

# 5 In the shadow of opium

## Tax farming and the political economy of colonial extraction in Java, 1807–1911

*Abdul Wahid*

## 5.1 Introduction

One of the crucial differences between the systems of colonial exploitation in the Netherlands Indies and the Belgian Congo was the role of local institutions assisting the colonial power to secure its imperial project. The fiscal system reflects these differences very well. In general, the Belgian Congo's fiscal system was based on taxing colonial products that had little foundation in indigenous socio-economic structures. In the absence of local contenders, the Belgians imposed their taxes almost without negotiation (see Gardner, Chapter 6 below). In contrast, the Dutch were dealing with better-established local social, political, and economic structures in the Netherlands Indies (Java in particular) from their earliest ventures in the archipelago. Despite holding political supremacy over the largest part of Java since the mid-eighteenth century, the Dutch colonial officers could not govern the island without the support of local elites. The Dutch took over the indigenous practice of tax farming to solidify colonial state revenue and engaged the Chinese immigrant minority to solve problems of agency (Wertheim 1964). This policy strengthened the role of the Chinese as the most important middleman minority in the Javanese economy, a role that is still perceptible.

Tax farming had been part of the Dutch fiscal strategy in Java since the VOC era (Vereenigde Oost-Indische Compagnie; see Thee, Chapter 2 above) and remained an important source of revenue until its abolition at the end of the nineteenth century. Dick (1993: 4) broadly defines tax farming as:

> A system by which the state leased, through auction to the highest bidder, the monopoly right to conduct a particular service, collecting taxes in particular, or to engage in a particular activity for profit, in return for an agreed fixed price paid in advance to the state on a routine basis.

Dick explains that in Java, as well as elsewhere in the archipelago and Southeast Asia, the colonial government chose Chinese businessmen as partners to act as tax farmers. The Dutch did not entrust local aristocracies with the task, fearing that they would use the collected revenue to strengthen their opposition against the Dutch (Dick 1993: 5). Moreover, the Dutch considered this system the best way to profit from the indispensable role in the economy played by the Chinese, with their vast trade network, capital, and knowledge of the local market (Giap 1989: 160–3).

Scholars hold differing opinions about the origins of tax farming, however. Some argue that the system only really evolved after the arrival of the first Europeans, others hold that the system, or similar practices, had existed in Java long before.[1] Reid (1993: 70), who favors the first position, argues that tax farming emerged as a result of intensifying trade contacts between the indigenous population and Europeans and foreign Asian migrants since the seventeenth century. Considering the absence of indigenous words for Dutch concepts like *pacht* or *verpachting* (lease, leasing), Reid assumes that the Dutch introduced the practice of tax farming with certain modifications for local tax practices and circumstances, starting in Batavia (Jakarta) and gradually spreading to other parts of the archipelago. Reid hypothesizes that the function of port administrator (*syahbandar*) in most of the Malay and Javanese ports came to incorporate practices of tax farming, because the port administrator served as a broker between the state authorities and the unassimilated commercial minority (Reid 1993: 72).

Kian (2006: 27) rejects Reid's view that tax farming emerged in Java only after the Europeans arrived. Citing archaeological works, she insists that some tax farming was practiced in Java in far earlier periods. She offers two examples of tax farms that existed from the ninth and tenth centuries: the tollgates along the overland route from Magelang to the north-central coast and those on the waterway along the Brantas River in East Java. According to Kian, local rulers deployed these practices for economic as well as political purposes. By farming out the right to collect taxes to outsiders, the rulers could gain more revenue than they could by managing the collections themselves. And from a political viewpoint, tax farms enabled local rulers to quell the rise of political competitors. These motivations probably explain why Chinese merchants – who were economically strong but politically weak – were selected for tax farm leases from their initial development (Kian 2006: 244).

Although scholars may differ on the origins of tax farming in Java, they agree that the Dutch institutionalized the system and introduced it to a wider area from the seventeenth century onwards. The founder of Batavia, Jan Pieterszoon Coen, farmed out the right to collect taxes on gambling and the weighing-house in 1620 and 1626, respectively, to the prominent Chinese merchant, Jan Con (Thomas 1893: 23). This agreement initiated the cooperation between the Dutch and the Chinese migrants in building Batavia and confirmed the VOC's trade supremacy in Java, which in the long run established the socio-political construction known in the literature as "Sino-European co-colonization" (Blussé 1988: 52).

After successfully subjugating the Sultanate of Mataram in 1755, the last stronghold of a local power contender, the Dutch extended tax farming to the majority of Java. As a result, by the end of the 1780s, the company officers reported that tax farming had become "the biggest income source of the Company so far" (Kian 2006: 77). In the meantime, the Chinese had secured their position as the favorite partner of the Dutch in revenue farming. From this strategic position, some elite Chinese families – such as the Tan family of Batavia, the Tan Bing family of Semarang, and the Han family of Surabaya – gained the economic prominence that they were to retain throughout the nineteenth century.

## 5.2 The expansion of tax farming under Dutch colonial rule

The nineteenth-century development of tax farming in Java can be divided into three stages, which are reflected in the overview of tax farm revenues presented in Table 5.1. In the formative stage (*c.*1807–35) the Dutch established full control over Java (for the Java War 1825–30 see Thee, Chapter 2 above), introduced the Cultivation System, and launched a major administrative reform program. From the mid-1830s onwards the Dutch consolidated the colonial fiscal system, expanded the administrative infrastructure and enhanced governmental efficiency. During the period 1830–70 tax farming contributed substantially to the Cultivation System's financial success and compensated for the financial losses of its abolition. The tax farm revenues reached a peak in the decade between 1885 and 1895. Finally, after 1895 the system was rapidly dismantled and during the first years of the Ethical Policy (see Thee, Chapter 2) the revenues declined to negligible amounts.

Table 5.1 shows that tax farm revenues continuously increased after 1816, with the exception of the decade between 1846 and 1855. Tax farm revenues contributed between one-fifth and a quarter of total government revenue from the mid-1820s onwards and this only changed significantly in the closing decade of the nineteenth century, when the yield declined to less than 100 million guilders and the share in total revenue dropped to 11.9 percent. The opium farm was the most important and profitable tax farm, contributing more than 138.5 million guilders per decade in the period 1866–95. Yet, taken together, the other small tax farms also offered a stable and significant contribution to the treasury, with an average of 31.2 million guilders per decade.

The expansion of the tax farm system closely corresponded with the attempts of successive political regimes to create a "modern" colonial state administration (Days 1900; Furnivall 1944). Succeeding administrations retained the tax farming system, with various degrees of modification, to finance their reform agendas (Ricklefs 2001: 143–50). Daendels (1814) started to revise the regulations: the auctioning of tax farm leases was tightened to counter the rampant corruption under the VOC officers. The auctions were held closer to the tax farm location and the extra 8 percent assessment for the Governor General was abolished. In addition, the successful bidder was freed from the obligation to deliver cotton thread and various other gifts to government officers (van Niel 2005: 204). Daendels made the Residents (district heads) the sole agents of opium distribution in their area and appointed specific controllers to supervise the tax farmers who retailed opium. In an official report of 1814, Daendels calculated that tax farming had contributed 5.25 million Rixdollars in silver coin and 5.07

Table 5.1 Income from tax farming in the Netherlands Indies, 1816–1925

| | Income from tax farming (in million guilders) | | | As % of state revenue in the Netherlands Indies | | |
|---|---|---|---|---|---|---|
| | Opium | Other | Total | Opium | Other | Total |
| 1816–25 | 14.8 | 12.8 | 27.6 | 8.2 | 7.1 | 15.3 |
| 1826–35 | 31.3 | 20.0 | 51.3 | 11.8 | 7.5 | 19.3 |
| 1836–45 | 65.4 | 39.8 | 105.2 | 16.7 | 10.1 | 26.8 |
| 1846–55 | 63.9 | 38.4 | 102.3 | 16.2 | 9.7 | 25.9 |
| 1856–65 | 96.6 | 27.5 | 124.1 | 17.6 | 5.0 | 22.6 |
| 1866–75 | 103.5 | 24.2 | 127.7 | 14.6 | 3.4 | 18.0 |
| 1876–85 | 158.3 | 33.4 | 191.7 | 16.8 | 3.5 | 20.3 |
| 1886–95 | 182.1 | 46.3 | 228.4 | 18.1 | 4.6 | 22.7 |
| 1896–1905 | 99.9 | 38.6 | 138.5 | 8.6 | 3.3 | 11.9 |
| 1906–15 | 21.6 | 33.9 | 55.5 | 1.1 | 1.8 | 2.9 |
| 1916–25 | – | 8.2 | 8.2 | – | 0.1 | 0.1 |

Source: Diehl (1993: 199).

million Rixdollars in paper currency during his administration, an impressive amount for those days (Daendels 1814: Vol. 3, Appendix 2).

During the British Interregnum (1811–16), Raffles sought to reform the fiscal system by introducing a new type of land taxation and by abolishing the existing feudalistic contingents and forced deliveries. He also replaced the tax farm system by direct collections through government officers (Knaap and Nagtegaal 1991: 127–57). Most of his reforms failed and had dire consequences for the state finances. In eastern Java, Raffles brought back the salt tax farms and turned them into a government monopoly, but local resistance, for example from the Sultans of Yogyakarta and Surakarta, halted reform of other tax farms.[2] For humanitarian reasons, he also intended to eliminate the opium farm, which he considered as harmful to the Javanese population. But his superiors pressed him to leave the opium trade unaffected, and Raffles abandoned the plan. Instead, he restricted the sale and consumption of opium to certain areas, such as the suburbs of Batavia, Semarang, Surabaya, and the Principalities of Yogyakarta and Surakarta, where he had no choice but to farm out the license to retail opium to the traditional players, the Chinese (Baud 1853: 156–7).

After the British returned Java to the Dutch in 1816, the new colonial government faced a difficult situation, politically and financially. The Dutch government extended the opium tax farm, reintroduced the Chinese gambling tax farm in 1817 – which had also been suspended under British rule – and introduced a tax farm on bazaars (*pasar*) in 1821. The exclusive long-term right to operate pawn shops was also extended to most districts of Java except the Principalities and the Priangan Regencies (Diehl 1993: 198).

The Java War (1825–30) caused a new financial loss to the governmental budget and temporarily suspended tax collections in central Java. In response, the Dutch launched the Cultivation System (see Thee, Chapter 2) and carried out a tax reform program that issued new regulations to boost fiscal efficiency and abolish ineffective taxes. The tax farms that were abolished were those with little financial importance, but which caused major grievances among the Javanese, such as the taxes on marriage in Tegal, on the sale of betel-chew leaves and fine chalk, on *ronggeng* dance performance, on the tollgates in Pekalongan, Kedu, Semarang, Surabaya, and the Principalities of Surakarta and Yogyakarta, and the bazaar tax farm (De Waal 1865b: 300–2). Suspension of the tollgates and bazaar tax farms was particularly important because they were considered the most abusive (Vitalis 1992: 39–41; van Zanden 2004: 1033), contributing to the revolutionary spirit during the Java War (Carey 1986: 55–137).

From 1834 onwards the government started to issue new regulations and split the tax farming administration into two groups: the opium tax farm (*opium pacht*) and the small tax farms (*kleine verpachte middelen*). The second group consisted of 15 tax farms on salt distribution and sales, cattle slaughtering, pig slaughtering, fish and fishing net sales, liquor sales, the Chinese poll tax, the crossing of rivers and sluices, bridge and ferry tolls, tobacco importation and cultivation, harvesting edible birds' nests, timber production, palm sugar sales, pawn shops, Chinese gambling and dance performances.[3] The new regulations

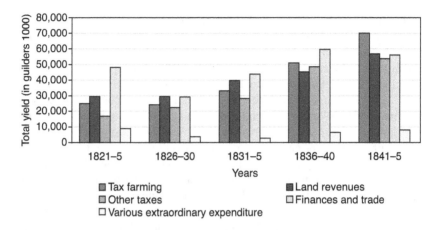

*Figure 5.1* Public revenue in the Netherlands Indies, 1821–45 (source: Koloniaal Verslag 1859, Appendix D, No. 5).

had a favorable impact on the colonial state budget, as tax farming revenue increased faster than any other government revenue source. Figure 5.1 shows that total tax farming revenue increased from 24.2 million guilders (21.9 percent of total revenue) during the war years of 1826–30 to 33.4 million (22.5 percent) in the period 1831–5, rising in the next five years to 51.6 million guilder (24.2 percent) and further to 69.7 million in the years 1841–5, by then comprising 33 percent of total revenue in the Netherlands Indies.

## 5.3  The opium tax farm

The tax reforms of the 1830s marked the beginning of a successful expansion of tax farm operations throughout the archipelago. By the mid-nineteenth century, the lucrative opium tax farm had been imposed throughout the territory under Dutch control, except for some opium-free zones (so-called "forbidden areas") such as Banten, the Priangan Regency, and several other smaller regions where Islamic influences or local rulers militated against opium consumption (Rush 1990: 25, 142–3). Opium smoking was originally introduced by the Chinese and became a common feature of urban and rural life from the early decades of nineteenth-century Java. Opium was not cultivated in Java, but was imported as a raw substance from Bengal and Turkey. The Dutch Trading Company (Nederlandsche Handel-Maatschappij, NHM) obtained a monopoly on the importation of opium in 1827. Opium farm activities were regulated by the opium ordinance of 1833, which stipulated a six-year term for farm rights, including the processing of raw opium, its distribution, its sale and the provision of public smoking places. In 1847, the ordinance was revised to provide for yearly contracts (van Dedem and Piepers 1889: 139–40).

Raw opium was refined for consumption and then sold in opium shops, built and maintained by opium tax farmers. In these shops, consumers could buy ready-to-use opium (*candu* in Javanese) of various qualities, as well as a smoking kit (*padudan*). Some shops also offered furnished smoking rooms for two or three persons. The best-quality opium, called *tiban* or *cako*, sold at the highest price and was affordable only by the indigenous elite (*priyayi*) and wealthy Chinese and Europeans. Chinese and Javanese commoners consumed lower-quality opium called *siram* or *cakat*. A colonial officer, De Waal, reported that in many cases smoking houses also functioned as brothels and gambling houses, attracting young Javanese and Chinese to spend their money (De Waal 1865a: 29–30; Boomgaard 1986: 35).

In his report of 1881, Charles TeMechelen, who was appointed chief of the anti-opium smuggling commission, wrote that opium users in Java could be categorized into three groups: () those consuming more than 20 *mata* (approximately 38 grams weight) of opium per day, who lived mostly in the principal towns and had higher incomes such as Chinese and other "foreign Orientals" and wealthy indigenous people; (2) those consuming less than 20 *mata* of opium per day, who lived mostly in the principal towns, also mainly Chinese; and (3) those consuming 2–5 *mata* per day, who were mostly commoners living in rural areas. Petty traders, workers, travelers, and those attending the traditional dance (*wayang*) performances – musicians, dancers, artists, and other performers – were the most frequent opium users among the Javanese commoners. According to TeMechelen, very few peasants smoked opium (TeMechelen 1885: 80–6).[4]

The Javanese consumed opium for different purposes and in different intensities. Among wealthy Javanese, opium was consumed for leisure or to entertain important guests at special occasions and ceremonies. Among poorer Javanese, opium was a remedy for various illnesses: headaches, fever and chills (including malaria), stomach aches, dysentery, asthma, tuberculosis, fatigue, and anxiety. Women used opium to relieve symptoms of venereal disease (*sakit perempuan*), and healers used it to mitigate pain caused by injuries such as dislocated or broken bones. But most of the Javanese laborers smoked or chewed opium as a stimulant (*obat cape*) and for pleasure (Rush 1990: 30–5). TeMechelen estimated that, in 1881, there were 748,603 opium users consuming a maximum of 20 *mata* of opium per day, while 228,122 persons consumed opium occasionally. He further estimated that a total of 977,557 people consumed some opium, which is 4.4 percent of a total population of 21,957,213. However, these are likely to be underestimates, as the legal and illegal market for opium was still growing (TeMechelen 1885: 86).

The auction of opium tax farms was a state occasion drawing higher- and lower-ranked Dutch and Javanese officials. The event was metaphorically referred to as a "battle of the kings" (*peperangan antara raja-raja*), where the wealthiest and most powerful Chinese in Java gathered to compete with one another for a concession (Joe 1933: 10; Rush 1990: 42). For the Chinese businessmen, the outcome meant control over the government's most valuable tax farm and the prestige and patronage that went with it. To the presiding Dutch official (the Resident), a farm's success meant a substantial contribution to his residency's state treasury, and indirectly, was an indication of his administration's success. Moreover, by holding the right to sell opium, the Chinese tax farmers could avoid the restriction of the pass system, which had been revived in 1823; they could freely travel to the countryside to conduct other economic activities, such as money lending and trade in rural commodities (Rush 1990: 44; Trocki 2002: 305).

To win the opium tax concession the Chinese participants made various preparations. They studied the local conditions to determine if the farm would be potentially profitable and worth a large investment, and they formed partnerships to win and operate the opium farm. These partnerships, commonly known as *kongsi*, would appoint two guarantors who, along with the tax farmer, would bind themselves to the farm contract. In many cases these three men represented a much larger association of *kongsi*, who financed the farms. Meanwhile, for its part, the government prepared for the auctions by investigating the *kongsi*'s performance to determine their reliability. Tax farmers were required to have at least two official guarantors to ensure the deliverance of the monthly tax fee (*pachtsom*). The government also tried to prevent prolonged domination by certain *kongsi*, so as to keep a level playing field (Rush 1990: 46–7).

The successful bidder signed a one to three-year contract with the government, giving the bidder the exclusive rights to retail opium in a clearly defined territory (*pacht gebied*). The contract also stipulated the price of the farm, that is, the farm fee plus the costs of purchasing official opium from the government. To operate the opium farm, a grantee *kongsi* usually divided its farm territory into smaller ones and leased them to a subcontracted farmer to facilitate the distribution of ready-to-use opium. The opium tax farmer handled the processing of raw opium and provided opium-smoking locations. The opium farmer took the necessary measures to protect his monopoly rights from intrusion by illegal opium retailers, for instance by employing Javanese spies (*mata-mata*) with martial arts skills and establishing good relationships with local Javanese authorities (TeMechelen 1885: 88).

De Waal, the ex-colonial officer who monitored the tax farming operations, reported a steady decrease in the number of granted opium farms, from 2738 in 1848 to 2321 in 1855 and 1812 in 1860, as the government sought to raise efficiency by granting fewer, but larger farms. The opium farms were concentrated in the north coast areas, and in the interior of central and eastern Java. The interior of central Java emerged as the most densely farmed areas, where each of the regencies had more than 100 opium farms in the 1850s. Yogyakarta and Surakarta taxed more than 200 opium farms a year, a number that increased constantly until the 1860s and marked the importance of these areas in opium farm concentration throughout the century. On the north coast of Java, the most important outlets for opium farms were the residencies of Tegal, Pekalongan, Semarang, and Surabaya. In eastern Java, the most important regencies were Madiun and Kediri, where more than 100 opium farms were granted annually. Even in the forbidden area of Priangan Regencies in western Java, opium was sold through clandestine trade and smuggling (De Waal 1865a: 35).

## 5.4 The small tax farms

Revenue from the small tax farms, also collected mostly in Java, was not as impressive as that from the opium farm. An exception was the salt farm, which was categorized as a small farm but was in reality a major source of revenue. Unlike the opium and salt tax farms, the smaller tax farms covered a limited geographical area and generated a smaller financial contribution. In principle, the terms and conditions for these small tax farms were similar to those for the opium farm, but the auction processes of these tax farms were less glamorous. A brief survey of these smaller tax farms reveals the fine-grained structure of the evolving colonial fiscal system in Java during the nineteenth century and the various political and economic aspects related to colonial taxation.

The Colonial Report of 1871 reported a total revenue of 1.3 million guilders from the small tax farms in the Netherlands Indies in 1870. This sum increased to 1.66 million guilders in 1880, then doubled to 3.03 million guilders in 1890, falling back to 1.6 million guilders in 1900 as some small tax farms were abolished (*Koloniaal Verslag* 1871–1901). Table 5.2 presents the data assembled by Mellegers (2004). It shows that the small farms operating in Java, such as the cattle slaughter, the pawn shop and the Chinese gambling farms were indeed small compared to the revenues drawn from the opium and salt farms, but their total value was not insignificant.

The salt tax farm – which for unclear reasons was administered as a small tax farm – was imposed during the VOC period. It was levied in particular on the sale and distribution of salt, in which the Chinese again played the leading role. Raffles abolished this tax farm in 1813 and transformed it into a direct state

*Table 5.2* The composition of tax farming revenue in Java, 1851–1900 (in thousand guilders)

| Years | 1851–60 | 1861–70 | 1871–80 | 1881–90 | 1891–1900 |
|---|---|---|---|---|---|
| Opium farm | 72,708 | 107,818 | 148,775 | 187,763 | 185,603 |
| Salt farm | 51,227 | 59,984 | 67,730 | 75,241 | 87,907 |
| Cattle slaughter farm | 4948 | 6487 | 8055 | 11,197 | 14,108 |
| Pig slaughter farm | 1204 | 716 | 521 | 591 | 546 |
| Pawn shop farm | 2911 | 3122 | 126 | 9016 | 10,824 |
| Liquor farm | 1741 | 2247 | 1882 | 1059 | 1764 |
| Gambling farm | 2415 | 2407 | 2631 | 9334 | 8018 |
| Other farms | 5503 | 6674 | 16,972 | 25,114 | 26,361 |
| Other leases & licenses | 10,719 | 6105 | 6876 | 13,777 | 13,018 |
| Total | 153,376 | 195,560 | 253,568 | 333,092 | 348,149 |

Source: Mellegers (2004) online dataset on www.cgeh.nl/indonesian-economy-history (accessed November 25, 2010).

monopoly that operated in Java, Madura, and Lampung. The Dutch administration reintroduced the tax farm system on salt in 1829. The government managed to collect more than 100 million guilders in the period 1851–70, which surpassed the yield of other small tax farms by far. This financial success, however, was accompanied by increasing abuses by Chinese tax farmers. Price and weight manipulation, usurious credit to salt-producing peasants, and other forms of corruption forced the government to stop the system and restore the state monopoly in 1882. Due to the strong grip of local aristocrats over several salt-producing areas, such as Bagan Siapi-api in North Sumatra and Pontianak in West Kalimantan, the government salt monopoly (*zoutregie*) was only enforced in the entire colony after 1914 (De Waal 1865b: 225; Diehl 1993: 230).

The fish farm, including fish, the supply of fishing nets, and the right to run fish markets, was leased for the first time as a single tax farm in 1817 and lasted until 1863. This farm was introduced in eight areas of fish production: Batavia, Bantam, Krawang, Tegal, Semarang, Surabaya, Pasuruan, and Besuki. In Krawang, the farm was abolished in 1832 because of the steady decrease in the catching and selling of fish. The tax on fish applied to the sale of fresh fish caught from the sea, rivers, or fishponds and of dried salt-fish, and other fish products in the government market, except for sea cucumber, seaweed, fish glue, and shark's-tail. The colonial ordinance of August 20, 1863 regulated fishing and fishery tax farms, and in the final years of their operation they contributed annually about 200,000 guilders to the government treasury.[5]

The tax on the sale of local liquor such as *arak, rum, ciu* and *araklikeur* restricted liquor sales to specific government-allocated locations. Other local liquors, such as *bandrik* or *brom*, which the Javanese produced and consumed in smaller amounts were free from the tax. The liquor tax farm was imposed in 1720 in Batavia by the VOC and expanded throughout Java in 1817. Licenses were for only one year, renewable every January 13. Violators of the rules received fines of 100 to 1000 guilders. Special regulations applied to the sale of liquor to military officers, Europeans, and indigenous people. The government ordinance of 1843 stipulated that military officers could drink liquor only in a special bar, canteen, or café, which opened only from 10 p.m. to 6 a.m. From 1850, liquor consumption in Java experienced a process of "Europeanization," as Dutch liquors such as *jenever* and *brandewijn* conquered the indigenous market. Religious leaders and some members of parliament viewed these liquors as a source of social problems. Consequently, despite the liquor tax farm's annual yield of approximately 200,000 guilders, the government abolished the liquor farm in 1872 and put the liquor tax under the schedule of excise duties one year later.[6]

The right to collect tax on animal slaughtering – including buffalo, sheep, goats, and horses – in Java and Madura was farmed out mostly to the Chinese. Available sources do not mention the exact year when the farm was introduced, but according to De Waal's report, this tax farm existed in 1817 in the most important residencies in Java, then contributing 62,400 guilders in total revenue. A government decree of 1851 set a tax of three guilders for slaughtering mature cattle, buffaloes and horses, and of one guilder for immature ones. The tax applied only to commercial slaughter, whereas slaughter for religious or charitable purposes was exempt (De Waal 1865b: 333). To operate the farm, the Chinese worked together with local authorities, in particular with the village head and the religiously legitimate butcher (*lebé*). This tax farm survived until 1894, and became an important source of local government revenue in cattle-breeding areas, such as East Java and Madura.[7]

The trade tax was a patent tax imposed only in Batavia and its suburbs. Originally, this tax was levied on vegetable stalls or shops, but after 1829 it was extended to other businesses. Businesses were classified into eight groups based on their scale, and assessed for monthly taxes of 15, 12, 8, 5, 4, 3, 2, or 1.5 guilders. This tax farm was closely connected with the bazaar farm tax, and the license was often held by the same person. The farm operated until the end of the 1860s, and was incorporated into the business tax in 1870 (De Waal 1865b: 403–4).

The Chinese poll tax and gambling tax applied mainly to the Chinese living in big cities in Java. The Chinese poll tax was an old tax, initially levied and farmed out in Batavia under the VOC administration. The tax was levied on Chinese individuals aged 14 to 60. People without work, the sick, district heads, and other officials were exempt. In 1860, the tax rate was 1.33 guilders per year for individuals employed as workers or small traders, and one guilder for individuals living in the Batavia suburbs. A government decree of 1823 extended the tax outside Batavia, namely to Krawang, Semarang, and Madura, where it was collected by Chinese leaders. In Krawang, the tax began promptly in 1826, collecting a sum of 700 guilders. In Semarang, this tax farm was begun in 1824 and lasted until 1851 when the business tax replaced it; in Madura the replacement occurred in 1865 (De Waal 1865b: 407).

The Chinese gambled in all corners of the archipelago, and they also held a virtual monopoly on the license to collect gambling taxes, as well as the right and obligation to control participants at the gambling houses. In Java and Madura, the tax farms were introduced only in the residencies of Batavia (except Buitenzorg), Semarang, Surabaya, and Madura. A government decree of 1849 established the first regulation of the gambling tax farm, stating that the tax license would be awarded only to those reliable and trustworthy Chinese who received the local authorities' permission to operate the farm. Article 11 stipulated that the gambling house could admit only Chinese adults older than 16; Europeans and indigenous people were not allowed. Those who broke the rules were fined 200 guilders, whereas the tax farmer was charged 1000 guilders for each illegal person. The Chinese gambling tax farm survived until the 1890s and became an important source of revenue for local authorities; but it also produced social problems because of uncontrollable illegal gambling activities in many areas of Java.[8]

Closely related to the gambling tax farm was the tax on traditional theater performances (*wayang*). Also dating to the VOC period, this tax was levied on indigenous and Chinese individuals who organized traditional theater performances.

From 1835 (as can be inferred from the government decree of 1849, no. 52), the tax was 80 guilders for a 24-hour women's performance, 60 guilders for a 24-hour men's performance, 30 guilders for puppet shows, and 20 guilders for a Chinese shadow play (*Schimmen*). Any show performed for religious purposes by indigenous people in their villages was exempt. After 1849, the yield of this tax farm was incorporated into that of the gambling tax farm (De Waal 1865b: 452–5).

The right to run a pawn shop was first farmed out in Batavia in 1814 and gradually extended to most districts in Java except the Principalities and Priangan Regencies. In 1840 the pawn shop farm yielded approximately 205,800 guilders annually, which rose slowly to an average of 269,000 in 1850 and 350,300 in 1860. In that year, 242 pawn shops were licensed, located mainly in large towns (Thomas 1893: 41–2; Vitalis 1992: 39–41). In 1870, the government introduced a license system that allowed those who could pay an annual fixed fee of 50 guilders to open a pawn shop with the local authority's permission. With this policy, the government hoped to increase competition that would lead to lower interest rates, an outcome that did not occur. Although the number of pawn shops increased considerably, from 242 in 1869 to 989 in 1879, the shops were monopolized by Chinese *kongsi*, which often had close relations with the opium farms. The license system held no advantage, and the government reintroduced the pawn shop tax farm in 1880, retaining it until the end of the nineteenth century (Vellema 1893: 1564–92; Diehl 1993: 224).

The tobacco tax farm, which operated only in the districts of Bantam, Batavia, Bogor, and Krawang, was introduced in 1817 and lasted until 1896. The farm was exceptional because elsewhere the business tax applied to tobacco sales. The edible bird's nest tax farm had existed since the VOC period in several areas in Java, such as Banten, Jepara, Rembang, Yogyakarta, Surakarta, Gresik, Pasuruan, Besuki, Probolinggo, Banjuwangi, and Kediri. The tax farm on forest products existed in Banten and Krawang from the VOC time and lasted until 1862. The tax on palm sugar sales was farmed out only in the Cianjur and Bandung districts in the Priangan Regencies, with its first annual revenue reported in 1834 and its last yield in 1863. The farm granted Chinese farmers access to the rural Priangan areas, which had been forbidden to them since 1824. The tax farms on tollgates and river crossings and the exploitation of small islands yielded negligible revenues; the former lasted until 1915, while the latter – including a tax on exploitation of the Kepulauan Seribu (*Duizend Eilanden*) north of Batavia and the Bawean Islands – lasted until 1863 (De Waal 1865b: 455–7, 461–3).

## 5.5  The end of tax farming and its long-term effects

Criticism of revenue farming started to emerge in the 1860s, and escalated a few decades later. A growing number of former colonial officers, journalists, and politicians in the Netherlands took a strong stand against tax farming in the colony. As transportation, telecommunication, and printing technology developed, a wider audience was engaged in the discourse. Information about real conditions in the colony was more easily accessible in the mother country, and moral considerations slowly started to play a role in assessing Dutch colonial affairs.

The growing interest in the nature and consequences of Dutch colonial policies was, of course, mainly fuelled by the debate on the Cultivation System, but the opium farm was also was subject to criticism. The colonial government was publicly condemned for selling (and thus supporting) a product that created so many social, economic, and health problems in Java and elsewhere. Various groups argued that the opium farm demoralized and impoverished the Javanese people, spread corruption and inefficiency among local ruling elites, and allowed the Chinese to capitalize and strengthen their economic influence in Java (Rush 1990: 201–2; Diehl 1993: 200).

In the meantime, the Chinese elite's conspicuous wealth and extravagant life style further increased worries among the Dutch about the negative effect of the growing Chinese influence in rural Java. Some civil servants started to blame the tax farm system for undermining government authority and the credibility of the legal system. In addition, the Javanese visibly suffered from the usurious interest rates charged by pawn shop keepers and Chinese money lending (*mind-ring*). The seriousness of abuses associated with slaughter tax collection and the corrupt practices of opium tax farms became a powerful ingredient for political campaigns demanding the improvement of Javanese living conditions (Claver 2006: 174).

Despite the public discussion, the political balance only started to shift seriously during the 1890s. In 1892, the Minister of Colonial Affairs van Dedem launched a thorough investigation of the economic position of "foreign Orientals" and their impact upon the indigenous life in Java and Madura.[9] The investigation was first entrusted to W.P. Groeneveldt, a respected member of the Indies Council (*Raad van Indië*) in Batavia, and then completed by F. Fokkens, the director of Plantation Affairs in the Netherlands Indies.[10] After a year's investigation, Fokkens presented two reports to the newly appointed Governor General van der Wijck.[11] Fokkens recommended the provision of cheap and easy credit facilities to the indigenous people and the abolition of the tax farm system. His reports also recommended a limited admission of foreign Orientals as agricultural planters, as government contractors in forest exploitation and transportation of people and products, and encouraged the government to create tighter supervision and control over the newly arrived migrants through a stricter implementation of the district and pass system (*wijken- en passenstelsel*).[12] By the end of that year, the colonial government decided to abolish the tax farm system.

Abolition of the opium farm and pawn shop tax farms and their transformation into a government monopoly began in 1894. The farms were phased out gradually because of their importance as a source of revenue and resistance among the Chinese tax farmers. However, the economic crisis of the 1880s, which deeply affected the agricultural sector, had already caused a serious blow to opium farmers. By 1889, only four of the 19 opium farms had survived the depression in the countryside, and farm debts to the state surpassed three million guilders. In 1893, the outstanding debt approached almost six million guilders (Rush 1990: 215; Claver 2006: 175). The collapse of major opium farms and other Chinese farms, and the perspective of declining auction revenues in the future, helped to build sufficient political support for a major tax reform program.

An experimental study in 1894 in Madura replaced the tax farm system with direct government control (*regie*). In 1897 the Dutch parliament gave final approval for the opium tax farm to be replaced throughout Java by a state monopoly. By 1904, the transition was made in Java, while the East Coast Province of Sumatra (now North Sumatra), Riau, and Aceh were the last regions to be included in 1911. With the introduction of *opiumregie*, the government controlled the entire opium business. The gradual transformation of the pawn shop tax farm into the government pawn shop administration followed, beginning in 1908 in Java and elsewhere in 1917 (Furnivall 1934: 5). Similarly, other small tax farms were converted: the slaughter tax farm became a direct slaughter tax in 1898, and the liquor tax farm became excise duties in 1925.

Although the colonial government formally abolished most tax farms at the turn of the twentieth century, the system's effects overshadowed state administrative practices and social relationships in Java until the end of colonial period and even further, until Indonesian independence. Two long-term effects were virtually inevitable: ethnic tension between the Javanese and the Chinese and a deeply rooted tradition of bureaucratic corruption.

As a minority group, the Chinese have always been under pressure because of their favorable economic, but vulnerable political, position. Carey (1984: 32–40) showed that the exploitative operation of tax farming in the hands of Chinese in south central Java was one of the primary causes of the Java War (1825–30).[13] The intensification of the tax farm system in the nineteenth century strengthened anti-Chinese resentment, as Chinese businessmen carried out the dirty work of the Dutch. These negative perceptions acquired a more solid basis as Chinese merchants expanded their activities as money lenders, retailers, and overseers during the Cultivation System (1830–70).[14]

Anti-Chinese resentment also grew among the Dutch administrators beginning in the mid-nineteenth century. Vitalis was among the first Europeans who fiercely criticized the Chinese role in tax farming activities (Vitalis 1851). Minister of Colonial Affairs Pieter Meijer was openly aggressive in a speech to the Dutch Parliament a few years later. He called the Chinese "the bloodsuckers of the Javanese," and warned: "It is dangerous to allow those foreigners to enter the rural areas unconditionally" (van Hoevell 1857). Baud, the former Minister of Colonial Affairs, put Meijer's statement into a wider context, stating that the Chinese opium tax farmers could jeopardize the political position of the Dutch in the Indies.[15] This discourse left its mark on the reform agendas of the late nineteenth century. The rise of anti-Chinese resentment went hand in hand with increased concern for indigenous welfare.

The tax farming system's second long-term legacy was bureaucratic corruption. Corruption undermined the reliability and legitimacy of the colonial state administration, and remained problematic for independent Indonesia. During the height of the tax farming operation, corruption was mostly apparent in opium smuggling. The government's failure to reduce opium smuggling was attributed to practices of corruption and collusion embedded within the institution itself. Plenty of evidence indicates that smuggling was organized partially by the Chinese *kongsi* and the official Chinese opium farmers with the support of indigenous officers.[16] In his opium investigation report, TeMechelen reckoned that the opium farm was indeed a hub of corruption, collusion, and abuse of power. As the opium farm structure was hierarchical, so was corruption in the opium business, permeating all levels. To meet their revenue target and to maximize profit, the opium farmers played around with opium regulations, with the pass and residency laws, and with the government administration in general. They bribed local officials, village heads, and police officers to get support for importing illegal opium from several smuggling entries in the north coast of Java and then distributed the contraband in their farm areas along with legal opium. The local indigenous officers helped the opium subcontractors for financial rewards.[17]

Corruption also obstructed the operation of the pawn shop, slaughter, and gambling tax farms. As Fokkens reported, changing the administration of pawn shops in the 1870s and 1880s from a license system to a farming system did not eradicate the abuse and corruption interwoven in pawn shop activities. The pawn shop license holders and the pawn shop tax farmers manipulated the existing regulations concerning maximum interest rates on loans, the evaluation of pawned goods, the accounting system, and the prohibition against using pawn shops as illegal opium shops. Moreover, they colluded with local police officers and even criminals to receive stolen goods in return for a cheaper loan. Similarly, the slaughter tax farmers exploited peasants in rural areas. In collusion with local officials, particularly village heads, the tax farmers often did not report the slaughter of stolen cows or buffaloes by criminals, but bought the slaughtered animal at a low price.[18] These corrupt and collusive practices made the Chinese farmers rich at the expense of the local population. Souterwoude (1890: 43), a prominent anti-opium activist, asserted that under the tax farming system the Chinese revenue farmers had emerged as "a power within the state" (*een macht in den staat*), and they found almost no restraint to building "an empire within an empire" (*een imperium in imperio*) in the colony.

Yet the colonial government failed to reduce corruption, even after the fiscal reforms in the early twentieth century. Annual reports of the government opium monopoly published from 1914 onward revealed that smuggling and corruption were still major problems. Seen in a longer perspective, bureaucratic corruption – in combination with a weak state and lack of law enforcement – remained one of the major obstacles that the new government had to face after Indonesia declared its independence in 1945.

## 5.6  Conclusion

This chapter has outlined the importance of tax farming in the wider context of Dutch colonial extractive policies in Java and Indonesia. The significance of tax farming was due not only to its financial contribution to the colonial government exchequer but also to its socio-political impact, as the system supported the consolidation of Dutch rule in Java, and the integration of this island into the wider territorial state of the Netherlands Indies. Two categories of tax farms – the opium tax farm and the small tax farms – operated through different administrative and supervisory arrangements, but both were awarded almost exclusively to the Chinese, who acted on behalf of the government. In this way, revenue farming was a strategy by which the colonial government in Java exploited the unique economic and political position of the Chinese immigrant minority. However, the tax farm system also depended on the support of the Javanese elite, who completed the colonial circle of rent-seeking elites.

Established initially as a secondary method of extracting surpluses, revenue farming developed into a highly efficient and profitable source of income in the course of the nineteenth century. Together with other taxes, particularly the land rent, it contributed indirectly to the success of the Cultivation System, as it gave the colonial government the financial means to expand territorial control and remit the profits of the CS to the Netherlands. To the colonial government, the tax farm system provided an attractive solution to the administrative and logistical problem of collecting taxes throughout a vast territory. For the Chinese, tax farms provided a way to expand their businesses and strengthen their socio-economic grip on the territories where they obtained their licenses.

But the system was not without socio-political costs. Many liberalists from the 1870s onward criticized the system as a source of corruption and exploitation, contributing to the impoverishment of indigenous people in the tax farm areas. As a response, from the mid-1890s the colonial government gradually dismantled most of the revenue farms in Java and Madura, and reformed the fiscal system to right past wrongs and injustices. This reform entailed three measures: complete abolition, change into direct taxation, and replacement with a direct administration or state monopoly.

After a century of operation, the tax farming system had also produced several serious long-term consequences for the state and society, both negative and positive. Anti-Chinese tensions were a consequence of the dominant role of the Chinese in the tax farming system as indigenous people viewed them as the right hand of the ruling colonial power. The problematic position of the Chinese in the socio-political and economic structure of modern Indonesia has remained more or less unchanged until the present. Similarly, the bureaucratic corruption inherent in tax farming persisted under different political regimes and remains a major problem in Indonesia today.

The positive long-term consequences appear when we contrast the fine-grained structure of the nineteenth-century colonial tax system in the Netherlands Indies with the virtual absence of a centralized fiscal apparatus in the Congo until, at least, the first decade of the twentieth century (see Gardner, Chapter 6 below). To achieve progress toward sustained modern economic growth requires a state capable of financing and securing the provision of certain critical public goods and services, as the chapters on education (Frankema, Chapter 7 below) and on the comparative economic policies of Mobutu and Suharto (Abbeloos, Chapter 12 below) clearly indicate. How far the Dutch fiscal legacy has helped to solidify a social, mental, and logistic infrastructure conducive to state taxation is an important question for future research. In fact, it is a question that warrants much more attention in assessing the long-term legacies of colonial rule in general.

## Notes

1 In the Netherlands, tax farming was well developed in the sixteenth century. Most of the tax farms were abolished in January 1806, when King Louis Bonaparte introduced a Napoleonic system of central administration (Tracy 1985: 180; Brugmans 1976: 8).
2 In this region, tax farms became an important factor in the conflict between the Sultan of Yogyakarta and Raffles (Carey 1984: 22–4).
3 The list of small tax farms is taken from the *Koloniaal verslag*, 1851.
4 TeMechelen found that addicted Javanese villagers who earned 0.25 guilders per day could spend up to 0.20 guilders per day on *candu*, for which they got no more than five or two *mata* of opium. Special permission had to be obtained to consume more than 20 *mata* of opium per day, for example at special celebrations (TeMechelen 1885: 80–6).
5 Arsip Nasional Republik Indonesia (hereafter ANRI), K.52.944, "Voorwaarden voor de pacht der Visscherijen in de oostvaart van Batavia gelegene residentiën, waar dit middel bestaat"; see also De Waal (1865b: 314–19).
6 ANRI, K.52.944, "Voorwaarden voor de pacht van de verkoop van Arak, Rum en Tjoe in het klein, op Java en Madura."
7 A similar pattern of organization was found in the pig slaughtering farm. However, since Muslims could not consume pigs, this tax farm yielded less revenue than the cattle slaughtering farm. Chinese tax farmers were obliged to arrange different places and butchers for the pig slaughtering farm. F. Fokkens, "Nota betreffende de vervanging door directe collecte dan wel eigen beheer van de op Java en Madoera voorkomende pachten der gewone of kleine middelen," Nationaal Archief, Ministerie van Koloniën, Inventaris Nummer 4837/ Verbaal 12 Juli 1894, no. 61 (hereafter NA/MvK).
8 ANRI, K.52.944, "Voorwaarden voor de pacht der Pho- en Topho of Chinesche dobblespelen, voor Batavia, Samarang, en Soerabaija."
9 NA/MvK, Verbaal 14 Maart 1892, no. 51/Inv. 4556.
10 NA/MvK, Verbaal 17 April 1896, no. 27/Inv. 5037.
11 NA/MvK, Verbaal 12 Juli 1892, no. 61/Inv. 4837, "Nota betreffende de vervanging door directe collecte dan wel eigen beheer van de op Java en Madoera voorkomende pachten der gewone of kleine middelen"; and NA/MvK, Verbaal 17 April 1896, no. 27/Inv. 5037, "Rapport betreffende het Onderzoek naar den Economische Toestand der Vreemde Oosterlingen op Java en Madoera en Voorstellen tot Verbetering."
12 NA/MvK, Verbaal 17 April 1896, no. 27/Inv. 5037, pp. 575–8.
13 The popular expression *Cina wurung, Londa durung, Jawa tanggung* – "No longer a Chinese, not yet a Dutchman, a half-baked Javanese" – showed their invidious position as foreigners and aptly reflected the Javanese perception of the Chinese at the time (Carey 1984: 5–9).
14 In 1910, for example, some Islamic merchants in Surakarta founded Sarekat Islam, the first mass organization in Java, as a political effort to counter Chinese economic domination in the batik industry (Shiraishi 1990).

15 As a solution, Baud required the colonial government to expel the Chinese from the opium tax system. See his view in "Zullen nu de Chinezen van de opiumpacht worden uitgesloten?," *Tijdschrift voor Nederlandsch-Indië*, Vol. 2, 1857, pp. 60–1. Baud's main idea was taken from a previous article on opium entitled "Proeve van eene geschiedenis van den handel en het verbruik van opium in Nederlandsch-Indië," *Bijdragen voor de Taal-, Land- en Volkenkunde van Nederlandsch-Indië*, Vol. 1, 1853, pp. 79–220.

16 A description of opium smuggling in Semarang run by a Chinese *kongsi* and its relation with the opium farmers can be found in Perelaer (1886) and Brooshooft (1888: 129–32).

17 In the Opium Report, the Resident of Semarang said that about 5475 *picol* of opium was distributed throughout Java, on which the population in general paid as much as 31.4 million guilders to the Chinese farmers and 24.5 million guilders to the smugglers (55.9 million guilders in total). "Opium Report...," (KITLV, H. 422 (a), fol. 1593) (a *picol* or *picul* is a traditional unit of weight; 1 *picol* is about 60.4 kg).

18 Fokken's report, folio 12–14, NA/MvK, Verbaal 17 April 1896, no. 27/Inv. 5037.

# References

## Primary sources

### The National Archive of Indonesia (Arsip Nasional Republik Indonesia – ANRI)

ANRI, K.52.944, "Voorwaarden voor de pacht van de Bazaars en Warongs (markten en kramen) op Java, met uitzondering van de Residentie Batavia en de afdeelingen Buitenzorg en Krawang."

ANRI, K.52.944, "Voorwaarden voor de pacht der Visscherijen in de oostvaart van Batavia gelegene residentiën, waar dit middel bestaat."

ANRI, K.52.944, "Voorwaarden voor de pacht van de verkoop van Arak, Rum en Tjoe in het klein, op Java en Madura."

ANRI, Departement van Financiën (1838) "Perdjandjian beja roemah-roemah pegadejan."

ANRI, Department van Financiën (1843) "Bepalingen, volgens welke aan de Chinesche bevolking op Java, met uitzondering van Batavia, Samarang en Soerabaya, verlof zal worden verleend tot het spelen van Chinesche dobbelspelen."

ANRI, Department van Financiën (1843) "Voorwaarden voor de pacht der Pho- en Topho of Chinesche dobbelspelen, voor Batavia, Samarang en Soerabaija."

ANRI, Department van Financiën (1853) "Reglement voor de Opium-pacht op Java en Madura."

ANRI, Departement van Financiën (1853) "Soerat peratoeran dari beja Apioen di Tanah Djawa dan Madura"; "Printah-printah atas mana nantie di djoeal beja djoealan Apioen dengan sediekit-sediekit di Tanah Djawa dan Madura dari tahun 1848."

ANRI, K.52.944, "Voorwaarden voor de pacht der Pho- en Topho of Chinesche dobbelspelen, voor Batavia, Samarang, en Soerabaija."

### The National Archive of the Netherlands (NA)

NA/MvK (Ministerie van Kolonien) (1892) Verbaal 14 Maart 1892, no. 51/Inv. 4556.

NA/MvK (Ministerie van Kolonien) (1894) Verbaal 12 Juli 1894, no. 61/Inv. 4837,

F. Fokkens, "Nota betreffende de vervanging door directe collecte dan wel eigen beheer van de op Java en Madoera voorkomende pachten der gewone of kleine middelen." NA/MvK (Ministerie van Kolonien) (1896) Verbaal 17 April 1896, no. 27/Inv. 5037, F. Fokkens, "Rapport betreffende het Onderzoek naar den Economische Toestand der Vreemde Oosterlingen op Java en Madoera en Voorstellen tot Verbetering."

## Secondary literature

Baud, J.C. (1853) "Proeve van eene geschiedenis van den Handel en het verbruik van opium in Nederlandsch Indië," *Bijdragen tot de Taal-, Land- en Volkenkunde van Nederlandsch Indië*, 1, 79–220.

Blussé, L. (1988) *Strange Company: Chinese Settlers, Mestizo Women and Dutch in VOC Batavia*, KITLV Verhandelingen Serie No. 122. Leiden: KITLV.

Blussé, L. (2005) "Changes of Regime and Colonial State Formation in the Malay Archipelago: an Invitation to an International Research Project," Working Papers series, No. 41, Singapore: Asia Research Institute NUS.

Boomgaard, P. (1986) "Buitenzorg in 1805: the Role of Money and Credit in a Colonial Frontier Society," *Modern Asian Studies*, 20, 33–58.

Brooshooft, P. (1888) *Memorie over den toestand in Indië, ter begeleiding van den open brief, op 7 Maart 1888 door 1255 ingezetenen van Nederlandsch-Indië gezonden aan 12 Nederlanders Heeren*, Semarang.

Brugmans, I.J. (1976) *Paardenkracht en Mensenmacht: sociaal-economische geschiedenis van Nederland, 1795–1940*, The Hague: Nijhoff.

Carey, P. (1984) "Changing Javanese Perception of the Chinese Communities in Central Java, 1755–1825," *Indonesia*, 37, 1–40.

Carey, P. (1986) "Waiting for the Ratu Adil: the Javanese Village Community on the Eve of the Java War (1825–30)," *Modern Asian Studies*, 20(1), 55–137.

Claver, A. (2006) "Commerce and Capital in Colonial Java: Trade, Finance and Commercial Relations between Europeans and Chinese, 1820s–1942," PhD Thesis, Vrije Universiteit Amsterdam.

Daendels, H.W. (1814) *Staat der Nederlandsche Oostindische Bezittingen, onder het Bestuur van den Gouverneur-Generaal Willem Daendels, Ridder, Luitenant-Generaal, in de jaren 1808–1811*, The Hague: Nijhoff.

Days, C. (1900) *The Policy and Administration of the Dutch in Java*, New York: The Macmillan Press.

De Waal, E. (1865a) *Aantekeningen over Koloniale Onderwerpen I, De Opiumpacht op Java*, The Hague: Martinus Nijhoff.

De Waal, E. (1865b) *Aantekeningen over Koloniale Onderwerpen IV, De Kleine Verpachte Middelen op Java*, Eerste Gedeelte, The Hague: Martinus Nijhoff.

Dick, H. (1993) "A Fresh Approach to Southeast Asian History," in J. Butcher and H. Dick (eds.) *The Rise and Fall of Revenue Farming: Business Elites and the Emergence of the Modern State in Southeast Asia*, New York: St. Martin's Press.

Diehl, F.W. (1993) "Revenue Farming in the Netherlands East Indies, 1816–1925," in J. Butcher and H. Dick (eds.) *The Rise and Fall of Revenue Farming: Business Elites and the Emergence of the Modern State in Southeast Asia*, New York: St. Martin's Press.

Furnivall, J.S. (1934) *State Pawnshop in the Netherlands Indies. Studies in the Economic and Social Development of the Netherlands East Indies*, Rangoon: Burma Book Club.

Furnivall, J.S. (1944) *Netherlands India: The Study of a Plural Economy*, Cambridge: Cambridge University Press.

Giap, T.S. (1989) "Socio-economic Role of the Chinese in Indonesia," in A. Madison and G. Prince (eds.) *Economic Growth in Indonesia, 1820–1940*, Dordrecht: Forris Publications.

Joe, L.T. (1933) *Riwajat Semarang: Dari Djamannja Sam Poo Sampe Terhapoesnja Kongkoan*, Semarang.

Kian, K.H. (2006) *The Political Economy of Java's Northeast Coast, c.1740–1800: Elite Synergy*, Leiden: Brill.

Knaap, G. and Nagtegaal, L. (1991) "A Forgotten Trade: Salt in Southeast Asia 1670–1813," in R. Ptak and D. Rothermund (eds.) *Emporia, Commodities and Entrepreneurs in Asian Maritime Trade, c.1400–1750*, Stuttgart: Steiner.

Koloniaal Verslag van 1851. Nederland (Oost-)Indië.

Koloniaal Verslag van 1855. Nederland (Oost-)Indië.

Koloniaal Verslag van 1871. Nederland (Oost-)Indië.

Koloniaal Verslag van 1881. Nederland (Oost-)Indië.

Koloniaal Verslag van 1891. Nederland (Oost-)Indië.

Mellegers, J. (2004) "Government Revenue in the Netherlands East Indies," online dataset available at www.cgeh.nl/indonesian-economic-history (accessed 25 November 2010).

Perelaer, M.T.H. (1886) *Baboe Dalima, Opium Roman*, Rotterdam: Elsevier.

Reid, A. (1993) "The Origins of Revenue Farming in Southeast Asia," in J. Butcher and H. Dick (eds.) *The Rise and Fall of Revenue Farming: Business Elites and the Emergence of the Modern State in Southeast Asia*, New York: St. Martin's Press.

Ricklefs, M.C. (1993, 3rd edn 2001) *A History of Modern Indonesia, c.1200*, Basingstoke: Palgrave Macmillan.

Rush, J. (1990) *Opium to Java: Revenue Farming and Chinese Enterprise in Colonial Indonesia, 1800–1910*, Ithaca, NY: Cornell University Press.

Schnijder, F. (1886) *De Verpachte Middelen voor Java en Madoera, zooals die tot op ultimo Juli 1885 zijn gewijzigd en aangevuld*, Semarang: Gebroeders Jansz.

Shiraishi, T. (1990) *An Age in Motion: Popular Radicalism in Java, 1912–1926*, Ithaca, NY: Cornell University Press.

Souterwoude, E. (1890) *De Opium-vloek op Java*, Batavia: Anti-opium Bond.

TeMechelen, C. (1885) "Rapport Uitgebracht in Voldoening aan 's Gouvernement Besluit d.d. 9 Juli 1885 No. 9," KITLV, H. 422 (a).

Thomas, T. (1893) *Eenige opmerking naar aanleiding van het Pachtstelsel op Java*, Leiden: E.J. Brill.

Tracy, J. (1985) *A Financial Revolution in the Habsburg Netherlands: Renten and Renteniers in the County of Holland, 1515–1565*, Berkeley: University of California Press.

Trocki, C.A. (2002) "Opium and the Beginnings of Chinese Capitalism in Southeast Asia," *Journal of Southeast Asian Studies*, 33(2), 297–314.

van Dedem, W.K. and Piepers, M.C. (1889) "De Opiumpacht in Nederlandsch-Indië," *Verslagen der Algemeene Vergadering van het Indische Genootschap*, The Hague, 139–70.

van Hoevell, W.R. (1857) "Sedert wanneer is het gouvernement zoo anti-Chinees worden?," *Tijdschrift voor Nederlandsch Indië*, 1, 169–71.

van Niel, R. (2005) *Java's Northeast Coast, 1740–1840: A Study in Colonial Encroachment and Dominance*, Leiden: CNWS.

van Zanden, J.L. (2004) "On the Efficiency of Markets for Agricultural Products: Rice Prices and Capital Markets in Java, 1823–1853," *Journal of Economic History*, 64(4), 1028–55.

van Zanden, J.L. (2009) "Credit and the Colonial State: the Reform of Capital Market on Java, 1900–30," in D. Henley and P. Boomgaard (eds.) *Credit and Debt in Indonesia, 860–1930: From Peonage to Pawnshop, from Kongsi to Cooperative*, Singapore-Leiden: ISEAS-KITLV Press.

Vellema, P. (1893) "Pandjeshuizen," *Tijdschrift van Nederlandsch-Indië*, 15(II), 1564–92.

Vitalis, L. (1851) "Over de pachten in het algemeen, de onzedelijkheid van sommige, en de verdrukking waaraan de overmatige misbruiken van andere Javaansche bevolking blootstellen," *Tijdschrift voor Nederlandsch Indië*, 13(2), 365–86.

Vitalis, L. (1992) "Effect of the Revenue Farming System," in M.R. Fernando and D. Bulbeck (eds.) *Chinese Economic Activity in Netherlands India: Selected Translations from the Dutch*, Singapore: ISEAS – RSPAS ANU.

Wertheim, W.F. (1964) *East–West Parallels: Sociological Approaches to Modern Asia*, The Hague: van Hoeve.

# 6 Fiscal policy in the Belgian Congo in comparative perspective

*Leigh Gardner*[1]

## 6.1 Introduction

> They grabbed what they could get just for the sake of what was to be got. It was just robbery with violence, aggravated murder on a grand scale, and men going at it blind.
>
> (Joseph Conrad, *Heart of Darkness*, p. 70)

Popular memories of the ravages of King Leopold II's rule of the Congo Free State, immortalized in Joseph Conrad's novel *Heart of Darkness*, have cast a long shadow over the assessment of Belgian colonialism in Central Africa. In 1956, Lord Hailey noted in the revised *African Survey* that

> the adverse impressions which were formed in the outside world during the regime of the Congo Free State have proved to be long lived, and there are still those who have in mind a picture of the Belgian Congo as a country of which the Administration lives in an iniquitous traffic in ivory and rubber.
>
> (Hailey 1957: 218)

That popular thinking still links King Leopold's regime with the depredations of the Congo's post-independence rulers is illustrated by the title of Michaela Wrong's profile of Mobuto Sese Seko, *In the Footsteps of Mr Kurtz*, in reference to Conrad's protagonist. Wrong (2000: 25) explicitly draws a comparison between Mobutu's kleptocratic regime and Leopold's, arguing that "Mobutu should not be regarded as sui generis, a monster out of time and place." In other words, the Congo's tragic history since independence can be traced to the legacy of the Congo Free State.

Making such a claim requires, in Cooper's words, "leapfrogging" the final 50 years of colonial rule, during which time the Congo was not the personal property of Leopold but rather a colony governed by agents of the Belgian state (Cooper 2005: 17). To link Mobutu to Leopold requires closer study of how and to what extent the policies and institutions of the Congo Free State influenced those of Belgian colonial rule after the transfer of power from Leopold to the Belgian government in 1908. Further, suggesting that the Congo's exceptional post-independence history is related to its exceptional colonial past makes it necessary to understand the extent to which Belgian colonialism differed from other contemporary regimes in Africa. However, the period from 1908 to 1960 is often neglected in histories of the Congo – Vansina (2010: 150) notes that this period "is often perceived as a single, rather uneventful era." This perception, Vansina argues, is inaccurate. The period from 1908 to 1960 saw a number of formative events in the history of the Congo, including the expansion of copper mining and the completion of the railway network, in addition to global events like the two world wars and the Great Depression, which had a profound impact on Belgian colonial rule in the Congo.

As this chapter will show, it was also during this period that the fiscal policies of the Belgian Congo became more like those of other colonies in Africa. The history of colonial taxation and public spending has been the subject of a number of recent studies attempting to assess whether colonial states were, in fact, "extractive" states, as argued by Acemoglu *et al.* (2001). This research, which has focused primarily on British Africa, has concluded that tax burdens in colonial Africa were relatively light (Frankema 2010). There are two principal reasons for this: the first was that the aim of British colonial governments was not necessarily maximizing revenue (Frankema 2011; Gardner 2012), and the second was that the capacity of colonial states to extract revenue was limited, particularly in the early decades (Gardner 2010b). This chapter compares the fiscal systems of British colonies in Africa with that of the Belgian Congo in order to understand the extent to which Belgian colonialism in the region differed from that of other colonial powers.

Taxation provides a particularly appropriate metric for comparison in this case. It is largely owing to the brutal system of in-kind tax collection under Leopold that the Congo is considered exceptional. In contrast to other colonial fiscal systems in the late nineteenth and early twentieth centuries, the tax system of the Congo Free State was designed to maximize revenue, and it made the Congo Free State the only territory in Africa to provide financial subsidies to its European ruler, rather than the other way around (Stengers 1957: 28–66). Reforming this system was one of the first steps taken by the new Belgian administration, which modeled the new colonial tax system on that of British colonies.

Correspondence between Belgian and British officials in the years following the transfer of power focused particularly on the tax system of the colony (Great Britain 1908a, 1908b, 1908c, 1911, 1912). British officials encouraged the Belgian government to abolish the collection of taxes in kind or in labor, to introduce currency and to limit exactions and interference with the market so as to encourage growth. The aim of early colonial taxation, in British practice, was not to maximize revenue in the short term but to establish institutions which could raise substantial revenue in later years when African participation in the commercial economy had increased (Lugard 1906: 86).

Further, the development of fiscal institutions provides a good indicator of the development of state institutions more broadly. Establishing a solid tax base was considered crucial for the success of post-independence development, which relied on the state's ability to raise considerable sums to support new expenditure on social services (Gardner 2010a). As shown in Chapter 5 above, the fiscal system of the Netherlands Indies was established in the early nineteenth century, while the development of fiscal institutions in the Congo did not really begin until after 1908. This late start not only placed the Belgian Congo behind the Netherlands Indies, but also made it difficult for the Congo to catch up even with neighboring British colonies.

This chapter will argue that although the fiscal policies of the Belgian Congo after 1908 did not differ greatly from those of British colonies in Africa, the early exactions of the Congo Free State made it particularly difficult for the Belgian administration to build a tax base. Contemporary observers noted that in-kind tax collection limited other kinds of production and encouraged flight from regions where the collection of "red rubber" was most punitive. The weak fiscal foundations of Belgian colonial rule manifested themselves in the continued reliance on concession companies and the reversion to policies of compulsory production during periods of declining revenue. It is this legacy which perhaps explains the tendency toward kleptocratic rule in the Congo after independence.

## 6.2  A difficult inheritance: the fiscal legacy of the Congo Free State

In his landmark study of the costs of the Congo and the colony's financial links with Belgium, Stengers (1957: 351) noted that the Congo was in his view the only colony to have generated a profit during the early years of colonial rule. He calculated that the metropolitan state (or, at least, the closest approximation thereof in the form of King Leopold II) had gained 26 million Belgian-francs (BEF) by the time power was transferred to the Belgian government in 1908, during years in which most other African colonies were in deficit (Gardner 2012: 32–3). However, as this section will show, this early profitability was not the result of sound fiscal management or of the Congo's inherent wealth, but a sign that the Free State administration prioritized short-term gain, taking advantage of the rising commodity prices of the late nineteenth and early twentieth centuries, over longer-term economic expansion through the creation of new industries. Though the Congo's early profits were notable by the standards of its contemporaries, they imposed costs on later administrations.

The distinction between the two methods of colonial development is analogous to the difference between roving and stationary bandits in Mancur Olson's famous model of state formation. According to this model, a "bandit" with a long-term interest in a territory will have an incentive to limit his predations so as to encourage the expansion of the economic surplus from which he draws his income. In contrast, bandits intent on moving on to terrorize other areas, who have a short-term interest in a particular region, will maximize their immediate gains (Olson 2000: 44). While Leopold's initial interest in the Congo cannot be characterized as short term – as Stengers and Vansina (1985: 317) put it,

"Leopold was a firm, and one might almost say a religious, believer in the economic profits of colonial exploitation" – he was facing short-term political pressures, including the threat of Belgian annexation, which gave him an incentive to maximize early revenue collections.

The Congo Free State officially came into being by the agreement of participants at the Berlin West Africa Conference in 1884–5, who gave international recognition to Leopold's growing influence in the Congo. The Conference had been called to lay down guidelines for the recognition of claims to paramountcy in Africa, in the context of growing European competition over colonial territory. Leopold's success, according to Sanderson (1985: 136), was due to his ability to offer a resolution to Anglo-French disputes over the Congo and his willingness to agree to free trade through the Congo Basin region (detailed in Figure 6.1). As this section will show, the financial challenges of governing such a large territory meant that Leopold did not honor that agreement.

*Figure 6.1* Map of the Congo Basin region (source: Gardner (2012), adapted from US Office of Strategic Services (1945)).

In the establishment of a skeletal administration in the Congo, Leopold and his deputies were faced with the same challenges as their counterparts in other colonies. Low population densities and high transport costs limited both the prospects of competitive export production and the size of the market for taxable imports (Austin 2008: 589–90). Achieving the financial self-sufficiency which Leopold had promised the Belgian parliament in seeking permission to claim sovereignty over the Congo would not be a trivial task. Leopold's insistence on the rapid expansion of his territory in the Congo added to the expense and the difficulty of making the territory self-supporting (Stengers and Vansina 1985: 317).

This rapid expansion was motivated by Leopold's determined optimism with regard to the profitability of his colonial territory. By contrast, in the British Empire, it was commonly agreed by both proponents and opponents of imperial expansion that most colonies would require significant subsidies from the imperial treasury before they were able to raise sufficient revenue to cover their own costs. Early investments in administration and infrastructure were required to build a tax base and provide the means for export production to grow before significant revenue could be raised. Sir Arthur Hardinge, the Commissioner of the East Africa Protectorate, observed with regard to the territory he governed that

> during the first few years after its occupation it is only natural that the expenditure in an undeveloped territory such as East Africa should be greatly in excess of its revenue, but as time goes on, there is every reason to hope that the latter will increase out of proportion to the cost of government.
>
> (Hardinge 1897: 42)

From 1901 to 1905, an average of 62 percent of revenue in the East Africa Protectorate was from grants-in-aid by the British government (East Africa Protectorate 1901–5). These funds were spent primarily on infrastructure, which the colonial administration believed would facilitate the expansion of cash crop production, thereby raising incomes and expanding the tax base.

As the Free State was the domain of King Leopold II rather than of the Belgian state, external funds could only come from Leopold's own personal wealth, which, though considerable, was insufficient for the task of developing a territory the size of the Congo (Anstey 1966: 4). In the years immediately following the Free State's legal foundation in 1885, local revenue could only cover a small proportion of total expenditure, leaving Leopold to cover the difference (Stengers and Vansina 1985: 318). Leopold contributed 40,000 BEF per year during much of the 1890s, and royal grants constituted an average of 15 percent of the total revenue of the Congo from 1891 to 1897 (Great Britain 1897).

Despite these contributions, the Congo remained on the verge of financial catastrophe, and Leopold was forced to turn to the Belgian government for assistance. A lottery loan raised in Belgium in 1888 was followed by a loan from the Belgian government of 25 million BEF spread over ten years issued in 1890 and a further seven million BEF in 1895 (Stengers and Vansina 1985: 318). Politically, these loans represented the failure of Leopold's pledge to the Belgian government that the colony would not require Belgian assistance, and therefore generated enormous pressure to make the colony self-supporting as quickly as possible. This pressure was heightened by the threat of Belgian annexation. In return for the 1890 loan, Belgium was given the right to annex the Congo if it decided to do so in 1901, though no further action was taken. In 1895, the king and the Belgian government agreed to immediate annexation pending the approval of parliament (Stengers and Vansina 1985: 323). Though that approval was never granted, the prospect that he would lose control of his African territory gave Leopold a powerful incentive to maximize revenue in the short term – as Stengers and Vansina (1985: 319) put it, Leopold "was preoccupied only with financial results."

The Congo's finances were saved in the short term by rising international prices for ivory and, more importantly, rubber (Munro 1976: 88; Stengers and Vansina 1985: 318). These were two products which the Congo could export at a profit, despite the high costs of transport by human porters prior to the completion of the railway. With few other forms of revenue, the Free State sought to exert an increasing degree of monopoly control over natural resources. A decree of July 1, 1885 established the administration's right to exploit directly or grant rights of exploitation over all uncultivated lands (Peemans 1975: 169). Though this constituted the majority of land in the Congo, land was not the most important resource in the colony, and prospects for the establishment of cash crop industries proved unattractive to investors. Five years later, "having failed to attract private Belgian and international sources of capital," the Free State administration claimed ownership of all natural products of the forest (Jewsiewicki 1983: 96). These claims provided the legal foundation for the collection of taxes in rubber and ivory. Africans were required to collect particular quantities of ivory and rubber (which varied by region) and deliver them to colonial officials, whose compensation was linked to the quantity of raw materials delivered (Anstey 1966: 5). This was one of the most infamous aspects of Leopold's regime in the Congo, and existing estimates of the tax burden imposed by the rubber and ivory tax suggest that it was onerous.

The Free State administration was incapable of exploiting directly all of the rights it had claimed to the Congo's natural resources. Instead, it "resigned itself to indirect management," and offered concessions on favorable terms to private companies who would organize production (Jewsiewicki 1983: 97). Under the terms of the concessions, companies received the sole right to purchase products from Africans, who were compelled to sell only to the concessionary company. The Congo administration retained a significant financial interest in the concessionary companies in exchange for the concession, and dividends from concessionary shares were a major source of revenue for the Free State administration (Harms 1975: 81; Jewsiewicki 1983: 97).

The profitability of Congo concessions, along with the Congo's wealth in natural resources, generated interest in colonial investment among Belgian corporations (Buelens and Marysse 2009: 141). However, concession companies in the Congo operated on the same principles as administrators working for the state, and gained their profits in the same way. Harms (1975: 79) describes the governance of the Anglo-Belgian India Rubber and Exploration Company (ABIR) concession, established in 1893, as "designed to maximize production." Company agents received financial rewards based on the quantity of rubber production, and financial sanctions for producing less than a specific quota.

In combination, the ruthless extraction of rubber and ivory along with dividends from concession companies made the Congo one of the only colonies to generate a surplus prior to World War I, and certainly the only one without a pre-existing export industry. However, these revenues were not sustainable, and the effects of the system compounded the existing difficulties of raising tax revenue in Africa. Both ivory and rubber were wasting resources, and the brutality of the collection methods used generated incentives for over-tapping and destruction of rubber trees (Harms 1975: 82). Harms (1975: 74) notes that production began to decline around the turn of the century, despite rising prices, due to the exhaustion of supplies. Further, flight from tax collectors working for both the Congo Free State and concession companies disrupted agricultural production and exacerbated the problems created by low population density in some parts of the Congo (Fetter 1983: 138; Harms 1975: 85–6; Stengers and Vansina 1985: 333).

One effort to encourage the opening of coffee plantations foundered as a result of such problems. As a British consular agent observed in 1897, any such plantation would face shortages in both labor and supplies. "The wholesale disarrangement of aboriginal existence has lessened the supply of food to such a degree that every estate would be a 'starvation camp' until it became independent of outside purchases" (Great Britain 1897: 5–6). Even without such problems, transport costs were too high for coffee production to be a paying proposition, being nearly double what was paid by coffee planters in Angola even if rates were kept artificially low (Great Britain 1897: 5–6). Similar efforts to establish rubber plantations in order to replenish supplies also failed, as neither concession company agents nor African workers had an incentive to invest in and care for rubber vines (Harms 1975: 82).

By the 1890s there were already distinct differences in both the quantity and type of revenue collected by the administration of the Congo and those of other colonies. In 1897, total revenue from taxes on imports and exports was just over 80,000 BEF, or 21 percent of total revenue. Per capita revenue figures provide a better indicator of the prosperity of colonial subjects and the ability of the colonial state to raise revenue. There are considerable uncertainties in population data for most African colonies in the early years of colonial rule, both in the British Empire (Kuczynski 1948) and for the Belgian Congo (Great Britain Naval Intelligence Division 1944: 249). However, taking an estimate of 9,314,475 for 1927 (Fetter 1983: 183) this amounted to just 0.01 BEF per capita. The Congo's total revenue in that year was 374,772 BEF or 0.04 BEF per capita. In the same year, the Gold Coast collected the equivalent of 3.39 BEF per capita in trade taxes, and 4.04 BEF per capita in total revenue. Landlocked Southern Rhodesia's total revenue in 1897 was 12.90 BEF per capita. In 1900, the first year that trade tax revenue for Southern Rhodesia is given, the colony collected 4.57 BEF per capita. Clarence-Smith (1983: 6) attributes the low collection of customs revenue in the Free State to the terms of the Berlin Act, but the greater revenue collected in British colonies which were also part of the Congo Basin suggests that the lack of investment in building a tax base was the more important factor. Nyasaland's per capita revenue in 1897 was 0.88 BEF, of which trade taxes comprised 0.22 BEF per capita.[2] Nyasaland was part of the Congo Basin; its low customs revenue was due to limited trade, as was also the case in the Congo, where low incomes kept imports low and exports beyond ivory and rubber were limited.

By the early twentieth century, rubber and ivory stocks were reaching the point of exhaustion and revenue declined even further (Young 1994: 104–5). The contrast between British and Belgian colonies remained stark after the transfer of power in 1908. In 1909 the value of the Congo's imports totaled 22,339,924 BEF, less than much smaller territories in West Africa like Sierra Leone (24,705,089 BEF), Southern Nigeria (100,960,000 BEF) and the Gold Coast (60,434,934 BEF). The Congo's imports were barely double those of tiny Gambia (10,211,094 BEF), which had a population of just over 146,000 as compared with over 9 million in the Congo. The British consul observed that the low value of the imports of the Congo resulted in a predictably low level of customs revenue, which for 1912 was estimated to be just 7,069,000 BEF (Great Britain 1912: 5). He pointed out that this was "not very much greater than that of the colony of Sierra Leone, thirty times less in area and with a population one-tenth that of the Congo." On a per capita basis this was just 0.76 BEF, substantially less than the customs revenue collected in the Gold Coast (12.34 BEF per capita) or Southern Rhodesia (8.36 BEF per capita). Only the more impoverished of Britain's colonies in Africa, such as Nyasaland (0.69 BEF per capita) or Northern Rhodesia (0.71 BEF per capita) collected less in customs revenue.[3] The rates of customs tariffs in the Congo were similar to those of other colonies (10–12 percent ad valorem), so the difference in customs revenue reflected the low value of imports. "That this has resulted largely from the policy of monopoly, restrictions on trade, and the operation of 'exploitation en régie' that have hitherto held sway here cannot, I think, be gainsaid" (Great Britain 1912: 5).

The legacy of Leopold's rule in the Congo was therefore a climate in which raising tax revenue was even more difficult than it would have been after the initial establishment of the Free State in 1885. Owing to Leopold's confidence in the economic value of colonial territory, and his impatience to substantiate his claims to the Belgian parliament, the Free State administration relied on maximizing the revenue from finite natural resources. While these were successful in generating early surpluses, the methods used led to both significant internal flight and falling agricultural production. The administration also exerted an increasing degree of control over production and trade, limiting incentives for private entrepreneurship. Peemans (1975: 172) notes that under the Free State's concession system "administrative constraint was used to incorporate the African population into the world market at an arbitrary level of remuneration," which "suppressed the profit motive in the development of production."

### 6.3 Reforming the Congo's tax system after 1908

In terms of tax revenue, the Congo after 1908 ranked among the poorest of Britain's landlocked colonies (see Figure 6.2). In 1912 the Congo's total revenue was 45,367,639 BEF or 4.87 BEF per capita. Nearly a third of that revenue was still generated by the sale of rubber and ivory, some of which had been stored in previous years (Great Britain 1912: 4). In contrast, the Gold Coast raised 20.66 BEF per capita, and Southern Rhodesia 25.20 BEF per capita. Nyasaland and Northern Rhodesia remained not far behind the Congo, with per capita revenue of 3.34 BEF and 3.88 BEF respectively. Both of the latter colonies would see significant growth in their revenue in the next decade; the challenge for Belgian authorities in the Congo was to do the same.

After 1908, the Belgian government was under considerable international pressure to bring its tax system, in particular, into line with the prevailing standards of the day. Much of this pressure came from Britain, which had played a leading role in the international campaign to end the abuses of Leopold's regime. By 1908, Britain was the leading imperial power in the region and the British government rationalized its efforts to influence Belgian colonial rule by noting that instability in the Congo could potentially influence its own colonies. A 1908 Foreign Office memorandum stated that because the Belgian territories shared a border with several British colonies, "it cannot therefore be a matter of indifference to His Majesty's Government how they are governed, inasmuch as the

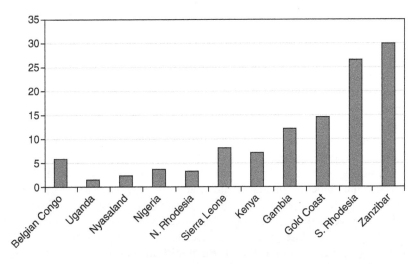

*Figure 6.2* Per capita revenue in the Belgian Congo and selected British colonies, 1911 (in BEF) (source: Great Britain (1912, 1926)).

maladministration of any one state cannot but react to the prejudice of its neighbours, more especially in a continent like Africa" (Great Britain 1908c: 3).[4]

The focus of British pressure was on both the hindrances to trade which had emerged in the Congo and the brutality of "red rubber" tax collections. It had been the concession system and its interference with free trade that had put Leopold and the Congo Free State on a collision course with the commercial interests of more powerful imperial rivals. It was a challenge to the concession system – originating in the French Congo rather than the Free State – which ultimately brought commercial interests to bear in growing protests against Leopold's regime. When the French colonial government began to emulate Leopold's concession strategy in an effort to develop a section of its African territories which had attracted little investment it created tensions between French and English companies. The latter complained that the French concessions interfered with the freedom of trade they were guaranteed under Article 1 of the Berlin Act (Cooksey 1966: 263). When a French company seized goods belonging to agents of John Holt and Company, the British trading company, Holt brought an action against the company, questioning the validity of concessions within the Congo Basin and contending that they interfered with the freedom of trade guaranteed by the Berlin Act. While his initial claim was dismissed, Holt later led a push by British commercial and industrial interests against the concession system (Cooksey 1968: 62–3). Linked with humanitarian interests by the argument that free trade was necessary to guarantee African welfare, this pressure was ultimately crucial in forcing Leopold to cede authority over the Congo to the Belgian government.

The Belgian government moved swiftly to address these criticisms after taking over administration of the territory. In April 1908, the Belgian government submitted a memorandum to the Foreign Secretary in Britain, reassuring the British government of its intentions with regard to the Congo, and emphasizing its commitment to free trade.

> The principle of individual liberty without constraint will be upheld, and the natives will not be compelled, either directly or indirectly, to furnish labour to the Concessionary Companies or to any other private enterprise. If they do voluntarily work for a private employer, it will be at a rate of wages to which the labourer has consented of his own free will.
>
> (Great Britain 1908b: 2)

Commerce and industry would be developed "in the most advanced and liberal manner," with no distinction made between Belgian and foreign companies (Great Britain 1908b: 2).

The opening of the territory to free trade was also intended to facilitate reform of the direct tax system. For colonial administrations in the first decades of the twentieth century, the ability to collect direct taxes from the African population was intimately linked with the expansion of both export production and monetization. In another notable departure from the practice of other colonies, the Free

State administration had not introduced a currency for fear that the ability to pay taxes in cash would reduce the supply of forced labor (Stengers and Vansina 1985: 344).[5] With regard to direct taxation, the Belgian government communicated to the British Foreign Office that it agreed that "the taxation of the natives of the Congo should be on a moderate scale, and in proportion to the circumstances of the taxpayers." The payment of taxes in labor by those without sufficient cash income would continue, but as "a temporary and provisional measure, destined to disappear gradually with the introduction and increased circulation of currency, which they will make every effort to encourage."[6]

The expansion of export markets and the adoption of colonial currencies was a slow process in most of colonial Africa, and therefore tax collection in kind was not uncommon even outside the Congo, and was, as Newbury (2004: 260) observes, "difficult to eradicate." However, the need to transport and either use or sell the proceeds of in-kind tax collection made it a relatively inefficient way of raising revenue – Lord Lugard (1919: 205) instructed that "tax must be collected in cash wherever possible, in order to avoid the transport of bulky produce, and the difficulty of its conversion into currency." Moving to a system of tax payments in money was therefore a priority for most colonial administrations. British officials attributed many of the abuses of the ivory and rubber taxes to the lack of an official currency in the Congo. Sir Edward Grey wrote to Hardinge, formerly administrator of British East Africa, that "as regards the question of taxation in labour, the abuses to which the system has given rise have only been rendered possible by the absence of a proper standard of value" (Great Britain 1908a: 3). As a result, he argued that "the only sure and efficacious means of precluding the existence of such abuses in the future is the introduction of currency throughout the state at the earliest possible date" (Great Britain 1908a: 3). This was established shortly after the transfer of power, with the incorporation of the Banque du Congo Belge, which was empowered to issue bank notes (Great Britain 1912: 3). A decree of August 17, 1910, which laid down conditions for labor contracts and recruitment, mandated that wages had to be paid in money (Great Britain 1911: 4). Jewsiewicki (1983: 98) describes the introduction of currency after 1908 as "the most important change to occur when Belgium took over the Congo colony."

Along with introducing a currency, the Belgian administration imposed a direct tax similar in structure to that imposed in other colonies. A decree of May 1910 established a poll tax to be paid by adult males, with an extra tax on wives above one. Rates were fixed annually by the Governor within a range of ten to 300 BEF. The actual rate charged varied within this range between districts. In addition, particular groups were exempt from the tax. This included chiefs and sub-chiefs, those who had done military or police service during the tax year, fathers of four or more children by a single wife, and teachers and missionaries (Hailey 1957: 673–4). Like all flat-rate taxes, the poll tax was regressive, bearing most heavily on poorer members of society, and less efficient than progressive income-based taxes introduced later, but it was nevertheless broadly in line with common colonial practice at the time (Hailey 1957: 652). Additional exemptions were granted in the first years of collecting the tax owing to economic conditions or a shortage of currency in particular districts. In the Kwango district, for example, half of the year's tax was remitted because there was insufficient demand for African produce. Some parts of Kasai district were granted exemptions due to poverty, while the Lubi-Bushimai district was exempted due to an epidemic of sleeping sickness (Great Britain 1912: 2).

By the late 1920s, the tax was well established and formed an important part of the revenue of the Belgian Congo. In the budget of 1930, the *impôt indigène* contributed nearly 17 percent of total revenue, forming the third most important source of revenue behind customs tariffs and a tax on company profits (Belgium 1932). Regional differences in the rates charged continued. Figure 6.3 shows the range of per capita contributions to hut tax revenue by province in 1929. The variation of hut and poll tax rates by region was a common practice in colonial Africa, where governments rarely had substantial data on the incomes of African taxpayers. In the absence of such data, regional variation of tax rates was a way of approximating the adjustment of tax rates to income. Regions perceived to be wealthier were charged higher rates while taxpayers in poorer regions paid lower rates – this was true not only in the Congo but also in Northern Rhodesia (Pim and Milligan 1938: 114) and Nyasaland (Hailey 1957: 657). As Figure 6.3 shows, per capita payments of poll tax were highest in the mining province of Katanga. This was not only due to higher rates of tax – Fetter (1983: 148) emphasizes that changing regional patterns of hut tax collections indicate regional variance in economic development, the spread of transport infrastructure, and the priorities of the colonial administration. After 1908, the Equateur province, which had been the center of rubber production, became less important as a producer of revenue, while Katanga and Orientale (particularly Stanleyville

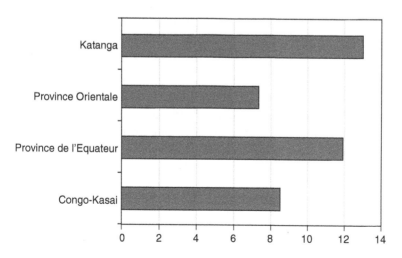

*Figure 6.3* Per capita hut tax payments by province, 1929 (in BEF) (source: calculated from Belgium (1930)).

and Aruwimi districts, which were on rail and steamer networks) became more important (Fetter 1983: Table 5.2).

An income tax was first imposed in 1920, around the same time as it was imposed in the Rhodesias – Northern Rhodesia mandated an income tax in 1921, while Southern Rhodesia's income tax was first introduced as a wartime measure in 1917 (Gardner 2012: 50; Hailey 1957: 649). In the Congo, the income tax actually incorporated several taxes depending on the form of income (e.g., rental income, salaries, etc.). The rate of income tax ranged from 1 to 25 percent of taxable income. Companies were taxed on a progressive scale according to their capital at rates from 10 to 25 percent of net revenue (Hailey 1957: 649–50).[7]

The taxation of metropolitan companies doing business in the colonies was a difficult problem in both Belgian and British colonies. Colonial administrations argued that the tax revenue derived from colonial commerce should stay within the colony, while metropolitan states claimed that companies based in the metropole should contribute to metropolitan public services from which they benefited (Stengers 1957: 14). In both cases, a compromise was reached through double taxation regulations, which divided the revenue between colonial and metropolitan governments. In British colonies, double taxation regulations limited colonial tax collections to half of the tax rate levied in Britain (Pim and Milligan 1938: 135–6). In the Congo, the division was approximately 25 percent for the metropolitan treasury and 75 percent for the colonial treasury (Stengers 1957: 12–13).

As revenue from income tax increased, the *impôt indigène* fell from just under 17 percent of total revenue in 1930 to only 3 percent in 1955. In contrast, income tax contributed over 30 percent of total revenue in 1955, up from 18 percent in 1930. Declining reliance on poll tax for revenue was a common pattern across most African colonies from the 1940s onwards. Lord Hailey observed that

> the procedure of taxation is shown to have been evolved in the majority of territories through a well-marked cycle. Starting from a hut tax it becomes a poll or capitation tax, usually graduated according to categories of taxpayers, though only in a few instances has it yet attained to the final stage of this process.
>
> (Hailey 1957: 676)

By the 1950s, therefore, the tax system of the Congo was broadly similar to that of other colonies surrounding it. The collection of taxes in rubber and ivory had been abandoned in favor of the introduction of currency and the collection of taxes in money. Regional variation of tax rates served as a rough method of varying tax rates by income, in the absence of systems for collecting accurate data on African incomes. African direct taxation became an important part of colonial revenue in the decades following 1908. However, it was eventually superseded by revenue from income taxes.

Despite these changes, the legacy of Leopold's regime was still visible, largely in the continuing use of concessions which free trade reforms after 1908 had not entirely eliminated. That this would be the case was not obvious in 1908, when the

Belgian government had made genuine efforts to remove the restrictions on free trade and competition imposed by the Free State regime. Peemans (1975: 187) characterizes the period from 1910 to 1915 as the most open in the colony's history.

Revenue from concessions (*produit de portefeuille*) had declined in importance in the years immediately following the transition to Belgian rule, from 3,162,350 BEF in 1910 to 157,700 BEF in 1911. This reduction followed a 1911 agreement which abolished the monopolies held by the ABIR, Anversoise and Kasai Companies (Great Britain 1912: 3–4). The British consul noted that "no part of the Government's policy throughout the year indicates more conclusively its reformatory trend" (Great Britain 1912: 3). However, these efforts were not to last, and revenue from shares in concession companies remained an important source of funds for the colonial state. The quantity of revenue received from income shares earned the colonial state the nickname "portfolio state."[8]

Revenue from such corporations came from two main sources: direct taxation of profits through income tax, and dividends on government-owned shares. As Figure 6.4 shows, such revenue remained an important part of the Belgian Congo's budget even in the final decade of colonial rule (Great Britain Naval Intelligence Division 1944: 441).

## 6.4 Public spending: a more familiar pattern

While the tax system of the Congo Free State had differed substantially from that of neighboring colonies, its public expenditure followed a more familiar

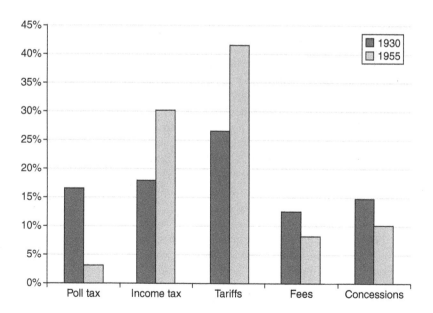

*Figure 6.4* Revenue by source, 1930 and 1955 (source: Calculated from Belgium (1932, 1957)).

pattern. Early expenditures were devoted primarily to conquest and the early establishment of the colonial administration. In subsequent decades, colonial budgets increasingly prioritized the expansion of the transport network. Following World War II, a more interventionist approach to colonial development saw the adoption of a development plan and increased spending on social services. Public spending in most African colonies followed the same pattern, which in many respects mirrored the expansion in quantity and scope of public expenditures around the globe over the course of the twentieth century (Tanzi and Schuknecht 2000: 3–22).

Early expenditures by the Free State were not dramatically different to those of other colonies. The dominant areas of expenditure were administration, defense and public works, as in other colonies. However, the Congo Free State spent a much larger share of its revenue on military and police than other colonial territories in the region. In the first decade of colonial rule, the British administration in Kenya spent an average of 25 percent of its total budget on military and police, as compared with an average of just over 46 percent in the Belgian Congo (Gardner 2012: 38). Contemporaries in other colonies were not unsympathetic to the need for such heavy expenditure on coercion. As a British consular agent reported to the Foreign Office in 1898, "with the best of intentions and the most humane of officials, no power in the world could make the tribes of Central Africa cohere as a peaceful nation without some amount of hammering" (Great Britain 1898: 7). However, such expenditures also reflected the consequences of a heavily extractive tax system – Africans responded to the demands for "red rubber" with tax revolts as well as flight, and the administration required a relatively large coercive apparatus to maintain order.

The Congo's early fiscal difficulties left it with a relatively large debt burden, which it carried with it from the Free State period into the period of Belgian rule. Servicing this debt absorbed a large percentage of the colony's resources at some points during its history. The year before the transfer, the Free State borrowed more than 100 million BEF, or more than double a single year's revenue. On the transfer of power to Belgium a further obligation of 50 million BEF was incurred as a *témoignage de gratitude* to King Leopold, to be paid in 15 annual installments. These loans, combined with debts taken on earlier in the Free State period, meant that in 1912 total public debt was nearly BEF 280 million (Great Britain Naval Intelligence Division 1944: 442). This was higher than in any of Britain's colonies, in Africa or elsewhere; the only colony to come close was Nigeria, which had a public debt equivalent to 250 million BEF (Great Britain 1926).

The 1920s saw extensive investments in public works, including improvements in ports, roads, and electrical supplies. The road network grew from 2400 km in 1920 to 30,000 km ten years later. New railway links and wireless stations were also constructed, and annual petrol consumption rose from 500 to 24,000 tons (Jewsiewicki 1986: 475, 1977: 155). In justifying expenditure on this expansion of infrastructure, Minister of Colonies Louis Franck echoed arguments made in British colonies in earlier decades, noting that although the colonial charter of 1908 had separated the Congo's budget from that of the metropole, it had not prohibited Belgium from practicing "a policy of wisdom and foresight." He argued that "no one who possessed new territory would think to extract resources from it without first advancing the capital necessary to develop them."[9]

These investments left the colony with a substantial debt burden (Jewsiewicki 1986: 462). Gann and Duignan claim that the Belgian Congo had the highest debt load of all African colonies (1979: 202–3). In 1930, debt charges represented just over 17 percent of the colony's total ordinary expenditure (Belgium 1932). Just a few years later, as public revenue contracted during the Great Depression, over a third of the budget was devoted to serving the public debt, up to a maximum of 44 percent in 1934. Figure 6.5 shows the allocation of ordinary expenditure during the 1930s.

After debt charges, the largest share of the budget was spent on local administration and defense, which absorbed about a quarter of the budget. Just under 20 percent of spending was devoted to public works, while social services claimed an average of 12.5 percent across the five years from 1933 to 1938 (Jewsiewicki 1977: 160). From a comparative perspective, the debt service payments of the Belgian Congo were high, but not exceptionally so. Kenya, over the same period, devoted just under a third of its budget to debt servicing (Kenya Colony 1933–8). Nyasaland spent 44 percent of its budget on servicing public debt, while Nigeria spent 31 percent (Frankema 2011: Appendix Table 1). The share of expenditure devoted to social services was low compared to British colonies, which by the late 1930s were devoting close to 20 percent of their budgets to social services (Frankema 2011: Appendix Table 1; Gardner 2012: 140–57).

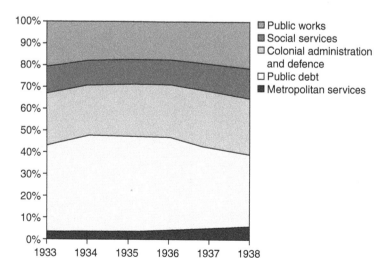

*Figure 6.5* Allocation of public spending in the Belgian Congo (source: Great Britain Naval Intelligence Division (1944)).

Comparing the 1955 budget with the budgets of the 1930s illustrates this transition. There were a number of similarities between the 1955 budget and the budgets of the 1930s. Figure 6.6 shows the allocation of ordinary expenditure in that year. Metropolitan services continued to absorb around 4 percent of total spending; around a quarter of the budget was still spent on administration, policing, and defense. However, spending on public works had expanded to nearly 28 percent of the budget, while debt servicing had dropped from well over a third to just over 8 percent. The biggest change was the increase in the proportion of public spending devoted to social services, from an average of 12.5 percent to over 30 percent.

This changing pattern of spending was largely the result of the Ten-Year Development Program, adopted in 1949 (Belgium 1949; Hailey 1957: 1340). In the Congo, as elsewhere, the period between 1945 and decolonization in 1960 was one of changing priorities in colonial development. This shift has been well documented in histories of the British Empire, one of which famously describes the unprecedented level of resources devoted to colonial economic development in the late 1940s as the "second colonial occupation" (Low and Lonsdale 1976: 12). In British colonies, post-war development plans were intended beyond the traditional focus on infrastructure to include a new focus on social services like health care and education, though in practice actual spending often failed to keep up with political rhetoric and infrastructure remained dominant (Havinden and Meredith 1993).

In comparison, spending on social services in the Congo looked relatively generous to contemporaries. Lord Hailey (1957: 220) observed that "there can be no better evidence of the interest shown by Belgium in the improvement of the social conditions of Africans than the large sums now being devoted to this object by the Ten-year Development Programme." As further evidence of this, Hailey also pointed to the establishment of a separate fund devoted to the welfare

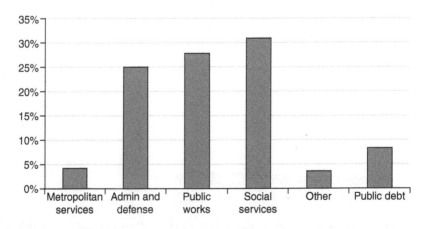

*Figure 6.6* Public spending in 1955 (source: Belgium (1957)).

of Africans (the *fonds du bien-être indigène*), established after World War II with a capital sum of just over 2000 million BEF with expenditures devoted largely to health services and rural development (Hailey 1957: 1340–1).

As in other African colonies, however, both public works and administration remained the largest items in the budget. Further, as Frankema illustrates in Chapter 7 below, the Congo's expenditures on social services may have been too late to have any real impact on economic outcomes after independence. Further, there was considerable regional variation in development efforts: Vansina (2010: 243) observes that in a large Kuba village at the end of the colonial period "there was no piped local water, no electricity, no advanced school, not even a complete elementary school, no health care."

## 6.5 Financial relations between the Congo and the Belgian state after 1908

How did these changes affect the financial links between colony and metropole? Section 2 argued, following Stengers, that the Congo was unique in colonial Africa for generating a sufficient surplus to contribute significant funds to public works projects in Belgium at a time when other African colonies were receiving large metropolitan subsidies. The methods by which these surpluses were achieved, however, compounded the existing difficulties of establishing a tax base in the Congo, and may have transferred some of the costs of doing so to the successor administration. If this was the case, Belgian grants and loans would be important in the Congo's budgets after 1908.

In the years following the transfer of power in 1908, the Congo ceased to generate profits for the metropole, though some portion of colonial expenditure still funded some metropolitan services. All imperial powers hoped to make at least most of their colonies financially self-sufficient after the initial period of conquest and establishment of infrastructure (Gardner 2012: 23–6). In 1908, the Belgian government sought to achieve that goal by separating the finances of the Congo from those of the metropolitan state in the colonial charter (Stengers 1957: 68). Such separation was common in the financial organization of the European empires, though it did not necessarily remove liabilities from the metropolitan state – Accominotti *et al.* (2011) find that British colonies were able to borrow at lower rates of interest because colonial status effectively removed the risk of default. Even with the official separation of budgets, financial links between the colony and metropole remained.

During the interwar period, the Belgian treasury contributed both to infrastructure spending during the 1920s and to the rescue of the colonial finances in the 1930s, when the effects of the Great Depression caused revenue collections to fall. From 1921–5, the Belgian treasury contributed around BEF 75 million to the colonial treasury in support of infrastructure investments. While this sum was initially in the form of an advance to be repaid, the loans were later forgiven and never repaid (Stengers 1957: 95–6). Despite the investments of the 1920s, the Congo struggled to cope with the falling prices of the 1930s. As Stengers

(1957: 101) observes, revenue fell by nearly 45 percent in the three years from 1929 to 1932, from 690 million BEF to 380 million BEF. To help make up this shortfall, the Belgian treasury made three annual grants of 165 million BEF between 1933 and 1935, a further grant of 155 million BEF in 1936, followed by smaller amounts through the late 1930s (Stengers 1957: 109). The 1933 grant represented 1.7 percent of Belgium's public expenditure that year – this was, as Stengers notes, a real sacrifice given conditions in Belgium at the time (Stengers 1957: 108). It was a sacrifice which was not made by other imperial governments. A 1932 report by the British Colonial Office noted that despite large and growing deficits in colonial budgets, "it is understood that no assistance from Imperial funds can be looked for" (Colonial Office 1932: 15).

The position changed after the start of World War II, when, like other colonies, the Congo became a valuable resource to the metropole. Even skeptical calculations of the costs and benefits of colonialism have observed that colonies became extremely valuable sources of raw materials, manpower, and even money during the two world wars (Havinden and Meredith 1993; Offer 1999). Loans from the Banque du Congo Belge provided nearly all of the foreign exchange available to the Belgian government in exile in London during the war (Stengers 1957: 11). Similarly, exports from the Congo remained an important source of dollars for the Belgian government after the end of the war (Eichengreen 2007: 128).

Belgium emerged from the war in a relatively weak economic position. It had suffered little damage to its industrial capacity owing to early occupation by the German army (Eichengreen 2007: 128). However, its growth rates following the end of the war were slow, like those of the UK and Ireland (Eichengreen 2007: 118). As a result, the colony funded the whole of its post-war development plans from local funds. This was unusual in comparison with other colonies, which received sometimes (but not always) substantial metropolitan subsidies in support of their post-war development efforts (Gardner 2012: 144–57).

Stengers (1957: 350) notes that the whole of Belgium's expenditure on the Congo was modest, totaling less than one-tenth of the Belgian state's annual expenditure in the mid-1950s, and less than the state budget for pensions in 1956. In this Belgium was not unique – studies of the costs and benefits of the British and French empires also suggest that total metropolitan spending was minimal, with local funds supporting the vast majority of expenditures (Davis and Huttenback 1986; Gardner 2012).

## 6.6  Conclusion: a colonial state struggling to catch up

Colonial state-building was in all contexts a slow process, vulnerable to setbacks caused by both political and economic shocks. Grier (1999) has argued that colonies held for longer periods of time have performed better after independence. This is one possible explanation for the better economic performance of former colonies in Asia relative to Africa, and the comparison of the Congo with the Netherlands Indies in this volume appears to support this hypothesis. Leopold's regime in the Congo, horrific though it was, did not necessarily doom the country to the difficulties it has experienced since independence. It did, however, leave little time for the Belgian administration to build a solid institutional foundation to be used by an independent Congo government. This process, which was incomplete even in the most successful colonies, was crucial for economic and political stability after the transfer of power.

For all colonial regimes in Africa, financial self-sufficiency was a major challenge owing to the size and sparse populations of the territories they were attempting to govern. British administrators managed to convince an often reluctant treasury in London that significant initial expenditure on infrastructure was required before a tax base could be established. Leopold, however, was under intense pressure to make his colony profitable as quickly as possible, and therefore focused on maximizing early revenue collections. The building of a tax base in the Belgian Congo did not really begin until 1908, when Belgian authorities introduced tax payable in currency, and removed monopolies on forest produce. From this point forward, the fiscal system of the Congo – in terms of both revenue and public spending – followed a very similar path to that of neighboring British colonies. This supports Vansina's argument that the Congo's "exceptionalism is often exaggerated: nearly all of its patterns of governance, economic exploitation, conversion to Christianity, and social modernization have on the whole been quite similar to those of other colonies" (Vansina 2010: 4).

Though the policies of the Belgian Congo may have been similar to those of other African colonies after 1908, the administration of the Congo had a much shorter period in which to construct the institutions of the colonial state – 50 years relative to the 60 or 70 available to other colonial administrations. Across such a short but influential period in Africa's economic history, decades mattered. The weakness of the Congo's fiscal system from 1908 led to a continued reliance on concession revenue as well as forced cultivation (Nelson 1994: 152–3). Increases in expenditure on social services and infrastructure came too late to build a foundation for growth which could be inherited by the government of the Congo after independence.

## Notes

1 I would like to thank Olivier Accominotti for access to exchange rate data and assistance with translations from French, and the editors and other contributors to this volume for their comments and suggestions. Any remaining errors in this chapter are mine.
2 Figures for British colonies calculated using data from Great Britain (1909). Revenue figures in sterling converted to francs at 25.14 BEF per £1.
3 Figures for British colonies calculated using data from Great Britain (1926). Revenue figures in sterling converted to francs at 25.24 BEF per £1.
4 Foreign Office memorandum composed in reply to letter from Belgian government, reprinted in Great Britain (1908c: 2–6).
5 This is not to say that the Congo was wholly without coin-based currency: evidence from British sources elsewhere indicates that rupees from Uganda were taken across the border in the early years of the twentieth century. However, such leakages were

likely to circulate in border areas only and could not make up for the lack of a currency issued and managed within the colony itself. And, crucially, currency that had crossed the border could not be used for the payment of tax. See UK National Archives (TNA) CO 536/6. I thank Karin Pallaver for drawing my attention to this reference.

6 Foreign Office summary of Belgian memorandum, June 23, 1908, reprinted in Great Britain (1908b: 2–3).

7 Details on the structure of income tax set down in a Decree of September 10, 1951, which consolidated regulations passed after the introduction of the tax in 1920.

8 Phrase coined by an unnamed Belgian Senator, quoted in Vellut (1983: 130).

9 Quoted in Stengers (1957: 88). Author's translation.

# References

Accominotti, O., Flandreau, M., and Rezzik, R. (2011) "The spread of empire: Clio and the measurement of colonial borrowing costs," *Economic History Review*, 64: 385–407.

Acemoglu, D., Johnson, S., and Robinson, J.A. (2001) "The colonial origins of comparative development: an empirical investigation," *American Economic Review*, 91: 1369–401.

Anstey, R. (1966) *King Leopold's Legacy: The Congo Under Belgian Rule, 1908–1960*, Oxford: Oxford University Press.

Austin, G. (2008) "Resources, techniques, and strategies south of the Sahara: revising the factor endowments perspective on African economic development, 1500–2000," *Economic History Review*, 61: 587–624.

Belgium (1930) *Rapport annuel sur l'administration de la Colonie du Congo Belge pendant l'année 1929*, Brussels: Chambre des Représentants.

Belgium (1932) *Rapport annuel sur l'administration de la Colonie du Congo Belge pendant l'année 1931*, Brussels: Chambre des Représentants.

Belgium (1949) *Plan Décennal du Congo Belge*, Brussels: Chambre des Représentants.

Belgium (1957) *Rapport annuel sur l'administration de la Colonie du Congo Belge pendant l'année 1956*, Brussels: Chambre des Représentants.

Buelens, F. and Marysse, S. (2009) "Returns on investments during the colonial era: the case of the Belgian Congo," *Economic History Review*, 62: 135–66.

Clarence-Smith, W.G. (1983) "Business empires in Equatorial Africa," *African Economic History* 12: 3–11.

Colonial Office (1932) *Financial and Trade Statistics of the Colonial Empire*, London: Her Majesty's Stationery Office.

Conrad, J. (1997) *Heart of Darkness*, New York: New American Library.

Cooksey, S.J.S. (1966) "The concession policy in the French Congo and the British reaction, 1898–1906," *Journal of African History*, VII: 263–78.

Cooksey, S.J.S. (1968) *Britain and the Congo Question, 1885–1913*, London: Longmans.

Cooper, F. (2005) *Colonialism in Question: Theory, Knowledge, History*, Berkeley: University of California Press.

Davis, L.E. and Huttenback, R.A. (1986) *Mammon and the Pursuit of Empire: The Political Economy of British Imperialism, 1860–1912*, Cambridge: Cambridge University Press.

East African Protectorate (1901–5) *Blue Books*, Nairobi: Government Printer.

Eichengreen, B. (2007) *The European Economy Since 1945: Coordinated Capitalism and Beyond*, Princeton, NJ: Princeton University Press.

Fetter, B. (1983) *Colonial Rule and Regional Imbalance in Central Africa*, Boulder, Colo.: Westview Press.

Frankema, E. (2010) "Raising revenue in the British Empire, 1870–1940: how 'extractive' were colonial taxes?," *Journal of Global History*, 5: 447–77.

Frankema, E. (2011) "Colonial taxation and government spending in British Africa, 1880–1940: maximizing revenue or minimizing Effort?," *Explorations in Economic History*, 48: 136–49.

Gann, L.H. and Duignan, P. (1979) *The Rulers of Belgian Africa, 1884–1914*, Princeton, NJ: Princeton University Press.

Gardner, L.A. (2010a) "An unstable foundation: taxation and development in Kenya, 1945–63," in D. Branch, N. Cheeseman, and L. Gardner, *Our Turn to Eat: Politics in Kenya Since 1950*, Berlin: Lit Verlag, 53–76.

Gardner, L.A. (2010b) "Decentralization and corruption in historical perspective: evidence from tax collection in British Colonial Africa," *Economic History of Developing Regions*, 25: 213–36.

Gardner, L.A. (2012) *Taxing Colonial Africa: The Political Economy of British Imperialism*, Oxford: Oxford University Press.

Great Britain (1897) *Report on the Trade and Finances of the Congo Independent State*, London: Her Majesty's Stationery Office.

Great Britain (1898) *Report on the Congo Independent State*, London: Her Majesty's Stationery Office.

Great Britain (1908a) *Africa No. 3 (1908) Correspondence Respecting the Taxation of Natives, and Other Questions, in the Congo State*, London: Her Majesty's Stationery Office.

Great Britain (1908b) *Africa No. 4 (1908) Further Correspondence Respecting the Taxation of Natives, and Other Questions, in the Congo State*, London: Her Majesty's Stationery Office.

Great Britain (1908c) *Africa No. 5 (1908) Further Correspondence Respecting the Taxation of Natives, and Other Questions, in the Congo State*, London: Her Majesty's Stationery Office.

Great Britain (1909) *Statistical Abstract for the Several British Colonies, Possessions and Protectorates in Each Year from 1894 to 1908*, London: Her Majesty's Stationery Office.

Great Britain (1911) *Africa No. 2 (1911) Correspondence Respecting the Affairs of the Congo*, London: Her Majesty's Stationery Office.

Great Britain (1912) *Africa No. 1 (1912) Correspondence Respecting the Administration and Finances of the Congo*, London: Her Majesty's Stationery Office.

Great Britain (1926) *Statistical Abstract for the Several British Overseas Dominions and Protectorates in Each Year from 1909 to 1923*, London: Her Majesty's Stationery Office.

Great Britain Naval Intelligence Division (1944) *The Belgian Congo*, London: Great Britain Admiralty.

Grier, R.M. (1999) "Colonial legacies and economic growth," *Public Choice*, 98: 317–35.

Hailey, W.M. (1957) *An African Survey, Revised 1956*. Oxford: Oxford University Press.

Hardinge, A. (1897) *A Report on the Conditions and Progress of the East African Protectorate from its Establishment to the 20th July, 1897*, London: Her Majesty's Stationery Office.

Harms, R. (1975) "The end of red rubber: a reassessment," *Journal of African History*, 16: 73–88.

Havinden, M. and Meredith, D. (1993) *Colonialism and Development: Britain and its Tropical Colonies, 1850–1960*, London: Routledge.

Jewsiewicki, B. (1977) "The Great Depression and the making of the colonial economic system in the Belgian Congo," *African Economic History*, 4: 153–76.

Jewsiewicki, B. (1983) "Rural society and the Belgian colonial economy," in D. Birmingham and P.M. Martin, *History of Central Africa*, London: Longman.

Jewsiewicki, B. (1986) "Belgian Africa," in A.D. Roberts (ed.), *The Cambridge History of Africa, Volume 7*, Cambridge: Cambridge University Press.

Kenya Colony (1933–8) *Blue Books*, Nairobi: Government Printer.

Kuczynski, R.R. (1948) *Demographic Survey of the British Colonial Empire*, Oxford: Oxford University Press.

Low, D.A. and Lonsdale, J.M. (1976) "Towards the new order 1945–1963," in D.A. Low and A. Smith (eds.) *History of East Africa*, Oxford: Clarendon Press.

Lugard, F.D. (1906) *Instructions to Political and Other Officers, on Subjects Chiefly Political and Administrative*, London: Waterlow and Sons.

Lugard, F.D. (1919) *Revision of Instructions to Political Officers on Subjects Chiefly Political and Administrative*, London: Waterlow and Sons.

Munro, J.F. (1976) *Africa and the International Economy, 1800–1960: An Introduction to the Modern Economic History of Africa South of the Sahara*, London: Dent.

Nelson, S.H. (1994) *Colonialism in the Congo Basin, 1880–1940*, Athens: Ohio University Press.

Newbury, C. (2004) "Accounting for power in Northern Nigeria," *Journal of African History*, 45: 257–77.

Offer, A. (1999) "Costs and benefits, prosperity and security, 1870–1914," in A. Porter (ed.) *Oxford History of the British Empire, Volume III: The Nineteenth Century*, Oxford: Oxford University Press.

Olson, M. (2000) *Power and Prosperity: Outgrowing Communist and Capitalist Dictatorships*, New York: Basic Books.

Peemans, J.-P. (1975) "Capital accumulation in the Congo under colonialism: the role of the state," in P. Duignan and L.H. Gann, *Colonialism in Africa 1870–1960, Volume 4*, Cambridge: Cambridge University Press.

Pim, A. and Milligan, S. (1938) *Report of the Commission Appointed to Enquire into the Financial and Economic Position of Northern Rhodesia*, London: Her Majesty's Stationery Office.

Sanderson, G.N. (1985) "The European partition of Africa: origins and dynamics," in R. Oliver and G.N. Sanderson, *The Cambridge History of Africa, Volume 6*, Cambridge: Cambridge University Press.

Stengers, J. (1957) *Combien le Congo a-t-il coûté à la Belgique?*, Brussels: Académie royale des Sciences coloniales.

Stengers, J. and Vansina, J. (1985) "Western Equatorial Africa: King Leopold's Congo, 1886–1905," in R. Oliver and G.N. Sanderson, *The Cambridge History of Africa, Volume 6*, Cambridge: Cambridge University Press.

Tanzi, V. and Schuknecht, L. (2000) *Public Spending in the 20th Century: A Global Perspective*, Cambridge: Cambridge University Press.

US Office of Strategic Services (1945), *Trade Policies in the Congo Basin*, Washington, DC: Office of Strategic Services Research and Analysis Branch.

Vansina, J. (2010) *Being Colonized: The Kuba Experience in Rural Congo, 1880–1960*, Madison: University of Wisconsin Press.

Vellut, J.-L. (1983) "Mining in the Belgian Congo," in D. Birmingham and P.M. Martin (eds.) *History of Central Africa*, London: Longman.

Wrong, M. (2000) *In the Footsteps of Mr Kurtz*, London: Fourth Estate.

Young, C. (1994) *The African Colonial State in Comparative Perspective*, New Haven, Conn.: Yale University Press.

# 7 Colonial education and post-colonial governance in the Congo and Indonesia

*Ewout Frankema*

## 7.1 Introduction

Education affects long-term social and economic development through at least three major channels.[1] First, education positively affects public health. Educated people possess a better understanding of the importance of hygiene, a more accurate knowledge of risks of disease and preventive measures, and tend to have better access to sources of medical knowledge. Studies have found a negative correlation between educational attainment and, for instance, infant and maternal mortality rates, the use of contraceptives, and fertility rates. Healthy people tend to be more productive, and the health effects of education tend to accumulate as they are transmitted between generations, a transmission in which maternal education plays a key role (Banarjee and Duflo 2011: 41–70; Klasen 2002; Lloyd *et al.* 2000; Mokyr 2002: 163–217).

Second, education contributes to the accumulation of productive skills and knowledge, which in combination with capital-embodied technology, raises opportunities for productivity growth according to standard production function theory (Mankiw *et al.* 1992). Education is not a sufficient condition for productivity growth, but it is a necessary condition to keep up with the technological innovations that sustain the process of modern economic growth (Helpman 2004; Kuznets 1966; Lucas 2002; Nelson 2000). For this reason, governments of modern welfare states have vastly increased their public education expenditure since the late nineteenth century (Lindert 2004). During the post-war era, most of the less developed countries exponentially increased their education budgets as well (Birdsall *et al.* 1997; Clemens 2004; Frankema 2009). The Congo is one of few examples, even among the least developed countries, where government spending on education collapsed in the closing decades of the twentieth century (Depaepe 1996: 153–6).

This chapter addresses a third channel that has received less attention in socio-economic historical literature. Education raises governance capabilities and increases the potential for popular checks on power. Governance capabilities are essential in the management of complex political, economic, and social affairs. A government capable of collecting useful information and acting upon the basis of information is a prerequisite for political and macro-economic stability. Stability of economic institutions (including financial market institutions) and government spending programs is vital to creating and sustaining a favorable climate for investors and optimizing conditions for private entrepreneurship. State capacity is also required to levy taxes and fees, and to reallocate public resources to sustain, amongst others, the public education effort. In addition to governance capacities, education also affects the socio-economic and political context in which government activities are embedded. When the state is controlled by a dominant coalition of rent-seeking elites who are overwhelmingly occupied with the preservation of personal interests, state policies tend to limit access to economic resources and political influence by the majority of the population (Khan 2000; North *et al.* 2009). A large group of "independent" intellectuals raises the probability of certain formal and informal checks on overt power abuse, as intellectuals are better positioned to lead political opposition and are usually better equipped to communicate calls for civil liberties (for example, freedom of speech and public assembly, independent jurisdiction, and political representation) in a more effective way (Hall *et al.* 1986). Again, educated leadership is by no means a sufficient condition for good governance, but it is a necessary condition for the decent management of complex societies.

Precisely for these reasons colonial governments have always been ambivalent toward providing higher education to indigenous subjects. On the one hand, colonial administrations required a certain number of skilled people in state service, including doctors to modernize the health care system and engineers and technicians to develop mines, plantations, and infrastructural networks. At the same time, colonial governments feared the rise of anti-colonial sentiments through popular education (Coleman 1954; Sutton 1965; White 1996). In the 1910s and 1920s, Dutch politicians openly ventilated their concerns about the growing white-collar proletariat in the Netherlands Indies, which they considered a threat to the stability of colonial society (Lelyveld 1996; van der Veur 1969). The Belgians in the Congo expressed similar concerns regarding the access of literate Congolese to subversive literature and anti-colonial ideologies, such as Pan-Africanism and Communism (Depaepe 1996: 147; Dunkerley 2009: 89–94).

This chapter explores the comparative nature of colonial educational development following the introduction of the Ethical Policy in Indonesia (1901) and the annexation of the Congo Free State by the Belgian state (1908). More specifically, this chapter focuses on the relationship between the education system and the development of indigenous nationalist leadership. The main argument suggests that the opportunities for Indonesian children to benefit from a full Western curriculum in primary, secondary, and tertiary education enabled a class of Indonesian intellectuals, however small it remained, to develop the leadership experience required to ensure, at least, the further development of educational capacity, which proved critical in the adoption of sound macro-economic policies under Suharto (1967–98). In the Belgian Congo, mission schools spread much faster than in most other African colonies, and primary school enrollment growth also outpaced the Netherlands Indies. However, the strict commitment to African–European segregation policies prevented Congolese access to the higher ranks of government administration, the military, and business management. Modern forms of higher education for the indigenous population were considered both unnecessary and potentially dangerous. This distinction in the level of education enjoyed by the early independence leaders in Indonesia and the Congo constitutes a fundamental part of the political context in which the Mobutu clan could ruin the national economy and destroy the fragile educational structures that evolved under Belgian rule.

## 7.2 Different approaches to colonial educational development

The advance of popular education constituted one of the cornerstones of the "civilizing mission" as envisaged by European colonial powers from, roughly, the start of the twentieth century. In the Netherlands Indies, the political initiative to expand school enrollment formed tangible proof of an important reorientation in colonial policy – a shift from excessive exploitation of indigenous labor and natural resources under the Dutch Cultivation System (*het Cultuurstelsel*, *c.*1830–70) toward a "paternalistic" mode of colonial rule, generally referred to as the Ethical Policy (*Ethische Politiek*) (see also Thee, Chapter 2 above). In the Belgian Congo, educational opportunities expanded at increasing rates after the transition from Leopold's "domanial regime" (*domaniale stelsel*, 1891–1908) toward Belgian colonial rule. The increased stability of the colonial state and rapid progress in tropical medicine opened up the horizon for missionaries to "conquer" the vast Congo basin through missionary education. Even though the state was unable to enforce any degree of standardization in the structure and content of colonial education before 1925, the Belgian government was keenly aware of the role education could fulfill in its attempt to dissociate itself from the atrocities committed under Leopold's rule (Dunkerley 2009).

The colonial administration in the Belgian Congo pursued a strategy that was common in large parts of non-Islamic Africa: they granted free entry to Catholic and Protestant missionaries who supplied the financial, human, and organizational capacity to set up networks of mission schools (Callego and Woodberry 2010; Cogneau and Moradi 2011; Frankema 2012; Nunn 2010). During the interwar years, the colonial government encouraged Belgian Catholic missions especially to upscale their activities. The subsidy program for the Catholic mission schools was formalized in the 1925 Projet d'Organisation de l'Enseignement libre, au Congo Belge et au Ruanda-Urundi avec le concours des Sociétes de Missions nationales.[2] Only in 1954, when the liberal–socialist government coalition broke the political dominance of the confessional party (Christelijke Volkspartij, CVP), did the colonial government claim primary responsibility and authority over educational affairs. The colonial government rapidly increased the education budget to also include Protestant mission schools in its subsidy program and create a new infrastructure for public lay education (*neutraal onderwijs*) (Depaepe and van Rompaey 1995: 185–99). The reforms implemented as the result of the second Belgian *schoolstrijd* led to deep conflicts with the Catholic establishment (Briffaerts 1999).

In the Netherlands Indies, Christian missionary societies never developed a comparable degree of control over the colonial education system. Despite support from the colonial administration to increase their activities during the mid-nineteenth century, the dominance of Islamic religious instruction posed a serious barrier to the diffusion of missionary stations and schools. The Dutch were reluctant to increase tensions by offering open support to Christian mission activities in Muslim communities and were even less inclined to support the expansion of indigenous Islamic education itself. Since the late nineteenth century, consecutive Dutch governments endorsed the liberal political viewpoint that a neutral colonial state should take the initiative in the development of colonial education (Hartgerink 1942: 45–53). In Belgium, a similar political debate about the primacy of secular over religious education (*de eerste schoolstrijd*) had ended in a landslide victory for the confessional parties (Witte *et al.* 2009). Mission schools in Indonesia only gained primacy in some of the Outer Islands (*de Buitengewesten*), such as the Minahassa (Sulawesi) and the Moluccas, where the opposition of local communities to Christian missionary encroachment was less vehement, and the colonial state had fewer interests in controlling the curriculum.

To secure British support for his private claim to the Congo domain at the Berlin Conference (1884–5), the Belgian King Leopold II committed himself to free trade and free entry of missionaries of all Christian denominations (Pakenham 1992: 247–50). Although the Protestant societies worked largely outside the orbit of the colonial administration, their presence added considerably to the supply of missionary schooling. The Belgian Catholic missionary societies actively cooperated in Leopold's colonial project. Leopold arranged land concessions to the missions in return for missionary schools focusing on agricultural training and manual labor. The fact that Leopold himself never visited his private domain for fear of catching a tropical disease (van Reybrouck 2010) indicates how vital the development of early mission stations was to the effective occupation of the vast Congo territory. In this early period, the Catholic missionary schools were also needed to train Congolese soldiers for the army (La Force Publique), native clerks for the lower ranks in the government administration, and technicians for developing transport and communications infrastructures (Dunkerley 2009: 34–5).

The primary goal of the missions was to convert as many indigenous souls as possible. The missionary effort thus focused on the diffusion of mass education with low-quality standards and limited opportunities to enroll in a post-primary school trajectory. In the distant rural areas, mission schools were generally ungraded and managed by one or two native missionary teachers with a curriculum confined to the lower grades of primary education. Post-primary education was offered in the larger cities, but initially focused on teacher training programs in order to enlarge the group of indigenous missionary teachers. Hence, the missions were regarded as an efficient medium to "civilize" and "socialize" colonial subjects without raising a class of indigenous intellectuals who could challenge the legitimacy and authority of the colonial state. The missions also operated at extremely low cost to a colonial state with limited budget possibilities because of its international commitment to free trade (no customs revenues).

Education policies did not immediately change after the transition of the territory in 1908 to Belgian rule. The region witnessed a steady expansion of missionary activities and primary schooling spread accordingly, especially in the villages located along the major navigable rivers (Johnson 1967). The public call for increased government involvement in African education, endorsed by the two reports of the Phelps-Stokes committees in 1922 and 1925, increased the pressure on the Belgian colonial government to expand its education budget.[3] The 1925 project in the Belgian Congo sought to standardize the colonial primary education system in three tiers, as illustrated in Figure 7.1. The first, two-year tier focused on acquiring manual skills and work discipline. In rural areas, the education focused particularly on agricultural labor activities, while in the urban areas more attention was focused on teaching basic literacy skills. A second, three-year tier of education in the urban centers gave value to contact with Europeans by emphasizing a wider range of subjects, including French language instruction and manual skills such as carpentry or woodwork. A third, rather exclusive, two-year tier was intended to steer talented urban students toward the jobs required by the colonial economy and polity. These schools separately prepared boys for work as tradesmen, lower-rank clerks, army officials, or missionary school teachers, and the girls for domestic-agricultural tasks (Dunkerley 2009: 39–45). These reforms obviously implied a reformulation of the responsibilities of the state and the missions in educational affairs. The Catholic missions became even more indispensable to the success of the Belgian colonial project (Depaepe and van Rompaey 1995: 60–3) than they had already been, but at the same time they fiercely resisted the plan to introduce state inspection in return for additional financial support and managed to postpone the implementation of the system until 1929.

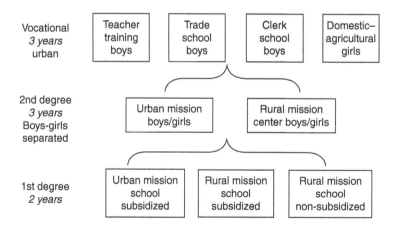

*Figure 7.1* The education system in the Belgian Congo after 1925/9 (source: Author's own figure based on Dunkerley (2009: 39–45)).

In the Netherlands Indies, the power contest between the state and the missions had been settled long before, and with a diametrically different outcome. The dominance of liberals in Dutch politics from 1848 led to a stricter policy of separation between state and church. In the last quarter of the nineteenth century, around a quarter of the students in "recognized schools" on Java and Madura attended mission schools (*zendingschool*), and in the Outer Islands the mission schools formed the majority (Hartgerink 1942: 39). Government-sponsored European schools were developed simultaneously and made accessible to children from the top layers of the Indonesian and Chinese elites. Between 1874 and 1895, the colonial government even refused to hand out any public subsidies to private mission schools (*bijzondere scholen*), in line with the policy advice dictated by the Dutch Schoolstrijd (1889–1917). In this period, the Dutch colonial government also annexed mission schools that were unable to stay in business or forced them to introduce lay education in return for continued financial support (Hartgerink 1942).

At the turn of the century a dual system of public education emerged in which the mission schools and the Islamic schools gradually gave way to publicly subsidized village schools.[4] In this dual system, European schools offered the standard Dutch curriculum to children of European and Indo-European descent. European schools prepared children for a career in the colonial administration and offered access to higher education in the Netherlands. The public schools for the common people (*Volksscholen*) served as a basic and cheap alternative to Western education (Brugmans 1938: 302–17; Lelyveld 1996), with the purpose of preparing Indonesians for a position in Indonesian society. As of 1907, the government launched a campaign to promote the development of village schools, the so-called *desa* schools, which became the major driver of increasing primary school enrollment rates between 1907 and the end of Dutch rule in 1942. Students enrolled in a three-year primary education program focused on the elementary principles of reading, writing, and calculating in the vernacular.

The possibilities for Indonesians to attain a standard Western primary education were gradually enlarged (Boone 1996). The Dutch–Chinese school (Hollands–Chinese School, HCS) emerged to prepare children of the Chinese minority for a position in the intermediary levels of business and state administration. The Dutch–Indonesian School (Hollands–Inlandse School, HIS) was founded in 1914 in response to growing discontent regarding the meager opportunities for high-quality education to Indonesians and the privileged position of the Chinese. As Figure 7.2 shows, these schools together with the so-called *schakel school* (literally "switch school") created opportunities to advance into Dutch-style secondary schools and further into tertiary education.[5] A survey from 1926 indicated that, despite the low numbers of indigenous children who eventually progressed into these higher echelons of the education system, access was certainly not restricted to the wealthiest indigenous families (van der Veur 1969: 3).

Another important Congo–Indonesia distinction was the earlier and much stronger rise of nationalist reform movements in Indonesia, movements with outspoken educational agendas. The Muslim reform movement that took root in the

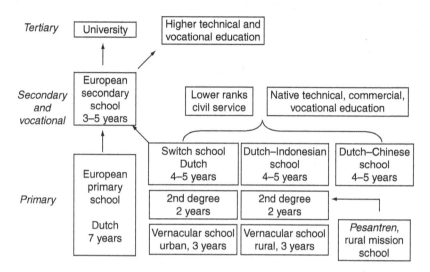

*Figure 7.2* The education system in the Netherlands Indies in the 1920s (source: Author's own figure based on van der Veur (1969)).

Minangkabau (Central Sumatra) during the 1900s provided as the basis of an influential political party (Sarekat Islam). Islamic anti-colonial ideology gener-ated a number of new educational institutions that aimed to offer a broader train-ing than the traditional *pesantren* (Islamic boarding schools) in order to prepare people for self-government. The leaders of the Islamic nationalists belonged almost without exception to the educated class of Islamic scholars (*ulama*) and were "teachers" of Islamic law. The rise of Islamic schools prompted a reappre-ciation of Christian mission schools by the Dutch colonial government, because they could help to limit the activities of Muslim missionaries in areas that were less affected by Islamic anti-colonial sentiment (Noer 1973: 162–75).

The Taman Siswa (Garden of Pupils) was another influential nationalist movement that aimed to unite and emancipate Indonesians from various social classes through a schooling campaign. The colonial government accused the Taman Siswa of spreading Communist ideology and implemented several laws in the 1920s and 1930s to prevent the spread of so-called *wilde scholen* (wild schools). These wild schools were not only beyond the control of the colonial administration; they were also suspected of teaching subversive ideas. The wild school ordinance of 1932 ruled that all teachers working in unrecognized schools should register themselves with the local authorities and undergo a "quality check" by an official state representative. This ordinance proved a formidable example of counter-productive policies; the protest against the ordinance led by the Taman Siswa became so vehement that the government had to repeal the law only a few months later and never again proposed such far-reaching measures to control the development of indigenous schooling (Tsuchiya 1987: 151–97).

The Belgian authorities also feared Islamic influence in Congolese schools, but the small size and concentration of the Islamic minority in the Eastern Province made this a more minor concern. Indigenous religious movements, such as Kimbanguism and Kitawala, were considered to be potentially far more dangerous. However, these movements differed in critical respects from those in the Netherlands Indies. They used animist rituals and mysticism to attract followers, but were essentially rooted in Catholic or Protestant orthodoxy. Second, these movements did not call for, let alone develop, their own educational institutions. The Belgian response was draconian. They suppressed these movements and forced them underground by brutal armed force. In areas where Kimbanguism gained popularity, the administration also started to establish special state-ordained schools as an alternative, prohibiting any type of religious instruction. But even the Catholic missions met with increasing suspicion as they were removing people from their traditional cultural values and, by doing so, at least to some extent supported "free-thinking" and "independent-mindedness" (Dunkerley 2009: 82–5).

Yet crucial to understanding the different features of post-colonial leadership is the twofold distinction between the education systems in the Netherlands Indies and the Belgian Congo: different opportunities of accessing post-primary education combined with different degrees of indigenous initiative in educational development at the local level. The post-independent Indonesian leaders were not only trained as university graduates in a Western education system; they were also able to tap into a deep pool of nationalist-religious ideology common to broad layers of society. Popular anti-colonial movements viewed education as the basic principle of self-determination. In the Congo, the involvement of the colonial state in schooling was evidently smaller, but its ability to contain the spread of politically subversive ideas through the education system was, paradoxically, bigger in many respects.

## 7.3 Comparing school enrollment rates, 1880–2000

A comparison of primary and post-primary school enrollment rates provides deeper insight into the effects of different educational policies on the expansion of educational access. Figure 7.3 shows the twentieth-century evolution of gross primary school enrollment rates for the 6–11 age group (the official school age in both countries during the post-independence era). The time series for the Netherlands Indies are taken from van Leeuwen (2007: 264–6). These include the enrollment of Indonesians, Europeans (mainly Dutch), and other Asians (mainly Chinese), but exclude the children enrolled in the so-called "unrecognized schools," that is, schools which did not receive state subsidies. The bulk of these unrecognized schools *pesantren* and mosque schools (*madrasah*), offering classes in religious philosophy and spiritual training (meditation), recitation of the Koran (in Arabic), martial arts, and a variety of manual skills (Steenbrink 1974). Colonial governments were reluctant to recognize these "traditional" schools because they were regarded as breeding grounds for anti-colonial sentiment and were accused of paying insufficient attention to the core values of Western primary education: reading, writing (literacy), and arithmetic.[6]

For comparative purposes, a rough idea of the relative share of unsubsidized schools is necessary. van der Wal (1963) offered an estimate of 2200 schools with an enrollment of 142,000 pupils in the late 1930s, but this figure is certainly too low because it excluded the Taman Siswa schools. Rather, this chapter combines the official enrollment rates in the unrecognized sector reported in the colonial annual accounts (*Koloniale Jaarcijfers*) of the 1880s (*c.*250,000–300,000) with Furnivall's estimate of 1938 (*c.*450,000). This figure implies that the relative share of unrecognized schools declined from approximately 75 percent to 16 percent of the official primary school enrollment estimates. The broken line for Indonesia reflects this trend.

For the Congo, the available data should be treated with even greater caution, especially for the years between 1885 and 1930, when education statistics were not collected on a systematic basis. Following the work of Liesenborghs (1939), Depaepe and van Rompaey (1995: 38, 247) estimated the number of students enrolled in 1908 at 46,000, of whom around 27,000 were enrolled in Protestant mission schools and 19,000 in Catholic ones. What seems more certain, however, is that the numbers increased spectacularly after 1908, to approximately 100,000 in 1913, 150,000 in 1921, and 350,000 in 1929. For the period

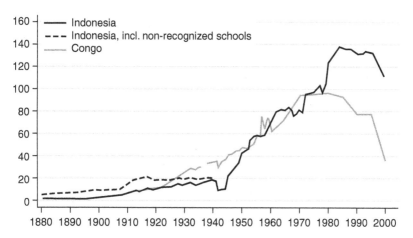

*Figure 7.3* Gross primary school enrollment rates (age 6–11) in the Belgian Congo and the Netherlands Indies, 1880–2000 (sources: Indonesian enrollment rates based on van Leeuwen (2007), Furnivall (1943), and on the *Jaarcijfers voor het Koninkrijk der Nederlanden (Koloniën)* 1880–1922, and Departement von Ekonomische Zaken, *Statistisch Jaaroverzicht van Nederlandsch-Indië* 1923–39. Data for the post-1950 years is from UNESCO, *Statistical Yearbooks*, various issues 1964–99; Data for the Congo is from Depaepe and van Rompaey (1995: 247) and the *Annuaire Statistique de la Belgique et du Congo Belge*, 1911–60. Data for the post-1960 years is from UNESCO, *Statistical Yearbooks*, various issues 1964–99).

1930–60, the Belgian *Annuaire Statistique* provided annual accounts of the number and type of schools and the number of students enrolled. For the post-colonial era, the official estimates presented in the UNESCO *Statistical Yearbooks* were used.

Another problem with the calculation of enrollment rates concerns the lack of reliable population data from the Congo. Census takers faced the impossible task of surveying immense hinterland areas with little logistical means. Moreover, the death toll due to the sleeping sickness pandemic, Leopold's aggressive rubber policies, and the drop in fertility caused by the spread of venereal diseases made it extremely difficult to estimate the size of the population on the basis of backward extrapolation from post-war census estimates (Vansina 2010: 127–49). The shortcut used here involves backward extrapolating the post-1950 population series with a fixed annual growth rate of 1 percent. However, changes in the assumed population growth rate (to 0.5 or 2 percent) will not alter the following general observations.

First, a dramatic collapse of school enrollment rates occurred in the Congo during the 1980s and 1990s, after a decade of stagnation in the 1970s. This decline was just one of the many tragic effects of the social, political, and economic deterioration that characterized most of Mobutu's 30-year rule. During this exact period, Indonesian gross enrollment rates started to exceed 100 percent, indicating that not only was the aim of universal primary education accomplished, but that it was also combined with a major reparation effort among higher age cohorts.

Second, Figure 7.3 shows that enrollment rates in the Belgian Congo surpassed enrollment rates in the Netherlands Indies in the three decades between 1920 and 1950. In the Belgian Congo, the expansion of enrollment followed a gradual upward trend between 1910 and 1970 with a few minor interruptions in the early 1940s and the late 1950s. In Indonesia, the colonial era was set apart from the post-colonial era by a major trend break. Before 1940, gross primary school enrollment rates did not go above 20 percent. During the years of the Japanese occupation (1942–5), enrollment rates even halved. The big push toward mass education occurred immediately after Indonesia's declaration of independence in 1945. Enrollment rates jumped from 20 percent to 80 percent of the school age population in less than two decades between 1945 and 1962.

Third, the relative success of the missionary approach in the Belgian Congo is also evident from an African comparative perspective. The Belgian Congo was part of a select group of mainly British African colonies such as Northern and Southern Rhodesia (Zambia and Zimbabwe), Nyasaland (Malawi), and Uganda where gross enrollment rates (age 5–14) were over 20 percent on the eve of World War II. This rate was higher than the British African average (18.2 percent) and much higher than the French (5.4 percent) or Portuguese African (5.3 percent) averages (Frankema 2012). Primary school enrollment in the Netherlands Indies, on the other hand, fell considerably behind those of its neighboring countries, such as British Malaya, Formosa (Taiwan), and the Philippines. In Thailand, enrollment rates were three times as high as in the Netherlands Indies (Furnivall 1943).

Notable similarities and differences are evident in the enrollment trends in secondary and tertiary education, as displayed in Figure 7.4. In both colonies, the expansion of post-primary school attainment was limited until independence. In Indonesia, a trend break in secondary schooling occurred after the mid-1940s. In the Belgian Congo, a similar trend break in the early 1960s occurred immediately after independence. This is not to say that the number of students in secondary school was stagnant before 1960, but rather that enrollment rates hardly outpaced population growth rates. The expansion of tertiary school enrollment followed a decade later in both countries.

Although secondary education expanded a few decades earlier in Indonesia, enrollment rates did not expand faster than in the Congo. In fact, in the two decades following independence in 1945 gross secondary school enrollment rates rose from around 1 percent to 13 percent. In the Congo, the rates increased from around 1 percent in 1960 to 20 percent in 1980. The key difference is that the expansion effort continued unabated in Indonesia and even sped up during the 1970s, whereas in the Congo enrollment rates stagnated and even declined after 1980.

Another major difference occurred in the expansion of tertiary education. In Indonesia, some 10 percent of all children continued their schooling careers into the post-secondary level in the last quarter of the twentieth century. In the Congo, tertiary school enrollment rates have never exceeded 1.5 percent until the present day. A survey of long-term enrollment rates thus reveals that the missionary approach in the Belgian Congo was relatively successful in expanding primary school enrollment rates, while the development of higher education, and especially tertiary education, lagged behind. The colonial government in the

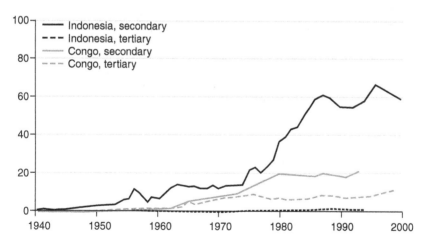

*Figure 7.4* Gross secondary and tertiary enrollment rates in the Belgian Congo and the Netherlands Indies, 1940–2000 (sources: see Figure 7.3).

Note
The age groups 12–17 are used for secondary schooling, and 18–23 for tertiary schooling.

Netherlands Indies performed moderately in expanding mass education, but compared to the Congo, the state-led education system laid a more solid foundation for access to and expansion of modern forms of higher education.

## 7.4 The success of the missionary effort in the Congo

The Congolese education system benefited from the presence of an exceptionally large number of Western missionaries. Table 7.1 shows that the number of foreign missionaries in the Belgian Congo came close to 4000 on the eve of World War II and continued to increase thereafter. To put this into comparative perspective, Oliver has estimated that the number of foreign Christian missionaries in the entire region of East Africa reached a maximum of approximately 3500 persons during the interwar years (Oliver 1962: 231–45). Foreign missionaries were of course crucial for the rapid spread of missionary schooling, but their presence also signaled comparatively favorable conditions for conversion. As argued elsewhere, the presence of foreign missionaries only made sense in areas with a revealed indigenous demand for missionary services and African demand was not self-evident (Frankema 2012). This demand for missionary services in combination with the virtual absence of institutional entry barriers sped up denominational competition. Another reason why Belgian missionary societies became actively engaged in the race against Protestant missions to conquer the "high-potential areas" had to do with the extremely strong roots of the Catholic church in Flanders, where religious intensity is comparable to that observed in Ireland and Poland. Almost every Flemish family had at least one member in a religious office and joining a mission in the Congo offered both a challenging and a prestigious opportunity to obey one's calling.

The table also shows that the number of foreign missionaries increased by a factor of 15, while enrollments rose by a factor of 37 between 1908 and 1957. This increase was only possible because of the rapidly growing involvement of native African missionaries and teachers. In 1958, no less than 6,934 Protestant

*Table 7.1* Absolute numbers and indices of missionary presence and students enrolled in the Belgian Congo, 1908–57 (1938 = 100)

|                       | 1908   | 1929    | 1938    | 1950    | 1957      |
|-----------------------|--------|---------|---------|---------|-----------|
| Foreign missionaries  | 500    | 2,500*  | 3,732   | 5,336   | 7,205     |
| Index                 | 13     | 67      | 100     | 143     | 193       |
| School enrollment     | 46,000 | 350,000 | 562,851 | 970,372 | 1,718,931 |
| Index                 | 8      | 62      | 100     | 172     | 305       |

Sources: 1908 based on Stengers and Vansina (1985); 1929 from Depaepe and van Rompaey (1995); 1938–57 from *Annuaire statistique de la Belgique et du Congo Belge* (1911–60).

Notes
The 1929 number of missionaries is an estimate based on 1931 figures from *Annuaire statistique de la Belgique et du Congo Belge* (1911–60).

mission schools were in the Congo and around 1,550 foreign Protestant missionaries. Most of these schools were thus run by Congolese converts. The Africanization of the missionary effort was a prerequisite for the impressive velocity and scale of expansion of primary education that occurred in the Congo.

An important factor in explaining this peculiar evolution is that the Congo was Belgium's only overseas possession.[7] Belgian citizens with overseas ambitions concentrated their efforts on the Congo, which especially appealed to Belgian Catholic missionaries. Moreover, the ratio of colonial versus metropolitan population remained low. Table 7.2 demonstrates that the metropolitan capacity, in terms of population size, made a significant difference. Indonesia was a similar "single big colony" for the Dutch, but in terms of demographic proportions, the Dutch–Indonesia relationship was more in line with the ratio of the British during the height of their imperial power.

The rather large carrying capacity of Belgian society was not confined to missionary societies. Richens has shown that in a sample of 33 African colonies in the late 1930s, the Belgian Congo had by far the highest number of European administrators: 728 against an African colonial average of 94. In British Nigeria, with more than twice as many inhabitants, the number of administrators was less than half (353) (Richens 2009: 21, 64–5). These numbers indicate a rather unusual feature of Belgian rule in Africa as they make clear how the Belgians managed to rule the single largest colonial territory in Africa without depending on indigenous representatives in the higher ranks of the state administration, the army, the judiciary, and the major companies.[8] Indeed, a policy of racial segregation is only possible with a minimum amount of settled Europeans occupying the key positions.

Johnson (1967) argued that the presence of navigable waterways also had a positive impact on the spread of missions in the Congo. She showed that the diffusion of mission stations in the Congo neatly followed the upstream courses of the Congo River and its tributaries. Water transport allowed missionaries to travel back and forth in a relatively efficient way and facilitated the delivery of the necessary supplies (school, medical, food, bibles, etc.). Many local communities lived close to a river because they depended on it economically. That the

*Table 7.2* The "population support ratio" in the British, Dutch, and Belgian colonial empires, *c.*1938

|  | *Metropolitan population (1) (× 1000)* | *Colonial population (2) (× 1000)* | *Population support ratio (2/1)* |
|---|---|---|---|
| United Kingdom | 47.5 | 358.1 | 7.5 |
| Netherlands | 8.7 | 68.3 | 7.8 |
| Belgium | 8.4 | 13.9 | 1.6 |

Source: Population data are from Maddison (2010); for the British Empire from the *Statistical Abstract for the British Empire* (1938–40).

Congolese river system facilitated the spread of missions seems clear, but the role of such natural advantages should not be overstated, especially in view of the huge risks missionaries were willing to take by working in the tropics in the first place. Moreover, the big population centers in Indonesia were also easy to reach for foreign missionaries, but in Indonesia the institutional constraints proved decisive.

The success of the missions in spreading education had much to do with their economic efficiency and flexibility: short lines of communication, high levels of personal responsibility entrusted to the people in the field, extremely low levels of labor remuneration, and a strong, religiously motivated spirit to endure. Colonial bureaucracies worked differently, which was one reason why enrollment rates in the Netherlands Indies grew at a slower pace, despite the much longer tradition of supplying formal education in the latter colony. Bureaucracies are designed to control, to work within delineated budgets and directives, and, most important, bureaucracies are not engaged in a competitive race for converts. In the Netherlands Indies, the teachers of the *desa* schools had to fulfill a number of teacher qualifications in order to receive a state salary. Teacher training schools (*de kweekscholen*) gradually expanded, but the pool of qualified students remained small. Moreover, the state had to provide official permission for the establishment of a new school if it was to receive state subsidies to pay for qualified and salaried teachers. The required investments, inspections, and feedback procedures took time. This situation also suggests that the quality standards in the public education system in Indonesia were higher than in the Congo.

## 7.5 Comparing the quality of education

Any scholar studying the comparative development of education in the Congo and Indonesia will be struck by the enormous difference in the availability and quality of education statistics. From the late nineteenth century, the Dutch colonial government recorded the number of schools, the type of schools, the number of students in school per grade, and the percentage of children who left school with a certificate. This percentage was extremely low in the late nineteenth century but improved quickly as more children continued into the third grade (Hartgerink 1942: 88–9, 136–7).[9] The fact that this information was centrally collected indicates the degree of control exercised by the colonial administration. The mission schools in the Congo enjoyed greater freedom because they lacked a central authority imposing and monitoring prescribed curricular standards until the 1950s. Perhaps a solid system of information collection is positively correlated with higher standards of quality control, but are there any indications that this was indeed the case?

The population censuses executed in 1961 in Indonesia and in 1962 in the Congo suggested that the education system in Indonesia was more effective in raising literacy rates, despite higher enrollment rates in the Congo between 1920 and 1950. The reported Indonesian literacy rate of the population over age 15 was 42.9 percent compared to 31.3 percent in the Congo (UNESCO 1965).[10] The literacy rates of consecutive Indonesian age cohorts reveal a steady improvement from the first decade of the twentieth century. Ten-year age cohorts who had reached the age of 15 in the 1910s, 1920s, and 1930s showed an increase in literacy rates of respectively 5.1 percent, 6.7 percent, and 10.8 percent compared to the preceding age cohort. After the 1940s, these rates improved even faster. The cohort of children attending primary school during the 1950s had a literacy rate of 72.1 percent (observed in 1961).

A comparison of government expenditure patterns provides further insight into possible quality differences. Between 1900 and 1940, the Dutch government gradually increased its investments in education from 2 to 5 percent of the total expenditure budget. From a global comparative perspective, this share was far from impressive (Frankema 2011), but it was much more than in the Congo. Figure 7.5 shows educational expenses per head of the population converted to current US dollars using official exchange rates. Exchange rates can deviate substantially from purchasing power parities and fluctuated, especially in the 1930s, yet the size and consistency of the gap in expenditure leaves little doubt that the difference was significant indeed. Prior to 1940, expenses in the Congo remained below US$ 0.10 per head of the population, which was roughly equal to the amount spent in the Indies before 1907. Between 1910 and 1940, the Dutch colonial government spent at least five times as much. Because enrollment rates in the Netherlands Indies were lower, the differences in government expenses per student enrolled reached an average rate of ten to one in this period.

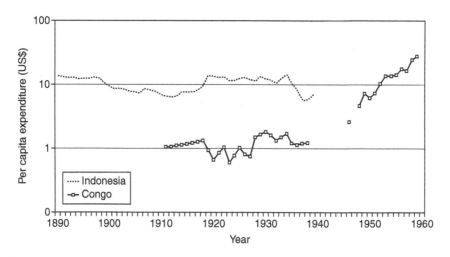

*Figure 7.5* Per capita government expenditure on education in the Netherlands Indies and the Belgian Congo, 1890–1940 (in current US$) (sources: Indonesia based on van Leeuwen (2007), including expenditure on the state level and provincial level; Congo based on the *Annuaire statistique de la Belgique et du Congo Belge* 1911–60).

Note
Dutch florins and Belgian francs have been converted to current US$ using official exchange rates.

Although the average amount of US$ 10 per student enrolled in the Netherlands Indies was quite respectable, the distribution around the average was highly unequal. In 1929, for instance, about half of the education budget was spent on European education, which was reserved for only about 10 percent of the total enrolled (van Leeuwen 2007). On the other hand, these government funds were increasingly absorbed by Indonesian and Chinese children as they started to outnumber the European children in the Dutch secondary schools during the 1920s (van der Veur 1969: 14). By the late 1930s, around 75 percent of the students enrolled in post-primary education were of Indonesian or Chinese origin (van Leeuwen 2007).

For the Belgian Congo, statistics do not allow for a breakdown between expenses on European education and subsidies to the Catholic mission schools. However, the missionary societies clearly remained the primary financiers of education at least until World War II. Protestant missions received no subsidies until 1947 and among the Catholic schools government funds were distributed rather unequally, with a strong bias toward the schools in the major urban centers. These central schools had to be better equipped because of their strategic importance; they trained the next generation of clerks and typists necessary for administrative tasks, the medical assistants, technicians, and agricultural experts necessary to develop the rural economy, and also the catechists and soldiers necessary to evangelize and secure order (Depaepe and van Rompaey 1995: 63–9).

The financial involvement of the Belgian Catholic missions in the Congo played a crucial role in the 1925 convention with the Belgian state. The Catholic schools would receive more financial support in exchange for extra efforts to spread mass education across the colony. The contract was not signed until 1929, however, because the missions rejected the proposal of state inspection to monitor the quality of missionary education. The Catholic missions eventually won this battle and extended their monopoly on the development of colonial education until 1954, just a few years before independence (Depaepe and van Rompaey 1995: 60–3).

The rise in government expenditures during the second half of the 1920s only sufficed to meet the increasing costs of enrollment expansion, especially as financial hardship increased during the interwar years. The number of mission schools and students expanded at a much faster rate than the domestically raised funds of the Christian missions. Local communities thus had to make substantial contributions in kind, such as food, clothing, and the supply of unpaid child labor on the mission fields. Agricultural work was a standard part of the curriculum in the rural mission schools and served a double purpose: it helped to teach discipline, docility, and organization, while generating an additional source of revenue to finance local missionary activities. On the other hand, the costs of Catholic mission schools could be kept at a minimum because priests and nuns went without salaries; they were only entitled to compensation for cost of living expenses.

Money makes a big difference. In the Netherlands Indies, the quality gap between the European schools (*gouvernement scholen*) and non-European schools was obvious to contemporary observers (Brugmans 1938). Applications to Dutch language schools were far higher than the available places. European schools could hire better-trained teachers, reduce class sizes, and buy more advanced teaching equipment. From the *Koloniale Jaarcijfers* (1934), it appears that pupil–teacher ratios were considerably lower in the European schools – in 1932–3, 31.6 pupils per teacher compared to 49.4 in the *desa* schools and 50.7 in the Dutch–Chinese schools.

In both colonies, however, the village schools, regardless of whether they were subsidized, constituted the backbone of the expansion of popular education. The key distinction between the village schools in Indonesia and the rural mission schools in the Congo relates to the secular nature of the curriculum in the former and the emphasis on religious and moral instruction in the latter. In the *desa* schools, reading and writing (in the vernacular) and arithmetic formed the core subjects. The curriculum was standardized, graded, and subject to state inspection. The primary objective of the missions in Congo was to spread Christianity. No hard evidence exists for the hypothesis that the quality of education was on average higher in the *desa* schools than in the rural mission schools in the Congo, but there are reasons to assume this was the case: children who entered a *desa* school could potentially make their way to a European university, which was unthinkable for a Congolese child.

## 7.6 Education for self-determination

Different colonial education systems shaped different contexts for post-colonial governance. This condition worked on at least three levels. First, the nationalist leaders who steered Indonesia toward independence had a distinctively better educational background than the Congolese leaders. Second, the Indonesian leaders such as Hatta and Sukarno could relate to major ideological undercurrents in society, which had a basis in indigenous education movements that were largely absent in the Congo. Third, although the numbers of university-educated were small, Indonesian leaders faced the checks and balances of an emerging intellectual class that was not entirely absent in the Congo, but certainly less developed.

The Japanese occupation of the Netherlands Indies uncovered the military and political weaknesses of the Dutch and furthered the diffusion of anti-colonial sentiment among the Indonesian population. The large-scale mobilization of Indonesian youth in the armed forces under Japanese rule connected an enormous amount of human energy to revolutionary ideas and military means of power. Moreover, the tyrannical rule of yet another foreign occupier endorsed the desire among the Indonesian people to determine their own future. In this respect, the Indonesian declaration of independence in 1945 was a logical consequence of the Japanese retreat, a consequence that the Dutch tragically failed to understand (Ricklefs 2008: 244–8).

The spirit of independence and revolution unleashed an enormous demand for schooling. Mass education now opened the doors to socio-economic mobility –

doors that had remained closed for as long as people remembered. Job opportunities in the civil service expanded enormously and were highly attractive to students and former soldiers. Politicians were eager to hand out higher-income jobs in return for political support. The Indonesian language became the standard throughout the education system and was also used in all official communications of the state and the mass media. A major achievement of the Sukarno regime (1945–67) was the facilitation of this great expansionist wave without a complete overhaul of the system. Grade repetition and pre-completion drop-out rates remained high in primary education (around 60 percent in the 1950s), but these rates did not inhibit the influx of a rapidly growing group of students into secondary and tertiary education (Ricklefs 2008: 274–5).

Universities were established in various parts of the country, and some of the long-established institutions achieved respectable standards. The University of Indonesia (Universitas Indonesia), which was one of these top-rated academic institutes, originated as a colonial school for medical assistants established in 1851. In 1898, the colonial government transformed this school into a full-fledged medical specialist training institute, called STOVIA (School tot Opleiding van Inlandsche Artsen). The nine-year education program combined aspects of non-academic and university education. The Bandung Institute of Technology, another top institute, was the oldest technology-oriented university in Indonesia and evolved out of the Technische Hoogeschool in Bandung established in 1920.

The graduates of these institutes were to fulfill a key role in Indonesia's independence movement. Sukarno himself was a product of the Indo-European school system. His father was a village school teacher at Java. Sukarno first completed three years of primary education in the vernacular and continued at a European primary school. In 1915, he attended the Hogere Burger School (HBS), which represented the highest level of Western secondary education. In 1920, he enrolled in the Technical School in Bandung and was among the first students to graduate as an engineer in 1925. His background in Western higher education had a decisive impact on his conception of the importance of education for self-determination, both on a personal and on a political level (Giebels 1999). Mohammed Hatta, Sukarno's closest companion, pursued a similar route. After his secondary school in Batavia he traveled to the Netherlands to study economics and business at the Higher Business School in Rotterdam (currently the Erasmus University). He stayed in the Netherlands for 11 years (1921–32). During this period, he began campaigning for non-cooperation and mass action against the colonial oppressor, activities for which he was detained in the Netherlands and again later in Indonesia.

The key figures dominating the political scene during the early years of independence in the Congo had a different background. They grew up when the segregation policies were still strictly maintained. Closed access to higher offices in the colonial administration and key positions in international commerce and the mining industry restricted the need to offer higher levels of non-vocational training to the indigenous population. The intellectual development of the early independence leaders was largely shaped by the jobs they fulfilled in the colonial economy. Lumumba, Kasavubu, Mobutu, and Tshombe, the four figureheads of the Congo crisis (1960–5), had all attended Christian mission schools. Lumumba began his working career as a postal clerk and a traveling beer salesman. His highest qualification was a one-year course at the government post office training school (McKown 1969). Kasavubu was trained as a teacher at a Catholic missionary school. Mobutu's educational career was completed in the army, at the School for Non-Commissioned Officers in Luluaburg, where he followed a two-year course in accounting and secretarial work. He rose to be a sergeant-accountant, the highest rank attainable for an African soldier in the Congolese army in his day (Etambala 1996). Tshombe was also trained as an accountant and pursued the career of his father in the Katangese retail business sector.

Although black children began to be admitted to European secondary schools in the 1950s, their numbers remained small. Lovanium, the first university in the Congo, was founded near Leopoldville (Kinshasa) in 1954. The university admitted black students but, ironically, the first cohorts of Congolese students had not completed secondary school yet. In 1956, a state university was established in Elisabethville (Lubumbashi) (Mantels 2007). On the eve of independence (1960) just a handful of Congolese were enrolled in tertiary education and even fewer actually held a university degree. In 1960, 13 students were enrolled in natural sciences at the tertiary level, 18 in engineering, 71 in the medical sciences, and 26 in agricultural sciences. Together this group formed 30 percent of the total 423 students. Most of the students were enrolled in the humanities and social science faculties, not in the technical faculties. Moreover, the majority of these students were European, many about to leave the country (Mantels 2007; UNESCO 1965).

Various accounts of the negotiations for independence at the 1960 round-table conference (*ronde tafel conferentie*) in Brussels stress the gap in political cunning between the young group of Congolese representatives and the *haute couture* of Belgium's professional politicians (Etambala 1996: 31–3; van Reybrouck 2010: 278–80). The Congolese delegation was supported by several Belgian advisors who had had a much more advanced education than the delegates themselves. The Congolese held jobs as accountants, clerks, journalists, school teachers, and tradesmen, but only a few of them held positions that provided a deep understanding of overarching national political and economic interests. Hence, naivety was the reason why the Congolese transition government agreed with the Belgian government to dissolve the Comité Spécial du Katanga, which formally left the new Congolese state with just a minority share in the Union Minière, the biggest mining operation in the Congo (Buelens 2007), one of the many opportunities that the independent Congolese leadership missed to preserve a sound fiscal state in the long run.

At just about the time that Mobutu conquered the stage in the Congo to hold power for more than three decades (1965–97), Suharto, the army general, displaced Sukarno. Suharto stayed in power for a similar period (1967–98). Suharto and Mobutu rank among the most cruel and conscienceless dictators of the

twentieth century. They have been responsible for mass murder and their appe-
tite for self-enrichment has become legendary. Their methods were similar. By
monopolizing the most profitable industries of the country (such as copper and
oil), they managed in no time to become the wealthiest persons of their country
(see Abbeloos, Chapter 12 below). Both dictators controlled power by combin-
ing an extensive system of political patronage, firm control over the army, and a
sustained threat of terror against political opponents. Both received support from
the Western world (especially the US) for their outspoken anti-Communism.

However, the economic policies of Mobutu's "Mobutuism" and Suharto's
"New Order" revealed sharp contrasts, not only in name. Suharto managed to
combine rent extraction for his personal clientele with an impressive record of
macro-economic growth, from which the vast majority of Indonesians eventually
reaped the benefits. Scholars widely agree that the macro-economic policies of
the Suharto government contributed positively to the structural transformation of
the Indonesian economy and the rapid reduction of urban and rural poverty rates
(Booth 1998; Dick et al. 2002; Frankema and Lindblad 2006; Hill 2000; Thee
2006; Warr 2006). With the benefit of hindsight, the start of the Suharto era in
Indonesia can be regarded as a structural break with a period of recurrent inflation, increasing state debt, declining foreign exchange reserves, and prolonged
economic stagnation (Glassburner 1971).

Can the success of Suharto's economic program and the failure of Mobutu's
be fully explained by personal differences in economic and political cunning?
This question is difficult to answer. Suharto did assemble a team of experts to
get the economy back on track in a deliberate attempt to restore social order.
These experts were capable of translating the New Order's development trilogy
"growth, stability, and equity" into a range of clearly defined objectives focusing
on achieving self-sufficiency in food production (namely rice) and, subsequently,
on an intensive program of industrialization based on Indonesia's comparative
advantages (Thee 2006). Suharto benefited not only from the available necessary
expertise of university-trained economists, but also, at a much broader level,
from the existence of a class of entrepreneurs sufficiently equipped with knowledge and organizational capacities to realize the potential of modern technology
in the major sectors of the economy. So it seems that the Indonesian education
system had prepared Indonesian society for rapid development in the technical
and economic realm.

Mobutu was aware of the importance of restoring economic stability for political survival in his early years and, like Suharto, squandered huge amounts of
money on megalomaniac projects (such as dams, steel mills, and an aircraft
industry) that never produced the envisaged return. But unlike Suharto, Mobutu
was known for his distrust of intellectuals, which some biographers have attributed to his removal from secondary school after extending his holidays without
permission (Zinzen 2010: 8). Mobutu allowed the education system to collapse
with the fiscal state, and the education system did not have the capacity to resist,
let alone to challenge, the personal power of a man who, over the years, became
increasingly detached from reality and managed to pull the rest of the country

into chaos with him. One cannot help but think that the virtual absence of any checks on Mobutu's power (except for international, namely Western, pressure that was deliberately kept minimal for political reasons) could only have occurred in a country where the basis of democratic control through intellectual leadership was so weak.

## 7.7 Conclusion

This chapter has offered a comparative analysis of the evolution of the colonial education systems in the Congo and Indonesia by arguing that the difference between the state-based education system in Indonesia and the mission-based system in the Congo was not impressive at the primary level. The average quality of education may have been better in Indonesia because of higher and more reliable budgets, teacher training programs, and curricular control, but enrollment expansion was more rapid in the Congo. The key differences were twofold. First, in Indonesia, access to higher forms of education was open to a small class of privileged Indonesians, while the doors remained strictly shut to even the brightest Congolese children after one or two years of secondary education. Second, in the wake of early nationalist tendencies, indigenous communities were allowed, within certain boundaries, to establish their own schools. Indonesian schooling movements, such as Taman Siswa, partly testified to a higher degree of political consciousness in the 1920s than was present in the Congo in the 1950s, and partly also to a less repressive response to the emergence of (presumed) anti-colonial and nationalist movements; the Dutch tolerated more not because they wanted to, but because they were forced to.

The prominent leaders of Indonesian independence, Sukarno and Hatta, had enjoyed a substantially better education than any of the Congolese independence leaders, but this does not automatically translate into different post-colonial economic policies. Mobutu's lack of understanding, or perhaps his unwillingness to understand, the prerequisite of solid debt management for the long-term stability of a national economy was in many ways comparable to Sukarno's blindness to the economic mechanisms behind hyperinflation. Under Sukarno, the economy and parts of the state administration fell into disarray, especially during the 1960s. However, the Indonesian education system did not collapse. Surprisingly, in retrospect, Suharto was able to bring the Indonesian economy quickly back on track, helped by a team of highly trained economic experts. Equally surprisingly in retrospect, Mobutu remained in power for more than 30 years in a state system that stopped providing even the most basic services to the common people. Only a few other countries in the world (such as Afghanistan, Somalia, and Haiti) have witnessed a similar collapse of their education systems, a collapse which has been detrimental to socio-economic progress in all of these countries. Whether this would have happened if a significant part of the Congolese elite had gained access to higher education and higher administrative offices is difficult to know, but it surely would have made this scenario less likely.

## Notes

1 I would like to thank all the participants of the workshops in Utrecht (December 2010) and Antwerp (October 2011) for their comments on earlier drafts of this chapter. I am grateful for financial support from the Dutch Science Foundation (NWO) to my VENI-research project on *The Colonial Origins of Inequality*.
2 The policy document is available online: www.abbol.com/ (see under "schoolbooks project," then under "Legislation and Curricula") (accessed 4 October 2011).
3 Phelps-Stokes is a privately funded non-profit organization based in New York, established by one of the first female philanthropists, Caroline Phelps-Stokes. The organization aimed to bridge intercultural differences and to improve the social and economic conditions of underprivileged communities and societies in and outside America, especially through educational development. The Phelps-Stokes fund was invited by the British Colonial Office to send a commission to investigate educational conditions in West, South, and Equatorial Africa. The reports of this and the second (1924) Phelps-Stokes Commissions to Africa provided the foundation of interwar British colonial education policy in Africa, but also affected policy debates elsewhere. See Jones (1922, 1925).
4 In the first decade of the twentieth century, the colonial government deliberately transferred part of its educational responsibility to the missions in some of the Outer Islands, such as the Moluccas, under the promise of state subsidies (Hartgerink 1942).
5 Dutch secondary education in the Netherlands Indies basically offered two types. The MULO (Meer Uitgebreid Lager Onderwijs) offered a lower-level, non-vocational sequel to primary education, and the HBS (Hogere Burger School) catered for the higher-level students.
6 The Christian mission schools were also criticized for their focus on religious education, but to a lesser extent.
7 After World War I, Belgium also acquired the mandate over Ruanda-Urundi, granted by the newly established League of Nations.
8 This is not to say that the Belgians adopted a model of full-scale direct rule. In the provinces, indigenous African leaders were either respected or appointed to rule and take care of local affairs.
9 These statistics also reveal that the *desa* schools on Java and Madura performed significantly better than in the Outer Islands.
10 The gender distribution of literacy was unequal in both countries: 57.2 percent male versus 29.6 percent female in Indonesia and 49 percent male versus 14 percent female in the Congo.

## References

*Annuaire statistique de la Belgique et du Congo belge* (1911–6) Brussels.

Banarjee, A.V. and Duflo, E. (2011) *Poor Economics. A Radical Rethinking of the Way to Fight Global Poverty*, New York: Public Affairs.

Birdsall, N., Ross, D., and Sabot, R. (1997) *Education, Growth and Inequality*, Washington DC: Inter-American Development Bank and Johns Hopkins University Press.

Boone, A.T. (1996) "Onderwijs en opvoeding in de Nederlandse koloniën 1595–1975," *Pedagogisch Tijdschrift*, 21: 87–99.

Booth, A. (1998) *Indonesian Economic Development in the Nineteenth and Twentieth Centuries: A History of Missed Opportunities*, London: Macmillan.

Briffaerts, J. (1999) "De schoolstrijd in Belgisch Congo 1930–1958," in E. Witte, J. de Groot and J. Tyssens (eds.) *Het schoolpact van 1958. Ontstaan, grondlijnen en toepassing van een Belgisch compromis*, Brussels: VUB Press.

Brugmans, I.J. (1938) *Geschiedenis van het Onderwijs in Nederlandsch-Indië*, Groningen: Wolters.

Buelens, F. (2007) *Congo 1885–1960: Een financieel-economische geschiedenis*, Berchem: EPO.

Callego, F.A. and Woodberry, R. (2010) "Christian Missionaries and Education in Former African Colonies: How Competition Mattered," *Journal of African Economies*, 19: 294–329.

Clemens, M.A. (2004) "The Long Walk to School: International Education Goals in Historical Perspective," Center for Global Development Working Paper No. 37, Center for Global Development.

Cogneau, D. and Moradi, A. (2011) "Borders that Divide: Education and Religion in Ghana and Togo since Colonial Times," CSAE Working Paper 2011/21, Centre for the Study of African Economies.

Coleman, J.S. (1954) "Nationalism in Tropical Africa," *The American Political Science Review*, 48: 404–26.

Depaepe, M. (1996) " 'Rien ne va plus'. De ondergang van de koloniale educatieve structuren in Zaïre (1960–1995)," *Pedagogisch Tijdschrift*, 21: 145–63.

Depaepe, M. and van Rompaey, L. (1995) *In het teken van de bevoogding. De educatieve actie in Belgisch-Kongo (1908–1960)*, Leuven: Garant.

Departement van Economische Zaken (1934) *Statistisch Jaaroverzicht van Nederlands-Indië over het jaar 1933*, Batavia: Landsdrukkerij.

Dick, H., Houben, V.J.H. Lindblad, J.T., and Thee K.W. (2002) *The Emergence of a National Economy. An Economic History of Indonesia, 1800–2000*, Leiden: KILTV Press.

Dunkerley, M.E. (2009) "Education Policies and the Development of the Colonial State in the Belgian Congo, 1916–1939," PhD thesis, University of Exeter.

Etambala, Z. (1996) *Het Zaïre van Mobutu*, Leuven: Davidsfonds.

Frankema, E.H.P. (2009) "The Expansion of Mass Education in Twentieth Century Latin America: A Global Comparative Perspective," *Revista de Historia Económica*, 27: 359–95.

Frankema, E.H.P. (2011) "Colonial Taxation and Government Spending in British Africa, 1880–1940: Maximizing Revenue or Minimizing Effort?," *Explorations in Economic History*, 48: 136–49.

Frankema, E.H.P. (forthcoming) "The Origins of Formal Education in Sub-Saharan Africa: Was British Rule More Benign?," *European Review of Economic History*.

Frankema, E.H.P. and Lindblad, J.T. (2006) "Technological Development and Economic Growth in Indonesia and Thailand since 1960," *ASEAN Economic Bulletin*, 23: 303–24.

Furnivall, J.S. (1943) *Educational Progress in Southeast Asia*, New York: Institute of Pacific Relations.

Giebels, L.J. (1999) *Soekarno. Biografie*, Amsterdam: Bakker.

Glassburner, B. (1971) *Indonesian Economic Policy after Sukarno*, Ithaca, NY: Cornell University Press.

Hall, R.L., Rodeghier, M., and Useem, B. (1986) "Effects of Education on Attitude to Protest," *American Sociological Review*, 51: 564–73.

Hartgerink, H.J.H. (1942) *De Staten-Generaal en het Volksonderwijs in Nederlandsch-Indië, 1848–1918*, Groningen: Wolters.

Helpman, E. (2004) *The Mystery of Economic Growth*, Cambridge, Mass.: The Belknap Press of Harvard University Press.

Hill, H. (2000) *The Indonesian Economy*, Cambridge: Cambridge University Press.

Johnson, H.B. (1967) "The Location of Christian Missions in Africa," *Geographical Review*, 57: 168–202.

Jones, T.J. (1922) *Education in Africa: a Study of West, South and Equatorial Africa by the African Education Commission under the Auspices of the Phelps-Stokes Fund and Foreign Mission Societies of North America and Europe*, New York: Phelps-Stokes Fund.

Jones, T.J. (1925) *Education in East Africa: a Study of East, Central and South Africa by the Second African Education Commission under the Auspices of the Phelps-Stokes Fund, in Cooperation with the International Education Board*, New York: Phelps-Stokes Fund.

Khan, M.H. (2000) *Rents, Efficiency and Growth*, Cambridge, Mass.: Cambridge University Press.

Klasen, S. (2002) "Low Schooling for Girls, Slower Growth for All? Cross-country Evidence on the Effect of Gender Inequality in Education on Economic Development," *The World Bank Economic Review*, 16: 345–73.

Kuznets, S. (1966) *Modern Economic Growth. Rate, Structure and Spread*, New Haven, Conn.: Yale University Press.

Lelyveld, J.E.A.M. (1996) "Koloniale pedagogiek in Nederlands-Indië," *Pedagogisch Tijdschrift*, 21: 101–14.

Liesenborghs, O. (1939) "Het Belgisch Koloniaal Onderwijswezen," *Vlaamsch Opvoedkundig Tijdschrift*, 21: 448–90.

Lindert, P.H. (2004) *Growing Public. Social Spending and Economic Growth since the Eighteenth Century*, Cambridge, Mass.: Cambridge University Press.

Lloyd, C.B., Kaufman, C.E., and Hewett, P. (2000) "The Spread of Primary Schooling in Sub-Saharan Africa: Implications for Fertility Change," *Population and Development Review*, 26: 483–515.

Lucas, R. (2002) *Lectures on Economic Growth*, Cambridge, Mass.: Harvard University Press.

McKown, R. (1969) *Lumumba: A Biography*, London: Doubleday.

Maddison, A. (2010) "Historical Statistics: Statistics on World Population, GDP, and Per Capita GDP, 1–2000 AD," www.ggdc.net/maddison/ (accessed April 21, 2012).

Mankiw, G.N., Romer, D., and Weil, D.N. (1992) "A Contribution to the Empirics of Economic Growth," *Quarterly Journal of Economics*, 107: 407–37.

Mantels, R. (2007) *Geleerd in de tropen, Leuven, Congo en de wetenschap, 1885–1960*, Leuven: Universitaire Pers.

Ministère de l'Intérieur (1911–60) *Annuaire Statistique de la Belgique et du Congo Belge*, Brussels: Imprimerie A. Lesigne.

Mokyr, J. (2002) *The Gifts of Athena. Historical Origins of the Knowledge Economy*, Princeton, NJ: Princeton University Press.

Nelson, R.R. (2000) *The Sources of Economic Growth*, Cambridge, Mass.: Harvard University Press.

Noer, D. (1973) *The Modernist Muslim Movement in Indonesia, 1900–1942*, Singapore: Oxford University Press.

North, D.C., Wallis, J.J. and Weingast, B.R. (2009) *Violence and Social Orders. A Conceptual Framework for Interpreting Recorded Human History*, Cambridge Mass.: Cambridge University Press.

Nunn, N. (2010) "Religious Conversion in Colonial Africa," *American Economic Review: Papers & Proceedings*, 100: 147–52.

Oliver, R. (1962) *The Missionary Factor in East Africa*, London: Longmans, Green.

Pakenham, T. (1992) *The Scramble for Africa. The White Man's Conquest of the Dark Continent from 1876–1912*, New York: Avon Books.

Richens, P. (2009) "The Economic Legacies of the 'Thin White Line': Indirect Rule and the Comparative Development of Sub-Saharan Africa," Working Paper No. 131/09, London School of Economics and Political Science.

Ricklefs, M.C. (2008) *A History of Modern Indonesia since c. 1200*, Basingstoke: Palgrave Macmillan.

*Statistical Abstract for the British Empire* (1938–40) London: HM Stationery Office.

Steenbrink, K.A. (1974) "Pesantren, Madrasah, Sekolah. Recente ontwikkelingen in Indonesisch islamonderricht," PhD thesis, Katholieke Universiteit Nijmegen.

Stengers, J. and Vansina, J. (1985) *King Leopold's Congo, 1886–1908*, Cambridge: Cambridge University Press.

Sutton, F.X. (1965) *Education and the Making of Modern Nations*, Princeton, NJ: Princeton University Press.

Thee, K.W. (2006) "Policies Affecting Indonesia's Industrial Technology Development," *ASEAN Economic Bulletin*, 23: 341–59.

Tsuchiya, K. (1987) *Democracy and Leadership: The Rise of the Taman Siswa Movement in Indonesia*, Honolulu: University of Hawaii Press.

UNESCO (1965) *Statistical Yearbook 1964*, Paris: UNESCO.

van der Veur, P.W. (1969) *Education and Social Change in Colonial Indonesia. Progress and Procrastination in Education in Indonesia prior to World War II*, Athens: Ohio University Press.

van der Wal, S.L. (1963) *Het onderwijsbeleid in Nederlands-Indië 1900–1940: Een bronnenpublikatie*, Groningen: J.B. Wolters.

van Leeuwen, B. (2007) "Human Capital and Economic Growth in India, Indonesia and Japan. A Quantitative Analysis, 1890–2000," PhD thesis, Utrecht University.

van Reybrouck, D. (2010) *Congo. Een Geschiedenis*, Amsterdam: De Bezige Bij.

Vansina, J. (2010) *Being Colonized. The Kuba Experience in Rural Congo, 1880–1960*, Madison: The University of Wisconsin Press.

Warr, P. (2006) "Poverty and Growth in Southeast Asia," *ASEAN Economic Bulletin*, 23: 279–302.

White, B.W. (1996) "Talk about School: Education and the Colonial Project in French and British Africa (1860–1960)," *Comparative Education*, 32: 9–25.

Witte, E., Craeybeckx, J., and Meynen, A. (2009) *Political History of Belgium from 1830 Onwards*, Brussels: ASP.

Zinzen, W. (2010) *Mobutu. De luipaard*, Antwerpen: Luster.

# 8 (Un)freedom

## Colonial labor relations in Belgian Congo and the Netherlands Indies compared

*Vincent Houben and Julia Seibert*

### 8.1 Introduction

The comparative study of colonial labor regimes is as old as colonialism itself. In the age of formal imperialism colonial powers were looking for ways of mobilizing the resources of the areas conquered in Asia and Africa to their own benefit. Specialists of the time were on the lookout for successful examples in neighboring European colonies and sometimes their findings resulted in books which are still well known (Day 1904; Furnivall 1948). To what extent colonial states were really successful in extracting surplus from their ventures overseas is a matter still discussed by historians today (Vanthemsche 2007; Maddison 1989). The long-term consequences of colonial rule, especially in the form of structural deficiencies leading to enduring poverty, have also been a topic of continuous expert debate (Rodney 1981; Austin 2008; Booth 1998). As part of the recent upsurge of world history or history of interconnectedness and entanglement, questions of how colonial states mobilized labor have reemerged (van der Linden 2008). Within the framework of global labor history a comparison between the Netherlands Indies and colonial Congo seems particularly promising, since the two are genealogically connected. It is a matter of fact that King Leopold II of Belgium got his inspiration for exploiting the Congo from the Netherlands Indies. The book by J.W.B. Money, published in 1861, on the Cultivation System in Java inspired him to set up a system of agricultural extraction in the Congo too (Stengers 1977; Wesseling 1991: 106).

The two country cases merit comparison whilst in both colonies a specific interplay between state and private capitalism produced a system of forced labor, which was marked by violence and coercion, yet had different long-term effects. It is obvious that the form that colonial exploitation took depended on local availability of economic resources, particularly land, natural resources and labor, which were necessary preconditions for setting up a line of production geared to the demands of the world market. In this way, world demand was supposed to function as a leverage to generate additional income in the mother countries concerned. During the earlier phases of colonial rule European regimes, with the exception of settler colonies of mass immigration like the USA or Australia, had to adapt to already present local systems of social organization and fiscal rule. From the 1880s onward,

Europe was able to lay down its own infrastructure in hitherto largely empty lands and import all the necessary factors of production to establish highly profitable ventures. In the Netherlands Indies the format of early colonial exploitation was that of the village, that of the late (and post-)colonial phase the plantation and mine. In early colonialism state agents often played the decisive role whereas during late colonialism private entrepreneurs and investors seemed to be in command. In the colonial Congo, however, both systems continued to coexist but the mining and plantation sector expanded rapidly in the first half of the twentieth century (Peemans 1997: 23–44). If this distinction between two phases of economic exploitation is accepted, the question needs to be raised of how the colonial economies of the Netherlands Indies and the Congo can be compared and what conclusions can be drawn for the kind of labor regime that emerged in their wake.

In the Congo, after a phase of very harsh exploitation under the flag of the Congo Free State, colonial rule by the Belgian state only started late, i.e., from 1908. In Java state exploitation on a grand scale began in 1830, although private plantations were set up much earlier, in West Java in the seventeenth century and in the Principalities of Central Java in the early 1800s. The state labor regime in Java was compulsory between 1830 and 1870 but was then phased out, whereas in the Congo the *culture obligatoire* – under a law which introduced forced crop growing into the village and household economy – started in 1917 and continued till the end of colonial rule in 1960. In contrast, outside Java the plantation coolie system was based upon indenture between 1884 and 1931 and then turned into "free" labor. In Congo coerced labor was the main source of colonial employed labor before 1908; thereafter the Belgian colonial authorities tried to establish a system of free wage labor but returned to compulsion during World War I (Seibert 2010). In the Netherlands Indies, on Java, the sequence went from private compulsory to public compulsory to free labor, whereas on the Outer Islands a coercive, public–private labor regime initiated in the 1880s was replaced by free labor only in 1931.

Besides Java being the initial source of inspiration for King Leopold II there existed no direct genealogical interconnection between the labor regimes in the Netherlands Indies and the colonial Congo. It is conceivable that the Belgians made use of colonial knowledge of Dutch or French provenance to set up their colony in the Congo, and that foreign specialists played a role in it, or that future Belgian colonial administrators were instructed in comparative colonialism at the *écoles coloniale*s in Brussels and Antwerp. However, a direct comparison between the two colonies might help us to understand in what way colonial labor regimes were shaped both by the dynamics of global demand and by local factors on the ground. Both colonial economies depended on an efficient use of production factors, of which land, natural resources, and labor were those dependent on local availability.

## 8.2 Colonial rural exploitation in Java

In West Java, an area close to the Dutch administrative center in Batavia and Buitenzorg, private domains (*particuliere landerijen*) were sold to individual owners from 1627 until the early 1830s. These estates were run as manorial properties in which the residents acted more or less as serfs. Some of these estates, such as Pamanukan and Ciasem, were very large and prefigured the format of late colonial plantations (Boomgaard 1989; Knight 1968: 43–7). A coercive labor regime also existed in the adjacent West Javanese area of Priangan, into which the Dutch East India Company introduced coffee cultivation under a system of forced delivery (see Thee, Chapter 2 above). This system was introduced during the early eighteenth century and lasted until World War I, prefiguring the predominant form of state exploitation in other parts of Java after 1830 (Breman 2010). Finally, starting from the 1820s and with the financial support of coastal trading houses, in the native states of Central Java local land leasers of Eurasian descent managed to set up their own estates. On these the resident population grew sugar cane, indigo, and tobacco, prefiguring large-scale private plantation agriculture, which emerged in Java toward the end of the nineteenth century (Houben 1994: 257–68).

The Cultivation System on Java, in place mainly between 1830 and 1870 in the areas under direct Dutch rule, was not a unified system but rather a collection of local arrangements. It has been defined as

> that form of agricultural-industrial exploitation of Java in which the government used its authority and influence to force the peasantry to grow tropical export products in return for payments that were unilaterally fixed and low; these products were sold for the benefit of the treasury.
>
> (Fasseur 1992: 27)

To be more concrete, the Javanese peasantry were compelled to devote up to one-fifth of the arable land to the cultivation of cash crops (mainly coffee, indigo, and sugar) and, at least in theory, also invested one-fifth of their labor in these forced cultivations. In return the peasants were paid a small cash wage but, contrary to earlier plans, were still liable to the land revenue tax – so-called land rent (Hugenholtz 2008). It is clear that the labor burden of the Cultivation System exceeded traditional forms of *corvée* by far and that, on top of cultivation services new forms of *corvée* were also demanded, especially for establishing a functioning infrastructure on the island (Boomgaard 1989: 34–6). Therefore the labor regime installed by this state-run system was highly exploitative; its output was so huge that it inspired colonial experts elsewhere (Money 1861; Day 1904).

How the Cultivation System functioned in practice and what its consequences were for Javanese society has been the subject of an extensive historiography. On the basis of local and regional colonial records, Elson (1994) produced an encompassing study, which has not been challenged. The Cultivation System in Java produced substantial social change, as village institutions were transformed and labor relations revamped. Spread-out hamlets were concentrated into larger, well-regulated villages; the role of the village chief was strengthened since he became the person in charge of the collection of the land revenue tax as well as the labor services for the Cultivation System. Thus instead of the Cultivation System acting as a leveling force spreading the burden of increased labor requirements among all peasants, hierarchies within the village were strengthened. An increasing number of people became landless and ended up at the bottom of Javanese society. The system turned out to be extremely remunerative for the Dutch, since they were able to build successfully upon existing local methods of mobilizing labor. As a big incentive to the European and local officials to cooperate, so-called cultivation percentages were paid out on an individual basis. Elson refutes the view that labor mobilization was simply a matter of strengthening the feudal character of socio-political relations, however. Regular and sustained maintenance of an intensified labor input required a new format of work, which the Dutch labeled cultivation services (*cultuurdiensten*) and to which more people were liable than ever before. Elson calls this a "peasant labor policy" characterized by a mixture of physical coercion and the offer of stakes in the form of crop payments and redistribution of village lands (Elson 1994: chapters 6 and 7). We should bear in mind, however, that due to a decline of mortality the Javanese population started to grow very rapidly in the nineteenth century and that therefore the supply of labor increased as well. Java had barely 4.5 million inhabitants in 1815 but in 1880 this figure had increased to 19.5 million and in 1900 to 28.3 million.

In the Dutch parliament in the middle of the nineteenth century the liberals carried the day and because of this and internal problems the Cultivation System was dismantled from 1870 onward to make room for private enterprise (see Thee, Chapter 2). This led to a marked increase in the amount of land leased out and a steep increase in the production of sugar, coffee, and tobacco on large private estates (Booth 1998: 30). Instead of colonial officials, now plantation staff got in contact with the chiefs of surrounding villages in order to recruit labor for the planting, harvesting, transportation, and eventual factory processing of export crops. In addition, because of further population growth, the number of landless peasants had increased to the extent that there was enough supply, so a system of "free" wage labor could be adopted. Wage levels were even dropping in a period in which demand for labor increased (van Schaik 1986: 106–13). However, it seems that even in an era of liberalism, compulsory labor did not disappear altogether. The peasant population was still taxed to deliver different kinds of services, and entrepreneurs were quick to pick up on this and the colonial administration slow to respond (Furnivall 1944: 185–7, 217). Although cultivation services were abolished, other labor services were still levied. More people than before were mobilized through more informal recruitment mechanisms based on the mediation of village chiefs (Breman 1983: 23–5). This liberal model of rural exploitation in Java continued until the end of the colonial period.

## 8.3 The labor regime on the Outer Islands

From the 1870s a spatial shift occurred in the colonial economy of the Netherlands Indies. Until then, Java was the major location of cash crop production, but subsequently, major plantations and mines were opened up on Sumatra, Borneo, and other islands of the archipelago, integrating the Dutch colony more fully into the global economy. New products also came to the fore, notably copra, rubber, tobacco, coal, and oil. Parallel to large-scale Western enterprise, for some products such as rubber an expansion of smallholder export production occurred (see Clarence-Smith, Chapter 9 below). The extension of colonial rule as well as an upsurge in private investment resulted in a new kind of alliance between state and capital, which again had severe implications for the labor regime in these locations. Nevertheless the huge insular zone covered by the so-called Outer Islands was marked by substantial economic differentiation, some areas remaining outside the forces of the world market and other fully enmeshed in it.[1]

Whereas in Java, as a result of fast population growth, labor had become abundant toward the end of the nineteenth century, in the Outer Islands labor was so scarce that recruitment from elsewhere was a precondition for setting up Western business. Thus, as in the Congo, the labor question started to preoccupy both politicians and entrepreneurs alike. Major issues included the recruitment and accommodation of hundreds of thousands of contract workers (so-called coolies) from Java, China, and India. Especially in Deli, on the northeast coast of Sumatra, a huge plantation area emerged, where by 1919 about 250,000 coolies were employed (see Thee, Chapter 2). By means of Coolie Ordinances, the first of which was issued in 1880, workers were tied to a particular employer for three years and subjected to a "penal clause" which made the breach of the work contract a criminal offence. Disciplinary measures, including corporal punishment, were regularly applied at work sites.[2] The system of Coolie Ordinances was abolished in 1931, when, as a consequence of the Great Depression, demand for labor plummeted and supply therefore became abundant.

Whereas rural exploitation in Java was located mainly in the village economy, the plantations and mining sites on the Outer Islands represented a form of capitalist production that could be found in many parts of the world during the late colonial period. Although elements of coercion were also prevalent on Java before and after 1870, forced labor was the cornerstone of the labor regime that drove the modern economy of the late colonial Netherlands Indies. As in Java, so-called "free labor" was not free at all; workers were subjected to various kinds of economic as well as extra-economic pressure and discipline. But the plantation, as a fenced-off site of large-scale export-oriented monoculture with a large, servile labor force, was a locus where exploitation was driven to the highest possible level. Nevertheless everyday realities for the workers differed substantially between regions, products, and phases of development. The linkages between the colonial administration and big business were also varied and even contentious at some junctures, despite the fact that state and capital both sought to maximize economic expansion.

## 8.4 New forms of unfree labor in the Belgian Congo

As in Java and the Outer Islands, the system of colonial exploitation in the Belgian Congo alternated between coercive and so-called free labor arrangements depending on the social, political, and economic context of the different regions in the territory. In 1908, when the Congo Free State became a Belgian colony, King Leopold's regime of force, which had been characterized by decades of brutal exploitation of Africans, was officially abolished. In the opinion of contemporary observers, the annexation marked the beginning of a "new era in Central African history" (Wauters 1911: 8). This sense of departure was furthered by a series of political, economic, and social reforms enacted by the Belgian parliament in 1908 and 1911, all of which were intended to readjust colonial policies in the Congo to make them more palatable to domestic and international audiences. Belgian colonial planners in particular tried to establish new ways for drawing economic benefits (*mise en valeur*) from the colony that was now administered by the state instead of a private individual.[3]

New policies focused on the depersonalization and bureaucratization of the exercise of power by Europeans. A new colonial constitution (*Charte Coloniale*) replaced Leopold's despotic form of rule with a Colonial Ministry and Colonial Council, whose policies were subject to parliamentary supervision and control. This new form of rule also made possible the adoption of a series of laws that allowed the administration to regulate the colonial economy in novel ways. New regulations in particular outlawed forced labor for private enterprises, imposed new taxes on the local population, and defined the rights and obligations of all parties to a labor contract. Altogether, these laws amounted to an attempt to establish European models of wage labor as the foundation for the mobilization of workers in the Congo – replacing, in effect, extra-economic force with contractual relations between employers and workers. The guiding idea was that imposing money taxes would force Congolese farmers and fishermen to earn cash incomes, giving them no choice but to engage with European-dominated sectors of the economy. Driven to earn wages, they would then find employment relations inspired by European models.

In the first years of Belgian rule, the colonial state focused in particular on the reorganization and development of the agricultural sector, especially the expansion of large-scale agricultural production, an effort which was characterized by close cooperation between the state and private interests. By the end of World War I, agricultural production was increasingly geared toward export cash crops, especially palm oil and cotton (see Buelens and Cassimon, Chapter 11 below). The British Lever Company was a driving force here, as it obtained huge land concessions, and, beginning in 1911, began to develop palm oil plantations in the northern and western part of the territory. In return for receiving these concessions, Lever developed the regional infrastructure, especially roads and railroads, which then could be used by the colonial state as well (Wilson 1968; Marchal 2008). The need for workers to harvest palm fruits and to build up a basic infrastructure for the processing and transportation of palm oil was enormous. Right from the beginning the newly established Lever Company in the Congo – the Huileries du Congo Belge (HCB) – was confronted with a severe labor shortage (Seibert 2012: 176–85). As in other sectors of the colonial economy, especially in the emerging mining sector in south Katanga, Belgian colonial planners and company managers did not succeed in mobilizing a sufficient number of Africans to engage in wage labor.

Africans remained reluctant to engage in wage labor supervised by Europeans, causing a chronic shortage of labor which came to affect all sectors of the colonial economy and led to stiff competition for labor among employers. The situation became more complicated, from the perspective of employers, because most workers signed labor contracts of only three or six months' duration, returning thereafter to their villages to reengage in subsistence agriculture. Employers had preferred such short-term contracts because neither the state nor employers had to pay benefits to these workers, knowing they would soon return to their villages. But the system could only succeed as long as there was a huge reservoir of workers in the countryside willing to sign these contracts, and this, increasingly, was not the case. Potentially, improving working conditions and paying higher wages might have motivated more Congolese to take up employment in the mines and on plantations – but neither employers nor the colonial administration favored such steps, and they thus played no significant role in the debates of the 1910s and 1920s.

However, there was more than just poor working conditions and low wages, along with a reluctance to leave their families behind, that kept Congolese men and women out of the plantations. An even more important reason for the slow acceptance of wage labor was that there still existed viable alternative uses for their time and effort that often were safer and more lucrative, and better fulfilled their personal preferences to maintain their traditional communal and social ties. One such activity was the production and sale of food crops to feed the workers on the plantations and mines. Because demand rose, prices were high, enabling African peasants to pay their cash taxes without having to resort to wage employment. This kind of work was not only more profitable; it also allowed local communities to organize their work efforts according to their own priorities and rhythms of daily life (Nelson 1994: 120). The colonial administration increasingly recognized that profitable trade in local food crops was a crucial factor behind their inability to recruit wage workers.[4] A report from Equateur, a province in the northern part of the colony, for example, stressed that peasants who traded in copal – a resin juice which was used in the manufacture of lacquers and varnishes – were unwilling to work on Lever's palm oil plantations (Engels 1921). The colonial state indeed feared that regions that were still largely dominated by subsistence farming, such as the east and north of the colony, would be economically so independent that they would escape the control of the administration (Engels 1921: 288–9). Indeed, expanding wage labor was thus a question not just of economic development but also of political control.

Yet Africans found wage labor unattractive not just because their own economy remained vibrant and profitable. They also feared the poor working conditions on plantations. Lever's plantations, for example, were infamous work sites among the Congolese, because cutting and collecting palm oil paid poorly and was physically demanding – so much so that plantation workers thought of themselves as slaves (Fieldhouse 1978: 512). Even Lever understood that things were difficult for its workers: its general manager, Sydney Edkins, reported that villagers refused to labor on a nearby plantation because they feared that taking on such work would mean an income so low that they would have to eat manioc without sauce, and would in addition take up the time needed to go fishing and hunting.[5]

To overcome the chronic labor shortage in the agricultural sector the government helped to reintroduce a system of forced labor. With the beginning of World War I the colonial state, together with private capitalists, legitimated the practice of forced recruiting of workers by an alleged need to overcome "African laziness," a powerful ideological trope that allowed for new degrees of violence.[6] As a result, coercion and violence spread across colonial work sites in the agricultural, mining, and transport sectors.[7] Another measure to motivate Africans to agree to more frequent and longer periods of employment with European firms was the imposition of the so-called poll tax. The poll tax itself was valued not only as a revenue source, but also because it forced people to work for wages, especially men, who were the main targets of labor recruiters. Indeed, tax increases were frequently and directly connected to local labor requirements. If a plantation required workers, it informed the colonial district officer, who then adjusted local poll taxes arbitrarily. Whoever was not able to pay the tax was immediately forced to sign up for compulsory labor.

Along with forced recruiting and taxation measures to mobilize workers, towards the end of World War I (in 1917) the colonial state introduced another form of forced labor inspired by the Cultivation System on Java. Edmond Leplae, agricultural expert in the Colonial Ministry in Brussels, introduced a program of so-called *cultures obligatoires* (forced cultivation) by which formerly independent peasants were compelled by law to grow certain crops – mostly cotton – for export markets (Likaka 1997: 45–6). From the distribution of seeds to the commercialization of the products, the colonial state controlled every step of the cultivation process. Rural cultivators who refused to produce these crops were penalized. The increase of peasant production not only brought economic benefits to the colonial state by drawing additional labor from extended families; it also allowed the state to tighten its grip on the everyday life of the rural population. State intervention in the production of agricultural commodities for global markets – such as cotton, coffee, and rice – helped to integrate more than one million peasants into the export economy in the 1920s (Peemans 1997: 34). Indeed, cotton production increased from 1000 tons in 1920 to 30,000 tons in 1930 (Brixhe 1953: 18–19).

Another consequence of the *cultures obligatoires* was the dissolution of local markets. Eventually, Belgian colonizers recognized that the reluctance of peasants to engage in wage labor on plantations was partly rooted in their continued ability to engage in a local economy not yet dominated by Europeans (Likaka 1997: 17–26). As a result, they set out to force peasants to sell cotton, rice, manioc, and coffee to European dealers at fixed prices. Pastor Referent Hensey, who was sent out by the Commission Permanente pour la Protection des

Indigènes – a colonial institution which was founded to protect the rights of the colonized – to investigate the situation of local people in the districts of Lulonga and Equateur in 1919, described local markets as a "comedy." Hensey observed that prices for cotton or food crops were not negotiated between the local producer or seller and the European dealers, but rather between the dealers themselves.[8] This clear abrogation of the free market, together with the introduction of forced crops, resulted in the reduction of local participation in the agricultural sector and, in general, dramatic changes for many Congolese subjects. Because their own economic initiative was systematically suppressed, the local peasantry became ever more dependent on the colonial export economy.

Market restrictions, forced labor recruitment, and direct taxes pushed Africans into wage labor. All these measures were a direct answer to the rising demand for, but lagged supply of, wage labor after 1910. Therefore, it is not surprising that punishment and violence have marked the collective memory of wage labor in the Congo. In nearly every oral history interview, recollections of labor during the interwar years are colored by memories of coercion. In fact, to this day, many Africans see wage work as a form of "slavery."[9]

## 8.5 Comparative observations

In both the Netherlands Indies and the Belgian Congo from, respectively, 1870 and 1908, the preferred system of labor mobilization was called a liberal system with "free" labor arrangements. However, in both cases "free labor" had to be molded by elements of coercion. The crucial difference, however, was that the system of compulsory cultivation was reintroduced in 1917 in the Congo, whereas the transition to liberalism in the Netherlands Indies was marked by the final abolition of the state-led Cultivation System but increasing use of indentured coolie workers in private domains on the Outer Islands (see the discussion on the Deli tobacco plantations in Sumatra by Thee, Chapter 2).

In the Congo the supply of labor was insufficient, but in Java it had become abundant in the course of the nineteenth century. Nevertheless, in both colonies labor codes were introduced that inserted coercion into free wage labor contracts and gave employers ample room for taking disciplinary measures. Despite the growing numbers of landless, many Javanese were not willing to move overseas (*tanah sabrang*) since they feared unknown places. Congolese peasants preferred to stay in their villages since there was enough work available there. Colonial discourse in both colonial situations attributed this behavior to a deficient work ethic (or "laziness") but there were rational considerations behind this. The global market, and especially business cycles, had a major impact on labor relations. As global demand rose, so did the demand for labor and the institutional mechanisms to provide for it; in times of depression this correlation turned the other way. Changes of product and production sites (the village or the plantation) were also dictated by developments in the global market and for this reason similar economic configurations came to the fore in the Congo and the Netherlands Indies.

The state was heavily involved in every form of labor regime in the Netherlands Indies and the Belgian Congo. The state had a direct stake in economic expansion, either through direct sales revenues (through the Cultivation System in Java or the *cultures obligatoires* in the Belgian Congo, for instance) or through the taxation of private trade. During the late colonial phase the state facilitated private investors by trying to offer them a good physical infrastructure and a favorable business environment, for instance by issuing labor codes that were biased in favor of the employer. The development of labor unions was restricted in both colonies. State officials had limited access to mines and private plantations and local forms of social organization were absent, giving large private enterprises almost total control over the organization of daily family life (Higginson 1989: 19–85). Though ruled by free market forces externally, these places were highly unfree internally, forced labor thus becoming a feature of the late colonial liberal economy, albeit in a different institutional setting than in village-based systems of colonial exploitation.

The labor regimes set up in the Netherlands Indies and the Belgian Congo altered existing modes of family income, away from a rural subsistence-based mode toward a wage-based mode. During colonialism there were attempts to calculate labor incomes in order to monitor the development of living standards and avoid social unrest due to impoverishment. However, it seems that attempts to define and monitor wage levels were much more effective in Indonesia than in the Congo. Besides being driven by colonial anxiety over revolt, or a possible decline in the supply of docile labor, in the Dutch case public pressure played a role too. Toward the end of the nineteenth century the debate concerning the Dutch debt of honor (*eereschuld*) led to labor and wage protection measures as part of the Ethical Policy (see Thee, Chapter 2). Already, from the introduction of the Cultivation System wage data had been collected by the colonial state. However, only at the very end of the colonial period was a large-scale official survey of coolie wages undertaken in Java (Huizinga 1958). A similar extensive database is lacking for Belgian Congo.

Assessing wage levels and comparing them between two colonies is a tricky undertaking, not only because of the differences in data collection, but also with regard to drawing conclusions from wage levels, particularly their rise or decline in relation to costs of living, a ratio that is often taken as a proxy for living standards in general. It is difficult to decide how differential wage levels, dependent on the kind of work performed, can be measured up against of expenses, and it is likewise very hard to account for regional and local differences, especially when undertaking a comparison between two countries in different continents. In addition, in colonial settings wage levels were not simply a reflection of supply and demand but also reflected distortions of the labor market as a consequence of compulsion (Frankema and van Waijenburg 2012). However, even under repressive conditions, some sort of incentive must have been provided in order to take up wage labor. The best one can do is to compare crude wage rates with the price of basic foodstuffs, which would be rice in the case of Java.

From the literature on wages in colonial Indonesia a number of rather disconnected observations emerge. Over a prolonged time period workers earned similar daily wages, those in Java being lower than on the Outer Islands. In the sugar industry in Java around 1855 a coolie earned between 12 and 20 cents per day for doing field work (Dros 1992: 45–9). In the 1930s daily income on enterprises was 20, 30, or 54 cents at most, field and factory workers earning substantially less, but still well above their expenses for daily necessities, which ranged from 8 to 12.5 cents per person per day (Huizinga 1958: 263–4, 267). During the booming 1920s, despite a sharp increase in the demand for coolies on East Sumatran enterprises, wages did not rise, whereas in the 1930s they fell. Coolies working in the rubber industry in the 1920s could earn 45 to 50 cents per day but only 35 cents in the 1930s. Rice prices, on the other hand, declined too, reaching 7 cents per kilogram in the 1930s, whereas in the previous decade 10 to 13 cents had to be paid (Leenarts 1999: Chapter 6). The sources on Indonesia thus seem to suggest that, although wage levels were low and inelastic, workers seemed to earn enough at least to cover their expenses. Major wage differences, however, existed between types of work done, gender, composition of the household, the type of industry, and its geographical context.

As far as the Belgian Congo is concerned, the colonial state fixed minimum wages and food rations for all sectors of the economy to stimulate wage labor. But especially in the agriculture sector plantation managers usually paid much less than the official wages. Lever, for instance, paid its workers ten to 30 Congolese cents per day, although the minimum wage agreed with the colonial state was 25 cents per day.[10] But not only did the wages remain low; the nutritional value and quality of the food distributed by Lever was modest at best. As a consequence, food rations became a permanent source of conflict between workers and the company. From the end of the 1920s wages and food rations became more stable – especially in the mining sector in the South Katanga – but in the rural areas the wages of workers remained low (Higginson 1989: 123). To buy one bicycle in the 1950s, for instance, would mean that a group of five or six plantation workers had to put their savings over more than one year together.[11]

The extremely low wages in the rural sector of the Belgian Congo did not represent the only crucial difference between the Belgian and the Dutch colony. It seems that in the Belgian Congo large parts of the local economy were destroyed in order to further the export sector. As the historian Osumaka Likaka (1997) has shown in his study on the production of cotton in the Belgian Congo, from the 1920s private companies and the colonial administration tightened their control over peasant household labor and local agricultural markets. The combination of the dissolution of local markets in favor of forced cotton production together with the forced integration of peasant labor power in the colonial export economy impacted directly on the material situation of many households and village communities: in some areas like the Uele district – in the northeast of the territory where in 1927 80 percent of the population was integrated in the production of cotton (Likaka 1997: 21) – the work load for households producing cotton was so high that local communities had difficulty producing enough food crops for their families and villages. Moreover, many peasant households were not able to produce other commodities besides cotton which made them even more dependent on the colonial export economy. After independence in 1960 the cotton sector broke down and peasant households lost their incomes, because alternative commodity markets were virtually absent. Indeed, the rural population in the post-colonial Congo had no access to regional, national, or international markets; they produced only for subsistence or for small local markets. Hence, colonial agricultural policies like the *cultures obligatoires* had long-term consequences for the rural sector in the Congo, as it destroyed the structures of household and village economies both driving local people out of the market and prevented households from producing agricultural surpluses (see also Booth, Chapter 3 above).

The Netherlands Indies was a huge insular expanse, which ensured that the impact of colonialism was felt in varying degrees in different locations. Remarkably, it was exactly at the high tide of imperialism that, at least for rubber, local entrepreneurs were able to establish a parallel line of production besides the Western one (see Clarence-Smith, Chapter 9 below). This was not the case in Congo, where the forced integration of the rural population into the cash crop and mining economies, together with the destruction of local markets, made the Congolese rural population much more dependent on the colonial economy than in Java, where the village economy was not completely taken over by colonialism. This might have been an important factor that enabled Indonesia to resume economic growth after 1965 more successfully than Congo.

## Notes

1 For a survey of economic developments during the 1870–1930 period, see chapters 4 and 5 by Thomas Lindblad in Dick *et al.* (2002) and Touwen (2001).

2 There exists an extensive historiography on late colonial labor relations in the Dutch East Indies, including Stoler (1985), Breman (1987), and Houben *et al.* (1999), challenging the historical treatment of colonial violence.

3 The concept of *mise en valeur* was elaborated by Albert Sarraut, the French Colonial Minister from 1920 to 1924 (Young 1994: 166).

4 This is shown by Samuel Nelson (1994: 120ff.), who focuses on the Tshuapa river region of the province of Equateur.

5 Musée Royal de l'Afrique Centrale (MRAC), Tervuren, Papiers Sydney Edkins, *Contrat Libre ou Travail Forcé*, no date, p. 5.

6 See, for example, Archives Africaines (AA), Brussels, Sous-comité Provincial de Recrutement d'Elisabethville, Compte rendu de la séance du 18 décembre 1920, AA/AI/1394, "Le noir est paresseux. Il travaille exactement le minimum possible...."

7 Bodily coercion and violence were also the subject of discussions within the colonial administration itself. See AA, Brussels, report about disciplinary action in Katanga, Elisabethville, 24 May 1917, AA/MOI/3605.

8 See: KADOC, Leuven, Bestand De Cleene/De Jonghe, Référend Hensey, Voeu Relatif aux Marchés de Produits d'Exportations, 1919.

9 These interpretations of colonial labor are also prevalent in oral history interviews that I conducted with workers in Katanga who remembered labor during the 1940s and 1950s. See Julia Seibert, Oral-History Projekt Lubumbashi/Katanga, August/September 2008, Interviewsammlung Julia Seibert. See also, Donatien Dibwe dia Mwembu and Bogumil Jewsiewicki (eds.), *Le Travail, hier et aujourd'hui. Mémoires de Lubumbashi* (Paris, 2004).

10  See: Convention entre Ministre des Colonies et Lever Brothers Ltd., Article 10, Bulletin Officiel (1911), S. 394.
11  Information about the real value of wages in the Belgian Congo originates from interviews with former mine or cotton workers during my field work in Lubumbashi, Katanga in 2008 and 2009 (Interviewsammlung Julia Seibert).

## References

Austin, G. (2008) "The 'Reversal of Fortune' Thesis and the Compression of History: Perspectives from African and Comparative Economic History," *Journal of International Development*, 20, 996–1027.

Boomgaard, P. (1989) *Children of the Colonial State. Population Growth and Economic Development in Java, 1795–1880*, Amsterdam: Free University Press.

Booth, A. (1998) *The Indonesian Economy in the Nineteenth and Twentieth Centuries. A History of Missed Opportunities*, Houndmills, Basingstoke: Macmillan.

Breman, J. (1983) *Control of Land and Labour in Colonial Java. A Case Study of Agrarian Crisis and Reform in the Region of Ceribon during the first Decades of the 20th Century*, Dordrecht: Foris.

Breman, J. (1987) *Koelies, planters en koloniale politiek. Het arbeidsregime op de grootlandbouwondernemingen aan Sumatra's Oostkust in het begin van de twintigste eeuw*, Dordrecht: Foris.

Breman, J. (2010) *Koloniaal profijt van de onvrije arbeid. Het Preanger stelsel van gedwongen koffieteelt op Java 1720–1870*, Amsterdam: Amsterdam University Press.

Brixhe, A. (1953) *Le Coton au Congo Belge*, Brussels: Direction de l'Agriculture des Forêts et de l'Elevage du Ministère des Colonies.

Day, C. (1904) *The Policy and Administration of the Dutch in Java*, New York and London: Macmillan.

Dibwe dia Mwembu, D. and Jewsiewicki, B. (eds.) (2004) *Le Travail, hier et aujourd'hui. Mémoires de Lubumbashi*, Paris: Harmattan.

Dick, H., Houben, V., Lindblad, T., and Thee, K.W. (2002) *The Emergence of a National Economy. An Economic History of Indonesia, 1800–2000*, Crows Nest, NSW: Allen & Unwin/Honolulu: University of Hawaii Press.

Dros, N. (1992) *Changing Economy in Indonesia*. Volume 13: *Wages 1820–1940*, Amsterdam: Royal Tropical Institute.

Elson, R.E. (1994) *Village Java under the Cultivation System 1830–1870*, Sydney: Allen & Unwin.

Engels, M. (1921) "L'Avenir économique de la Province l'Equateur," *Congo, Revue Générale de la Colonie Belge*, 2, 288–9.

Fasseur, C. (1992) *The Politics of Colonial Exploitation. Java, the Dutch, and the Cultivation System*, Ithaca, NY: SEAP Cornell.

Fieldhouse, D.K. (1978) *Unilever Overseas. The Anatomy of a Multinational 1895–1965*, Stanford, Calif.: The Hoover Institution Press.

Frankema, E.H.P. and van Waijenburg, M. (2012) "Structural Impediments to African Growth? New Evidence from British African Real Wages, 1880–1965," *Journal of Economic History*, 72, 895–926.

Furnivall, J.S. (1944) *Netherlands India. A Study of Plural Economy*, Cambridge: Cambridge University Press.

Furnivall, J.S. (1948) *Colonial Policy and Practice. A Comparative Study of Burma and Netherlands India*, Cambridge: Cambridge University Press.

Higginson, J. (1989) *A Working Class in the Making. Belgian Colonial Labor Policy, Private Enterprise, and the African Mineworker, 1907–1951*, Madison: The University of Wisconsin Press.

Houben, V. (1993) "Private Estates in Java in the Nineteenth Century: a Reappraisal," in J.T. Lindblad (ed.), *New Challenges in the Modern Economic History of Indonesia*, Leiden: Programme of Indonesian Studies 1993.

Houben, V. (1994) *Kraton and Kumpeni. Surakarta and Yogyakarta 1830–1870*, Leiden: KITLV Press.

Houben, V., Lindblad J.T., *et al.* (1999) *Coolie Labour in Colonial Indonesia. A Study of Labour Relations in the Outer Islands, c.1900–1940*, Wiesbaden: Harrassowitz.

Hugenholtz, W.R. (2008) "Landrentebelasting op Java 1812–1920," Unpublished PhD Dissertation, University of Leiden.

Huizinga, L.H. (1958) *Het koeliebudgetonderzoek op Java in 1939–40*, Wageningen: Vada.

Knight, G.R. (1968) "Estates and Plantations in Java," 1812–1834, Unpublished PhD dissertation, University of London.

Leenarts, E. (1999) "Coolie Wages in Western Enterprises in the Outer Islands, 1919–1938," in V. Houben, J.T. Lindblad, *et al.* (1999) *Coolie Labour in Colonial Indonesia. A Study of Labour Relations in the Outer Islands, c.1900–1940*, Wiesbaden: Harrassowitz.

Leplae, E. (1930) *Les Cultures obligatoires dans les pays d'agriculture arriérée*, Brussels.

Likaka, O. (1997) *Rural Society and Cotton in Colonial Zaire*, Madison: Wisconsin University Press.

Maddison, A. (1989) "Dutch Income in and from Indonesia 1700–1938," *Modern Asian Studies*, 23–4, 645–70.

Marchal, J. (2008) *Lord Leverhulme's Ghost. Colonial Exploitation in the Congo*, London: Verso.

Money, J.W.B. (1861) *Java; or How to Manage a Colony: Showing a Practical Solution of the Questions now Affecting British India*, London: Hurst and Blackett.

Nelson, S. (1994) *Colonialism in the Congo Basin 1880–1940*, Athens: Ohio University Press.

Peemans, J.P. (1997) *Le Congo-Zaïre au gré du XXe siècle. Etat, économie, société 1880–1990*, Paris: Harmattan.

Rodney, W. (1981) *How Europe Underdeveloped Africa*, Washington: Howard University Press (rev. edn published in 1981 by Vincent Harding, William Strickland and Robert Hill).

Seibert, J. (2010) "More Continuity than Change? – New Forms of Unfree Labor in the Belgium Congo 1908–1930," in M. van der Linden (ed.), *Humanitarian Intervention and Changing Labor Relations: The Long-Term Consequences of the Abolition of the Slave-Trade*, Leiden: Brill.

Seibert, J. (2012) "Arbeit und Gewalt: Die langsame Durchsetzung der Lohnarbeit im kolonialen Kongo: 1885–1960," Unpublished PhD dissertation, University of Trier.

Stengers, J. (1977) "La Genèse d'une pensée coloniale. Léopold II et le modèle hollandais," *Tijdschrift voor Geschiedenis*, 90, 46–71.

Stoler, A.L. (1985) *Capitalism and Confrontation in Sumatra's Plantation Belt, 1870–1979*, New Haven, Conn., and London: Yale University Press.

Touwen, J. (2001) *Extremes in the Archipelago. Trade and Economic Development in the Outer Islands of Indonesia, 1900–1942*, Leiden: KITLV Press.

van der Linden, M. (2008) *Workers of the World. Essays toward a Global Labor History*, Leiden: Brill.

van Schaik, A. (1986) *Colonial Control and Peasant Resources in Java*, Amsterdam: University of Amsterdam.

Vanthemsche, G. (2007) *La Belgique et le Congo. Nouvelle Histoire de Belgique*, Volume 4, Brussels: Editions Complexe.

Wauters, A.J. (1911) *Histoire politique du Congo belge*, Brussels.

Wesseling, H.L (1991) *Verdeel en heers. De deling van Afrika 1880–1914*, Amsterdam: Bert Bakker.

Wilson, C. (1968) *The History of Unilever. A Study in Economic Growth and Social Change in Three Volumes*, London: Cassell.

Young, C. (1994) *The African Colonial State in Comparative Perspective*, London: Yale University Press.

# 9 Rubber cultivation in Indonesia and the Congo from the 1910s to the 1950s

## Divergent paths

*William G. Clarence-Smith*

### 9.1 Introduction

After the global wild rubber boom ended in the early 1910s, the rubber econo-mies of the Congo and Indonesia diverged markedly. The Congo's output fell sharply, to the point of almost disappearing altogether during the price collapse of the early 1930s when it stood at only around 100 tonnes a year (Vandewalle 1966: 11). In stark contrast, Indonesia, fast catching up with Malaya, produced some 250,000 tonnes a year in the early 1930s, accounting for about a quarter of the world's total output (Bauer 1948: 377). An international price cartel, formed in 1934, reversed the trend to a modest degree, as Indonesia was subject to restrictions that were not applied to Africa (McFadyean 1944).

The Japanese conquest of Southeast Asia, complete by March 1942, offered a much more substantial opportunity to the Congo to improve its relative position, but it was only half-heartedly taken up. There was indeed an intense upsurge in Congolese production during the Allied "battle for rubber" between 1942 and 1945, but it proved to be a straw fire. The new state of Indonesia again pulled far ahead of the Congo, despite the turbulent process of Indonesian independence after 1945. In 1959, the Congo reached an output of 40,000 tonnes, but this was overshadowed by Indonesia's production of some 700,000 tonnes (Baulkwill 1989: 47). Indeed, other African territories in the front line of World War II's "battle for rubber" did better than the Congo after 1945, notably Nigeria and Liberia (Clarence-Smith 2012; Mitchell 2007: 277; Helleiner 1966; Schulze 1973).

This outcome does not seem to have owed much to factor endowments or to most other aspects of economic context. The Congo was certainly at something of a disadvantage in terms of disease, soils, transport, and the growth of local manufacturing. However, these obstacles seem insufficient, even cumulatively, to explain the divergence with Indonesia, especially as a few factors favored the Congo. Furthermore, policies concerning large plantations were broadly similar, even if shortages of labor were probably more marked in Africa.

It is argued here that official handling of smallholders may hold the key to explaining differing outcomes. Smallholders were by far the most cost-efficient producers of natural rubber, as Peter Bauer (1948) elegantly demonstrated in his path-breaking research on Southeast Asia. Indeed, it was the dynamism of small indigenous farmers that turned southern Sumatra into the center of gravity of the global natural rubber economy from the 1920s. To be sure, both the Dutch and the Indonesian governments placed obstacles in the path of small producers, while clumsily seeking to favor inefficient large plantations. However, the Dutch very rarely forced Indonesian peasants to cultivate rubber, and gradually relaxed measures protecting large plantations. The Japanese hesitated, during their brief occupation, but Sukarno gave smallholders their head after 1945, if only by default, due to the Indonesian state's incapacity to prevent massive smuggling to Singapore.

In contrast, the Belgians applied debilitating constraint to smallholders, after a brief interlude of agricultural liberalization following their take-over of the Congo from King Leopold in 1908. Belgian officials soon drifted back to the king's authoritarian policies, even if they did not engage in the excesses of wanton brutality that had characterized the Congo Free State. The Great Depression led to a further hardening of attitudes. From 1933, the Belgians obliged Africans to plant rubber in designated locations and in officially determined ways, paying low fixed official prices. Pressure intensified during World War II. To be sure, the Belgians relaxed these constraints after 1949, but they failed to adopt resolutely pro-smallholder policies. Many resentful Congolese smallholders then abandoned their rubber plots to the forest, or converted them to food crops.

That said, the Congo may have simply specialized in a different crop through a combination of chance and "path dependence." Oil palms were indigenous to Equatorial Africa, and grew in much the same ecological niche as latex-yielding plants. Thus, the skills for tending and harvesting oil palms were already in place in the Congo Basin by the time that rubber became significant. A similar argument could be made for West Africa, where both oil palms and cocoa, the latter a native of the Americas, proved to be effective replacements for rubber. Southeast Asia, where neither crop was indigenous, opted for rubber, and "path dependence" then reinforced this initial choice for some decades. The fact that the planting of both oil palms and cocoa trees has recently boomed in Southeast Asia, and that tropical Africa is undergoing a more modest surge in rubber planting, might underpin this argument.

## 9.2  Factor endowment in Indonesia and the Congo

Large areas of lowland Indonesia and the northern Congo are suited to *Hevea brasiliensis* in terms of soils and climate. The tree does best in wet equatorial lowlands, sheltered from high winds, and with rainfall of 2000 to 4000 millimeters, evenly spread throughout the year. *Hevea* adapts to a multitude of soils, although not to highly acid or highly alkaline ones. Moreover, it does not tolerate a permanently high water table. Nutritional deficiencies in soils can be countered through fertilization, albeit at a price (Watson 1989). Soils in the Congo's Cuvette Centrale were often poor and water-logged, and the area was at a rather higher altitude than corresponding regions in Indonesia (Laclavère 1978: 22–3; Nelson 1994: 16, 24). Plantation companies complained about the low fertility of soils, compared to those of Southeast Asia (AS). However, poor and swampy soils were also common in South Sumatra and Southeastern Borneo (Kaliman- tan), both vital centers of Indonesia's rubber economy (Purwanto 1992: 228–9; Donner 1987: ch 1). Conversely, the rich volcanic soils of Java and East Sumatra were largely reserved for other crops.

In terms of plant disease, *Hevea brasiliensis* was native to the Amazon Basin, where South American leaf blight, caused by the fungus *Microcyclus ulei*, pre- vented dense planting. Indeed, Henry Ford's attempts to develop gigantic planta- tions in the Brazilian Amazon turned into one of the most spectacular fiascos in the history of capitalism (Dean 1987). While leaf blight spread all over the tropi- cal Americas, it never left the New World, making Africa and Asia equally well suited to the commercial planting of *Hevea*.

That said, African trees suffered from a form of root rot caused by the "honey fungus," *Armilliaria mellea*, which was absent in Asia. It was possible to control the incidence of the fungus by managing wild tree hosts, but this implied costs, especially in terms of labor (Johnston 1989). Although this fungus has not been indicted as a major factor affecting Africa's competition with Southeast Asia, it is possible that its impact has been underestimated.

In terms of labor, Indonesian and Congolese forests were both thinly popu- lated, but Indonesian producers could draw on abundant workers from the wider region, whether from Java or from nearby South India and South China (Houben *et al.* 1999). However, Indonesian smallholders, the most dynamic rubber pro- ducers, did not have ready access to such foreign labor. Conversely, the volcanic and densely populated Rift Valley of Africa, which supplied many workers to the Katanga mines, was not geographically distant from the Congo's Cuvette Centrale (Northrup 1988).

Once turned into dried sheets, rubber is fairly bulky and heavy, and transport costs thus weigh on profits. Indonesia's rubber production zones were all close to the sea, or had easy access to navigable rivers quickly emerging into the sea (Knaap 1989; Dick 1990). The great Congo riverine network was also navigable, but production zones lay further from the ocean, and break of bulk was neces- sary at Leopoldville (Kinshasa), where a railway took goods to the Atlantic port of Matadi. Transhipment in Leopoldville was expensive, and was prone to bot- tlenecks (Huybrechts 1970). That said, Matadi was closer to major consuming industries in North America and Europe than were rubber ports in Indonesia.

In terms of regional markets for raw rubber, Asia developed manufacturing industries earlier than Africa, and on a larger scale. Japan's rubber industries flourished from around 1900, and coastal China began to catch up in the 1920s (Allen 1940: 559–60; Lieu 1936: 49–51; Coble 2003: 195–200). In Southeast Asia itself, the manufacture of rubber footwear spread out from Singapore in the 1920s, and Goodyear began producing car tires in West Java in 1935 (Tan 1994; Allen and Donnithorne 1962: 262; O'Reilly and Keating 1983: 78, 101). Indone- sia was well placed to sell to this burgeoning Asian market. That said, the Czech

Bata company was producing footwear in the Leopoldville area by 1942 (*Encyclopédie* 1949–52: III, 408, 415). Moreover, the world's raw rubber was still overwhelmingly sold to the West in this period, notably to the United States (Bauer 1948).

In short, Indonesia enjoyed a number of minor benefits in terms of growing *Hevea brasiliensis*, but also some disadvantages. On balance, it is hard to discern any determining trend. It is true that no attempt has been made to quantify Indonesia's overall comparative advantage over the Congo. However, *prima facie*, other reasons are required to explain the enormous disparity between the output of natural rubber in the two areas.

## 9.3   Large plantations in Indonesia

By 1940, large plantations, belonging to Western and Japanese individuals and corporations, controlled 46 percent of the area planted in rubber, which amounted to some 1,400,000 hectares (Barlow and Drabble 1990: 187). Given that large plantations were inefficient dinosaurs, the prominence of estates owed much to Dutch prejudices, similar to those of the British in Malaya. Estates suffered from an excessive reliance on borrowed capital, high unskilled labor costs, stratospheric skilled labor expenditures, and expensive and counter-productive agricultural strategies. They enjoyed no economies of scale in growing rubber, or in tapping trees, and experienced considerable diseconomies of scale, especially in the deployment of labor (Bauer 1948; Thee 1977: 24–5).

Economies of scale were slightly more evident in primary processing, but remained restricted. To coagulate, wash, roll, dry, smoke, press, and bale rubber demanded little capital or know-how. Even if more sophisticated processes emerged over time, together with more diversified products, it is far from clear that the advantages were worth the costs involved. To be sure, estate output was generally of higher quality than that coming from smallholdings, but it was a moot point whether this improved prices to the point of making up for costs. Unprepossessing "slab" rubber purchased from smallholders could easily be remilled in specialized factories in Singapore, and commercial intermediaries, mainly Chinese and Arabs from Hadhramawt in modern Yemen, were efficient providers of processing services. The only exception lay in the preparation of liquid latex for export from the 1930s, which was utilized for special applications, such as making surgical gloves. Latex for this purpose had to be processed quickly and carefully immediately after tapping, giving estates a real comparative advantage, but this was a niche product with a limited market (Morris 1989).

Dutch support for European plantations was therefore crucial to their continued prominence. Settlers and companies enjoyed an initial advantage, springing from being "prime movers," better placed to learn about how to grow, tap, and process *Hevea brasiliensis*. Rubber estates surged to the fore as a result of the great speculative share boom of 1909–12, which served quite effectively to spread knowledge about the crop (Allen and Donnithorne 1962: 117–20). Later, however, Westerners clamored for protection against swelling smallholder competition, on the unacceptable grounds that indolent and ignorant "natives" were incapable of properly growing the exotic newcomer and processing its latex (Bauer 1948).

Large rubber plantations benefited from government support in a number of ways. Corporation tax was low, at 10 percent, and there were no export taxes until the 1930s. From 1934, estate exports were taxed at 5 percent, much more lightly than those of smallholders, and were favored in terms of export licenses. The state granted land concessions to "Europeans," including all those legally classified as such, albeit usually only as long leases. Conversely, the authorities generally refused leases to "Foreign Orientals," mainly Chinese and Arabs, or to indigenous applicants. Officials facilitated the flow of Javanese and Chinese contract labor to estates, and controlled indentured workers by applying penal sanctions for breaches of contract. The botanical gardens at Buitenzorg (Bogor) directed almost all their initial efforts to supporting European planters, pioneering the first commercially applicable system of bud grafting of rubber in 1916. Allowing for the clonal reproduction of more productive trees, this led to a rough doubling of latex yields. By 1940, 36 percent of estate rubber in Indonesia was bud grafted. That said, estates planted their trees too wide apart, insisted on counter-productive clean weeding, and did little to interplant catch crops apart from occasionally putting in some low-grade Robusta coffee (Barlow and Drabble 1990: 199, 201–3; Touwen 2001: 107; Thee 1977: 26–8; Allen and Donnithorne 1962: 117–18, 125–6; Clarence-Smith 1997a).

Estate rubber remained geographically circumscribed in Indonesia, spreading little outside Java and East Sumatra's *Cultuurgebied* (cultivation) zone. Planters first experimented with types other than *Hevea brasiliensis* as supplementary crops on existing coffee and tobacco plantations. Monocropping of *Hevea brasiliensis* only became typical of regions to the north and south of East Sumatra's tobacco area, as well as in parts of the far west and far east of Java. In these areas, with relatively fertile soils, smallholder output was deliberately restricted by official land policies (Barlow and Drabble 1990: 190, 195; Thee 1977; Pelzer 1978: 39, 50–4; Purwanto 1992: 11–12).

Japanese occupation from 1942 has often been portrayed as the nemesis of rubber estates, but the reality was quite different. The Japanese did little damage to rubber plantations, displaying more interest in first transferring them to Japanese owners, and then attempting to use them as bargaining chips with the advancing Allies. Moreover, mature *Hevea* trees were much harder to uproot and replace with food crops than many other cash crops, such as tobacco. Only small acreages of rubber trees were thus felled, often consisting of immature trees. Export markets almost vanished, and tapping ground to a halt, but the trees were able to rest and store up their precious latex (Nawiyanto 2005: 128–31, 159; Prillwitz 1947: 13–15).

It was the chaotic process of independence from 1945 that really harmed large rubber estates in Indonesia, although deliberate policy was only part of the story. Initially, it was rebellions, strikes, land disputes, thefts of latex and processed rubber, high export duties, foreign exchange shortages, and heavy taxes on remittances of profits that caused most operators to cease investing. Some simply sold up and left in despair (Allen and Donnithorne 1962: 134–7; Booth 1988: 208). The nationalization of 542 legally Dutch estates in 1957, about three-quarters of the total, was the last straw. The state plantations that emerged in 1957 were able to coerce labor and ignore peasant land claims, but they were badly managed and starved of investment. Above all, they could not smuggle rubber to Singapore. By 1967, large plantations thus accounted for only about a quarter of value added in overall cash crop production (Booth 1988: 198, 208).

## 9.4  Large plantations in the Congo

Estates growing *Hevea brasiliensis* sprang up in the Congo somewhat earlier than in Indonesia, but they failed to become of much significance. Hevea trees were first planted in the coastal Boma region in 1896 (AGR). The Urselia estate in the coastal Mayumbe enclave, concentrating on cocoa at this time, experimented with *Hevea brasiliensis* (Vandervelde 1909: 66–7). From 1899, *Hevea* spread upriver to the regions of Coquilhatville (Mbandaka) and Nouvelle Anvers (Makanza) (AGR undated).

Labor problems were put forward as the key to stunted growth. Adrien Hallet started his career growing oil palms in the Congo, and was from 1905 the chief architect of the expansion in Southeast Asia of what became the Société Financière des Caoutchoucs (Socfin). This specialized Franco-Belgian corporation, also known as the Rivaud–Hallet Group from 1919, came to possess immense rubber plantations in Java, Sumatra, Malaya, and Indochina (Clarence-Smith 1997a; de Vathaire 2009; Clarence-Smith 2010). Hallet explained his shift of geographical interest in terms of inadequate labor supplies in the Congo Basin, together with poor transport links (Baudhuin 1944: 241–3). In 1923, he stated that he was reluctant to invest in the Congo until the labor question there had been solved. He was careful to say that he was not asking the administration to provide forced labor, but merely general support (AA 1923).

In the mid-1920s, there were only about 2000 hectares of estate land devoted to *Hevea brasiliensis* throughout the colony, consisting largely of mature trees planted before World War I (Whitford and Antony 1926: 5–6, 91–3). By 1932, as the world price fell to its nadir, this fledgling sector was in a poor state, and many of the plantations were derelict (Great Britain Naval Intelligence Division 1944: 388).

Somewhat paradoxically, the Great Depression then acted in favor of the renaissance of rubber estates. In 1933, the Belgians promulgated a plan to react to the severity of the world slump. They envisaged, *inter alia*, a "vast extension of European palm, rubber and coffee plantations," to provide work for unemployed Africans (Nelson 1994: 152–3). From 1934, the case for rubber became more compelling, as the International Rubber Regulations Agreement (IRRA) did not apply to Africa, allowing the continent to become a "free rider" on the slowly rising world price engineered by this cartel (McFadyean 1944). While rubber prices recovered, the same could not be said of the crop's main competitors in the Cuvette Centrale, palm products and copal (Nelson 1994: 155).

The gathering clouds of war in the Far East also led the Belgians to consider securing supplies of this strategic commodity from their colony. The King of the Belgians personally intervened to persuade Socfin to consider operating in the northern Congo (Anciaux 1955: 136). An exploratory mission was dispatched in 1937 (Fincol 1937). As a result, the group set up two new rubber plantation companies in the Tshuapa region, in 1937 and 1939. Socfin boasted that it had transferred advanced Southeast Asian methods, especially bud grafting, to the heart of Africa (van den Abeele 1968: 451; Anciaux 1955: 136).

Other corporations adopted similar measures. Overgrown plantations were reconditioned, and the area planted with rubber on estates rose from some 4500 hectares in 1934 to about 14,000 in 1940 (Great Britain Naval Intelligence Division 1944: 276–7, 292, 388–9; Becquet 1945: 73). The Société Anonyme Belge pour le Commerce du Haut Congo enlarged an existing *Hevea* plantation to 300 hectares (Nelson 1994: 179). By 1938, there were 46 rubber estates, and new plantings were mainly in bud-grafted trees (*Encyclopédie* 1949–52: I, 389, and III, 392). This was still far behind the roughly 640,000 hectares planted on Indonesian estates in 1940, but it was a rapid rate of growth.

Although shortage of labor remained the leitmotiv of Congolese rubber planters, they did manage to attract some local workers, especially as alternative opportunities in the mines remained depressed. Typically coming on 60- to 90-day rolling contracts, men were attracted by the availability of trade goods. Moreover, they could set their stints of estate work against official demands for corvée labor (Nelson 1994: 178–9, 183–90).

As war engulfed the world, public pressure to produce more rubber moved into high gear, especially after the Japanese had seized most of the world's *Hevea* trees in early 1942. At this time, a shortage of natural rubber, essential for large tires, threatened to undermine the entire Allied war effort (Clarence-Smith 2009). To deal with the immediate crisis, estates mainly sought to boost output from existing mature trees (Becquet 1945: 72–3). This included rehabilitating estates that had remained abandoned since the Great Depression, and tapping rubber trees that were employed to shade coffee (*India-Rubber Journal*, July 4, 1942: 1). The Institut National pour l'Étude Agronomique du Congo Belge (INEAC) stepped up the struggle against various diseases of *Hevea* (Henry 1983: 365). To attract more labor, planters stocked estate shops with scarce imported goods (Cornelis 1983: 60–1, 70).

Although planting new trees was unlikely to affect the course of the war as a *Hevea* tree took up to seven years to enter into production, estate companies prepared themselves for future decades in an uncertain world (Cornelis 1983: 60). INEAC distributed 86,000 *Hevea* seeds, and 66,000 bud grafts (Henry 1983: 339). Some 7000 hectares were ultra-dense plantings of precocious trees, tapped when they were only two years old, but this bold experiment did not work well (Becquet 1945: 73; Henry 1983: 396, note 47; *Bulletin Agricole* 1961: 102; AS 1985).

INEAC was meant to support both smallholders and large planters, but it initially concentrated on estates (Schoofs 1944: 84). Of the over 50,000 hectares estimated as being planted at the end of 1943, some 30,000 hectares were in European hands (Becquet 1945: 73). Planting of another 10,000 hectares was forecast (Schoofs 1944: 84). In 1948, the total in European hands stood at 54,514 hectares, ten times what had existed in 1934 (*Encyclopédie* 1949–52: I, 589). About two-thirds of these trees were located in Equateur province, and nearly all the rest in Congo-Ubangi province (Belgium 1950: 264). Companies with other interests entered the field of rubber. Thus, in 1942, the Huileries du Congo Belge, a subsidiary of the Anglo-Dutch Unilever group that specialized in oil palms, planted *Hevea* on two of its plantations, at a time when it possessed some 73,000 hectares of land (Edington 1991: 11–12; Fieldhouse 1978: 529).

There was one more burst of planting, during the Korean War of the early 1950s, but thereafter estates tended to coast along, tapping existing trees. Companies were worried about price levels, and believed that the growth of synthetic rubber production in the West would make matters worse, abetted by the falling price of oil, from which synthetic rubber was made. By 1955, the proportion of immature trees on estates had fallen to 18 percent, compared to 54 percent in 1949, although there was a slight rise up to independence in 1960 (Vandewalle 1966: 115–16). In 1958, estates had 57,976 hectares in production (*Bulletin Agricole* 1961: 181). About 25 percent was in the hands of two companies belonging to the Socfin group, with another 12 percent belonging to the Huileries du Congo Belge (Joye and Lewin 1961: 256; Fieldhouse 1978: 530). In short, despite estates being central to the Congo's rising rubber exports after 1945, this was not a strikingly dynamic sector (Peemans 1997: 126).

The chaotic process of independence then led to an absolute decline in output, worsened by the nationalization of most plantations in 1973–5. Socfin's properties were taken over in 1974 (AS). As a result of some deft political footwork, the Unilever estates, known as Huileries du Congo Belge and renamed Plantations Lever au Congo and then Plantations Lever au Zaïre, were spared "Zaïrianization." However, they operated at low levels of output, in a very difficult economic context (Shapiro and Tollens 1992: 9–11, 102–3).

## 9.5 Smallholdings in Indonesia

Smallholdings in Indonesia, accounting for an estimated 54 percent of the area planted in rubber by 1940, were strongly associated with free peasant cultivation (Barlow and Drabble 1990: 187–8). Local officials did attempt to oblige Sumatran peasants to grow indigenous *Ficus elastica* in the late nineteenth century, and briefly made the cultivation of *Hevea brasiliensis* compulsory in Jambi, in southeastern Sumatra, from 1906 to 1908. However, these half-hearted and poorly enforced initiatives, lacking support from Batavia (Jakarta), had no real consequences, and left no collective memory of coercion (Purwanto 1992: 132–3, 197–9). This was partly a question of the timing of the introduction of *Hevea*. The Dutch had been slowly winding down the Cultivation System since

1870, finally ending it for coffee in 1917, and they were not keen to embrace new crops (Clarence-Smith 1994).

The Dutch thus played almost no part in the massive adoption of *Hevea* by smallholders from 1909, which turned the southeastern Sumatran regions of Jambi and Palembang into the global heart of smallholder rubber. There were other Sumatran concentrations in Tapanuli, Aceh, and Riau. In Borneo (Kalimantan) too, rubber spread in the southeastern and western provinces (Purwanto 1992: 113–14; Barlow and Drabble 1990: 190; Lindblad 1988: 58–78). The most that smallholders could generally expect from Dutch officials was benign neglect, although there were exceptions, as in western Borneo, where the Dutch actively fostered the growth of smallholdings. After the British introduced the Stevenson restriction scheme in 1922, attempting to raise rubber prices by limiting production, the Dutch refused to join. They then became increasingly concerned about the tremendous smallholder boom that the scheme engendered in their "Outer Islands." They thus established arbitrary and unhelpful quality control measures on planting in 1923 and 1928, and imposed a 5 percent export duty on smallholder rubber leaving Sumatra in 1925 (Purwanto 1992: 184, 285; Touwen 2001: 181).

The crucial external players in the dramatic story of Indonesia's smallholder rubber boom were non-Western, notably "Foreign Oriental" traders, who were mainly southeastern Chinese and Hadhrami Arabs (Vleming 1926; Clarence-Smith 1997b). They brought information and seeds from the Malay peninsula, with assistance from a "Malay international," notably composed of *hajji* (who had made the pilgrimage to Mecca). Traders purchased "slab" rubber, transported it on steamers often owned by members of their own community, and sold it to efficient and profitable remilling factories in Singapore (Purwanto 1992: 189–91, 225; Pelzer 1978: 53; Thee 1977: 17–18; Barlow and Drabble 1990: 190; Touwen 2001: 177–80; Lindblad 1988: 58; Vleming 1926: 242–3, 258–60, 266). The Dutch made strenuous efforts to encourage the development of Western remilling factories in Sumatra and Borneo, but they proved unable to sustain Chinese competition. It was Japanese and Arab entrepreneurs who provided the only effective competition to Chinese mills, whether locally or in Singapore (Purwanto 1992: 280–4, 296; Touwen 2001: 180).

Smallholders obtained additional seeds, as well as basic tapping skills, from working on estates, and they integrated rubber almost seamlessly into existing patterns of cultivation. Forest land was effectively free to people of the area, and much forest clearing was gradually undertaken with existing tools in slack periods of the year. Before the canopy formed, smallholders interplanted rapidly maturing food crops, as well as cash crops ready in a few years such as coffee and pineapples. They scattered plots in the forest, which reduced the incidence of disease. They planted *Hevea* trees close together, which kept down weeds, while also raising yields per hectare. It was estimated that only 2 percent of smallholder trees were bud grafted by 1940, but other techniques improved quickly over time. Indeed, yields per hectare on smallholdings were generally as high as those on estates, or even higher, despite a constant stream of Dutch criticisms of the "bad methods" employed by indigenous farmers. Coagulants probably represented the largest single expenditure on imported inputs, and even they involved no major outlay in cash (Purwanto 1992: 116, 202–3, 220–3, 230, 237–8; Barlow and Drabble 1990: 190, 203, 208; Touwen 2001: 177–8; Lindblad 1988: 59–68).

Most important to smallholder success were agreements with sharecroppers, who initially supplemented family labor, and who soon became the main source of labor. Oral contracts were generally on a 50:50 basis (*bagi dua*), and drew in workers from a wide area around smallholdings. Because a share of the physical harvest was specified in the contracts, changes in the price of rubber caused none of the interminable negotiations that estates suffered from. Moreover, workers did not have to be employed in slack periods of the year. Many Javanese "coolies" were seduced away from European plantations to engage in these flexible and effective labor agreements, which enabled the smallholding sector to move effortlessly beyond family production (Purwanto 1992: 152, 202–3, 234–5, 244–5, 252–66; Touwen 2001: 182–3; Lindblad 1988: 61).

The smallholder boom created an unmistakable aura of prosperity in the 1920s. In this golden decade, not only were rice and textiles consumed on an ever increasing scale, but also bicycles, cars, sewing machines, gold, and jewels. Wedding feasts expanded, and new houses were built. Perhaps most striking to Western observers were the crowds of pilgrims going to Mecca, many of them several times over, which turned Indonesian and Malayan smallholder rubber zones into some of the largest sources of pilgrims in the Islamic world (Lindblad 1988: 70–1; Purwanto 1992: 326–36).

After the shock of the sharp fall in prices of 1929–32, the Dutch signed the International Rubber Regulations Agreement of 1934, determined to make smallholders bear the brunt of restrictions in exports. The authorities aimed at a rough export ratio of 10:7 for planter to smallholder produce. Whereas European estates paid only a 5 percent export duty, smallholders were subjected to a variable "special tax," which could amount to as much as two-thirds of the average price of rubber. Although the money thus collected was to be directed back to smallholders, there was much "leakage." Some of the income from these taxes even went into the registration of smallholdings from 1935, in order better to control their output. When the infamous "special tax" was ended in 1937, export licenses were unfairly biased toward estates, causing a vigorous secondary market in licenses to spring up. The Dutch also attempted to impose counter-productive rules about spacing rubber trees widely, which merely encouraged weeds and lowered yields per hectare. A more positive Dutch policy consisted in new regulations fostering local primary processing, with indigenous smokehouses sprouting up in large numbers (Purwanto 1992: 184, 215–17; Barlow and Drabble 1990: 205–6; Thee 1977: 27–8; Touwen 2001: 189–91; Lindblad 1988: 74–7; Allen and Donnithorne 1962: 125; Bauer 1948: 151–70).

Given these generally biased and vindictive Dutch measures, it was all the more impressive that smallholder output of rubber continued to surge forward in the 1930s, overtaking that of estates by the end of the decade. In essence, small-holders were reaping the benefits of the planting boom of the 1920s, while pushing up output as much as possible to compensate for low prices, especially as rubber prices were somewhat firmer than those for competing product, such as coffee (Purwanto 1992: 317).

The period of Japanese occupation, from 1942 to 1945, marked a pause, but smallholders were able to fall back on subsistence crops. Even more than in the case of estates, the Japanese were reluctant to chop down the rubber trees of smallholders, as they feared the social and political consequences. Rubber trees were thus able to rest, becoming all the more productive when tapped again after the war (Anonymous 1947: 167).

Indonesian independence after the war witnessed slow but generally positive output growth to the mid-1960s, despite the prolonged violence that accompanied the birth of the republic, and devastating economic mismanagement. The main reason for this paradoxical outcome was growing smuggling of small-holder rubber to Singapore, which assumed colossal proportions. This allowed rubber smallholders to operate as though they were semi-detached from the deepening economic catastrophe that was enveloping Indonesia (Booth 1988: 198, 208–9). An ancillary reason for the rise in smallholder output was that Indonesian farmers increasingly adopted bud-grafting techniques from estates (Coates 1987: 332).

## 9.6 Smallholdings in the Congo

Indigenous production in the Congo was indelibly bound up with official coercion. There were vivid memories of the great "red rubber" scandal under the Congo Free State regime, when thousands of Africans had died because of the imposition of the forced collection of wild rubber. Indeed, it was this scandal that had principally forced the Belgian state to take over the Congo from King Leopold in 1908 (Harms 1975).

The Belgians thus began by abolishing forced cultivation, and dismantling the commercial monopsonies that had accompanied obligatory collection. Taxes were paid in cash, trading posts multiplied, and Africans sold freely produced commodities. Among these were small quantities of wild rubber, which rose slightly in the mid-1920s as the Stevenson restriction scheme in British Asia pushed up the world price (Peemans 1997: 27). In the northern Congo, the dominant commercial diaspora came to consist of Muslim Gujarati Indians. The pioneer in Coquilhatville had been in Java for a time before being called by a relative to the eastern Congo in 1929 (Lufungula 2002). Coming the other way, up the Congo river system, were Portuguese entrepreneurs (Vellut 1991).

Old habits die hard, however, and the crisis of World War I led to the reestablishment of forced cultivation by decree in 1917. Although initially limited to cotton and foodstuffs in the east, the coercion of peasants gradually spread geographically in the 1920s, and was extended to other crops, notably palm products. Villages had to collect produce from the wild, or cultivate a designated area in a given crop. The authorities fixed a minimum price, which in practice was the only price, and often reserved the purchasing of produce to certain settler and corporate operators. The purposes were declared to be to "educate" Africans, wean them away from "idleness," ensure food security, and diversify the economy (Peemans 1997: 28–9, 34, 73, 88; Jewsiewicki 1983: 16, 47).

Rubber was marginal to forced cultivation in the 1920s, although the government appears to have imposed some planting, or at least strongly encouraged it. Africans were often told to plant less productive trees than the *Hevea brasiliensis* adopted by estates, notably drought-resistant *Manihot glaziovii* (Ceará rubber) in the Lower Congo and Uele regions, and *Funtumia elastica*, native to Africa, in the Middle Congo (Whitford and Antony 1926: 90–2). Smallholders accounted for only around a fifth of the colony's tiny and falling rubber exports in 1930, by which date the collection of wild rubber had temporarily ceased (Peemans 1997: 124; Great Britain Naval Intelligence Division 1944: 425).

The Great Depression resulted in a hardening and widening of administrative compulsion, for the unfortunately named "Total Civilization" plan of 1933 generalized forced cultivation across the colony. Although there was much talk of *paysannats africains*, idealized nuclei of sturdy African yeomen proprietors, the reality quickly became one of naked force, dressed up as saving Africans from idleness and ignorance (Nelson 1994: 152–3, 157–8, 161–4; Jewsiewicki 1983: 18–19, 46, 49–51; Peemans 1997: 29, 73). Elderly Mongo oral informants in the Cuvette Centrale recalled the workings of the 1933 plan with considerable bitterness (Nelson 1994: 168).

*Hevea brasiliensis* came into its own at this point, as one of three perennial cash crops chosen for forced cultivation in the Cuvette Centrale, together with oil palms and coffee. By 1940, some 2000 hectares of *Hevea* had been planted in the region. Administrators extracted corvée labor to build new dirt roads, and the agricultural service selected lands allegedly suitable for rubber, usually on the side of these new roads. Officials then obliged villagers to plant rubber communally, on plots from 25 to 40 hectares in size, using their own axes and machetes. The administration imposed and supervised weeding, pruning, and tapping operations, in a kind of "micro-management" which was simultaneously burdensome and ineffective. In law, Africans owed 60 days of labor a year, but in practice they were made to complete fixed tasks, which required considerably more time than this. Officials fixed the prices at which the latex was to be sold to a European monopsonist, who then carried out primary processing tasks (Nelson 1994: 162, 168–9, 171–4).

In typical colonial fashion, it was thought that *Hevea brasiliensis* "seems hardly the type of tree which natives will naturally plant, cultivate and tend." (Great Britain Naval Intelligence Division 1944: 382) It was noted that in 1937, 60,000 seedlings had been distributed and planted by "natives" near Bongandanga, in the region of Coquilhatville (Great Britain 1944: 382). Paradoxically, Africans began to collect wild rubber again in 1937, not because of compulsion, but as a rational response to high taxes and low fixed official prices for cultivated products (Great Britain 1944: 425; Nelson 1994: 167).

In the great crisis caused by the Japanese seizure of Southeast Asia in 1942, the Belgians once again emphasized the forced gathering of wild rubber, which was authorized by a decree of March 1942 (Henry 1983: 396, note 47). Wild rubber leapt from 7 percent of total rubber exports of just over 1000 tonnes in 1939, to 70 percent of nearly 8000 tonnes in 1945 (*Bulletin Agricole* 1961: 107). However, these demands raised the ghosts of the repudiated Leopoldian past (Vink 2001). The authorities therefore provided carrots for collectors in this hour of need, establishing favorable producer prices to stimulate the flow of latex, and making scarce consumer goods especially available to sellers of crude rubber (Cornelis 1983: 60–1, 70, 86). Whether raw rubber really was wild rubber remains far from clear in many cases, as the tapping of abandoned groves, especially of *Manihot glaziovii* and *Funtumia elastica*, was typically classed as collection from the wild (Becquet 1945: 72–3).

The forced planting of *Hevea* was also tied to the war effort, sometimes taking the form of experimental "ultra-dense" stands (Peemans 1997: 126; Serier 1993: 199). Whereas "natives" officially had 2099 hectares in *Hevea* in 1941, by 1945 this had shot up to 28,143 hectares (*Bulletin Agricole* 1961: 102). High hopes were placed on this spurt of planting for the expansion of a substantial rubber peasantry in the post-war years (Crubilé 1950: 318).

The taint of coercion appears to have been responsible for a sharp decline in smallholder rubber in the post-war Congo. The area planted fell to only 19,000 hectares in 1951, and it was tellingly noted that this was "under government control" (*Encyclopédie* 1949–52: I, 589, III, 393). In 1950, "native rubber" represented a mere 2 percent of exports of over 9000 tonnes. However, a resolutely optimistic official tone was maintained, as it was declared that rubber trees planted during the war were not yet bearing (Belgium 1950: 197, 254).

Forced cultivation was considered to have ended in 1949, although a decree of 1957 still assumed the existence of such regulations, and emphasis was rather placed on *paysannats africains*, which had already been foreseen in the 1930s. In theory, the *paysannats* were to create a rural petty bourgeoisie, enjoying individual title to surveyed land, and working together in cooperatives. In practice, the heavy hand of the administration was pervasive, and primary processing continued to be reserved to settlers and companies. Africans were particularly resentful of the strong pressures applied to grow certain crops for "educational" reasons (Jewsiewicki 1983: 19–20, 46, 53; Peemans 1997: 73).

*Hevea*, together with oil palms and coffee, was earmarked as one of the chief perennials to be grown on the *paysannats africains* of the forest zone from 1949, with great hopes placed in developing "rational cultivation." However, risks were borne by Africans, while the profits of primary processing remained essentially with settlers and companies (Jewsiewicki 1983: 19, 53). There were some positive results, but smallholder rubber in 1958 accounted for only 3576 tonnes, or just under 10 percent of a total harvest of 37,422 tonnes (*Bulletin Agricole* 1961: 132).

After independence in 1960, many of the crops imposed or "encouraged" by the colonizers simply returned to bush, or were replaced by other cultigens

(Jewsiewicki 1983: 53). In the case of rubber, the state fixed a producer price for peasant rubber that became absurdly low due to rampant inflation, and this was probably the single main cause for a rapid decline in output (Peemans 1997: 248). Unlike their Indonesian counterparts, Congolese smallholders were generally unable to counter the fall in real prices through smuggling, due to the tyranny of geography and the nature of neighboring countries. A free rubber peasantry, so often proclaimed since the end of King Leopold's violent tyranny, had yet again failed to materialize.

## 9.7  Conclusion

The causes for the divergent paths of rubber cultivation in Indonesia and the Congo still remain to be fully elucidated. It would be necessary to refer to detailed calculations of costs, prices and yields over the long run to be sure of the scale of Indonesia's natural comparative advantage, and it is far from clear whether archival and published materials would allow for such an exercise. In particular, the impact of disease might repay closer attention. Moreover, serendipity and "path dependency" need to be factored in.

In terms of the agents involved in cultivation, large rubber corporations in the two areas were not dissimilar, and the mighty Brussels-based Socfin group was active in both. The main argument put forward by rubber planters for preferring Indonesia to the Congo was more abundant and cheaper labor in the former territory. It is also possible that the productivity of rubber workers in Indonesia was higher than in the Congo, whereas palm fruit cutters in Equatorial Africa had learned skills from their parents that were not present in Southeast Asia. It thus took special circumstances, such as the international cartel of 1934 and global warfare, to make the Congo appear attractive to capitalists as a place in which to cultivate *Hevea*.

The crux of the matter appears to lie in policies toward smallholders. While no government in the Congo or Indonesia ever systematically took the side of smallholders in the period under consideration, degrees of discrimination varied. The heavy-handed dirigisme of the Belgian authorities contrasted with a more laissez-faire attitude on the part of the Dutch. As for the independent Indonesian state, it developed its own brand of benign, if unintended, neglect. As a result, the sullen and resentful cultivation of *Hevea* rubber by North Congolese smallholders was a world apart from the eager and voluntary adoption of the same crop by their counterparts in Sumatra and Borneo.

## References

AA = Archives Africaines, Brussels, 3602, 163, A. Hallet to Minister of Colonies, April 5, 1923.

AGR = Archives Générales du Royaume, Brussels, Eetvelde Papers, 161, "Note sur les Hevea Brasiliensis au Congo," undated [c. 1905].

Allen, G. C. (1940) "Japanese industry: its organization and development to 1937," in

E. B. Schumpeter (ed.), *The industrialization of Japan and Manchukuo*, New York: Macmillan, 477–786.

Allen, G. C. and Donnithorne, A.G. (1962) *Western enterprise in Indonesia and Malaysia*, London: George Allen & Unwin, 2nd printing.

Anciaux, L. (1955) *La participation des Belges à l'oeuvre coloniale des Hollandais aux Indes orientales*, Brussels: Institut Colonial Royal Belge.

Anonymous (1947) "The native agriculture and its recovery," *The Economic Review of Indonesia*, 1, 11, 165–9.

AS = Archives de la Société Financière des Caoutchoucs [Socfin], Brussels, Veldekens, Biography of Robert Hallet.

Barlow, C. and Drabble, J. (1990) "Government and the emerging rubber industries in Indonesia and Malaya, 1900–1940," in A. Booth, W. J. O'Malley, and A. Weidemann (eds.), *Indonesian economic history in the Dutch colonial era*, New Haven, Conn.: Yale University Press.

Baudhuin, F. (1944) *Histoire économique de la Belgique*, Brussels: E. Bruylant.

Bauer, P. T. (1948) *The rubber industry, a study in competition and monopoly*, London: Longmans Green.

Baulkwill, W. J. (1989) "The history of natural rubber production," in C. C. Webster and W. J. Baulkwill (eds.), *Rubber*, Harlow: Longman.

Becquet, A. (c.1945) "Le caoutchouc," in *Congo Belge 1944*, [Léopoldville]: Imprimerie du Gouvernement-Général, 72–3.

Belgium (1950) *Rapport sur l'administration de la colonie du Congo Belge pendant l'année 1950, présenté aux chambres législatives*, Brussels.

Booth, A. (1988) *Agricultural development in Indonesia*, Sydney: Allen and Unwin.

*Bulletin Agricole du Congo Belge et du Ruanda–Urundi, volume jubilaire, 1910–1960* (1961) Brussels: Ministère du Congo Belge et du Ruanda–Urundi.

Clarence-Smith, W. G. (1994) "The impact of forced coffee cultivation on Java, 1805–1917," *Indonesia Circle*, 64, 214–64.

Clarence-Smith, W. G. (1997a) "The Rivaud-Hallet plantation group in the economic crises of the inter-war years," in P. Lanthier and H. Watelet (eds.), *Private enterprises during economic crises: tactics and strategies*, Ottawa: Legas.

Clarence-Smith, W. G. (1997b) "Hadhrami entrepreneurs in the Malay World, c. 1750 to c. 1940," in U. Freitag and W. G. Clarence-Smith (eds.), *Hadhrami traders, scholars and statesmen in the Indian Ocean, 1750s to 1960s*, Leiden: E. J. Brill.

Clarence-Smith, W. G. (2009) "The battle for rubber in the Second World War: cooperation and resistance," Open University and Institute for the Study of the Americas, Commodities of empire working paper No. 14 (electronic publication: www.open.ac. uk/Arts/ferguson-centre/commodities-of-empire/working-papers/abstract-william-clarenc-smith-nov09.htm).

Clarence-Smith, W. G. (2010) "La Socfin (Groupe Rivaud) entre l'Axe et les Alliés," in H. Bonin, C. Bouneau, and H. Joly (eds.), *Les entreprises et l'outre-mer pendant la Seconde Guerre Mondiale*, Pessac: Maison des Sciences de l'Homme d'Aquitaine.

Clarence-Smith, W. G. (2012) "Grands et petits planteurs de caoutchouc en Afrique, 1934–1973," *Economies Rurale, Agriculture, Alimentations, Territoires*, 330–1, 88–101.

Coates, A. (1987) *The commerce in rubber: the first 250 years*, Singapore: Oxford University Press.

Coble, P. M. (2003) *Chinese capitalists in Japan's new order: the occupied lower Yangzi, 1937–1945*, Berkeley: University of California Press.

Cornelis, H. A. A. (1983) "Belgisch Congo en Ruanda-Urundi tijdens de Tweede

Wereldoorlog: de economische en financiële situatie," in *Le Congo Belge durant la deuxième guerre mondiale*, Brussels: Académie Royale des Sciences d'Outre-Mer, 51–81.

Crubilé, D. (1950) "Le caoutchouc," in E. Guernier (ed.), *Afrique Equatoriale Française*, Paris: Encyclopédie Coloniale et Maritime.

Dean, W. (1987) *Brazil and the struggle for rubber, a study in environmental history*, Cambridge: Cambridge University Press.

de Vathaire, A. (2009) "Les écrivains-planteurs français de caoutchouc en Malaisie, 1905–1957," Doctoral thesis, Université de La Rochelle.

Dick, H. (1990) "Interisland trade, economic integration, and the emergence of the national economy," in A. Booth, W. J. O'Malley, and A. Weidemann (eds.), *Indonesian economic history in the Dutch colonial era*, New Haven, Conn.: Yale University Press.

Donner, W. (1987) *Land use and environment in Indonesia*, London: C. Hurst.

Edington, J. A. S. (1991) *Rubber in West Africa*, London: Rex Collings.

*Encyclopédie du Congo belge* (1949–52), Brussels: Editions Bieleveld.

Fieldhouse, D. K. (1978) *Unilever overseas, the anatomy of a multinational, 1895–1965*, London: Croom Helm.

Fincol (Financière des Colonies) "Rapport annuel."

Great Britain, Naval Intelligence Division (1944) *The Belgian Congo*, Oxford: His Majesty's Stationery Office.

Harms, R. (1975) "The end of red rubber: a reassessment," *Journal of African History*, 16, 1, 73–88.

Helleiner, G. K. (1966) *Peasant agriculture, government, and economic growth in Nigeria*, Homewood, Ill.: Richard D. Irwin.

Henry, J.-M. (1983) "L'INEAC en Afrique pendant la seconde guerre mondiale," in *Le Congo Belge durant la deuxième guerre mondiale*, Brussels: Académie Royale des Sciences d'Outre-Mer, 313–97.

Houben, V. J. H. *et al.* (1999) *Coolie labour in colonial Indonesia: a study of labour relations in the Outer Islands, c.1900–1940*, Wiesbaden: Harrassowitz.

Huybrechts, A. (1970) *Transports et structures de développement au Congo: étude de progrès économique de 1900 à 1970*, Paris: Mouton.

*India-Rubber Journal*, London.

Jewsiewicki, B. (1983) "Modernisation ou destruction du village africain: l'économie politique de la 'modernisation agricole' au Congo Belge," *Les Cahiers du CEDAF*, 5, 1–79.

Johnston, A. (1989) "Diseases and pests," in C. C. Webster and W. J. Baulkwill (eds.), *Rubber*, Harlow: Longman.

Joye, P. and Lewin, R. (1961) *Les trusts au Congo*, Brussels: Société Populaire d'Editions.

Knaap, G. J. (1989) *Changing economy in Indonesia, Volume 9, Transport 1819–1940*, Amsterdam: Royal Tropical Institute.

Laclavère, G. (ed.) (1978) *Atlas de la République du Zaïre*, Paris: Editions Jeune Afrique.

Lieu, D. K. (1936) *The growth and industrialization of Shanghai*, Shanghai: China Institute of Pacific Relations.

Lindblad, J. T. (1988) *Between Dayak and Dutch: the economic history of southeast Kalimantan, 1880–1942*, Dordrecht: Foris.

Lufungula L. (2002) "Patel Ismail Youssuf: un bâtisseur de Coquilhatville, 1934–1969," *Annales Aeqatoria*, 23, 217–44.

McFadyean, A. (1944) *The history of rubber regulation, 1934–1943*, London: George Allen and Unwin.

Mitchell, B. R. (2007) *International historical statistics: Africa, Asia and Oceania, 1750–2005*, Basingstoke: Palgrave Macmillan, 5th edn.

Morris, J. E. (1989) "Processing and marketing," in C. C. Webster and W. J. Baulkwill (eds.), *Rubber*, Harlow: Longman.

Nawiyanto, S. (2005) *The rising sun in a Javanese rice granary: change and the impact of the Japanese occupation on the agricultural economy of Besuki residency, 1942–1945*, Yogyakarta: Galang Press.

Nelson, S. H. (1994) *Colonialism in the Congo basin, 1880–1940*, Athens: Ohio University Press.

Northrup, D. (1988) *Beyond the bend in the river: African labor in eastern Zaïre, 1865–1940*, Athens: Ohio Center for International Studies.

O'Reilly, M. and Keating, J. T. (1983) *The Goodyear story*, Elmsford, NY: Goodyear Tire and Rubber Company.

Peemans, J.-P. (1997) *Le Congo-Zaïre au gré du XXe siècle: état, économie, société, 1880–1990*, Paris: L'Harmattan.

Pelzer, K. J. (1978) *Planter and peasant: colonial policy and the agrarian struggle in East Sumatra, 1863–1947*, Leiden: Royal Institute of Linguistics and Anthropology.

Prillwitz, P. M. (1947) "The estate agriculture during the Japanese occupation," *The Economic Review of Indonesia*, 1, 1, 13–17.

Purwanto, B. (1992) "From *dusun* to market: native rubber cultivation in southern Sumatra, 1890–1940," PhD Thesis, University of London.

Schoofs, M. (1944) *La préparation du caoutchouc en Extrême-Orient*, Brussels: Ministère des Colonies (initially published in *Bulletin Agricole du Congo Belge*, 35, 1, 1944).

Schulze, W. (1973) *Liberia: länderkundliche Dominanten und regionale Strukturen*, Darmstadt: Buch Gesellschaft.

Serier, J.-B. (1993) *Histoire du caoutchouc*, Paris: Desjonquères.

Shapiro, D. and Tollens, E. (1992) *The agricultural development of Zaire*, Aldershot: Avebury.

Tan, K.K. (1994) *The memoirs of Tan Kah-kee*, Singapore: Singapore University Press.

Thee, K.W. (1977) *Plantation agriculture and export growth: an economic history of East Sumatra*, Jakarta: LEKNAS-LIPI.

Touwen, J. (2001) *Extremes in the archipelago: trade and economic development in the Outer Islands of Indonesia, 1900–1942*, Leiden: KITLV Press.

van den Abeele, M. (1968) "Hallet, Robert," in *Biographie belge d'outremer*, Brussels: Académie Royale des Sciences d'Outre-Mer, vol. 6, columns 450–2.

Vandervelde, E. (1909) *Les derniers jours de l'Etat du Congo: journal de voyage, juillet–octobre 1908*, Mons: La Société Nouvelle.

Vandewalle, G. (1966) *De conjuncturele evolutie in Kongo en Ruanda-Urundi, van 1920 tot 1939, en van 1949 tot 1958*, Ghent: Rijksuniversiteit Gent.

Vellut, J.-L. (1991) "La communauté portugaise du Congo belge, 1885–1960," in J. Everaert and E. Stols (eds.) *Flandre et Portugal: aux confluents de deux cultures*, Antwerp: Fonds Mercator.

Vink, H. (2001) "La guerre de 1940–45 vécue à Coquilhatville (Mbandaka, R. D. du Congo)," *Annales Aequatoria*, 22, 21–101.

Vleming, J. L. (ed.) (1926) *Het Chineessche zakenleven in Nederlandsch-Indië*, Weltevreden: Volkslectuur.

Watson, G. A. (1989) "Climate and soil," in C. C. Webster and W. J. Baulkwill (eds.), *Rubber*, Harlow: Longman.

Whitford, H. N. and Anthony, A. (1926) *Rubber production in Africa*, Washington, DC: US Department of Commerce and Trade (Promotion Series, No. 34).

# 10 Manufacturing and foreign investment in colonial Indonesia

*J. Thomas Lindblad*

## 10.1 Introduction

The Rotterdam-trained economist Sumitro Djojohadikusumo was a key figure in shaping economic policy and promoting the science of economics in newly independent Indonesia. As minister of trade and industry in the Natsir cabinet, a position to which he was appointed at the age of 33, he took the initiative of drafting a full-scale scheme for industrialization in Indonesia, the so-called Economic Urgency Plan, also referred to as the Sumitro Plan. The plan was released in April 1951, when the Sukiman cabinet had already taken charge, with another minister of trade and industry. It is interesting to note that the final thrust towards industrialization in the Belgian Congo took place at virtually the same time, during the final decade of Belgian colonial rule.

Sumitro had an acute grasp of the pressing need in Indonesia for balanced economic growth based on both agricultural and industrial development (Thee 2010: 49–50). Despite short-term gains for Indonesia from the Korean War boom due to rising demand for oil and rubber, a solid manufacturing base was lacking which could have reduced the nation's extreme dependence on world markets for exports of primary products. In the event, such an industrial base only materialized under Suharto's New Order government. When assessing the economic repercussions of colonial rule in the Netherlands Indies as compared to the Belgian Congo, we need to understand why so little industrialization had taken place prior to Indonesian independence.

The Sumitro Plan was highly ambitious. Total outlays during the first two years of execution alone required a capital injection of Rp.920 million, a figure corresponding to one-third of total export revenue in 1950 (Lindblad 2008: 81, 224). The Indonesian government obviously had no capacity to finance investment at such an order of magnitude, even aside from the huge demands on public finance for current expenditure. Only large-scale foreign investment could have ended the bottleneck in financing long-term investment undertakings, but such inflows were for a variety of reasons drying up precisely when they were most needed. This signified a reversal of the trend during the late-colonial period when foreign direct investment had played an increasingly large role in propelling the Indonesian economy. This brings us to a second issue. Why was foreign investment, in particular from the colonial mother country, so strongly biased against the secondary sector of the Netherlands Indies?

This chapter consists of three sections, apart from the introduction and conclusion. The first section assesses the efforts at early industrialization during the late-colonial period and immediately after independence, whereas the second section concerns foreign investment under colonialism in Indonesia. The third section offers a brief case study concerning the subsidiary set up in colonial Indonesia by Anglo-Dutch giant Unilever in the 1930s. Occasional comparisons with the situation in the Belgian Congo are inserted wherever applicable.[1]

## 10.2 Modernity in a traditional context

Indonesia today is a far cry from the stereotyped image of a predominantly agrarian economy that is often projected in memories of colonial days. In 2010, manufacturing accounted for almost 55 percent of Gross Domestic Product (GDP), twice as much as the tertiary sector and more than three times as much as agriculture.[2] The decisive transformation in the nation's economic structure took place between 1965 and the 1980s when the secondary sector bypassed the primary sector as the prime engine of economic growth (World Bank 1992: 222). But the real breakthrough in restructuring toward an industrial economy only occurred in the 1980s and early 1990s when stabilization, or even decline of world oil prices, convinced the Suharto government of the necessity to move away from dependence on unprocessed exports. Interestingly, various projects proposed in the Sumitro Plan that had remained on paper, such as the Asahan aluminum smelter (North Sumatra), were then dusted off and implemented (Hill 2000: 156–75; Dick *et al.* 2002: 220–3). By 1990, the share of agriculture in total employment, which is likely to exceed its share in GDP, had fallen below 50 percent Dick *et al.* 2002: 199). Such statistics testify to the presence of a huge unused potential for industrialization during earlier phases of economic development, including the late-colonial period. The question is: Could the industrial breakthrough have taken place at about the same time in the Belgian Congo, with initial progress during the 1910s and 1920s and a final thrust during the 1940s and 1950s?

Discussions on the right moment for industrialization are invariably contingent upon the quality of statistics. The rich statistical heritage of Dutch colonial rule in Indonesia has permitted a reconstruction of national accounts that provides us with a useful point of departure, even if historical GDP estimates need to be used with caution because of the sometimes bold assumptions made.[3] The contribution of manufacturing to GDP in the Netherlands Indies, as projected by Pierre van der Eng (2002: 172), remained stable at a level of approximately 15 percent throughout most of the late-colonial period (Figure 10.1). The pre-1940 share of manufacturing in GDP in the Netherlands Indies was, therefore, not markedly different from the one reported for the Belgian Congo in the late 1950s. Yet, whereas the Belgian Congo stood out among neighboring countries, ranking second in sub-Saharan Africa, the Netherlands Indies clearly lagged

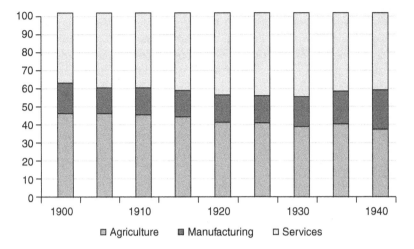

*Figure 10.1* Sectoral composition of Indonesian GDP, 1900–40 (source: van der Eng 2002: 171–2).

Note
Gross Domestic Product estimated at 1983 level market prices in Rp. billion.

behind Asian nations such as Japan and India. The high degree of stability over time in the composition of GDP in colonial Indonesia is borne out by the position of the services sector. Tertiary economic activities occupied a rather constant proportion of GDP, between one-third and 40 percent, throughout the entire twentieth century (Marks 2009: 80).

The strength of the bias against industrialization is evident from immediate post-independence developments when a "structural retrogression" of sorts seems to have taken place. The less modern parts of the economy allegedly gained at the expense of those with a greater potential for technological progress, a development obviously at variance with professed priorities of economic policy as well as expectations among development economists. In the early 1950s, manufacturing was estimated to account for merely 8.5 percent of GDP, far less than in the late 1930s. But the trend against modernization does not appear to have been sustained for very long. Calculations show that manufacturing accounted for 13.5 percent of national income in 1958, an increase of almost 60 percent in only a few years; the percentage stayed at virtually the same level up to the mid-1960s (Booth 1998: 70; Mangkusuwondo 1975: 13; World Bank 1992: 220). These simple statistics reveal that there was considerable scope for far more industrialization prior to Indonesian independence. This does not appear to have been the case in the Belgian Congo.

There was a wide spectrum of manufacturing activity in all parts of the late-colonial economy. Numbers of factories and workshops in the Netherlands Indies showed a steady increase during the 1910s and 1930s in particular, coinciding with similar developments in the Belgian Congo (Figure 10.2). A few examples serve to illustrate the industrial expansion that did take place. The number of rice mills, mostly in Java, climbed from about 200 around 1910 to more than 800 in the mid-1930s. There were nearly 200 sugar processing plants in East and Central Java at the time of World War I, but this number was reduced to some 130 by a succession of mergers and closures during the worldwide depression in the 1930s. Large, modern oil refineries were operated in North Sumatra (then East Sumatra) and East Kalimantan (then Dutch Borneo), there was a proliferation of textile factories in West Java, numerous installations for manufacturing *kretek* cigarettes in Central Java, shipyards and engineering firms in Batavia (now Jakarta) and Surabaya. The first cement factory in the Dutch colony, located near Padang in West Sumatra, began producing in the early 1910s, predating the first cement factory in the Congo by less than a decade.

The indigenous population in colonial Indonesia was large and growing fast, numbering almost 60 million people by 1930. Unlike the Belgian Congo, demand for cheap, unskilled labor did not have to create a bottleneck in setting up industrial ventures. The industrial labor force increased gradually, reaching some 140,000 persons by 1930 (Segers 1987: 59–61, 77). In addition, it must not be overlooked that many rural dwellers, identified in the census as being engaged in agriculture, in fact pursued part-time economic activities in the secondary sector as well (Alexander *et al.* 1991). This, again, may not have applied to the situation in the Belgian Congo, where labor was in chronically short supply and industrial development, especially in the mining areas, almost fully detached from rural subsistence production (see Houben and Seibert, Chapter 8 above).

Indigenous entrepreneurship played a particularly prominent role in *kretek* cigarette manufacturing and textile production. Following the establishment of a

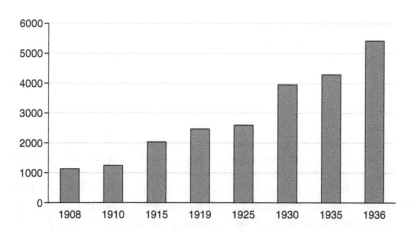

*Figure 10.2* Number of factories in the Netherlands Indies, 1908–36 (source: Segers 1987: 59–61).

Note
Numbers of factories and workshops as registered under the Factory Act of 1905.

large-scale cigarette factory in 1910, Kudus in Central Java turned into a predominantly industrial town, a most unusual development in the Indonesian countryside at the time. By 1933, Kudus counted 15 large factories, 48 medium-sized plants and 800 small production units (Lindblad 2008: 30). The Sundanese textile industry emerged at a slightly later stage, supported by government promotion of mechanization in the 1920s and increasingly replacing imports of textiles during the economic depression in the 1930s. Production was centered in Majalaya in West Java, which by the late 1930s alone counted 275 weaving mills and almost 3300 handlooms (Lindblad 2008: 32). Kudus and Majalaya both used labor-intensive production techniques and relatively simple technologies while benefiting from unlimited access to a large and growing domestic market of consumers. By contrast, indigenous industrial activities were virtually absent in the Belgian Congo.

Ethnic Chinese often mixed trading with activities in the secondary sector. The foremost example of a late-colonial Chinese tycoon, erecting a virtual empire of firms, is Oei Tiong Ham in Semarang, whose concern included sugar mills and light manufacturing. There are other examples such as Tiong A Fie in Medan in the early 1920s (Claver 2006: 366–9). Ethnic Chinese were also successful in already existing branches such as the Sundanese textile industry or *kretek* manufacturing in both Kudus and the Brantas Valley in East Java. Here indigenous producers increasingly operated as subcontractors to Chinese factory owners with more capital. Chinese entrepreneurs also played an important role in copra oil refining, operating three out of four oil mills at the end of the colonial period. The fourth one, Archa, was acquired by Unilever after the Pacific War (Wamsteker 1993: 47).

The distinguishing characteristic of manufacturing initiated by European investors in the colony was access not only to capital but also to modern technology. The refinery built by Shell at Balikpapan in the late 1890s was known as one of the most technologically advanced in the region, clearly outpacing the rival one at Pangkalan Brandan (North Sumatra), erected earlier by Royal Dutch (Koninklijke). After having been set up as a jointly owned subsidiary by Royal Dutch and Shell, the BPM (Bataafsche Petroleum Maatschappij) counted as the colony's single largest industrial enterprise. Sugar factories using the newest machinery mushroomed in the Javanese countryside during the 1920s. By the late 1930s, there were about 125 of them and the industry has aptly been characterized as "a first-world industry in a third-world field" (Lindblad 2008: 53; Knight 1996: 155). Industrial ventures outside the oil sector were not confined to Java. An enterprise named *Insulinde*, for processing copra from Sulawesi (then Celebes), underwent a very rapid expansion during the late 1910s but went bankrupt in the early 1920s (Kamerling 1982).

During the 1920s and 1930s, a whole host of leading international concerns erected modern factories in and around Batavia, catering to a rapidly growing domestic market. Production included automobiles at General Motors, tires from Goodyear, Bata shoes, electrical appliances from Philips, and soap and margarine produced by Unilever. Late-colonial Indonesia thus became self-sufficient in a wide range of industrial consumer goods, for instance cigarettes, beer, shoes, and confectionery, whereas margarine, biscuits, batteries, and bicycles were also being produced on a significant scale (Dick *et al.* 2002: 160–1). The proliferation of manufacturing enterprises during the final decade of uncontested colonial rule is corroborated by information from an annual directory of private business firms, incorporated under Western law, which, incidentally, would exclude virtually all indigenous operations (Handboek 1888–1940). According to an informal estimate, Java alone counted about 4000 individual factories of varying size at the time of the Japanese occupation in 1942 (Wamsteker 1993: 40).

Colonial economic policy played a key part in the somewhat haphazard and inconsistent industrial development from the late nineteenth century until the end of effective Dutch colonial rule over the entire archipelago in 1942. From the 1870s onward, liberal economic policies had successively replaced the state-run commercial agriculture of the Cultivation System in Java, which arguably inspired King Leopold when he erected his Congo Free State. Extreme liberalism held sway in economic policies as implemented in the Netherlands Indies for more than six decades, up to the early 1930s when the worldwide economic depression necessitated other policies (see Thee, Chapter 2 above). Liberalism implied both virtually unlimited access for imports in the domestic market and free play for foreign direct investment. The former reduced the scope for import-substituting industrialization under the protective umbrella of import tariffs whereas the latter linked much new industrial activity to the simultaneous expansion of exploitation of natural resources with the use of foreign capital and technology. Foreign imports benefited from the increasing demand for industrial consumer goods and foreign firms were mostly interested in enhancing capabilities in export production. In the absence of an explicit industrial policy, there was an inherent bias against "easy" industrialization and in favor of specific types of "difficult" industrialization during most of the late-colonial period.

As main suppliers of primary products in world markets, both the Belgian Congo and the Netherlands Indies were severely hit by the depression of the 1930s. In the Netherlands Indies, declining incomes and rising competition from cheap Japanese imported goods prompted a shift away from liberalism toward protectionism. The Crisis Import Ordinance of 1933 was effectively, if not overtly, directed against Japanese industrial products. In 1934 it was followed by an Industry Regulation. This was the first step toward a comprehensive policy of industrialization, although it had been preceded by the promotion of mechanization in textile production in West Java during the 1920s. A major aim of the colonial government was to streamline efforts toward industrialization, for instance by imposing capacity controls on production in order to prevent excessive competition (van Oorschot 1956: 46). Local industry centers were set up from 1936 to further support industrialization. In the late 1930s, the newly created Department of Economic Affairs in Batavia expanded rapidly and began designing a strategy of full-fledged industrialization, which, interestingly, included some projects that were later to figure in the Sumitro Plan. In 1941, on the eve of the Japanese occupation, when the colonial mother country itself was occupied, the so-called Visman committee was busy formulating specific targets of industrialization. It proved too late.

A chief bottleneck in sustaining industrial development in the Belgian Congo obviously lay in human capital formation. This applied to the Netherlands Indies as well, albeit to a less extreme degree. There was an intermediate ethnic group, consisting largely of Chinese, boosting a strong tradition of entrepreneurship and trading. Even if Dutch colonial policies were geared to maintaining ethnic segmentation in society, most of all by differential access to education, a tiny indigenous elite still did emerge, which found no counterpart in the Belgian Congo prior to 1954. Finally, as mentioned, indigenous entrepreneurship had proved viable in certain specific branches of manufacturing, in which Western firms showed little or no interest, notably *kretek* cigarette manufacturing and textile production.

Returning to the question of the timing of a possible industrial breakthrough, we consider three options: at an early stage, very late, and not at all. The first possibility has been suggested, somewhat provocatively, by Dick, putting Surabaya on a par with Bombay and Osaka in terms of industrial development in the 1880s or 1890s. For a variety of reasons, the take-off achieved by Japan failed to materialize in Java at the turn of the century (Dick 1993: 138, 2003: 255–61). The second option rests upon the counterfactual hypothesis that the Japanese army did not invade Indonesia and – by logical corollary – Indonesia remained a Dutch colony a bit longer. Then Indonesia would have been the first to industrialize in Southeast Asia, not a late-comer lagging behind its neighbors (Dick *et al.* 2002: 162). In the final analysis, the third option, coinciding with historical reality, appears the most probable, all the more since van der Eng's optimistic assessment that manufacturing by 1940 contributed one-fifth of GDP cannot be taken at face value (van der Eng 2002: 172). The climate had never been conducive to industrialization except for a few years toward the very end of the late-colonial period. Despite the tremendous hardships, it is unlikely that the Japanese occupation and the Indonesian Revolution would have completely annihilated an industrial base, if there had been one in 1942.

## 10.3 The different faces of capitalism

Private foreign investment only developed in the Netherlands Indies during the late-colonial period and required a relatively long gestation period after the colonial state had withdrawn from direct involvement in production, from 1870 onward. A significant increase in foreign-held asset holdings only occurred in the very early twentieth century, especially in regions outside Java that had just or barely been brought under effective colonial rule. Accumulated foreign direct investment rose from 750 million guilders in 1900 to 1.7 billion guilders in 1914. A specular increase followed during World War I and the 1920s, pushing the accumulated aggregate toward four billion guilders by 1930, an amount to be adjusted downwards by divestment during the depression of the 1930s. Dutch firms accounted for about 70 percent of the total. More than one-half of all foreign investment was in estate agriculture and almost one-fifth in the oil industry alone (Lindblad 1998: 14). Only a small proportion of foreign direct investment entered manufacturing, which is all the more striking considering the strong reliance on foreign capital in the final thrust toward industrialization during the 1970s and 1980s (Hill 1988: 80–3).

In order to understand the apparent bias against the secondary sector in incoming foreign investment during the late-colonial period, we need to take a closer look at the character and function of such investment. A significant feature was the skewed size distribution, with a small number of large enterprises as well as large numbers of small- and medium-sized firms. The foreign-owned enterprise at the top, BPM, had a registered paid-up equity of 300 million guilders. Two other leading Dutch-owned concerns, NHM (Nederlandsche Handel-Maatschappij, Netherlands Trading Association) and KPM (Koninklijke Paketvaart-Maatschappij, Royal Packet Company), were good for respectively 80 and 30 million guilders of equity (Lindblad 1998: 77).

The skewed size distribution needs to be linked with the identity of firms. The context of colonialism offered a peculiar distinction based on degree of foreignness. Dutch-owned companies were obviously foreign compared to indigenous ones but less so than firms with British or American owners since they operated under the same authorities and in the same legal system as at home in the Netherlands. It also made a difference whether a Dutch-owned firm was run from headquarters in the Netherlands or in the colony. In the latter case, the firm was technically not foreign but it was managed in the interests of overseas owners. The large Dutch-owned firms were generally run from the Netherlands. Around 1930, companies in this category held at least 70 percent of all foreign-owned equity against only 14 percent held by Dutch-owned firms with headquarters in the Netherlands, a category making up almost one-half of all companies known to have foreign proprietors (Lindblad 1998: 77, 79). The fine distinctions with regard to identity are completed by adding the numerous firms owned by ethnic Chinese residents in the colony. These firms were technically not foreign at all but were effectively treated as such, a tendency that was only to be reinforced after independence.

Investing in the Netherlands Indies held a threefold attraction for Dutch owners of capital. In the first place, the Indonesian archipelago offered – just like the Belgian Congo – unique opportunities for the exploitation of rich natural resources. The Netherlands Indies possessed fertile soils for growing sugar, tobacco, rubber, coffee, tea, and palm oil, to name only the most successful cash crops, and mineral wealth, in particular oil and tin. Massive access to cheap, unskilled labor was not in itself conceived as a major asset of the colonial economy, but only when labor-intensive techniques were applied in the exploitation of natural resources, especially in estate agriculture. This was indeed different from the situation in the Belgian Congo.

The second source of attraction for Dutch investors lay in colonial rule itself, a feature that obviously applied to the Belgian Congo to at least the same degree. Colonial rule offered advantages that would not have been easily obtained elsewhere with regard to language, institutional connections, legal protection, and political leverage, even affinity with social and cultural life. It was no coincidence that the Dutch ranked first and the British second in the Netherlands whereas it was exactly the other way around in British Malaya.

The third reason to invest in the Netherlands Indies was connected to the increasing globalization of major Dutch corporations, using Southeast Asia in general and colonial Indonesia in particular as a vehicle for expansion. Bilateral trade between the Netherlands and its colony had been of paramount importance until the late nineteenth century but in the twentieth century this trading relationship was dwarfed by the interests of investment capital (Dick *et al.* 2002: 128–30). In the Belgian Congo, by contrast, investment activities appear to have been more exclusively confined to the mineral resources offered on location.

The strong orientation toward exports of primary products to the world market is crucial to our understanding of why so much foreign direct investment resulted in so little industrialization. This may be substantiated by comparing export figures with estimates of investment commitments over a period of time. Trade figures are readily available but investment commitments on an annual basis can only be inferred for Dutch equity from extrapolations from claims for indemnification submitted by Dutch companies after nationalization by the Sukarno administration in the late 1950s.[4] The time series of total exports and estimated accumulated Dutch-held equity do indeed show a high degree of congruence during the three decades between 1910 and 1940 (Figure 10.3). The visual correspondence between the two variables can be corroborated by simple regression analysis producing a statistically significant correlation ($R^2 = 0.66$).[5]

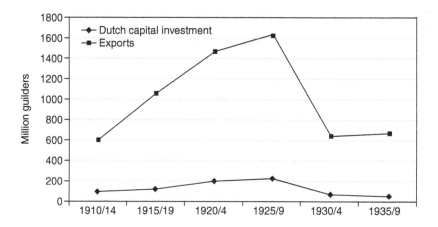

*Figure 10.3* Dutch capital investment and exports from the Netherlands Indies, 1910–39 (sources: Creutzberg 1977: 17–18; Korthals Altes 1987: 41).

Note

Five-year averages of estimated new investment of Dutch capital and value of foreign exports at current prices.

Profitability was rumored to be high in colonial investment, both in the Netherlands Indies and in the Belgian Congo. Examples of spectacular returns on invested capital are not lacking for colonial Indonesia. In the second half of the 1920s, profits from the tin mines of Billiton permitted a pay-out ratio of 70 percent to shareholders, whereas a leading manager of agricultural estates such as HVA (Handels Vereeniging "Amsterdam," Amsterdam Trading Association) paid out dividends at 30 percent or more during the same decade. The jointly owned subsidiary of Royal Dutch and Shell, BPM, generated such lavish profits that even the firm's experienced directors began feeling embarrassed (Lindblad 1998: 58, 82; van Zanden and Jonker 2007: 267). Judging from dividend payments in the 1920s, profits were also lavish at famous Dutch enterprises such as the Billiton tin mining company on the island of Belitung and the Deli tobacco company in North Sumatra (Lindblad 1996: 218). Generally speaking, a dividend ratio of 11 percent of paid-up equity was normal in the late 1920s, with sugar and oil scoring better than average (Lindblad 2008: 23). This level of profits was respectable by any business standards in the Netherlands, given also that part of the profits may not have been designated for dividend payment but rather for reinvestment in the company.

The case for high and sustained levels of profitability in foreign direct investment in the Netherlands Indies is reinforced by an argument pertaining to the time horizon in management strategy. Colonial rule offered an environment for foreign investment that for decades appeared extremely safe. Rather than any urgent need for the short-run priority of making profits as soon as possible, there was considerable scope for long-term commitment. This becomes apparent when we compare the late-colonial situation with the turbulent 1950s, when extraordinary opportunities to reap gains abroad from the Korean War boom coincided with unprecedented and mounting pressures in the domestic economy. At that time, remittance of profits to the metropolitan country was awarded top priority, which often meant tedious controversies in dealing with the Indonesian authorities (Lindblad 2008: 159). Unlike the period before independence, and indeed in stark contrast to the situation at the time in the Belgian Congo, little fresh capital investment was made by Dutch firms. In fact, virtually the only foreign direct investment of importance during the Sukarno period, up to the mid-1960s, was in the oil industry where American firms took over the lead from Anglo-Dutch Shell.

Foreign direct investment is generally welcomed not so much for filling in the savings gap in developing countries as for providing access to the newest technology. In this regard, we notice a wide variety of technological applications in the late-colonial context, ranging from extremely labor-intensive production using little technology in estate agriculture to highly capital- and technology-intensive processing in oil refineries and sugar factories. Mechanization was only sparingly introduced, for instance in tin and coal mines depending on large workforces. Spill-over effects from scattered instances of the use of advanced technologies imported directly from the metropolitan country are likely to have been few and far between in the Netherlands Indies. It is also worth noting that the promotion of mechanization in the textile industry in the 1920s, following the establishment of the Textile Institute in Bandung in 1919, was directed primarily at Sundanese or Chinese producers, not foreign-owned firms (van Oorschot 1956: 43).

The relationship between foreign firms and domestic demand also needs to be kept in mind. Foreign firms producing manufactured goods in the Netherlands Indies would in effect be competing in the domestic market with imports from the Western world, supplied by related companies or even, on occasion, by the very same business concern. Import substitution was not in the interest of foreign firms. This state of affairs formed a logical corollary to the extreme liberalism in colonial trade policy prevailing from the early 1870s until 1933.

There are two good reasons why foreign direct investment retained its built-in bias against undertakings in manufacturing. The first stems from the character and functionality of foreign direct investment in the colony. It was geared toward exports and participation in the world market, not toward meeting demand in the domestic market. As such, it was highly profitable. There was simply no urgency to change direction. The second reason has to do with colonial economic policy. There was no overt policy with respect to foreign direct investment, except openness. No effort was made to channel incoming investment into lines of production with a greater potential for sustained economic growth.

## 10.4 Unilever Indonesia

Lever's Zeepfabrieken (Soap factories), forerunner of today's Unilever Indonesia, officially opened its doors in Batavia in December 1933. A few weeks later, the firm was formally incorporated as a limited liability company with an equity capital of two million guilders, all issued and held by the mother company in Rotterdam and London. Lever's Zeep (Soap), as it was colloquially called, accounted for only a small proportion of total investment commitments by Unilever all over the world (Baudet and Fennema 1983: 236). Nevertheless, it remains a particularly interesting case study of foreign investment in a colonial setting precisely because it anticipated a profound change in the structure of the Indonesian economy. At the time of incorporation, the firm's objective was stated as follows: "manufacturing of, and trade in, oils and fats, soap and other detergents and related commodities, including required raw materials" (Handboek 1935: 1024). Together with several other foreign-owned manufacturing companies, Lever's Zeep represented a new trend in the economy of colonial Indonesia, a trend away from traditional export-oriented production using the archipelago's endowment of raw materials, onto processing manufactured goods targeting a rapidly growing domestic market. In the context of our comparative endeavor, it is noteworthy that Unilever operated a similar plant in the Belgian Congo.

Both the Margarine Union in the Netherlands and Lever Brothers in the United Kingdom, the two partners in the 1930 fusion that created Unilever, had at an earlier stage been exploring connections with the Netherlands Indies. Anton

Jurgens at the Margarine Union procured copra oil for processing elsewhere during World War I and immediately afterwards, yet abandoned his trade in 1921 after having suffered considerable losses. In 1928 and again in 1932, Charles Tatlow journeyed to the Netherlands Indies for Lever Brothers to investigate prospects of setting up production facilities in the Dutch colony. He was at first skeptical about the idea, fearing cut-throat competition from the many small-scale producers in the local market. Nor was he enthusiastic about the proposed location for a factory, Cirebon, on Java's north coast. But calculations at the head office in London predicted a potential annual profit of £40,000 and Tatlow was again dispatched to Batavia in late 1933, this time in order to find a suitable production site on the outskirts of the colony's capital (Wilson 1954: II, 181–2; Wamsteker 1993: 15–25). Significantly, the initiative to start producing in the Netherlands Indies emanated from the British partner in Unilever, not the Dutch one. This only underscores the international character of fresh investment entering the Netherlands Indies during the 1920s and 1930s. In 1937, British investors accounted for 16 percent of accumulated foreign investment in colonial Indonesia, ranking second after Dutch capital (Lindblad 1998: 14).

The product range of Lever's Zeep consisted of two commodities: soap in two different varieties, hard soap and toilet soap, known under the brand names Sunlight and Lux, as well as margarine of the familiar brand Blue Band. Hard soap was intended for both laundry and personal use. The market for hard soap was substantially larger than the one for toilet soap but competition was fiercer and profit margins narrower. Lever's Zeep increased output at a rapid pace during the second half of the 1930s. By 1940, the Unilever subsidiary commanded a market share of about 10 percent in hard soap and 32 percent in toilet soap. Blue Band, marketed from 1936 onward, had one major rival, Colgate-Palmolive's Palmboom, apart from a substantial number of small-scale Chinese and even Japanese producers. Total sales of Blue Band climbed to 9000 tons, which in 1939 corresponded to a market share of 60 percent. It is unlikely that Unilever could have made such inroads in the colony's soap and margarine markets if it had kept to relying on imports rather than embarking on producing locally. Nevertheless, the Far East accounted for just a small proportion of total worldwide sales, in 1937 merely 2.5 percent against 20 percent for Africa, including the Belgian Congo (Wilson 1954: II, 397, 408; Wamsteker 1993: 31–5).

The factory in Batavia employed some 150 persons, far less than the main competitor in toilet soap manufacturing, the German-owned Dralle factory in Surabaya (Wamsteker 1993: 116). During the company's first eight years of operations, up to the arrival of Japanese troops in 1942, the factory had two managers, one for soap, the other for margarine, one Englishman and one Dutchman, as was more often than not the case in Unilever subsidiaries. On the British side, H.G. Sandy was replaced in 1939 by Robert Graham MacMorran, who died in 1943 in a Japanese prison camp. The first Dutch manager of Lever's Zeep, Herman Bicker Caarten, was to resume his position upon the conclusion of the war. Bicker Caarten and MacMorran were jointly responsible for the first major expansion of Lever's Zeep, the acquisition in September 1941 of the Dralle factory in Surabaya, which had been seized by the Netherlands Indies authorities after the German invasion of the Netherlands. Lever's Zeep paid 225,000 guilders for the factory itself, now renamed "Colibri," and another 400,000 guilders for stocks of raw materials and finished goods. As a result, Lever's Zeep became market leader in toilet soap while extending the product range to include toothpaste as well. Employment rose to almost 1000 laborers, divided between the plants in Batavia and Surabaya (Wamsteker 1993: 35–40).

The Japanese occupation (March 1942 – August 1945) inflicted severe damage on the entire manufacturing sector in Indonesia, including the two Unilever plants where production came to a virtual standstill. But recovery after the war was relatively quick, especially since both factories were located in Dutch-controlled territory during the Indonesian Revolution (August 1945 – December 1949). Noud Caron, who succeeded Bicker Caarten as the firm's sole manager in 1947, secured a substantial loan from the leading Dutch-owned bank in Indonesia, the NHM (Nederlandsche Handel-Maatschappij, Netherlands Trading Association), whereas the returning Dutch colonial administration allocated a generous quota of 65 percent of the country's margarine production to Unilever, twice as much as its main competitor, American-owned Procter & Gamble. Already in 1947, the combined production of soap and margarine amounted to some 21,000 tons, or about the same as in 1941. A second round of expansion took place in the same year with Unilever's purchase of the Archa oil mill for 600,000 guilders. This plant, conveniently located near Unilever's Jakarta factory, had been operated by Dutchmen since the early 1920s, supplying inputs for the manufacturing of soap and margarine (Wamsteker 1993: 40–7).

Just as with developments in manufacturing and foreign investment sketched above, the story of Unilever's operations under the aegis of Dutch colonialism needs to be rounded off by touching briefly on the situation in the 1950s. At the aggregate level, the economic structure changed in the "wrong" direction for a time whilst flows of incoming foreign investment capital dried up (except in the oil sector where special privileges applied). Sentiment at Unilever's plant in Indonesia oscillated between optimism and grave concerns about the future. Total sales in the Far East region, which included Indonesia but excluded China, more than doubled during the 1950s, eventually touching 1 billion guilders. Demand for soap and margarine from Unilever was continuously reported to be increasing, at any rate up to 1957. Out of total employment in Unilever's Far East division, Indonesia accounted for at least 10 percent. In 1952, a major investment was undertaken at the Jakarta plant at a total cost of 5.5 million guilders, enabling an increase of output by 1953 at three times the level of 1941. The year 1955 saw another round of new investment at both factories, in Jakarta and Surabaya, and in the main office in downtown Jakarta (Unilever 1949–60; Unilever-Populair 1951–2; Wamsteker 1993: 50–1).

Flourishing business contrasted sharply with the deterioration of general conditions of operations of foreign firms in Sukarno's Indonesia, caused by, amongst others, wage hikes demanded by militant trade unions and severe restrictions on remittance of profits to overseas owners. Dividends could only be transferred to the Netherlands by Lever's Zeep up to 1955. The situation was aggravated for Dutch-owned firms by the escalating conflict between Indonesia and the Netherlands about the possession of western New Guinea (West Irian, now Papua). Unilever occupied a peculiar position here since it was half-Dutch, half-British. Paul Rijkens, executive manager of the concern until 1954, even attempted to create a lobby consisting of businessmen who discreetly let it be known that they did not agree with the firm Dutch stance on the issue of New Guinea. The initiative met with limited response among Dutch businessmen but surely contributed to good relations with the Indonesian government. When Dutch corporate possessions were finally expropriated in December 1957, the Unilever subsidiary was spared on account of its alleged British identity. Out of precaution, the company now replaced Dutch staff by employees of other nationalities, usually British; replacements were completed in 1958 (Baudet and Fennema 1983: 144; Unilever 1957, 1958; Wamsteker 1993: 70; Wilson 1968: 245).

Expropriation only struck at Unilever's Indonesian subsidiary some years later, in 1964, when British and American companies were seized in the framework of the so-called *Konfrontasi*, the armed conflict between Indonesia and Malaysia and its Western allies (1963–6) (Redfern 2010: 334–9). Keeping in mind the eventual fate of Dutch private firms – formal nationalization in 1959 – the management could do little but inform the shareholders that "We do not know what the future will bring in Indonesia" (Unilever 1964). In 1967, Unilever's possessions were returned to the lawful owners and in 1980 the firm was reconstituted as a limited liability company, Unilever Indonesia (P.T., Perseroan Terbatas in Indonesian), with shares issued on the Jakarta Stock Exchange and an Indonesian national, Yamani Hassan, as its chairman (Wamsteker 1993: 75–7). Unilever Indonesia has since reinforced its position as a leading foreign-owned manufacturer of light consumer goods in Indonesia. By the late 1990s, the company operated five factories, all in Java, employing more than 3000 personnel. It has gained a reputation for efficient transfers of technology to Indonesian staff, in part by maintaining limited R&D facilities in Jakarta (Lindblad 1999: 77–82). Unilever's success as a foreign-owned producer in Indonesia has been aided by both its orientation towards light manufacturing and its partial non-Dutch identity.

## 10.5 Conclusion

An oft-quoted statement by Governor-General B.C. de Jonge in the early 1930s expressed the conviction that another 300 years of Dutch colonial rule would be needed before Indonesia was ready for independence. Although this may have sounded like a far cry from the thousand-year interval deemed to be necessary in the Belgian Congo, such a statement demonstrates, if anything, that colonial rule was losing touch with reality. There were stronger forces at work that would lead to independence at a far earlier stage than anticipated, both in Indonesia and in the Congo. The salient, more general question concerns the type of heritage bequeathed to Indonesia and the Congo by the former colonial rulers. Here we can only answer that question with regard to industrial development in Indonesia. Yet suffice it to say that post-independence developments in Indonesia and the Congo do suggest that the colonial heritage differed profoundly. Indonesia was at one stage hailed by the World Bank as a Southeast Asian Newly Industrializing Country, one of the so-called Highly Performing Asian Economies, whereas the Congo gained notoriety as a "failed state" (World Bank 1993). Up to 1972, GDP per capita was higher in the Democratic Republic of the Congo than in Indonesia (see Introduction, Figure 0.4).

This chapter set out to answer two questions. Why did so little industrialization take place in the Netherlands Indies during the late-colonial period? Why was foreign direct investment in the colony biased against manufacturing? In both cases, it is instructive to distinguish between fundamental currents in macro-economic development on the one hand and colonial economic policy on the other.

Macro-economic determinants of development are governed by long-term perspectives of gain. In this respect, colonial Indonesia was – like Suharto's Indonesia during the oil boom of the 1970s – in a sense cursed by its exceptionally favorable endowment of resources. There was little urgency to develop other lines of production than those directly linked to the availability of natural resources. Only the obvious potentials inherent in mass consumption of *kretek* cigarettes and cheap textiles offered an impetus for industrial ventures but these were not enough to achieve full-scale industrialization and a take-off into sustained economic growth. The lack of urgency applied not least to those entrepreneurs who would have been best equipped to undertake manufacturing investment and harness sophisticated technologies, that is, the foreign firms that played such a vital role in the late-colonial economy. The lack of urgency to change the direction of economic development grew into a path dependency that was to affect, or haunt, Indonesia for most of the twentieth century.

The role of the colonial government reinforced the strength of the path dependency. Far-reaching economic liberalism explains both the absence of any industrial policy until it was too late and the lack of market incentives for import substitution. Such policies were intrinsically bound up with the colonial context, a context in which the economic development of the colony does not necessarily warrant priority in its own right but is rather seen as complementary to development of the metropolitan economy, in particular the internationalization of private companies operating there. Industrialization failed to take place in the Netherlands Indies despite ready access to investment capital precisely because it was a colony.

The general impression that more could have been achieved in terms of industrialization using foreign capital and know-how is borne out by the brief case study on Unilever's subsidiary in Indonesia. With its very orientation toward producing light consumer goods for a growing domestic market, Unilever in

Indonesia represented a new trend to the country, a trend away from the traditional structure of the colonial economy and toward emphasis on manufacturing production, which eventually became the hallmark of the modern Indonesian economy. Unilever Indonesia combined modernity with inflows of foreign investment capital and know-how. Optimism and expansion characterized operations during the 1930s and the years immediately following Indonesian independence and the transfer of sovereignty. On account of its partly British identity, Unilever Indonesia escaped the fate of most Dutch-owned companies during the economic decolonization of Indonesia in the 1950s, which in turn laid the foundation for its post-Sukarno performance.

## Notes

1  I am grateful to my assistant Thomas de Greeve for helping me to compile the case study on Unilever in Indonesia. For references to industrialization in the Belgian Congo, see Chapter 11 below by Frans Buelens and Danny Cassimon.
2  OECD data from: https://stats.oecd.org.
3  The most easily accessible tables are in van der Eng (1992, 2002).
4  Balance of payments data on incoming capital transactions offer only a partial picture since much new investment was done by reinvesting profits.
5  Recalculation to express these variables in constant prices would admittedly offer a more adequate representation of changes in magnitude over time but would make no difference with regard to the comparison of variations around the mean in the two variables.

## Bibliography

Alexander, P., Boomgaard, P., and White, B. (eds.) (1991) *In the shadow of agriculture; non-farm activities in the Javanese economy: past and present*, Amsterdam: Royal Tropical Institute.

Baudet, H. and Fennema, M. (1983) *Het Nederlands belang bij Indië*, Utrecht/Antwerpen: Spectrum.

Booth, A. (1998) *The Indonesian economy in the nineteenth and twentieth centuries; a history of missed opportunities*, London: Macmillan.

Claver, A. (2006) "Commerce and capital in colonial Java; trade, finance and commercial relations between Europeans and Chinese, 1820s-1942," PhD thesis, Free University of Amsterdam.

Creutzberg, P. (1977) *Changing economy in Indonesia: III. Expenditure on fixed assets*, The Hague: Nijhoff.

Dick, H.W. (1993) "Nineteenth-century industrialization: a missed opportunity?," in Lindblad, J.T. (ed.), *New challenges in the modern economic history of Indonesia*, Leiden: Programme of Indonesian Studies.

Dick, H.W. (2003) *Surabaya, city of work: a socioeconomic history, 1900–2000*, Singapore: Singapore University Press.

Dick, H.W., Houben, V.J.H., Lindblad, J.T., and Thee, K.W. (2002) *The emergence of a national economy: an economic history of Indonesia, 1800–2000*, Crows Nest, NSW: Allen & Unwin.

Handboek (1888–1940) *Handboek voor cultuur- en handelsondernemingen in Nederlandsch-Indië*, Amsterdam: De Bussy (published annually).

Hill, H. (1988) *Foreign investment and industrialization in Indonesia*, Singapore: Oxford University Press.

Hill, H. (2000) *The Indonesian economy since 1966*, Cambridge: Cambridge University Press.

Kamerling, R.N.J. (1982) *De N.V. Oliefabrieken Insulinde in Nederlands-Indië; Bedrijfsvoering in het onbekende*, Franeker: Wever.

Knight, G.R. (1996) "Did 'dependency' really get it wrong? The Indonesian sugar industry, 1880–1942," in Lindblad, J.T. (ed.), *Historical foundations of a national economy in Indonesia, 1890s–1990s*, Amsterdam: North-Holland.

Korthals Altes, W.L. (1987) *Changing economy in Indonesia:; VII. Balance of payments, 1822–1939*, Amsterdam: Royal Tropical Institute.

Lindblad, J.T. (1996) "Business strategies in late colonial Indonesia," in Lindblad, J.T. (ed.), *Historical foundations of a national economy in Indonesia, 1890s-1990s*, Amsterdam: North-Holland.

Lindblad, J.T. (1998) *Foreign investment in Southeast Asia in the twentieth century*, London: Macmillan.

Lindblad, J.T. (1999) "European and Asian styles of foreign investment in Southeast Asia: a preliminary exploration," in Knipping, F., Bunnag, P. and Phatharodom, V. (eds.), *Europe and Southeast Asia in the contemporary world: mutual influences and comparisons*, Baden-Baden: Nomos.

Lindblad, J.T. (2008) *Bridges to new business. The economic decolonization of Indonesia*, Leiden: KITLV Press.

Mangkusuwondo, S. (1975) "Indonesia," in Ichimura, S. (ed.), *The economic development of East and Southeast Asia*, Honolulu: University of Hawaii Press.

Marks, D. (2009) *Accounting for services: the economic development of the Indonesian service sector, ca. 1900–2000*, Amsterdam: Aksant.

Redfern, W.A. (2010) "Sukarno's Guided Democracy and the takeovers of foreign companies in Indonesia in the 1960s," PhD dissertation, Ann Arbor: University of Michigan.

Segers, W.A.I.M. (1987) *Changing economy in Indonesia: VIII. Manufacturing industry 1870–1942*, Amsterdam: Royal Tropical Institute.

Thee K.W. (2010) "The debate on economic policy in newly-independent Indonesia between Sjafruddin Prawiranegara and Sumitro Djojohadikusumo," *Itinerario*, 34, 35–56.

Unilever (1947–64) *Jaarverslag [Annual report]*, Rotterdam: Unilever.

Unilever-Populair (1951–2) *Populair jaarverslag*, Rotterdam: Unilever.

van der Eng, P. (1992) "The real domestic product of Indonesia, 1880–1989," *Explorations in Economic History*, 29, 343–73.

van der Eng, P. (2002) "Indonesia's growth performance in the twentieth century," in Maddison, A., Prasada, D.S., and Shepherd, W.F. (eds.), *The Asian economies in the twentieth century*, Cheltenham, UK, and Northampton, Mass.: Elgar.

van Oorschot, H.J. (1956) *De ontwikkeling van de nijverheid in Indonesië*, The Hague: van Hoeve.

van Zanden, J.L. and Jonker, J. (2007) *A history of Royal Dutch Shell: I. From challenger to joint industry leader, 1890–1939*, New York: Oxford University Press.

Wamsteker, H.W. (1993) *60 years Unilever in Indonesia; 1933–1993*, Jakarta: Unilever Indonesia.

Wilson, C. (1954) *Geschiedenis van Unilever; Een beeld van economische groei en maatschappelijke verandering*, The Hague: Nijhoff.

Wilson, C. (1968) *Unilever 1945–1965: challenge & response in the post-war industrial revolution*, London: Cassell.

World Bank (1992) *World development report 1992*, New York: Oxford University Press.

World Bank (1993) *The East Asian miracle: a World Bank policy research report*, New York: Oxford University Press.

# 11 The industrialization of the Belgian Congo

*Frans Buelens and Danny Cassimon*

## 11.1 Introduction

It is widely recognized that sustained economic growth involves structural changes away from agriculture, toward industry and modern service activities.[1] Industrial production is usually characterized by higher levels of labor productivity and the terms of trade for manufactured goods are more advantageous and less volatile than for raw materials. Moreover, the process of industrialization entails a rather intensive process of technology adoption and diffusion, including the relevant knowledge, part of which spills over to non-industrial sectors. Finally, higher levels of labor productivity and income enhance domestic demand for consumer goods and fine-grained financial services. Thus, industrialization functions as a flywheel to economic development (Murphy *et al.* 1989; Rodrik 2004).

The historical examples of the United States and Japan demonstrate the importance of catching up through industrialization. Furthermore, the example of China makes clear that rapid catching up is possible for those countries that have (for whatever reason) not industrialized until now. However, the "Chinese route" seems not to be applicable to a lot of countries, especially most of the former African colonies. They do not seem to be able to make the step toward a diversified industrialized economy. One of the most "hopeless cases" at present is the Democratic Republic of the Congo (DRC), one of the poorest countries in the world. For this reason it is interesting to analyze how the country industrialized under Belgian rule and why it lost that heritage so quickly after independence.

In 1885 the Congo was a sparsely populated region in the middle of Africa. Its economic activities were restricted to hunting, fishing, and agriculture. When the Belgian Congo became independent in 1960 it had one of the most industrialized economies of Africa. The Congo had obtained the second highest level of industrialization of sub-Saharan Africa, after South Africa (Huybrechts 2010). Of a total GDP of 63 billion Belgian francs (BEF), industrial production amounted to 9 billion BEF, which makes the industrial sector represent about 14 percent of GDP, and in some regions (such as Leopoldville, now Kinshasa) this share exceeded 25 percent (Table 11.1). Industrialization was intimately related

Table 11.1 GDP (1958) (value added by industry)

| Sectors | Total (billions of BEF) | Percentage |
| --- | --- | --- |
| Agricultural production (commercialized) | 3.7 | 5.89 |
| Agricultural production (for export or industry) | 7.7 | 12.11 |
| Mining | 5.0 | 7.94 |
| Industrial production (export) | 4.8 | 7.56 |
| Industrial production (home market) | 4.3 | 6.75 |
| Total | 25.5 | 40.25 |
| Transport | 4.6 | 7.26 |
| Electricity and water | 1.0 | 1.64 |
| Real estate and public works | 2.2 | 3.50 |
| Administration, education, defense | 8.6 | 13.55 |
| Commerce | 4.7 | 7.37 |
| Other services | 4.1 | 6.41 |
| Total | 25.2 | 39.72 |
| Indirect taxes | 5.2 | 8.12 |
| GDP (commercialized) | 55.9 | 88.09 |
| Non-commercialized production | 7.9 | 11.91 |
| GDP | 63.4 | 100.00 |

Source: Lacroix (1967: 30).

to the growth of Congolese mining activities and the production of tropical cash crops such as palm oil, cotton, and coffee.

The pace of industrial growth was impressive for an African colony. Taking into account that the population of the Belgian Congo and Belgium were similar at the end of colonization, comparing data for these two countries shows that in some sectors the Belgian Congo was highly developed. Electricity in the Belgian Congo was about 18.4 percent of Belgian production; this is perhaps the best indicator of the level of industrialization of the Belgian Congo (Table 11.2). Nevertheless, in the decades after 1960 this vast industrial and mining structure would collapse (Buelens 2007).

This chapter explores how Congolese industrialization evolved over time, dividing the industrialization process into three sub-periods. Section 2 discusses the era of "Raubwirtschaft" (plunder economy) under King Leopold II (1885–1908). Section 3 addresses the first period of industrialization (1920–40), in the years following the Belgian take-over (1908) and World War I. This first wave of industrialization was centered on the export of raw materials, including tropical cash crops and minerals (especially copper) and supported by state investments in physical infrastructure. Section 4 discusses the second wave of industrialization (1940–58), from World War II up to independence. This period was characterized by a growing domestic market, a tendency to import substitution and a changing class structure. By the end of the colonial era a third period emerges with big plans for the development of the capital goods sector. However, these plans were never realized during the colonial era (Section 5).

*Table 11.2* Comparing industrial production for Belgium and the Belgian Congo in 1957

| Commodity | Unit | Belgium | Belgian Congo | as a Percentage of Belgium |
|---|---|---|---|---|
| Electricity | Millions KWH | 12,611 | 2320 | 18.4 |
| Sugar | Tons | 369,335 | 19,332 | 5.2 |
| Beer | 1000 hl | 10,185 | 1382 | 13.6 |
| Water + lemonade | 1000 hl | 2966 | 320 | 10.8 |
| Margarine | Tons | 95,253 | 669 | 0.7 |
| Cigarettes | Millions | 10,546 | 4045 | 38.4 |
| Cement | Tons | 4,705,000 | 463,952 | 9.9 |
| Lime | Tons | 29,249,000 | 100,460 | 0.3 |
| Bricks | 1000 | 2,242,933 | 293,876 | 13.1 |
| Ceramics | 1000 m² | 1625 | 137 | 8.4 |
| Shoes | 1000 pair | 12,117 | 2851 | 23.5 |
| Fabric | 1000 m² | 702,105 | 52,982 | 7.5 |
| Blankets | 1000 pieces | 11,768 | 1976 | 16.8 |

Source: Centrale Bank van Belgisch-Congo en Ruanda Urundi (1959).

Later on, during the Mobutu dictatorship, some of these plans were partially realized and new ones were made (Lacroix 1966), although the overall economic structure collapsed (Section 6). Section 7 summarizes and concludes.

## 11.2 "Raubwirtschaft" (1885–1908)

In 1885 the Congo Free State was born under the reign of King Leopold II, who was also king of Belgium (and from then on king of the two countries). The Congo at the time did not exist as a political entity; it became a unified territory under colonial domination. The Berlin Act of 1885 gave some official status to this acquisition.[2] King Leopold II took for granted that overseas colonies should contribute to the well-being of the mother country (Stengers 1977). Colonization started with the expropriation of land. By ordinance on July 1, 1885 the principle of "free estates" ("terres vacantes") was established. The overwhelming part of the Congo territory became state-owned (Dubois 1913: 13). Only those small territories in which people lived remained free of state ownership. The colonial state used these estates to hand out big land concessions (mining and other, for a long period of time) or to sell to colonial investors. In exchange, the colonial state received equity shares in those colonial companies, making the colonial state the biggest investor in the Congo. The high dividends paid by colonial companies would enable the colonial state to finance most of its activities from its "Congo Portfolio" (Buelens and Marysse 2009; see also Gardner, Chapter 6 above).[3]

The early colonial state prioritized the development of transport infrastructure to facilitate resource extraction. The main "natural highway" in the Congo was the Congo River, but to make it an efficient means of transport it had to be complemented by railways. The railway network would eventually comprise over 5000 kilometers in 1960, nearly twice as much as in Nigeria at the eve of independence (Mitchell 2007: 721–2). In the wake of these infrastructural investments several construction companies were created in the early period.[4]

There can hardly be any doubt that the primary (and nearly sole) objective during the first stage of colonization was to extract as much profit as possible from the exploitation of Congolese natural resources. Rubber, ivory, and copal were the main products extracted by a cruel system of forced labor, based on excessive violence (Gann and Duignan 1979: 30; Jewsiewicki 1983). Other tropical crops such as timber from the forests of Mayumbé (near the Atlantic Ocean) would follow. The system of exploitation has rightly been characterized as "Raubwirtschaft." Population would sharply diminish during this era, and although it is unclear how far excess mortality was caused by human intervention rather than invisible biological processes, there is no doubt that colonial policies aggravated the deprivation (Vansina 2010). The atrocities led to a stylized image of the Congo in the public and academic literature as an extreme example of an extractive state (Young 1994; Acemoglu *et al.* 2001; Hochschild 1999).

The "Raubwirtschaft" met fierce resistance from the international community at the time, forcing King Leopold II to transfer the Congo in 1908 to the Belgian state. The "Belgian Congo" was born. But perhaps more importantly, economic power switched to the Société Générale de Belgique, one of the strongest holding companies in Europe at the time (Ndaywel è Nziem 1998: 28–30).[5] The Société Générale de Belgique was highly interested in the mining potential of the Congo. Already during the final years of Leopoldian rule ivory, rubber, and copal were replaced by copper and other metals as the main export "staples." This shift can be dated more precisely with the founding of the "three mining companies of 1906": UMHK (Union Minière du Haut Katanga), Forminière (Société Internationale Forestière et Minière du Congo), and BCK (Compagnie du Chemin de Fer du Bas-Congo au Katanga). Each of these companies received enormous concessions and land grants and soon became daughter companies of the Société Générale de Belgique.

## 11.3  The first wave of industrialization (1920–40)

The Belgian administration would change the way the Congo was ruled, although the bare essence of an extractive state remained in place. The key difference was that the exploitation of resources became organized in a more "rational," even "scientific," way. This did not mean the Congo would be developed in the interests of its people. Belgium maintained the classic mercantile colonial opinion that colonies had to supply the "mother countries" with raw materials, at a time when the Dutch were pursuing their "Ethical Policy" in the Netherlands Indies. In exchange for minerals and tropical crops from the Congo, Belgium would export manufactured products, exploiting its strong position in metalworking and machinery in particular. Besides, Belgian investors would receive huge amounts of dividends in return for foreign direct investment in the colony. Belgian exporters pursued an aggressive strategy to contain foreign competition in the Congo and only favored the development of industries that complemented the activities of Belgian companies.

Hence, the first wave of industrialization was directly linked to the emerging mining sector, to the expansion of commercial centers' activities and to the cultivation of tropical cash crops. Industrial development was mainly financed by Belgian investors. As can be seen in Table 11.3, foreign direct investment in the Belgian Congo rose sharply in the period 1920–8: the capital account balance exploded from 92 million BEF in 1920 to 1530 million BEF in 1928, mainly due to private foreign investment. Investment in the Congo in the interwar period represented 11.7 percent of total capital invested in Africa, whereas the vast French and Portuguese colonial empires received only 4.2 and 5.4 percent, respectively, of total investment in Africa (Vanthemsche 2007: 167).

*Table 11.3* Balance of payments of the Belgian Congo and Ruanda–Urundi (1920–39) (million BEF)

| Year | Capital account | | | Current account | Overall balance |
|------|------|------|------|------|------|
|  | *(1)* | *(2)* | *(3)* | *(4)* | *(5)* |
| 1920 | 84 | 8 | 92 | 57 | 149 |
| 1921 | 39 | 47 | 86 | −110 | −24 |
| 1922 | 120 | 77 | 197 | −78 | 119 |
| 1923 | 162 | −47 | 115 | 25 | 140 |
| 1924 | 64 | 121 | 185 | 42 | 227 |
| 1925 | 369 | 170 | 539 | −250 | 289 |
| 1926 | 587 | 450 | 1037 | −540 | 497 |
| 1927 | 720 | −45 | 675 | −530 | 145 |
| 1928 | 1614 | −84 | 1530 | −409 | 1121 |
| 1929 | 989 | 210 | 1199 | −343 | 856 |
| 1930 | 1236 | 261 | 1497 | −284 | 1213 |
| 1931 | 736 | 341 | 1077 | −279 | 798 |
| 1932 | −24 | 581 | 577 | −238 | 319 |
| 1933 | −108 | 376 | 268 | −77 | 191 |
| 1934 | −3 | −326 | −329 | 186 | −133 |
| 1935 | −198 | −456 | −654 | 287 | −367 |
| 1936 | −955 | 1126 | 171 | 218 | 389 |
| 1937 | −119 | −328 | −447 | 537 | 90 |
| 1938 | −78 | −204 | −282 | 82 | −200 |
| 1939 | −9 | 109 | 100 | 106 | 206 |

Source: Vandewalle (1966: 77).

Notes
1 Capital operations in the long run (private capital).
2 Capital operations in the long run (state capital).
3 Capital account balance (long run).
4 Current account balance.
5 Overall balance.

In the 1920s several new industries were established, such as cement (1920), soap (1922), beer (1924), cotton fabrics (1925), sugar (1925), and even some metal fabrication companies (Lacroix 1967: 21). Industries catering for the home market developed in cases where it was cheaper to produce in the Belgian Congo (for example, beer, cotton fabrics, cement) or where manufactures were vital for the production of export commodities (for example, cement, electricity, and certain chemicals for the mining companies). However, industrial activities were also developed to facilitate the export sector for two other reasons: first, because some products were too costly to export in unprocessed form (for example, copper) and, second, because some products could not be transported in raw form for technical or biological reasons (for example, palm oil)[6] (Ahrens 1953: 31). The remainder of this section will discuss these linkages in more detail.

## Mining

The Congo was, and still is, extremely rich in minerals. Its soils contain gold, copper, cobalt, tantalite, coltan, columbite, cassiterite, uranium, tin, and dozens of other minerals. Especially in Katanga, where the major copper mines were located and the UMHK established its headquarters, mining-related industrial development was impressive. The remoteness of Katanga, at a great distance from the Atlantic Ocean without a navigable water connection, was a critical factor. The raw copper ore had to undergo preliminary processing in order to lower transport costs. Since Katanga was sparsely populated and did not produce enough food for the rapidly increasing mining workforce, food industries had to be developed such as grain mills and meat-producing farms. In 1923 the Brasseries du Katanga (Brassekat) was founded (brewery), in 1924 the Compagnie d'Elevage et d'Alimentation du Katanga (Elakat), in 1929 the Minoteries du Katanga, and in 1930 the Compagnie des Grands Elevages Congolais (Grelco). The housing needs of the staff and the construction needs of the mining companies gave rise to the development of all kinds of construction-related firms, such as Ciments du Katanga (Cimenkat) (founded in 1922) and the Compagnie Foncière du Katanga (1922). The mining activities also required inputs from chemical factories, huge amounts of electricity, and fabricated metals.

The UMHK had the highest power generation capacity in the Belgian Congo; in other mining regions, such as Kilo-Moto (gold), power plants were founded as well but of lower capacity. Traditional thermal processes were used at first by the UMHK, notwithstanding the extremely high cost of coke (which at first had to be imported from Europe, afterwards from Southern Rhodesia). In 1930 the UMHK switched to using hydraulic resources (Gouverneur 1971: 57). Indeed, the Belgian Congo offers great possibilities for generating electricity, as its hydraulic power potential is enormous. From 1930 on the Société Générale des Forces Hydro-Electriques du Katanga (Sogefor), a subsidiary of the UMHK, developed a series of hydroelectric power plants in Katanga; Sogelec (Société Générale Africaine d'Electricité; a subsidiary of Sogefor) was in charge of their exploitation. Hence, a vast network of interconnected firms was needed to start and maintain mining activities in Katanga. In other regions mining was far from absent, but diamond production in Kasai and gold production in Kilo-Moto did not give rise to a similar level of industrial development as there was in Katanga.

## *Tropical cash crops*

African agriculture became the handmaiden of colonial economic development. Mining needs posed severe consequences for African agriculture. As the country was thinly populated (approximately ten million people around 1908; 14.4 million in 1959) (Huybrechts 2010: 25) and the need for miners was high, mining companies such as subsidiary UMHK tried to attract laborers from villages in other regions. Massive mining recruitment campaigns deprived African villages of the majority of their young and strong workers, leaving older people, women, and children to till the land. This labor migration impoverished large rural areas and contributed to the highly uneven development of the Belgian Congo (see also Clement, Chapter 4 above).

The reallocation of labor resources away from subsistence agriculture was aggravated by the introduction of a system of compulsory crop cultivation in 1917, with cotton being the main crop from 1920 on (in addition to other tropical products such as palm oil, coffee, cacao, timber, and tobacco). In 1959 nearly 800,000 villagers were engaged in compulsory cotton growing (Foutry and Neckers 1986: 124). Large areas of the Congo such as Uélé, Maniema, Ubangi, Kivu, Lualaba, and Lusambo became compulsory cotton-producing regions (Foutry and Neckers 1986: 122–4; Vellut 1979: 370). Compulsory cotton production served the interests of the vast textile industry in Belgium, which would no longer be dependent on raw materials from other countries (Fransolet 1947). In 1920, the Cotonco company was founded and obtained a monopsony on the cotton produced by African farmers (Cotonco did not have its own cotton plantations). The purchase of raw cotton took place at a (low) state-defined minimum price in order to strengthen Belgian textile companies' international competitiveness. In 1947, Cotonco had 73 factories located all over the Congo. The cotton plantations were comparable in size to those of the southern United States.

Palm oil was another major crop (second after cotton) for which compulsory labor was used, with the Belgian Congo becoming the second exporter in Africa after Nigeria (Lacroix 1967: 243). Unilever controlled most of the production (see Lindblad, Chapter 10 above, for the activities of Unilever in the Netherlands Indies). By 1911, the Lever Company had acquired vast territories in the Belgian Congo. Lord Lever acquired five big "circle areas" in the Congo. Production was carried out by salaried workers and small farmers. Since it was impossible to export the unprocessed oil, the preliminary processing had to be organized on site. This gave rise to a large number of plants set up by the Huileries du Congo Belge (founded in 1911).

## Commercial centers: the role of Leopoldville

Not all the cotton production was for export. In 1925, a Belgian firm, Texaf, was founded that would produce vast amounts of textiles for the domestic market, especially in the Leopoldville region. The fast-growing commercial township of Leopoldville, one of the two main centers of urban growth in the Belgian Congo (the other being Katanga), was a logical choice. The town was situated on the Congo River, some 400 km from the coast. It was the central place for acquiring trading products from elsewhere in the Congo (transported mainly by the Congo River) and for transporting them further by the Congo railway (connecting Matadi with Leopoldville) to avoid the non-navigable parts of the lower Congo. This strategically located trading hub became the capital of the Belgian Congo, replacing Boma (near the Atlantic Ocean), and gained importance as the main administrative center of the colony.

Several industries were developed in the surrounding area, all of them to serve the immediate needs of the growing city (and region). Breweries were started from 1923 on, with the establishment of the Brasserie de Leopoldville. In 1925 the sugar industry was started with the Compagnie Sucrière Congolaise (at Moerbeke-Kwilu). This latter company was a typical example of a Congolese firm: it not only produced sugar but also developed activities in construction, metal working, the timber industry and hospitals (Lippens 1953: 65). As in Katanga, construction was an important business, focusing on the rising demand for production sites, residences, and construction inputs such as cement. In 1920, a cement industry was created in Lukula (Ciments du Congo); in 1928, the Compagnie Immobilière du Congo became responsible for housing (Kipré 1993). Additionally, investments were made in shipbuilding (and maintenance activities) to facilitate transport on the Congo River. In 1928 Chanic (Chantier Naval et Industriel du Congo) was founded, near Leopoldville. Before World War II, Chanic was active in assembling components for ships from Belgium (Cockerill Yards, Hoboken, near Antwerp) as well as in maintenance activities. Finally, just as in Katanga, there was a huge need for energy. In 1923 the Société Coloniale d'Electricité (Colectric) was founded. It would distribute electricity from the electric power plant in Zongo. Additionally, in 1930 the Forces Hydro-Electriques de Sanga would start production using the Sanga Waterfalls on the Congo River (near Leopoldville). Texaf itself would become a holding company in 1934, transferring its textile manufacturing activities to the Usines Textiles de Leopoldville (UtexLeo).

The first wave of investment came to an end with the economic crisis of the 1930s. Prices of exports of raw materials as well as export volumes were shrinking. Foreign investment dwindled and colonial companies were severely hit. For example, one out of three soap companies was liquidated (Lacroix 1967: 169). Several companies started to replace expensive European labour with cheap "upgraded" African labor. Industrial production for the domestic market also diminished. Between 1930 and 1935 overall domestic market demand fell below the 1920 level. Production for the domestic market would only reach the 1929 level again in 1944 (Lacroix 1967: 169). Examples are numerous and well documented by Lacroix: cement production fell from 64,000 tons (1929) to 21,000 tons (1944), beer production from 24,000 hl (1929) to 8700 hl (1934), and internal consumption of sugar from 2100 tons (1929) to 937 tons (1933), rising to 2125 tons in 1938 (Lacroix 1967: 169–70). Only from 1935 did the economic situation start to improve, as investments slowly picked up. The multinational shoe company Bata would found the Société Bata Congolaise in 1937 (Joye and Lewin 1961: 273) with a manufacturing unit in Leopoldville. But the real upswing would come with World War II.

## 11.4 The second wave of industrialization (1940–58)

World War II (and its aftermath) fundamentally changed the Congolese economy. The Allied war effort required huge supplies of minerals and crops and productive capacity had to be increased to meet this boom. In the period between 1935 and 1949 industrial production rose at an average annual rate of at least 14 percent (Lacroix 1967: 21–2). The number of enterprises sharply increased from 7396 in 1948 to 11,784 in 1952. For example, the number of construction companies would rise from 104 in 1948 to 402 in 1952 (Derkinderen 1953: 42–51). In 1951, tropical agricultural product exports stood at 7694 million BEF and total exports at 20,406 million BEF, compared to just 388 million BEF and 1533 million BEF in 1937 (Ahrens 1953: 31).

The wartime boom had several consequences (see also Peemans 1975a). First, the available transport infrastructure no longer sufficed. It attracted huge investment after the end of the war. Second, to meet the increase in production the number of miners and workers increased sharply, from 480,000 in 1940 to 800,000 in 1945. New recruitment efforts intensified the unevenness of development between rural areas and industrial centers (and towns). Third, as World War II temporarily cut the links between Belgium and the Belgian Congo, and the demand for employees was rising, companies were forced to upgrade the skills of their African workers: at the end of the war highly skilled workers and lower-skilled clerks occupied positions they could not have held before the war. Fourth, companies made enormous profits. The accumulated reserves would be used to finance large-scale post-war investments. The Congo was even forced by the Belgians to finance the Belgian government in exile.

Fifth, since goods from Belgium could not be imported during the war and colonial companies saw competition from European rivals diminish, industry in the Belgian Congo was able to expand into regular activities and develop in niches it had not yet explored. A typical example is Chanic. It developed into a real metalworking conglomerate with diversified production. During World War II, Chanic's activities took over. It became involved in every stage of the construction of ships, which led to a real shipyard industry emerging in the Congo. Chanic diversified its production to canned food and took on the distribution of products from Caterpillar and other (mostly American) companies. Moreover, Chanic would help to found other companies such as Cegeac (Compagnie

Générale d'Automobiles et d'Aviation du Congo) and Congacier. It had staff of more than 3000 after World War II.

Surprisingly, once the war was over, growth rates continued at the same high levels. The Cold War, the Korean War, strategic stockpiling by Allied powers and fear of a third world war kept the Congolese economy on the same rapid growth path. Production growth rates were especially high in the mining sector. Growth rates for some minerals such as tantalite-columbite boomed to more than 722 percent between 1946 and 1952. Wolfram production grew at 396 percent, cobalt 217 percent, zinc 183 percent and even copper at 42 percent. Consequently exports also grew. The total value of mineral exports rose from 3314 million BEF (in 1946) to 12,108 million BEF (in 1952) (Marthoz 1953: 71).

Besides economic changes, a fundamental change at the social and political level took place following the war. The attitude to colonialism changed. Neither the Soviet Union nor the United States accepted old-fashioned European colonialism. Independence movements gained momentum throughout Africa. Perhaps more than in any other African colony, the class structure of Congolese society had changed, with a growing (lower) middle class, an industrial working class and an impoverished agricultural population. The participation rate of workers in the "formal economy" stood at 59 percent of the total workforce. About 30 percent of them were salaried workers, one of the highest rates in Africa at that time (Lacroix 1967: 26–8). Belgian official colonialist doctrine changed its focus from "exploitative colonialism" toward "developmental colonialism" in response to the growing assertiveness of post-war Congolese society.

Resistance to Belgian domination was growing. Consequently, during the 1945–58 period, the Congolese domestic market developed through a policy of increasing wages, improving social security systems (pensions and child allowances), and even establishing a minimum wage. Apart from increasing sales of consumer goods in a well-developed domestic market, the political motive was extremely important, as stated by Derkinderen:

> the Government wants to support the middle classes, in order to stabilize the home-market ... these middle classes are necessary, if only to act as intermediaries between big capital and the aboriginal proletariat. These classes, to which natives should be admitted, will further a peaceful evolution.
>
> (Derkinderen 1953: 52)

In the meantime, on the economic side, a ten-Year Plan (1949–59) was drafted. The plan proposed huge investments in the Congo and was essentially aimed at adapting and developing transport infrastructure. Between 1950 and 1957 additional (public and private) investment amounted to 124 billion BEF (on average) or 27.5 percent of GDP per year (Peemans 1975b: 187–93; Vanthemsche 1993: 345). Financing came mostly from new loans. Planning was a popular policy tool, partly due to the perceived economic success of the Soviet system, and partly due to the Keynesian answer to the crisis of the 1930s. But in the ten-Year

Plan there was hardly any meaningful investment in African agriculture. Moreover, some very promising objectives, such as the foundation of a Société de Développement Colonial (to stimulate the development of "strategic sectors") and a Société pour le Développement de l'Economie Indigène (to stimulate the development of small enterprises by Africans), were not carried through.

As the Congo economy enjoyed healthy growth rates, there was an additional factor at play: a widespread fear that a third world war was near. This fear forced the Société Générale to explore other regions for investment, with Canada and the Belgian Congo becoming the most favored destinations. The result was an additional boost to foreign direct investment in the Belgian Congo, as shown by the balance of payments for 1948–58 (see Table 11.4). The flow of private capital into the Congo (18.6 billion BEF) continued to increase, together with the export of capital out of the Congo, sometimes leading to a negative balance of payments. Meanwhile, investments financed by the increasing self-financing capacity of existing companies were growing rapidly. Hence in 1953, for example, the per capita investment level in the Congo was US$25, compared to US$19 per capita in French Africa, US$15 in British Africa and only US$3.5 in Portuguese Africa (Vanthemsche 2007: 167). At the same time, the Congolese economy was also able to sustain a massive transfer of dividends (mainly to Belgium). In the period 1948–58, at least 26 billion BEF in dividends were distributed (Table 11.4).

*Table 11.4* Capital account of the Belgian Congo and Ruanda–Urundi (1948–58) (million BEF)

| Year | Private capital | | | State capital | | | |
|------|------|------|------|------|------|------|------|
| | (1) | (2) | (3) | (4) | (5) | (6) | (7) |
| 1948 | 531 | 396 | 135 | 4 | 31 | −27 | 1019 |
| 1949 | 336 | 681 | −345 | 0 | 36 | −36 | 1256 |
| 1950 | 876 | 498 | 378 | 2564 | 7 | 2557 | 1295 |
| 1951 | 1252 | 321 | 931 | 230 | 394 | −164 | 1316 |
| 1952 | 1058 | 295 | 763 | 2576 | 115 | 2461 | 1778 |
| 1953 | 1581 | 1456 | 125 | 2623 | 21 | 2602 | 2212 |
| 1954 | 1532 | 1858 | −326 | 2615 | 100 | 2515 | 2459 |
| 1955 | 2685 | 2549 | 136 | 3028 | 192 | 2836 | 3266 |
| 1956 | 2375 | 2998 | −623 | 4728 | 402 | 4326 | 4411 |
| 1957 | 3565 | 3200 | 365 | 569 | 493 | 76 | 3569 |
| 1958 | 2812 | 2991 | −179 | 6021 | 556 | 5465 | 3476 |

Source: Vanthemsche (2007: 352).

Notes
1 Capital operations in the long run (private capital): imports into the Belgian Congo.
2 Capital operations in the long run (private capital): exports out of the Belgian Congo.
3 Capital operations in the long run (private capital): balance.
4 Capital operations in the long run (state capital): imports into the Belgian Congo.
5 Capital operations in the long run (state capital): exports out of the Belgian Congo.
6 Capital operations in the long run (state capital): balance.
7 Dividends, interests, and bonuses paid to foreign investors.

Between 1950 and 1957, not only was the mining sector growing fast, but the annual average growth rate of industrial production was also extremely high at 14.3 percent (Lacroix 1967: 22). This growth is reflected in the volume index of industrial production (see Table 11.5). Between 1939 and 1957, the index grew by 622 percent for food, 2843 percent for textiles, 1251 percent for chemicals and 2489 percent for construction.

Existing companies witnessed some magnificent years. For example the shoe industry produced three million pairs of shoes in 1959, which represented 25 percent of the production volume of Belgian shoe companies (Joye and Lewin 1961: 107). The growing domestic market also saw many new activities springing up. For example, in 1947 the Brasseries de Léopoldville founded a new company, Bouteillerie de Léopoldville. The brewery sector witnessed a tremendous expansion with the foundation of breweries all over the country. Textiles also expanded further: in addition to UtexLeo (spinning and weaving of cotton; printing of fabrics), the Société Coloniale de Textiles (Socotex, 1946, blankets) and Tissaco (Filatures et Tissages de Fibres au Congo, 1947, jute bags) were founded in the region of Leopoldville (Moxhon 1953). But also in other regions such as Katanga new companies were created, such as the Société Métallurgique du Katanga (1948) and Ciments Métallurgiques de Jadotville (1951). Construction activities were booming; metal and chemical industries were developing rapidly too (Dumortier 1947). This turned the Katanga region into a highly developed industrial area, largely thanks to the UMHK's activities (Brion and Moreau 2006).

*Table 11.5* Evolution of the volume index of industrial production (1939–57) (base year: 1947–9 = 100)

| Year | Food | Textiles | Chemicals | Construction | Others | Total |
|------|------|----------|-----------|--------------|--------|-------|
| 1939 | 41   | 21       | 35        | 19           | 10     | 29    |
| 1940 | 44   | 25       | 44        | 15           | 9      | 30    |
| 1941 | 45   | 27       | 53        | 28           | 26     | 38    |
| 1942 | 59   | 27       | 75        | 30           | 27     | 46    |
| 1943 | 69   | 44       | 70        | 44           | 29     | 54    |
| 1944 | 72   | 42       | 71        | 54           | 32     | 59    |
| 1945 | 73   | 69       | 75        | 52           | 52     | 64    |
| 1946 | 79   | 67       | 81        | 58           | 60     | 71    |
| 1947 | 89   | 81       | 91        | 87           | 61     | 82    |
| 1948 | 100  | 102      | 76        | 105          | 95     | 99    |
| 1949 | 111  | 116      | 133       | 108          | 144    | 119   |
| 1950 | 124  | 160      | 145       | 201          | 147    | 147   |
| 1951 | 146  | 327      | 154       | 244          | 175    | 179   |
| 1952 | 158  | 392      | 196       | 283          | 218    | 206   |
| 1953 | 186  | 446      | 304       | 339          | 267    | 250   |
| 1954 | 212  | 524      | 330       | 413          | 280    | 280   |
| 1955 | 237  | 601      | 412       | 432          | 310    | 315   |
| 1956 | 272  | 697      | 448       | 462          | 336    | 349   |
| 1957 | 296  | 618      | 473       | 492          | 387    | 377   |

Source: CBBCRU (1959: 4).

Many foreign multinational companies entered the market but so did a lot of Belgian companies such as the fibre cement-producing company Eternit, a Belgian multinational company that founded Eternit-Congo in 1947. As the Congolese economy was booming, Belgian exporters tried all kinds of strategies to protect and increase the exports of their products. They were actively supported in this endeavor by the colonial authorities. For example, in 1951, a commercial register was introduced, protecting entrepreneurs from rogue competitors; measures to protect trademarks had the same objective (Cleys 2002). The giant Belgian business organization Fabrimetal opened an office in Leopoldville and actively sought to explore the Congolese market (Brion and Moreau 1996: 97). The results were not disappointing: the average return on investment (net profits/capital plus reserves) for industrial companies was consistently above 12 percent during 1950–7 (CBBCRU 1959: 11).

## 11.5 Planning for the development of heavy industries (1958–60)

Despite the rapid pace of industrialization after 1940, the capital goods sector remained underdeveloped. In the course of the 1950s several far-reaching ideas were developed to promote heavy industries. Since transportation had been the prime focus of the completed ten-Year Plan, it was considered to be the right time for the establishment of huge energy-producing industries. Plans were envisaged for a petroleum refinery near Kitona on the Atlantic Ocean, but the greatest potential lay in the field of electricity provision. As stated earlier, electric power plants had already been developed, but they were rather unevenly distributed throughout the country. Plans to construct the Inga hydraulic power plant were not new: the Syneba Syndicate (Syndicat d'Etude du Bas Congo) examined the issue as early as 1929, but aborted the idea during the crises (see Willame 1986: 29–30). The Inga Falls are among the largest waterfalls in the world: the Congo River drops 96 meters and the average flow is 42 cubic meters per second. The Falls are near the Atlantic Ocean, some 40 km from Matadi, and the potential electricity-generating capacity would make it possible to develop steel mills, aluminum mills, and chemical industries.

Policymakers envisaged that once a minimum threshold of firms had been attracted to the region, industrial development would automatically follow. The colonial government founded the Inga Institute (Institut National d'Etudes pour le Développement du Bas-Congo) in 1957. A Belgian consortium (Sydelinga) was interested in investing; it included companies such as Traction et Electricité, Electrobel and Sofina, while others such as the Cominière holding company and Abelinga (Association Belge pour l'Etude de l'Aménagement Hydroélectrique d'Inga) were also eager to invest (Mollin 1996). The plans were developed, but the project had not been realized before the rather sudden and unexpected granting of independence of the Congo. The Inga project would only be partially realized after independence (Willame 1986).

## 11.6 The collapse of the Congolese industrial complex

The new political leaders of the independent Congo were well aware of the vast growth potential of the country's economy and there was a substantial degree of continuity in key economic policies from the late colonial era into the early independence years. In his famous speech during the official hand-over in June 1960, Prime Minister Patrice Lumumba declared that he wanted to continue the economic policy pursued by the Belgians, although he added that he also wanted to end exclusive dependence on Belgium (De Villers 2012: 130). Mining would remain the engine of industrial growth and the foundation of state finances. To diversify the Congo's economic relations, Lumumba signed a convention between the Congo state and an American company, CIMCO (Congo International Management Corporation), in July 1960, on financial assistance to the Inga Falls project and the valorization of the Congo's mineral wealth for a 50-year period, dividing the profits between the two partners (Kaplan 2010: 65, Willame 1986: 40).[7]

Likewise Mobutu, who came to power in 1965, initially supported the Belgian colonial style of economic management. He envisaged a number of "mega-projects," such as the Inga project, the giant steel works at Maluku and a high voltage line (of 1800 km) between Inga (in the west) and Shaba (Katanga, in the southeast), to be financed with loans, repayable in interest payments and mining revenues. Indeed, especially after World War II the Belgians had made comparably big investments in industrial and infrastructural projects, and these had also been financed by large loans, while the copper mines of the UMHK financed the colonial state. As demand for all kind of minerals was extremely high in the 1940s and 1950s (due to World War II, strategic stockpiling after the war, and the Korean War), this strategy resulted in notable industrial progress. Moreover, the Congo was not the only country that tried to service its debt on the basis of expected revenues from industrial investment schemes. However, a combination of factors, some of which were clearly exogenous, caused the complete collapse of the industrial complex in the 1970s and 1980s.

First, the Congolese lacked sufficient technical competence to monitor and withstand rent-seeking foreign enterprises. Industrial development in the Congo depended heavily on foreign know-how, but the foreign firms engaged in turnkey projects (a booming business in Third World countries at that time) took as little responsibility as possible for the final result. This was a direct consequence of Belgian colonial policy: suppressing the development of indigenous intellectual, political, and economic capacity by keeping Africans out of leading positions (see Frankema, Chapter 7 above). Compared to most other colonial powers, Belgian policies had not supported the education or training of highly skilled Africans. The Belgians relied largely on Belgian administrative and management skills and many believed that Belgium would rule the Congo for centuries to come. Not a single African was allowed to follow university courses until 1954, nor did any of them have the opportunity to acquire practical skills in a top job in the administration, politics, the army, or business. As a result, it was extremely difficult for Africans to take over the Congo after 1960. For instance, when Mobutu decided to nationalize the copper mines in 1966–7, the Congo state still had to apply for technical assistance from the UMHK to operate the mines, a call that came at a huge price (Verhaegen 1972). The neglect of human capital development would prove to be a disaster not only in the political arena but also, and especially, in the management of enterprises, state finances, and the economy at large.

Second, the money-squandering mega-projects suffered increasingly from a lack of entrepreneurial common sense, especially under Mobutu. The Inga Falls project became a disaster. Demand for the enormous supply of energy produced by the hydro-electric power plant was simply not there. The rural market remained underdeveloped and lacked the necessary electricity infrastructure, while urban and industrial demand was insufficient to make the Inga Falls profitable. The idea of attracting a range of industries that would make use of the low-cost energy was not bad in itself, but putting this grand scheme into practice required effective solutions to a wide array of problems. One of the industries that the Congo wanted to attract was aluminum production. Big firms like Kaiser Aluminum promised to invest in the Inga region but never did so. Mobutu ordered the building of a very high voltage line to Shaba (Katanga) but this line eventually offered electricity at four times the normal price. Mobutu also ordered the construction of a big steel works at Maluku but it worked far below its capacity. It was extremely badly located in a mountainous area, 80 km from Kinshasa, without a good connection to the ports or the road network. Since its iron ore had to come from elsewhere, transport costs were huge. Remarkably, Maluku was not the original location for this steel plant, but was chosen after a personal intervention by Mobutu (Willame 1986: 74). The poor management of nearly all of these mega-projects contributed to a large extent to the creation of untenable levels of Congolese state debt which eventually resulted in complete financial collapse.

Third, political instability during the first five years of independence (1960–5), partly reinforced by foreign interference, severely undermined economic stability and worsened the investment climate. When in 1960 Patrice Lumumba became the first democratically elected Prime Minister of the Belgian Congo, both the Belgian government and the Société Générale feared a switch to radical nationalist policies, regarding Lumumba as a potential Soviet ally. The United States shared this concern. The Congo became a hot issue in Cold War politics and preventing the country from joining the Soviet bloc became an obsession. Instead of giving full support to the first elected government, Belgium supported the secessionist agenda of the (rich) Katanga and Kasai provinces. This culminated in the Congo Secession War, followed by the civil war, and ending in the Mobutu dictatorship in 1965. Patrice Lumumba was murdered with the consent, and probably also the direct support, of Belgian officials (De Vos *et al.* 2004; van Reybrouck 2010: 325–7). During the war, infrastructure was damaged severely and production was disrupted: demand for steel had reached 350,000 tons in 1957 but fell back to 60,000 tons by 1968 (Willame 1986: 71).

Furthermore, the national liberation war in neighboring Angola (a Portuguese colony), followed by the civil war between the liberation movements UNITA, MPRA, and FNLA after 1975 (when Angola became independent from Portugal), led to the closing of the Benguela railroad, which was a crucial artery for exports from the Katanga copper mines as well as for imports of machinery and petroleum.

Fourth, during the 1970s global economic conditions changed unexpectedly and the critical reliance of state investment schemes on mining revenues soon proved to be erroneous. The Mobutu era experienced some very good economic years in the late 1960s and early 1970s. There was a huge demand for copper partly due to the protracted war in Vietnam, Laos, and Cambodia and copper prices boomed until 1973. But then the oil crisis started to hit many countries with soaring inflation due to oil price hikes. For the Congo, collapsing copper prices were far worse. It erased the foundation of state revenue, just as falling mining revenues had done in the 1930s. However, this time, it was not a business cycle phenomenon but a structural decline. In terms of non-ferrous metals, world demand for aluminum had risen from 6 percent in 1939 to at least 50 percent in the 1980s, whereas the share of copper had diminished from 35 percent to 25 percent. Alternatives to copper were on the rise, especially optical fibers for telecommunications (Willame 1986: 135). The Congo's finances switched from copper revenue to massive loans, bringing the state debt to nearly 100 percent of GDP. This led to a cessation of payments by the Congo state and the intervention of the IMF in 1976–7. A new devaluation of the national currency of about 42 percent followed in 1976. The Congo joined the club of the highly indebted countries such as Mexico, Argentina, and so many others in that period. But the Congo would never leave it.

Fifth, the ever-expanding predatory practices of the Mobutu clan destroyed all prospects of recovery after 1973. Notwithstanding the fact that Mobutu presented himself as a stable factor after the years of the "weak state" (1960–5), that he relied on strong foreign support as a Western ally in the Cold war era, and had some economic successes in the early years of his reign, his kleptocratic dictatorship proved disastrous in the long run. In 1966 Mobutu launched the *Bakajika* law by which the colonial concession policy was revised and most former concessions were revoked and renegotiated. Foreign companies operating in the Congo were obliged to have their headquarters in the Congo under penalty of loss of commercial registration. Despite resistance from the UMHK, most companies obeyed. Mobutu tried to favor industrialization by founding in 1969 the Société Congolaise de Financement du Développement (Socofide, later renamed Sofide) (Moll *et al.* 1994: 119). Like communist China under Deng Hsiao Ping a decade later, he launched an open door policy in 1969 with a renewed Code des Investissements (Congo 1969), exempting foreign enterprises from import taxes and profit taxes. This move led to a considerable inflow of foreign capital from multinationals such as General Motors, Goodyear, and Fiat, and industrial production rose during the period 1966–72 by 50 percent (Chomé *et al.* 1977: 120). Yet, this inconsistency in Mobutu's economic policy was just a portent of what was to come.

Witnessing the boom in copper revenues until 1973, Mobutu thought the Congo would become the most developed economy of Africa within a few decades. But for Mobutu big was never big enough and economic common sense was increasingly lacking. Besides the Inga project, several giant industrial projects were started, for instance in the agro-industry sector (tomatoes, soap), telecommunications, steel, and cement. All of these projects produced huge losses (Willame 1986: 26). Mobutu's personal interventions in investment schemes were often politically inspired, the best example being the construction of the very high voltage line between Inga and Shaba. This line was primarily intended to increase Katanga's dependence on the western part of the Congo. Economic objections to the line from the management of Gecamines[8] (the firm that had taken over the UMHK's sites in Katanga) were brushed aside. A series of other measures made things even worse. In the context of his Zaïrianization program (launched in 1971), Mobutu nationalized most enterprises in 1973–4. As during Russia's turn to capitalism some decades later, nearly all these enterprises were handed over to the new elite, who in turn supported his regime. Many of these enterprises went bankrupt within a few years due to general mismanagement or deliberate stripping of critical productive assets. Mobutu himself gathered a fortune of nearly US$3 billion. Corruption spread at an incredible pace. The kleptocratic system undermined the effectiveness of the state administration and made sound business activities nearly impossible. The informal economy became the only way to survive (Bartlett 1990).

Mobutu's nationalization program not only led to a complete collapse of the industrial complex. It also triggered a free fall in food crop production within a short period of time. Seeing the disaster, Mobutu announced the (partial, 40 percent) restitution of nationalized assets on November 25, 1975 (followed in 1976 by the announcement that 60 percent would be restituted) but the damage was already tremendous and nearly irreparable (Moreau 2012: 176–7). Mobutu's dictatorship was extremely cruel and ruined the economy, but he continued to receive full support not only from Belgium but also, and especially, from the United States (Young 1994). He was thus able to plunder the Congo until he was finally driven out of power in 1997, after 32 years of dictatorial rule.

## 11.7 Summary and conclusions

The high level of industrialization of the Belgian Congo compared with the Netherlands Indies (see Lindblad, Chapter 10 above) and many other African colonies is relatively easy to explain. It was not the result of some kind of "enlightened government," as the Belgians would often have it. First, a certain level of industrialization was necessary in order to make the exploitation of the Congo's mineral wealth possible. In order to operate the mines in Katanga, for instance, electricity plants, mechanical engineering, food processing, and construction materials were needed. Second, the export of minerals and tropical produce often required an initial stage of processing. It was simply too costly to export raw copper or cassiterite ore, as the key mining regions were too distant from the Atlantic Ocean. Palm oil products have to be submitted to a first treatment for technical reasons. Industrialization was thus linked to the colonial model of exploitation, focusing on the export of minerals and tropical cash crops, giving rise to the formation of certain industrial "islands" within the Congo economy.

Additionally there was a Belgian-specific reason. Due to the enormous coal fields in the Walloon region of the country, Belgium had a comparative advantage in mining: many engineers had acquired high skills in the mining industry. Based on mining, Belgian capitalism in the nineteenth century had developed as a real form of industrial capitalism, whereas the Netherlands, for example, had more historical experience with a trade capitalist system (see also Abbeloos, Chapter 12 below). The industrial strength of the Belgian economy was reflected in the composition of the board of the Société Générale itself, which mainly comprised industrial engineers. Indeed, to some extent Belgium reproduced its own development model in the Congo.

The industrialization of the Belgian Congo went through different stages. It took off in the 1920s in two major growth centers: Leopoldville and Katanga (UMHK). The first region was highly focused on developing consumer goods for the domestic market; the second was based on linkages with the booming mining sector, providing consumer goods as well as intermediary products for mining. Substantial company profits were generated, to be transmitted to Belgium or used to finance the colonial state. Rapid industrialization was made possible by big investments from Belgian companies, but also through harsh exploitation of African labor. The forced recruitment of Congolese peasants literally separated indigenous agriculture from the fast-growing administrative capital and the mining regions. These recruitment policies were largely responsible for the impoverishment of the Congolese countryside and the uneven development of the Congolese economy in the long run.

With World War II, some important changes can be observed in the Belgian Congo. These were mainly caused by the explosive growth of the Congolese economy during and after the war (due to its unique position as a main supplier of minerals and tropical products for the Allied forces). As a consequence, wages and consumption began to increase and a lot of new manufacturing activities were developed. As the domestic market expanded, a new middle class emerged for the first time. The changing class structure gave birth to an historic alliance between the new middle class and the poor peasant population, as well as to an army of industrial and mining wage workers. These alliances would eventually overthrow colonial domination.

Among the many factors that contributed to the collapse of the industrial complex under Mobutu, the lack of colonial investment in human capital was perhaps the most decisive. Neither in administrative nor in entrepreneurial skills were Africans allowed to acquire the experience (and the instruction) needed to assure successful leadership of the country's resources. Opportunities were restricted to (at maximum) highly skilled technical jobs and lower-level office jobs. During the turmoil of the first years of independence, after the Belgians withdrew from the Congo, and also withdrew a large part of their capital investments, they basically decapitated the Congolese economy. The structures they left behind were insufficiently resilient to survive the extreme forms of kleptocracy inflicted upon the Congo by three decades of Mobutu rule.

## Notes

1 We thank the participants of the workshops in Utrecht and Antwerp for their useful remarks on earlier drafts of this chapter. Many thanks to Thomas Lindblad for his extensive review of our chapter and in particular also to Ewout Frankema for his stimulating suggestions and useful remarks.

2 The Act would play an important role in the way the economic structure of the country developed. Indeed, it forbade colonial rulers from developing a protectionist policy toward other countries. The Berlin Act defined the Congo Free State as a free trade zone, prohibiting Belgium from establishing a preferential trade tariff there; no "infant industry policy" was allowed. Later on, this would imply that Belgian-owned companies were founded in the Belgian Congo in order to confront foreign competition. In 1925, for example, the textile company Texaf was founded in order to address the systematic dumping practices of Japan, which were used to try to conquer the Congo market (Lacroix 1967: 19).

3 Later on, during World War II, the Congo would even finance the Belgian government in exile as well as provide for the servicing of the Belgian debt (Huybrechts 2010).

4 Such as Socol (Société Colonial de Construction) which was founded in 1911 for the construction of the railway Elisabethville–Bukama.

5 When in 1928 the Banque d'Outremer merged with Société Générale, the most important Congo holding company, the CCCI (Compagnie du Congo pour le Commerce et l'Industrie) provided the Société Générale with near total control of the Belgian Congo.

6 All technical details about Congo-specific products are in Lacroix (1967: 240–94). With regard to palm oil the author states: "The oil contained in the pericarp of the fruit should be removed as soon as possible after cutting, otherwise the oil content decreases rapidly while acidity increases" (Lacroix 1967: 240, translated).

7 This agreement was concluded with a speculator, however, and the Congo state soon had to retreat from its commitment. In 1963 Prime Minister Cyrille Adoula signed an agreement with the Italian––Congolese firm SICAI (Société italo-congolaise de développement industriel) to continue the work on the Inga power plant.

8 Gecamines (Générale des Carrières et des Mines) was the successor of Gecomin (Société Générale Congolaise des Minerais), that in 1967 took over the former UMHK mines.

## References

Acemoglu, D., Johnson, S., and Robinson, J.A. (2001) "The Colonial Origins of Comparative Development: An Empirical Investigation," *American Economic Review*, 91: 1369–401.

Ahrens, L. (1953) *Agricultural industries of Belgian Congo: The industrial potential of Africa*, Ghent: International Days for African Studies of the International Fair of Ghent.

Bartlett, B.R. (1990) "Capitalism in Africa: A Survey," *The Journal of Developing Areas*, 24 (3): 327–35.

Brion, R. and Moreau, J.L. (1996) *Fabrimetal. 50 ans au coeur de l'industrie*, Brussels: Editions Racine.

248 *F. Buelens and D. Cassimon*

Brion, R. and Moreau, J.L. (2006) *van Mijnbouw tot Mars. De ontstaansgeschiedenis van Umicore*, Tielt: Lannoo.

Buelens, F. (2007) *Congo 1885–1960. Een financieel-economische geschiedenis*, Antwerp: Epo.

Buelens, F. and Marysse, S. (2009) "Returns on Investments during the Colonial Era: The Case of the Belgian Congo," *The Economic History Review*, 62: 135–66.

Cattier, F. (1906) *Etude sur la situation de l'état indépendant du Congo*, Brussels: Larcier.

CBBCRU (Centrale Bank van Belgisch-Congo en Ruanda Urundi) (1959) "De vorderingen van de industrialisering in Belgisch-Congo," *Tijdschrift van de Centrale Bank van Belgisch-Congo en Ruanda Urundi*, 8: 1–16.

Chomé, J. and Zaïre Komitee (1977) *Zaïre.Ketens van Koper*, Louvain: Kritak.

Cleys, B. (2002) "Andries Dequae. De zelfgenoegzaamheid van een koloniaal bestuur (1950–1954)," Louvain: KULeuven, Master thesis.

Congo (1969) Code des Investissements: ordonnance-loi no. 69–032 du 26 juin 1969, Kinshasa: Ministère de l'Economie Nationale, de l'Industrie et du Tourisme.

Derkinderen, G. (1953) *Trade and minor industries in Belgian Congo, The industrial potential of Africa*, Ghent: International Days for African Studies of the International Fair of Ghent.

De Villers, G. (2012) "Du Congo au Zaïre. Epilogue d'une décolonisation," in M. Dumoulin, A.S. Gijs, P.L. Plasman and C. van de Velde (eds.), *Du Congo Belge à la République du Congo 1955–1965*, Brussels: Peter Lang.

De Vos, L., Gerard E., Raxhon P., and Gérard-Libois J. (2004) *Lumumba. De Complotten? De moord*, Louvain: Davidsfonds.

Dubois, E. (1913) "Le Congo Belge. Historique et organisation politique et administrative," in *Conférences faites au VI Cours International d'Expansion Commerciale organisé à l'Institut Supérieur de Commerce d'Anvers*, Brussels: Misch & Thron, VIII-20.

Dumortier, P. (1947) "L'industrie chimique au Congo Belge," in Association des Ingénieurs sortis de l'Ecole de Liège, *Centenaire de l'Association des Ingénieurs sortis de l'Ecole de Liège. Congrès 1947. Section Coloniale*, Liège: Association des Ingénieurs sortis de l'Ecole de Liège.

Foutry, V. and Neckers, J. (1986) *Als een wereld zo groot waar uw vlag staat geplant*, Louvain: Nauwelaerts.

Fransolet, F.J.F. (1947) "L'industrie textile coloniale belge," in Association des Ingénieurs sortis de l'Ecole de Liège, *Centenaire de l'Association des Ingénieurs sortis de l'Ecole de Liège. Congrès 1947. Section Coloniale*, Liège: Association des Ingénieurs sortis de l'Ecole de Liège.

Gann, L.H. and Duignan, P. (1979) *The rulers of Belgian Africa*, Princeton, NJ: Princeton University Press.

Gouverneur, J. (1971) *Productivity and factor proportions in less developed countries: the case of industrial firms in the Congo*, Oxford: Clarendon Press.

Hochschild, A. (1999) *King Leopold's ghost. A story of greed, terror, and heroism in Colonial Africa*, Boston, Mass.: Mariner Books.

Huybrechts, A. (2010) *Bilan économique du Congo 1908–1960*, Paris: l'Harmattan.

Jewsiewicki, B. (1983) "Rural Society and the Belgian Colonial Economy," in D. Birmingham and P.M. Martin (eds.), *The history of Central Africa*, vol. 2, New York: Longman.

Joye, P. and Lewin, R. (1961) *Les trusts au Congo*, Brussels: Société Populaire d'Editions.

Kaplan, L.S. (2010) *Nato and the UN: a peculiar relationship*, Columbia and London: University of Missouri Press.

Kipré, P. (1993) "Industrial Development and Urban Growth," in A. Mazrui (ed.), *General history of Africa. Africa since 1935*, vol. 8, Paris: Unesco.

Lacroix, J.L. (1966) "Principes pour une stratégie du développement industriel du Congo," in OECD, *Industrialisation problems in Africa*, Leopoldville: OECD.

Lacroix, J.L. (1967) *Industrialisation au Congo. La transformation des structures économiques*, Paris: Mouton.

Lippens, R. (1953) *The industrial culture of sugar-cane in Belgian Congo. The industrial potential of Africa*, Ghent: International Days for African Studies of the International Fair of Ghent.

Marthoz, A. (1953) *The mining industry of Belgian Congo and Ruanda–Urundi. The industrial potential of Africa*, Ghent: International Days for African Studies of the International Fair of Ghent.

Marysse, S., Cassimon, D., De Herdt, T., Tshiunza Mbiye, O., Verbeke, K., and Visser, M. (2011) *Evaluation de l'allégement de la dette en RDC. Final Report*, Antwerp: Institute of Development Policy and Management, University of Antwerp.

Melville, E. (1953) *The industrial future of British African colonies. The industrial potential of Africa*, Ghent: International Days for African Studies of the International Fair of Ghent.

Mitchell, B.R. (2007) *International historical statistics: Africa, Asia & Oceania, 1750–2005*, Basingstoke: Palgrave Macmillan.

Moll, M., Couvreur, J.P., and Norro, M. (1994), *Zaïre. Secteur des parastataux. Réactivation de l'économie. Contribution d'entreprises du portefeuille de l'etat*, Brussels: Société Nationale d'Investissement.

Mollin, G. (1996) *Die USA und der Kolonialismus: Amerika als Partner und Nachfolger der Belgischen Macht in Afrika*, Berlin: Akademie Verlag.

Moreau, J.L. (2012) "De la colonisation à la zaïrianisation. Le sort des capitaux belges au Congo," in M. Dumoulin, A.S. Gijs, P.L. Plasman and C. van de Velde (eds.), *Du Congo Belge à la République du Congo 1955–1965*, Brussels: Peter Lang.

Moxhon, H. (1953) *The textile industry in Belgian Congo and Ruanda-Urundi. The industrial potential of Africa*, Ghent: International Days for African Studies of the International Fair of Ghent.

Murphy, K.M., Shleifer, A., and Vishny, R. (1989) "Income Distribution, Market Size, and Industrialization," *The Quarterly Journal of Economics*, 104: 537–64.

Ndaywel è Nziem, I. (1998) *Histoire générale du Congo. De l'héritage ancien à la République Démocratique*, Paris and Brussels: De Boeck & Larcier.

Peemans, J.P. (1975a) "Capital Accumulation in the Congo under Colonialism: The Role of the State," in L.H. Gann and P. Duignan (eds.), *Colonialism in Africa 1870–1960, 4, The economics of colonialism*, Stanford, Calif.: Hoover Institution Press.

Peemans, J.P. (1975b) "The Social and Economic Development of Zaire since Independence: An Historical Outline," *African Affairs*, 74: 148–79.

Rodrik, D. (2004) "Industrial policy in the twenty-first century." Paper prepared for UNIDO. Online. Available at www.ksg.harvard.edu/rodrik (accessed July 10, 2011).

Stengers, J. (1977) "La genèse d'une pensée coloniale. Leopold II et le modèle hollandais," *Tijdschrift voor Geschiedenis*, 90: 46–71.

Vandewalle, G. (1966) *De conjuncturele evolutie in Kongo en Ruanda-Urundi van 1920 tot 1939 en van 1949 tot 1958*, Ghent: Hogere School voor Handels- en Economische Wetenschappen.

van Reybrouck, D. (2010) *Congo. Een Geschiedenis*, Amsterdam: De Bezige Bij.

Vansina, J. (2010) *Being colonized: The Kuba experience in Rural Congo, 1880–1960*, Madison: University of Wisconsin Press.

Vanthemsche, G. (1993) "Une politique de développement économique colonial. Le 'plan décennal' du Congo Belge 1949–1959," in E. Aerts, B. Henau, P. Janssens, and R. van Uytven (eds.), *Studia historica oeconomica. Liber amicorum Herman van der Wee*, Louvain: University Press.

Vanthemsche, G. (2007) *La Belgique et le Congo*, Brussels: Editions Complexe.

Vellut, J.L. (1979) "De Kongo 1910–1940," in P. Blok (ed.), *Algemene Geschiedenis der Nederlanden*, 14, Haarlem: Fibula-van Dishoeck.

Verhaegen, B. (1972) "La Société Générale et l'Union Minière," *La Revue Nouvelle*, 371–4.

Willame, J.C. (1986) *Zaïre: l'épopée d'Inga: chronique d'une prédation industrielle*, Paris: l'Harmattan.

Young, C. (1994) "The Shattered Illusion of the Integral State," *The Journal of Modern African Studies*, 32: 247–63.

# 12  Mobutu, Suharto, and the challenges of nation-building and economic development, 1965–97

*Jan-Frederik Abbeloos*

## 12.1 Introduction

This chapter takes a closer look at the post-colonial divergence between the Congo and Indonesia during the regimes of Suharto and Mobutu, between 1965 and 1997.[1] The data summarized in Table 12.1 indicate just how dramatic this divergence was in terms of economic growth and the structures of production and export underpinning it. After 1965, the Congo changed from an export-driven economy harboring one of the few industrializing enclaves on the African continent into a low-growth, predominantly agricultural subsistence zone with only a small industrial base, dependent on fluctuating foreign demand for its natural resources. In contrast, Indonesia enjoyed strong and persistent economic growth per capita, and has gradually upgraded its export structure in recent decades to include more labor-intensive and capital-intensive merchandise.

Starting out with higher GDP per capita levels than Indonesia, the Congo turned into one of the least developed economies in the world. This gloomy picture is the result of a long negative slide since the 1970s. By 1975 the Congo's per capita GDP stood at its 1960 level. Afterwards, things went downhill. The economy finally hit rock bottom during the 1990s, with an annual contraction of 8.4 percent. Congo's small domestic product today is over 47 percent dependent on its primary sector and 28 percent on services; only around 24 percent of added value is realized in industry – with a negligible share of manufacturing activities. These figures reflect a serious deindustrialization of the Congolese economy, which thanks to the Katangese copper processing industry in the first decade of independence had an industrial share in GDP rivaling South Africa. However, after 1990 copper production remained at a virtual standstill until 2003. Since then, relative domestic stability and high international copper prices have renewed foreign interest and production. Overall, Congolese merchandise exports narrowed down to a handful of primary commodities over the post-colonial period (Figure 12.1).[2] Although official figures after 1990 are hard to find and even harder to trust, exports have become very concentrated in copper, cobalt, and diamonds at different stages of the processing stage – although never fully processed.[3] Whereas 8 percent of total merchandise trade in 1965 consisted of manufactures, the share of manufactures in today's exports

Table 12.1 Divergence in growth, structures of production, and export between the Congo and Indonesia, 1960–2010

| GDP per capita (2000 US$) | 1960 | 1965 | 1970 | 1980 | 1990 | 2000 | 2010 |
|---|---|---|---|---|---|---|---|
| Indonesia | 201 | 196 | 233 | 390 | 592 | 773 | 1144 |
| Congo | 325 | 319 | 332 | 260 | 210 | 87 | 104 |

| Sectoral composition of GDP (%) | 1960–70 | | | | 2001–10 | | | |
|---|---|---|---|---|---|---|---|---|
| | Agriculture | Industry | Manufacturing | Services | Agriculture | Industry | Manufacturing | Services |
| Indonesia | 50.9 | 14.8 | 9.1 | 34.2 | 14.8 | 47.1 | 28 | 38.2 |
| Congo | 19.9 | 35.2 | n.a. | 44.9 | 47.3 | 24.7 | 5.8 | 27.9 |

| Composition of merchandise exports (%) | 1960–70 | | | | 2001–10 | | | |
|---|---|---|---|---|---|---|---|---|
| | Agriculture | Food | Ores and fuels | Manufacturing | Agriculture. | Food | Ores and fuels | Manufacturing |
| Indonesia | 33.1 | 20.0 | 45 | 1.3 | 5.2 | 13.0 | 34.3 | 47.5 |
| Congo | 3.9 | 13.7 | 74.9 | 7.5 | 8.2 | 3.9 | 83.4 | 3.2 |

Source: World Bank Development Indicators 2012.

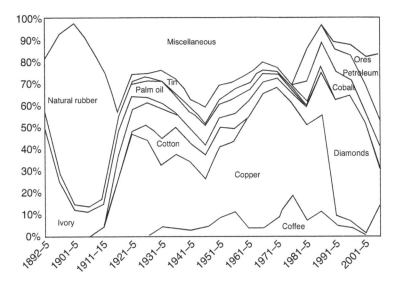

*Figure 12.1* The Congo's merchandise export composition, 1892–2010 (sources: 1892–1960: Mitchell (1998); 1965–78: UN Comtrade; 1980–8: Tshishimbi and Glick (1993: Appendix Table 18); 1990: Kisangani and Bobb (2010: Table 2); 1995–2010: UN, UNCTAD Statistics).

has shrunk below 3 percent. These deplorable statistics illustrate the erosion of Congo's manufacturing capabilities.

Indonesia, starting out as one of the least developed economies in 1960, on the contrary underwent rapid growth after 1965, up to the 1997–8 financial crisis, and growth levels have again picked up since, amounting to an overall average annual growth rate of 4 percent since 1965. During this time, Indonesia's economic structure strongly shifted out of the primary and into the secondary sector. About 47 percent of added value was realized in the secondary sector over the period 2001–10, half of it in manufacturing. Agriculture meanwhile has fallen back to 15 percent of GDP. The predominance of rubber in merchandise exports noted upon independence gradually gave way to dependence on petroleum, which made up a staggering 70 percent of total exports by 1975 (Figure 12.2). After the negative oil price shocks of the 1980s, the share of primary commodities in total exports fell drastically. Vice versa, manufactures, which were less than 10 percent of GDP in 1966, grew to 57 percent by 2000. The subsequent commodity boom once again pushed up the share of primary commodities in exports, especially palm oil, natural gas, and oil. But symbolizing the general industrialization and growth of the economy, Indonesia actually became a net oil importer by 2004, withdrawing from OPEC in 2008.

As regards political development, the comparison shows a different pattern. To be blunt, the Congo today is a poor but relatively unified country with a strong

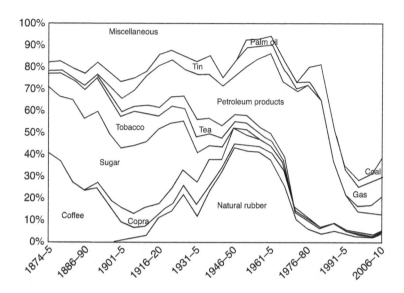

*Figure 12.2* Indonesia's merchandise export composition, 1874–2010 (source: 1891–1938: Kano (2008: Table 2–7b, Table 2–11a); 1940, 1949, 1950: Mitchell (1998); 1951–66: Woo and Nasution (1989: Table 2.6); 1967–2010: UN, Comtrade Database).

sense of shared nationhood which continues to amaze students of the region (Schrank 2009). Paradoxically, Indonesia since Suharto is a much richer country that suffers from stronger centrifugal tendencies; plenty of ethnic and nationalistic killings have taken place in regions such as Aceh, East Timor, Maluku, Java, West Kalimantan, West Papua, and elsewhere. Of course, this does not mean that in contrast the Congo is a peaceful or stable country, far from it. Civil war since 1997 has claimed millions of victims, particularly in the Eastern Kivu region, and economic failure is reflected in a weak central government that cannot claim to be able to project its power across the country (Englebert 2000; Herbst and Mills 2009; Young 1994). However, despite these destabilizing forces, the Congolese people continue to share a sense of national feeling, and at two separate polls, in 1998 and 2001, a large majority of them – respectively 89 and 70 percent – declared themselves against a partition of the country (Raeymaekers 2009). To be sure, the perceived political unity across the Congo can be interpreted as a consequence of its economic decline, given that the state is unable to govern much more than the public's imagination and aspirations. In other words, the idea of shared nationhood is "all that remains to a people that has been dispossessed of its wealth, its peace and much of its dignity" (Englebert 2002: 592). Nationalist pride can thus be seen as a reaction against economic hardship, creating an imagined stability in a society where there is little security to be found. But whatever the viability or political potential of this imagined community, for our purposes it is important that, contrary to Indonesia, the numerous political and economic conflicts in the Congo deal with access to state power, not the desire to break away from state power or to realize regional self-determination (Englebert 2002).

The political/economic divergence forces us to tackle a fundamental question: why did Indonesia grow rich yet disunited, and not the Congo? Why did Indonesia under Suharto enjoy far stronger economic growth, perhaps paying the price of a more fragile political unity? At this point the comparison between Suharto and Mobutu becomes really interesting, given that both regimes at face value were so much alike. The generals' rise to power ushered in three decades of authoritarian rule situated on the anti-communist side of the Cold War ideological spectrum. Both regimes were firmly backed and funded by the West. Just as in Mobutu's Zaïre, political and economic power under Suharto – and Sukarno – derived from patron–client relationships across networks encircling the presidency. Public offices were distributed among relatives, friends, and clients in order to exploit them, and private interests were pursued within a political structure that only had a legal-rational façade. In this respect, both regimes have been identified as being *neo-patrimonial*, with a corps of power holders around the presidency acting as gatekeepers to monopolies, offices, and contracts (Budd 2004: 10; De Herdt 2002; Willame 1972; Abbott 2003: ch. 3; MacGaffey 1987: 17; Ricklefs 2001: 313; Robison 2009; Thomson 2000: 109).[4]

Given their neo-patrimonial similarities, what makes for the divergence in development between the countries during the Mobutu and Suharto regimes? The short answer is that seemingly similar regimes nevertheless pursued different policies. Much of the literature points out how Suharto's neo-patrimonial regime did get its economic policies right, whether by distributing oil rents and targeting inflation in order to dampen regional and social inequality, countering exchange rate overvaluations in order to maintain strong non-oil tradable (e.g., manufacturing) sectors, investing in agricultural productivity in order to avoid food import dependence, or promoting import substitution-based and export-oriented industrialization (for more detailed discussions of these policies see Woo and Nasution 1989; Hill 1992; Rock 1999; Dove and Kammen 2001; Ishida 2003). What characterizes these policies is that they actively supported the intensification of agriculture and the upgrading of manufacturing. And the policies paid off. By the mid-1980s, Indonesia was self-sufficient in rice, and from 1972 to 1981 non-mining GDP expanded by over 8 percent a year (Perkins *et al.* 2006: 680).

Similar developmental policies meanwhile were never actively pursued under Mobutu, even when occasional lip service was paid to them (Maton and Lecomte 2001). In contrast to Indonesia, Congo was self-sufficient in food at independence. But by the 1980s it was importing large quantities of food products, consumer goods, and transportation and construction equipment. Whereas Suharto kept inflation in check, it skyrocketed under Mobutu. For 23 years following independence, the Congo's currency exchange rate was not managed so as to promote export competitiveness, but set at unrealistically high levels. Stringent management under Suharto of the money supply and the budget to protect foreign exchange reserves contrasts with the Mubutu government's tendency to borrow from the treasury to meet its budget deficits. Shortages of foreign exchange gave rise to a thriving parallel market, in which the US dollar often traded at three to seven times its official exchange rate (Kisangani and Bobb 2010: 125). The list of contrasting policy choices can easily be extended.

The straightforward argument that Suharto made the right policy choices begs the question of why Mobutu somehow made all the wrong choices. It will not do to argue that Suharto was simply a better leader than Mobutu, or that Mobutu was somehow bent on ruining his country. Accusations fall short as explanations and they overlook the incentives, interests, and circumstances that steer human agency and its effects. This chapter therefore frames the actions and policies of the Mobutu and Suharto regimes in the specific political economic contexts in which both generals attained power around 1965. These contexts conditioned the economic and political outlook of both leaders, influenced their development priorities, and determined the institutional environment in which they could operate.

Two contrasting features of these political economic contexts in particular seem important. The first is that Suharto inherited a country that under Sukarno had "fallen apart" as an economy but already had "become one" as a nation (Ricklefs 2001: 311). Suharto consequently prioritized economic capacity building, inviting Western capital back into the country, even dealing with the publicly mistrusted Sino-Indonesian entrepreneurial class, all in order to achieve food security and industrial upgrading (Rock 1999: 692). This does not mean that Suharto did not have to suppress ethnic conflicts and regional uprisings – in fact they were more frequent in Indonesia than in the Congo.[5] But it is crucial that when the blueprint of the New Order regime was being drafted, the political and economic situation of the 1960s dictated that economics would come first. This is in sharp contrast with the Congo, where Mobutu, in 1965, especially faced a country torn apart by political conflict based on ethnic and regional divisions. The country's macro-economic performance meanwhile was reasonably solid though overly dependent on the booming copper business in Katanga, a region with an outspoken secessionist agenda. Given the ethnic and secessionist tensions Mobutu had to overcome, politics came first, with the implicit assumption that economic growth would follow as long as political unity was achieved.

A second difference concerns the power balance between rural and urban interests. In the Congo, the predominance of copper had already infused colonial policies with a strong urban and industrial bias, with agriculture as the handmaiden of (mining) industry. This was a developmental stereotype that Mobutu confirmed rather than challenged. In Indonesia, however, the importance of natural resources such as sugar, coffee, and rubber had already influenced a different kind of colonial policy that was less concerned with uprooting the peasantry and more with agricultural intensification.

As a consequence, the two regions reacted differently to a shifting post-1973 global economy that saw, amongst other transformations, two oil crises, the emergence of a floating exchange rate regime, volatile primary commodity markets, a slowdown of growth in the industrial world, a subsequent boom in transnational investment and finance, and delocalization plus slicing up of the value chain. At the heart of these shifts – often summed up as globalization – sits an important relocation in global production. Due to falling private savings, fiscal imbalances, or budget deficits, a number of industrial countries swung from being creditor to debtor nations, including the global economic leader. The United States swung from the world's largest creditor to being a debtor nation in the 1980s, from net foreign assets of 11 percent of GDP in 1970–5 to –22 percent by 2004 (Cline 2005: 21). The redirection of foreign capital this entailed in recent decades has allowed the United States in particular to run large deficits in the balance of trade in recent decades. This in turn kept up demand for a range of consumer manufactures that to a growing extent could be produced more cheaply elsewhere.

As pointed out by Giovanni Arrighi (2002: 22–3), low-income countries that could compete for a share of the expanding demand for cheap industrial products profited twice. The improvement in their balance of payments lessened the need to compete with richer countries in world financial markets, while the shift into manufactures created technological and capital spill-overs and other linkage effects throughout the economy. Following this formula, many East Asian countries, including Indonesia, have seen their economies grow and their position in the global wealth of nations upgraded, to the point where China and Taiwan have even become creditor nations. Developing countries that missed out on the opportunity, however, tended to run into balance-of-payment difficulties, debt crises, and stunted growth. In this category we find most sub-Saharan economies, especially the Congo – and many Latin American economies for that matter (Becker and Craigie 2007; Kohli 2009).

## 12.2 Similar challenges, different circumstances

The starting point of the present chapter is that the outcome of the Congo's and Indonesia's colonial transformation in at least one respect was comparable: both were low-income countries with economic structures and socio-political institutions that were geared toward the production and export of primary commodities. The Dutch and Belgian colonial projects had combined a concern to improve *native welfare* with the practice of *mise en valeur*, basing economic activity on the rising demand across industrializing countries for primary commodities such as coffee, sugar, rubber, copper, or cotton. This dual mandate, suggested as a model for British colonies by Frederick Lugard (1922) and for the French colonies by Albert Sarraut (1923), was also visible in Dutch and Belgian colonial policies (Booth 1998: 2–6, 2007: 5; Furnivall 1967: 346; Ndaywel è Nziem 1998: 362; Stengers 1989:180). Primary export promotion and control did not require the colonial administration to fully penetrate society in terms of fiscal requirements or direct control over the entire colony. Instead, the sort of economic and institutional structures developed in both regions were those managed by what Frederick Cooper has called a gatekeeper state (Cooper 2002:

5, 2005). The notion of a gatekeeper state was developed by Cooper with specific reference to the ideal-typical African colonial experience of "being systematically conquered but not so systematically ruled." Cooper thus underlines how
the (African) colonial state managed and profited from the interface between a
colonial territory and the world market, maintaining narrow links to specific
areas of the interior while displaying weak overall control over interior spaces.
In these respects, both Belgian and Dutch colonizers have been said to have
established limited connections with their colonies, projecting power through
systems of indirect rule, and primarily controlling the link between local production and outside demand for natural resources that fuel industrialization elsewhere (Bowie and Unger 1997: 45; Gondola 2002: 78; Touwen 2001).

Of course – as previous chapters illustrate – there were ample differences
between the ways in which the dual mandate was put into practice in the Congo
and in Indonesia, and I will stress one fundamental difference later on. Budget
constraints and the relatively small numbers of administrators controlling a vast
territory also limited the effective implementation of gatekeeper policies
(Richens 2009; van der Eng 1996; Lindblad 2002:120).[6] Moreover, the colonial
administration was not the only stakeholder steering the Congo's and Indonesia's colonial transformation. Different social agents influenced the process,
including the demands made by European business, missions, settler and indigenous communities, and the local labor force. But whatever the limits of their
*respective* agency, the *combined* agency of all these stakeholders structured the
institutions and relations of production to the extent that the outward projection
– or extroversion (Bayart 2000) – of the economy and of the institutions underpinning it substantially ordered the degrees of freedom for post-colonial growth
and development. By the time Indonesia and the Congo could organize their own
economic policies, colonialism had imposed a degree of path dependence on
their economies toward specialization in the production and export of primary
commodities (Kano 2008; Peemans 1975: 153). As both countries were more
firmly integrated in international networks of trade and power than they were
domestically, post-colonial governments inherited neither a strong national
economy nor a well- developed national bureaucracy nor a population trained to
work together under a shared government that would embody a national interest
of sorts. The result of the colonial transformation was not a national economy
but a dual economy, with serious uneven development between commercial and
industrial centers on the one hand – such as Java or Katanga – and rural periph-
eries on the other hand – such as the Outer Islands or central Congo.

In sum, *despite* colonial differences, the Congo and Indonesia, like so many
former European colonies, faced a similar post-colonial challenge of forging
political unity out of diversity and managing and upgrading an economic
product largely dependent on global natural resource markets. The colonial dual
mandate had to be countered by what might be considered a post-colonial dual
challenge: to unify politically and diversify economically, turning colonial subjects into national citizens, consumers, and entrepreneurs. This dual challenge
was central to the speech by Patrice Lumumba on the proclamation of Congo's

independence in 1960 in which he stressed how Congolese citizens had to leave their "tribal quarrels" behind and create a national economy that would ensure economic independence (McIntire 2009: 438–40; De Witte 2001: 177). Similar opinions surfaced frequently in Indonesia after the uncertainties of the 1940s, when Japanese forces overthrew the colonial administration in 1942 before surrendering to the Allied forces. In the four years of political and diplomatic strife that led up to independence in 1949, Indonesian politicians articulated a vision of an *ekonomi nasional* that would replace the *ekonomi colonial* (Chalmers 1997: 7).

However, this does not mean that by the time Mobutu and Suharto achieved power around 1965 they enjoyed similar conditions when facing the post-colonial challenge of nation building and economic capacity building, quite the contrary. As said earlier, especially regarding the balance between economic versus political stability and rural versus urban interests, the Congo and Indonesia by 1965 were very different cases. The next sections look deeper into these differences.

## 12.3 Political versus economic capacity building

Starting with Indonesia, the government under Sukarno, especially during the first decade of independence, had been preoccupied with domestic political and military problems – such as the restoration of sovereignty on West Irian – and with political recognition in world forums. Little attention or resources were devoted to economic development, resulting in serious economic problems. As Anne Booth points out (1998: 7), Indonesia under Sukarno was viewed by both foreign and Indonesian economists as "a developmental catastrophe," "a chronic dropout," or "the number one economic failure among the major underdeveloped countries." Under Sukarno's rule, food production was falling behind population growth, export earnings were declining, successive budget deficits were fuelling runaway inflation, infrastructure was deteriorating, and real per capita income was almost certainly lower than it had been in the late 1930s, and probably lower than in 1913 (Booth 1998: 7). However, despite this economic catastrophe, the people of Indonesia, in the words of Ricklefs (2001: 310), "had achieved one extraordinary victory: Indonesia was a single nation." Not that political and social unrest was lacking under Sukarno, but even dissident regional movements under the Guilded Democracy protested at the way the nation was structured and governed, not at its existence (Ricklefs 2001: 310). Like Mobutu's a decade later, Sukarno's economic decisions were also considered instrumental to this nationalist revolution, taking over Dutch enterprises and discouraging so-called neo-colonial foreign direct investment.

The economic chaos of the 1958–65 period left such a deep impression that Suharto gave priority to economic capacity building. Suharto therefore appealed for economic support from the West and brought into his government a number of American-trained economists, the so-called Berkeley Mafia headed by Widjojo Nitisastro. At their urging, in 1967 the Inter-Governmental Group on

Indonesia (IGGI) was set up, and, together with the World Bank and International Monetary Fund (IMF), it provided more than 75 percent of development expenses during Suharto's early years. The technocratic Berkeley Mafia introduced orthodox monetary and macro-economic policies – such as keeping a balanced budget – but these liberal policies had to be accommodated with the more micro-economic developmental goal of industrial upgrading, which was heavily championed by a second, more amorphous, group of technicians-turned-managers, military advisors, and economists with structuralist inclinations (Woo and Nasution 1989). The First Five-Year Program announced in 1969 designated fertilizers, cement, and agricultural machinery as priority areas for industrialization and by 1970 Indonesia had successively adopted such measures as import tariff hikes and import bans targeted at specific industry sectors, while the bulk of foreign direct investment flowed into synthetic fibers and other spinning sectors (Ishida 2003). Within Indonesia, the use Suharto made of the Sino-Indonesian groups illustrated to what extent the nationalist tendencies visible under Sukarno had to make way for a more pragmatic approach that prioritized economic growth over nationalist pride.

Whereas Suharto especially faced dire economic conditions upon achieving power, Mobutu especially faced dire political conditions. Mobutu's rise to power had depended on external support from Belgium, France, and the CIA (Nzongola-Ntalaja 2002: 142–3). His coup ended a five-year post-colonial transition period – the so-called First Republic – during which civil war, ethnic pogroms, military mutiny, and regional rebellions tore the country apart. One of the main victims of the chaos was Lumumba, and the dream of a unified Congo seemed dead and buried with him. I lack the space to review the complex and ever shifting power balance that typified this Congo crisis, but for the present purpose the Katanga secession in 1960–3 is of particular importance. The region had already under colonialism been an economic enclave and during the post-colonial turmoil it saw the chance to break away from the rest of the country – which at that point would have caused national bankruptcy (Saideman 2001: ch. 3). The secession did not succeed – despite Belgian support – but it did lay bare the dependence of Congo on the copper-rich province. Mobutu's main goal therefore, like Sukarno's, was to forge political unity, promoting so-called "Authenticity policies" that were aimed at abolishing tribalism and regionalism and developing a sense of nationhood among the people. And like Sukarno's, Mobutu's economic policies largely served this nationalist agenda. The *Bakajika* Law, passed in 1966, stipulated that all public land was a domain of the state and paved the way for the nationalization one year later of the local copper business of the Union Minière du Haut Katanga (UMHK). Also in 1967, the Congolese franc was replaced by a new currency, called the zaïre (Z), which was exchanged at the rate of US$2 for 1 zaïre.

To be sure, the nationalist policies served their political purpose. Under Mobutu people started to feel Zairian. Mobutu's achievement was quite remarkable, and people recognized Zairian identity as a legitimate supra-identity that united the different regions within Congo (van Reybrouck 2010: 374). Blinded by the copper boom and what seemed an authoritarian yet perhaps developmental government, foreign investment peaked in the early 1970s, when foreign banks granted large loans for ambitious infrastructure and industrial development projects based on projected revenues from Congolese mineral exports, which at the time were enjoying historically high prices. The government launched the Politique des Grands Travaux (Great Works Policy), which focused on building large-scale development projects aimed at transforming the country into a modern industrial state. From 1967 to 1973, Mobutu's economic model actually seemed to work relatively well, and the Congo was even considered as a rival to Nigeria and South Africa for economic leadership of Africa – symbolized for example by the Organization of African Unity summit conference in 1967 in Kinshasa (Trefon *et al.* 2002: 380).

But taking the copper wealth for granted, Mobutu's political project largely neglected rebuilding economic capacity. High copper prices masked the fact that the private economy outside the copper business, and especially agriculture, had suffered badly during the transition period. In the rush to claim national independence, the question of economic independence was hardly given a thought, while Belgian capital, know-how, and managers had mostly left the country between 1960 and 1965. After independence, Authenticity policies did not imply the development of a local bourgeoisie. Given Mobutu's primary goal of forging a national unity around a personal axis, Dunning (2005) points out that generating an entrepreneurial class with an interest in industrial transformation was as dangerous as promoting the political organization of a civil society. A broad transformation of the relations of production with the potential rise of a domestic bourgeoisie was consequently not high on the agenda. And again, such a transformation did not seem urgent as copper continued to pay the budget and secure foreign loans.

To be sure, the political motivations that fueled Mobutu's tactics were not necessarily alien to Suharto. He too would have been reluctant to create a bourgeois class that could demand political reform, while his repressive regime equally fueled social protests and political opposition. Dunning (2005) underlines that Suharto, in sharp contrast to Mobutu, was able to reduce the political risk of diversification by promoting the private activities of economically powerful but politically weak groups of ethnic Chinese entrepreneurs. Rather than promote private business among indigenous Indonesian entrepreneurs (known as *pribumi* enterprises), Suharto developed tight relationships with a quite small number of Sino-Indonesian entrepreneurs (*cukong*), who were offered tariff protection, preferential access to monopoly licenses and contracts, subsidized credits and other benefits. Mobutu's harsh anti-colonial rhetoric and Authenticity policies would have made it harder for him to call upon such a foreign entrepreneurial class if there had been one in the Congo. The Belgian state had not been willing to open the Congolese gate to other European, let alone extra-European, communities (Vanthemsche 2007: 274–5). One of the goals of Belgian policy had been to *Belgify* the Congo, much as it had been Mobutu's goal to *Zaïrianize* the country afterward. In both projects, there was little room for outside participation.

## 12.4 Urban versus rural interests

Woo and Nasution (1989) underline that Suharto's willingness to use active exchange rate policy to maintain competitiveness, along with incentives for agriculture and light manufacturing, arose from the desire to retain political support in rural areas. They identify two political concerns that have significantly influenced Suharto's choice of economic policies.

The first was to avoid conditions favorable to the revival of the Indonesian Communist Party (Purtai Kommunis Indonesia or PKI). The PKI had been an important pillar of support to Sukarno and in the years before 1965 it was starting to pose a threat to the other important force in Indonesian politics, the army (Angkatan Bersenjata Republik Indonesia, ABRI). The coup by Suharto effectively tipped the balance of power in favor of the military. Yet despite the large-scale killings of PKI supporters – particularly in the countryside – and the purge of pro-Sukarno elements of the armed forces, the specter of a communist return nevertheless influenced New Order politics. Since the PKI was primarily a Javanese peasant-based movement, the policy implication was that conditions in the rural areas had to be improved. The second concern was to display equitable treatment of the Outer Islands, given their still fresh history of secessionist movements under Sukarno. Since the economy of the Outer Islands depended heavily on tree crop exports, this further strengthened the case for promoting agricultural development.

Whereas political calculations stimulated Suharto to consider agricultural and rural interests in developing his economic policies, Mobutu's Authenticity policies were especially geared toward securing urban support. The dependence on copper in particular biased policies against rural interests (Nzongola-Ntalaja 1986: 9). This actually confirmed Belgian colonial policies, which had equally prioritized development of the copper sector over the agricultural sector. As discussed in greater detail by Booth (see Chapter 3 above), the Belgians were in any case less concerned with agricultural intensification or promoting indigenous agricultural production than the Dutch. Or put differently, managing a gate for minerals such as diamonds, uranium, and copper in the case of the Congo implied that much more had to be done in order to connect local production to global demand. According to Geertz, Dutch colonial economic interests from 1619 to 1942 continued to be first and foremost mercantilist. They aimed "to pry agricultural products out of the archipelago, and particularly out of Java, which were saleable on world markets without changing fundamentally the structure of the indigenous economy" (Geertz 1963: 47). Bringing sugar, coffee, and later rubber onto the world market of course still implied penetrating domestic markets and plugging into existing relations of production and exchange in order to control the gate between local production and global demand. However, once put into our comparative framework, it is clear that there were differences in the way in which the Dutch and the Belgian colonizers managed the gate. Whereas the Dutch could initially redirect existing cash crop commerce, there was no existing copper production to redirect in the Congo – whatever production there once had been was in serious decline once the Europeans penetrated Katanga.

Starting up production in the sparsely populated inland region of Katanga created huge problems in terms of labor, energy, and transport. Overcoming these obstacles turned the Congo in what Gareth Austin typifies as a settler colony, where the profitable exploitation of copper and diamonds required that the cost of labor be reduced far below what the physical labor–land ratio implied (Austin 2010). During its earliest period, the development of the mining sector was the result of low-wage migrant labor, and thereafter, its stabilized and relatively better-paid manpower was provided with food bought at low prices from peasants, or produced by capitalist farming companies using low-cost agricultural wage workers (Peemans 1975: 150). Only in the final decade of colonization were efforts made to raise agricultural productivity. The paradox associated with this transformation is that this actively pursued proletarianization of the original producers, although classically associated with the origins of economic growth across Europe, has become one of the biggest barriers to successful economic development across southern Africa (Arrighi *et al.* 2010). As in many other African countries, this colonial pattern of *accumulation by dispossession* lived on in Mobutu's reluctance to invest heavily in mobilizing or unlocking rural areas, despite the often larger population in these areas (Arrighi and Saul 1968; Bates 1981: 33; Cooper 2002: 5; Herbst 2000: 17). Unfortunately, by restraining the growth of agricultural productivity and domestic markets, this pattern perpetuated the dependence of African economies on the growth of world demand for primary products (Arrighi 2002: 11).

## 12.5 The reversal of fortune

The different priorities of Mobutu and Suharto conditioned how well or ill prepared both regimes were in dealing with the rising volatility from the 1970s on the markets for their main export commodities, oil and copper. The price trends plotted in Figure 12.3 indicate that both the copper and the oil markets, like so many other primary commodity markets, suffered from strong volatility under the post-1973 global flexible exchange rate regime, displaying violent and frequent boom and bust cycles (Cashin and McDermott 2001). Of course, the first of these shocks in 1973 boosted oil prices while severely depressing copper prices. It is undeniably true that Indonesia's growth acceleration was aided by a dramatic improvement in the country's terms of trade, due mainly to the improvement in the price of oil (Figure 12.4). Vice versa, the Congo's economic decline coincides with a series of negative price shocks for copper from 1973 onward, bringing down the country's more advantage terms of trade. However, oil prices crashed after 1981, falling back to their 1973 level by 1998. Revenue from oil and gas, which in the early 1980s generated three-quarters of Indonesia's exports and two-thirds of government receipts fell sharply after 1982 (Hill 1992: 352). Nevertheless, Indonesia's economic growth immediately recovered from this negative shock, depending less on primary commodity exports and more on manufacturing – in the end consuming more oil than it produced domestically. It is precisely this pattern of sustained economic growth beyond the

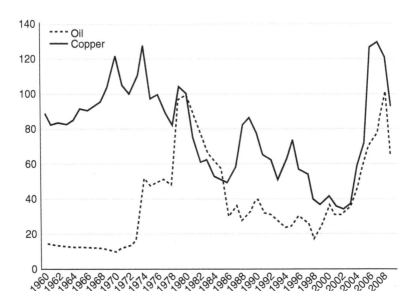

*Figure 12.3* Evolution of the average annual crude oil and copper prices, 1960–2008
(1980 = 100) (source: Oil prices ($/tonne) provided by *BP Statistical Review
of World Energy*, June 2010, London, UK. 1945–83 Arabian Light posted at
Ras Tanura. 1984–2009 Brent dated. Copper prices ($/tonne) are estimated
from the Annual Average US Producer Copper Price which diverged only
marginally in the longer run with prices set at the London Metal Exchange).

initial acceleration, and despite the subsequent negative shocks, which explains
Indonesia's success (see Hausmann *et al.* 2005). Vice versa, no copper boom so
far has turned the tide of the Congo's economic downturn, even though each
commodity boom fuels such hopes.

To sum up, the story of the divergence goes beyond the market outcome of
the leading export sectors involved. This does not mean that the major primary
commodity markets or the timing of their boom and bust cycles play no role in
the divergence. Their role is crucial, but even more important is the political
channel through which their role is mediated (Robinson *et al.* 2006). For
example, even when commodity prices swing in the right, upward, direction and
the terms of trade are advantageous to primary commodity exporters, the effects
of such a boom can still hamper economic development, for example because of
the negative macro-economic effects that stem from a strengthening of the
exchange rate (the so-called Dutch Disease). The problem with such a scenario
is that it can make other export activities uncompetitive, even if it would enhance
technological processing of employment opportunities (Auty 1993: 15). A comparison of Nigeria and Indonesia between 1973 and 1984 immediately shows
that a booming oil business does not automatically imply a booming national
economy. If anything, the oil windfall in the Nigerian case stimulated budget

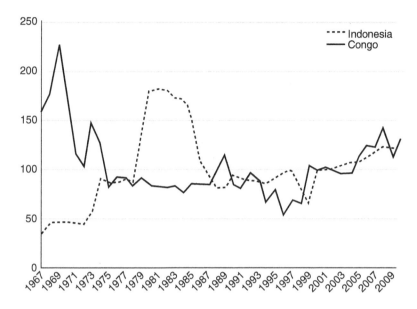

*Figure 12.4* Indonesia's and the Congo's net barter terms of trade, 1967–2009 (sources: Congo 1980–2010: World Bank Development Indicators; Congo 1967–79: Tshishimbi and Glick (1993: Appendix Table 20); Indonesia 1981–2010: World Bank Development Indicators; Indonesia 1967–80: van der Eng (2002: Figure 4); Rosendale (1975: Appendix Table 6)).

Note
Net barter terms of trade index is calculated as the percentage ratio of the export unit value indexes to the import unit value indexes, measured relative to the base year 2000.

deficits, rising inflation, and declining agricultural output per capita – illustrations of economic decline we equally find in the Congo (Lewis 2007). Whether booming prices turn out to be a good or a bad thing has thus much to do with how these prices and rents are dealt with. Vice versa, the sort of commodity bust experienced by the Congo in the 1970s could equally have stimulated government to put its fiscal eggs into more baskets, aiming to diversify the economy and become less dependent on the volatile income base provided by the leading export commodity. This would in practice be stimulated by depreciating exchange rates that make more export industries internationally competitive.

As said above, the resource-dependency risks were fairly dealt with under the Suharto regime given the macro-economic and investment policies that had been put in place after 1965 – putting Indonesia on a path of consistent growth despite negative exogenous shocks in the 1980s and 1990s. A mixture of macro-economic constraints and micro-economic stimuli allowed Indonesia to channel its oil windfalls and avert an overly specialized economy, despite reports on the excesses of crony capitalism. A survey made by Hal Hill in 1992 of Indonesia's provincial development since 1965 concludes that the oil revenues were actively redistributed, keeping regional economic and social inequality (infant mortality, lack of education, poverty) relatively in check. Hill points out how Indonesia's oil boom could have actually operated as a centrifugal force, heightening social and regional inequalities. Instead, during the era of rapid growth

> Indonesia's record of regional economic development was remarkably good; its social achievements were equally impressive; and a strong central government flushed with oil money and a commitment to the uniform development of physical and social infrastructure was a major explanation of this success.
>
> (Hill 1992: 371)

For about a dozen years, the oil boom put a developmental shine on Suharto's New Order while drawing attention away from the far less impressive social, democratic, and human rights record of the regime. Both for the middle and lower classes, Suharto seemed to guarantee that the specter of underdevelopment, rampant inflation, and abject rural poverty which haunted the early postcolonial decade would not return. Once oil prices plummeted in the 1980s, the government unleashed a string of liberalization packages on trade and investment, including the relaxation of restrictions on foreign investment, tariff cuts, and the abolition of non-tariff trade barriers such as import restrictions. Meanwhile, from around 1989 ever more foreign direct investment from Japan and Asian New Industrializing Economies began to flow into labor-intensive manufacturing, which helped the Indonesian economy register strong growth from 1989 to early 1990 and usher in a strong diversification away from primary commodity exports (Ishida 2003). Once these investment flows threatened to shift toward China and Vietnam, the Indonesian government in May 1994 backed down on the restrictions on foreign capital introduced in 1974 and set forth a new policy allowing full ownership by foreign companies.

The financial liberalization was not so carefully guided as the oil windfall had been, and the financial crisis of 1997 hit Indonesia harder than any other Asian country. At that moment, Suharto's critics changed his popular nickname *father of development* into *father of bankruptcy* (Anderson 2008: 40). While the Congo's downward spiral reached its nadir in the warlord economy of the 1990s and Mobutu's overthrow and death in 1997, Indonesia's financial crisis cascaded into a political crisis that led to widespread rioting and eventually to Suharto's resignation in May 1998. GDP contracted by about 15 percent in 1998 before the economy finally began to stabilize in 1999, and it took many years for it to recover. Since about 2004 the economy has been back on track, riding the wave of a global commodity and economic boom that of course has recently come under pressure. All the while, the making of a national economy is still a work in progress. In the words of Hill, Suharto's ousting meant the end of a "hard, authoritarian, corrupt but growth-oriented state," making way for a new type of "messy, weakened, democratic, corrupt state … with the political leadership not yet able to provide a clear and unambiguous commitment to growth" (Hill 2007:

140). A weaker cabinet and presidency created a welcome breathing space for civil society and ushered in a decentralization of power. Resource-rich regions have been the major beneficiaries, however, since they are now allowed to keep most of the locally generated revenue that formerly went to the center (Hill 2007: 157). Partly as a consequence, decentralization has sharpened social and ethnic tensions.

As for the Congo, by November 1973, at the height of the economic boom and amid popular support for Authenticity, the Mobutu government overplayed its hand when it nationalized all businesses with annual revenues of more than Z1 million ($2 million) and all foreign-owned businesses in certain strategic sectors. The more attractive concerns wound up reserved for the top echelon of politicians and army officers, often acting through wives or relatives. Vast disruption of the commercial sector followed, as the Zaïrean *acquéreurs* generally lacked commercial experience, access to credit, and contacts with suppliers (Young 1984: 741). Zaïrianization led to a flight of foreign capital, leaving the copper sector to serve as the only pillar supporting the economy and government. The copper bust that followed in 1974 could thus hardly have come at a less opportune moment, as both state finances and the economy were under a lot of pressure and highly dependent on the copper business, probably even more so than during colonial times. In other words, despite Mobutu's early nationalistic policies, things went fairly well for the Congo as long as copper prices kept booming. But when prices began to drop during 1974 as a consequence of the industrial recession in the developed countries and the large-scale sales of Japanese surplus stocks, the economic situation took a turn for the worse. Government revenues tumbled, and the Mobutu government was obliged to borrow increasingly large sums to cover a growing balance of payments deficit (Radmann 1978: 46). Retrocession was decreed in December 1974, which allowed up to 40 percent and later up to 60 percent foreign ownership in Zairianized businesses. Despite these and other incentives, the collapse of commodity prices, the well-remembered policies of Zaïrianization and the subsequent recession in 1975 kept new investment away. The income shock that the collapse of copper brought about in the 1970s was all the more dramatic because it was not buffered by appropriate insurance and credit mechanisms. This in turn testifies to the local misunderstandings by the Mobutu regime of the world copper industry, underestimating the vulnerability of non-vertically integrated national producers, while overestimating the possible strength of a copper producer's cartel (CIPEC) of exporting countries (Shafer 1983).

In sum, by the mid-1970s the falling price of copper meant a huge income shock for a budget and economy already plagued by a regime that neglected the economic aspect of the post-colonial dual challenge. Almost nothing was done to take fiscal or budgetary measures that could stimulate internal demand or entrepreneurship, promote regional diversification, or at least secure agricultural production. Instead, the regime was in denial, maintaining a ridiculously lean monetary policy which caused inflation to sky-rocket. Stagflation is a serious euphemism when describing the Congolese combination of a completely depressed economy and a veritable flood of all too easily printed money. Mobutu, much like Sukarno, was unable and unwilling to change his nationalist tactics, and soon put the personal before the political or the economic – which he could because of enduring foreign support. Rising inflation, food shortages and institutionalized corruption throughout the body politic caused a collapse of the economy, finally leading to the pillages and civil war of the 1990s.

Instead of benefiting from the employment and technological spill-over effects that stem from attracting investment into manufacturing, the Congo, like so many African countries, missed out on the global shift in manufacturing capabilities toward developing economies during the 1990s.

In the end, the Congo's economic decline was part and parcel of Mobutu's political calculations, which, unfortunately for the Congolese people, proved to be correct as regards the enduring support he received from the West. Only after the dissolution of the Soviet bloc had reduced Mobutu's geopolitical value did he have to accommodate to the growing opposition to his regime. In the early 1990s, the Congo thus entered a new transition period during which Mobutu's position weakened but opposition failed to remove him. It once again took outside – especially Rwandese – support to overthrow Mobutu and help Laurent-Désiré Kabila into power.

## 12.6  Conclusion

The Congo's and Indonesia's different economic trajectories are defined by policy and institutional responses to path-dependent market environments and political economic contexts. This is true for both the colonial and the post-colonial period. In the colonial era, the colonial systems the Dutch and the Belgians devised differed in degree, but the transformation that took place under colonialism was one in kind. Both countries inherited technological, economic, and institutional structures geared toward the development of the regions' comparative advantage in the primary resource business. As a result, both the Congo and Indonesia faced a similar post-colonial developmental challenge to create a political nation and manage, upgrade, and diversify a primary resource-dependent economy. Nevertheless, by the time Suharto and Mobutu seized power around 1965 they enjoyed different conditions when facing this post-colonial challenge. Suharto inherited a country from Sukarno that was relatively politically unified but economically ruined, whereas Mobutu inherited a country whose copper business still fueled economic development but which faced territorial disintegration, above all in copper-rich Katanga. As a consequence, Suharto's New Order policies prioritized economic capacity building that focused on manufacturing and agricultural upgrading. This allowed for a balanced management of the unforeseen oil windfalls of the 1970s and the subsequent oil collapse of the 1980s.

Mobutu, on the other hand, invested heavily in creating political unity around his own personal rule, making the economy instrumental to this purpose – much like Sukarno. Little therefore was done to prepare the country for the negative copper shocks after 1973. Afterwards, Mobutu was unable and unwilling to change his tactics, putting the personal before the political or the economic. In the end, the Congo's economy collapsed and most of its formal institutions and relations of production disintegrated. What did not disintegrate, however, was a strong sense of shared nationhood amongst the Congolese, in sharp contrast to the regional claims for self-determination that are fueling political conflicts in Indonesia. This political divergence is partly a consequence of the economic divergence, given that economic growth heightens regional sensitivities to uneven development whereas economic uncertainties can fuel a desire for an imagined national community. But the question of why Indonesia grew rich yet divided while the Congo in the end became one as it fell apart was also a matter of the options taken by the Suharto and the Mobutu regimes after seizing power, options that were determined by the political and economic situation they faced at that point.

## Notes

1 I thank the participants to at workshops in Utrecht and Antwerp and referees for their many useful remarks on earlier drafts of this chapter. Many thanks also to the organizers/editors for the meticulous organization of the workshops.
2 The role of services in Indonesia's and the Congo's trade profiles is still limited and as such not discussed here. For the period 2003–9, Indonesia's share of services in total trade on average was 10.6 percent, whereas the missing data for the Congo probably hide lower levels of service trade. In comparison, Belgium and the Netherlands have service shares of 15.2 and 16 percent, a couple of percentages below the share of services in global trade, which has fluctuated around 19 percent since 1990. These figures confirm the enduring global importance of merchandise trading to developing economies, which in total control only 25 percent of global service exports (Mattoo *et al.* 2008: 9).
3 Of course official figures are highly problematic in a country where, according to a local source quoted in a report by *Global Witness* (2006: 4), about three-quarters of the copper minerals exported from Katanga are taken out of the country illicitly. If anything, official figures seriously underestimate the natural resources flowing out of the country. However, it is more doubtful whether the *structure* of exports would change dramatically if informal and illegal flows were taken into account.
4 A notorious symptom of this neo-patrimonialism was the apparent unwillingness to distinguish between state finances and personal finances. According to an online research report by the French-based NGO CCFD-Terre Solidaire, Suharto is believed to have embezzled three to seven times more state funds than Mobutu, roughly between $15 billion and $35 billion (Dulin and Merckaert 2009: 202).
5 According to the scale of episode(s) of ethnic violence composed by the Center for Systemic Peace (www.systemicpeace.org), Indonesia suffered much more ethnic violence than the Congo, both during and after Suharto.
6 Given that Belgium basically had only one colony to worry about, the Congo was actually relatively heavily ruled in comparison to other sub-Saharan colonies. As Gann and Duignan point out, the colonial *Force Publique* was one of the largest armies in all of sub-Saharan Africa, larger than the armed forces in the whole of German Africa and the peace-time army maintained by the Union of South Africa, while the Belgian administration was more heavily staffed than the colonial services that administered the British and German colonies (Gann and Duignan 1979: 66, 184). The snapshot of the Congo by Richens (2009) confirms the comparatively intense rule in the Congo,

with an estimated 728 administrators governing approximately 10,981,320 Congolese in 1937. As a result, the Congo ranks eighth in his sample of 33 colonies, preceded only by the French Congo, Swaziland, Gabon, Zambia, Botswana, Senegal, and Benin. But this "comparatively intense rule" in Congo still relied on small numbers.

# References

Abbott, J. (2003) *Developmentalism and Dependency in Southeast Asia: the case of the automotive industry*, London: Routledge.

Anderson, B. (2008) "Exit Suharto: obituary for a mediocre tyrant," *New Left Review*, 50: 27–59.

Arrighi, G. (2002) "The African crisis: world systemic and regional aspects," *New Left Review*, 15(2): 5–36.

Arrighi, G. and Saul, J.S. (1968) "Socialism and economic development in tropical Africa," *The Journal of Modern African Studies*, 6(2): 141–69.

Arrighi, G., Aschoff N., and Scully, B. (2010) "Accumulation by dispossession in its limits: the Southern Africa paradigm revisited," *Studies in Comparative International Development*, 45: 410–38.

Austin, G. (2010) "African economic development and colonial legacies," *Revue Internationale de Politique de Développement*, 1(1): 11–32.

Auty, R.M. (1993) *Sustaining Development in Mineral Economies: the resource curse thesis*, London and New York: Routledge.

Bates, R. (1981) *Markets and States in Sub-Saharan Africa*, Berkeley: University of California Press.

Bayart, J.-F. (2000) "Africa in the world: a history of extraversion," *African Affairs*, 99(395): 217–67.

Becker, C.M. and Craigie, T.-A. (2007) "W. Arthur Lewis in retrospect," *Review of Black Political Economy*, 34: 187–216.

Booth, A. (1998) *The Indonesian Economy in the Nineteenth and Twentieth Centuries: a history of missed opportunities*, London: Macmillan Press.

Booth, A. (2007) *Colonial Legacies: economic and social development in East and Southeast Asia*, Honolulu: University of Hawaii Press.

Bowie, A. and Unger D. (1997) *The Politics of Open Economies: Indonesia, Malaysia, the Philippines, and Thailand*, Cambridge: Cambridge University Press.

Budd, E. (2004) *Democratization, Development, and the Patrimonial State in the Age of Globalization*, Lanham, Md.: Lexington.

Cashin, P. and McDermott, J.C. (2001) "The long-run behavior of commodity prices: small trends and big variability," *IMF Working Paper*, No. 01/68.

Chalmers, I. (1997) "Introduction," in I. Chalmers and V.R. Hadiz (eds.) *The Politics of Economic Development in Indonesia: contending perspectives*, London: Routledge.

Cline, W.R. (2005) *The United States as a Debtor Nation: risks and policy reform*, Washington, DC: Institute for International Economics.

Cooper, F. (2002) *Africa since 1940: the past of the present*, New York: Cambridge University Press.

Cooper, F. (2005) "From colonial state to gatekeeper state in Africa," *The Mario Einaudi Center for International Studies Working Paper Series*, No. 04–05.

De Herdt, T. (2002) "Democracy and the money machine in Zaire," *Review of African Political Economy*, 29(93/94): 445–62.

De Witte, L. (2001) *The Assassination of Lumumba*, London: Verso.

Dove, M.R. and Kammen, D.M. (2001) "Vernacular models of development: an analysis of Indonesia under the 'New Order'," *World Development*, 24(4): 619–39.

Dulin, A. and Merckaert, J. (2009) "Biens mal acquis: à qui profite le crime?," Rapport du CCFD-Terre Solidaire (Comité catholique contre la faim et pour le développement) http://ccfd-terresolidaire.org/BMA/ (accessed March 21, 2010).

Dunning, T. (2005) "Resource dependence, economic performance, and political stability," *Journal of Conflict Resolution* 49: 451–82.

Englebert, P. (2000) *State Legitimacy and Development in Africa*, Boulder, Colo.: Lynne Rienner.

Englebert, P. (2002) "A research note on Congo's nationalist paradox," *Review of African Political Economy*, 29(93/94): 591–4.

Furnivall, J.S. (1967) *Netherlands India: a study of plural economy*, Cambridge: Cambridge University Press.

Gann, L.H. and Duignan, P. (1979) *The Rulers of Belgian Africa, 1884–1914*, Princeton, NJ: Princeton University Press.

Geertz, C. (1963) *Agricultural Involution: the processes of ecological change in Indonesia*, Berkeley and Los Angeles: University of California Press.

Global Witness (2006) "Digging in corruption: fraud, abuse and exploitation in Katanga's copper and cobalt mines," *Global Witness Report*. Online. Available HTTP: www.globalwitness.org (accessed March 21, 2012).

Gondola, C.D. (2002) *The History of Congo*, Westport, Conn.: Greenwood Press.

Hausmann, R., Pritchett, L., and Rodrik, D. (2005) "Growth accelerations," *Journal of Economic Growth*, 10: 303–29.

Herbst, J. (2000) *States and Power in Africa: comparative lessons in authority and control*, Princeton, NJ: Princeton University Press.

Herbst, J. and Mills, G. (2009) "There is no Congo," *Foreign Policy*, March 18.

Hill, H. (1992) "Regional development in a boom and bust petroleum economy: Indonesia since 1970," *Economic Development and Cultural Change*, 40(2): 351–79.

Hill, H. (2007) "The Indonesian economy: growth, crisis, and recovery," *The Singapore Economic Review*, 52(2): 137–66.

Ishida, M. (2003) "Industrialization in Indonesia since the 1970s," IDE Research Paper No. 5. Online. Available www.ide.go.jp (accessed March 21, 2012).

Kano, H. (2008) *Indonesian Exports, Peasant Agriculture and the World Economy, 1850–2000: economic structures in a Southeast Asian state*, Singapore: NUS Press.

Kisangani, E.F. and Bobb, F.S. (2010) *Historical Dictionary of the Democratic Republic of the Congo*, 3rd edn, Lanham, Md., Toronto, and Plymouth: The Scarecrow Press.

Kohli, A. (2009) "Nationalist versus dependent capitalist development: alternate pathways of Asia and Latin America in a globalized world," *Studies in Comparative International Development*, 44: 386–410.

Lewis, P. (2007) *Growing Apart: oil, politics, and economic change in Indonesia and Nigeria*, Ann Arbor: University of Michigan Press.

Lindblad, J.T. (2002) "The late colonial state and economic expansion, 1900–30s," in D. Howard, V.J.H. Houben, J.T. Lindblad, and Thee K.W. (eds.) *The Emergence of a National Economy: an economic history of Indonesia 1800–2000*, Sydney: Allen and Unwin.

Lugard, F. (1922) *The Dual Mandate in British Tropical Africa*, Edinburgh/London: William Blackwood & Sons.

MacGaffey, J. (1987) *Entrepreneurs and Parasites: the struggle for indigenous capitalism in Zaire*, Cambridge: Cambridge University Press.

272   J.-F. Abbeloos

McIntire, S. (2009) *Speeches in World History*, New York: Facts On File.
Maton, J. and Lecomte, H.B.S. (2001) "Congo 1965–99: les espoirs déçus du Brésil africain," *OECD Development Centre Working Paper*, No. 178.
Mattoo, A., Stern R.M., and Zanini, G. (2008) *A Handbook of International Trade in Services*, Oxford: Oxford University Press.
Mitchell, B.R. (1998) *International Historical Statistics: Africa, Asia and Oceania 1750–1993*, Basingstoke: Macmillan.
Ndaywel è Nziem, I. (1998) *Histoire générale du Congo: de l'héritage ancien à la République Démocratique*, Paris/Bruxelles: De Boeck & Larcier.
Nzongola-Ntalaja, G. (1986) *The Crisis in Zaire: myths and realities*, Trenton, NJ: Africa World Press.
Nzongola-Ntalaja, G. (2002) *The Congo from Leopold to Kabila: a people's history*, London: Zed Books.
Peemans, J.P. (1975) "The social and economic development of Zaire since independence: an historical outline," *African Affairs*, 74(295): 148–79.
Perkins, D.H., Radelet S., and Lindauer, D.L. (2006) *Economies of Development*, 6th edn, New York: W.W. Norton.
Radmann, W. (1978) "Nationalization of Zaire copper: from Union Minière to Gécamines," *Africa Today*, 25(4): 25–47.
Raeymaekers, T. (2009) "Who calls the Congo? A response to Jeffrey Herbst and Greg Mills." Online. Available http://rubeneberlein.wordpress.com (accessed March 21, 2012).
Richens, P. (2009) "The economic legacies of the 'thin white line': indirect rule and the comparative development of Sub-Saharan Africa," *London School of Economics Economic History Working Papers*, No. 131/09.
Ricklefs, M.C. (2001) *A History of Modern Indonesia since c. 1200*, 3rd edn, Basingstoke: Palgrave.
Robinson, J.A., Torvik, R., and Verdier, T. (2006) "Political foundations of the resource curse," *Journal of Development Economics*, 79: 447–68.
Robison, R. (2009) *Indonesia: the rise of capital*, Jakarta: Equinox Publishing.
Rock, M.T. (1999) "Reassessing the effectiveness of industrial policy in Indonesia: can the neoliberals be wrong?," *World Development*, 27(4): 691–704.
Rosendale, P. (1975) "The Indonesian terms of trade 1950–73," *Bulletin of Indonesian Economic Studies*, 11(3): 50–80.
Saideman, S.M. (2001) *The Ties that Divide: ethnic politics, foreign policy, and international conflict*, New York: Columbia University Press.
Sarraut, A. (1923) *La Mise en valeur des colonies françaises*, Paris: Payot.
Schrank, D. (2009) "68 million Congolese can't be wrong," *Foreign Policy*, 9 April.
Shafer, M.D. (1983) "Capturing the mineral multinationals: advantage or disadvantage?," *International Organization*, 37(1): 93–119.
Stengers, J. (1989) *Congo mythes et réalités: 100 ans d'histoire*, Paris and Louvain-la-Neuve: Editions Ducolot.
Thomson, A. (2000) *An Introduction to African Politics*, London: Routledge.
Touwen, J. (2001) *Extremes in the Archipelago: trade and economic development in the Outer Islands of Indonesia 1900–42*, Leiden: KITLV Press.
Trefon, T., van Hoyweghen, S. and Smis, S. (2002) "State failure in the Congo: perceptions and realities," *Review of African Political Economy*, 29(93/94): 379–88.
Tshishimbi, W.B. and Glick, P. (1993) "Economic crisis and adjustment in Zaire," *Cornell Food and Nutrition Policy Program*, Monograph 16.

United Nations, Comtrade database, http://comtrade.un.org./db/default.aspx (accessed March 1, 2012).

United Nations, UNCTAD Statistics, http://unctad.org/en/Pages/Statistics.aspx (accessed March 1, 2012).

van der Eng, P. (1996) *Agricultural Growth in Indonesia: productivity change and policy impact since 1880*, London: Macmillan.

van der Eng, P. (2002) "Indonesia's growth experience in the twentieth century: evidence, queries, guesses." Online. Available www.iisg.nl/research/ecgrowtheng.pdf (accessed March 21, 2012).

van Reybrouck, D. (2010) *Congo. Een geschiedenis*, Amsterdam: De Bezige Bij.

Vanthemsche, G. (2007). *Congo. De Impact van de Kolonie op België*, Tielt: Lannoo.

Willame, J.-C. (1972) *Patrimonialism and Political Change in the Congo*, Stanford, Calif.: Stanford University Press.

Woo, W.T. and Nasution, A. (1989) "Indonesian economic policies and their relation to external debt management," in J.D. Sachs and S.M. Collins (eds.) *Developing Country Debt and Economic Performance Volume 3: country studies – Indonesia, Korea, Philippines, Turkey*, Chicago and London: The University of Chicago Press.

World Bank, World Development Indicators Database, http://data.worldbank.org/datacatalog/world-development-indicators (accessed March 1, 2012).

Young, C. (1984) "Zaire, Rwanda and Burundi," in J.D. Fage and R. Oliver (eds.) *The Cambridge History of Africa Volume 8: from c. 1940 to c. 1975*, Cambridge: Cambridge University Press.

Young, C. (1994) "Zaire: the shattered illusion of the integral state," *The Journal of Modern African Studies*, 32(2): 247–63.

# Conclusion

*Ewout Frankema and Frans Buelens*

This study set out to explore how two distinct systems of colonial exploitation, in the Belgian Congo and in the Netherlands Indies, have affected the long-term course of economic development in the two countries into the post-independence era. To what extent can their post-colonial economic divergence be explained by differences in their colonial exploitation? Before we offer our main conclusions, we should acknowledge that colonial legacies only have a long-term impact in *interaction* with post-colonial developments. It is tempting to trace the post-colonial divergence of Indonesia and the Congo back in time and interpret the variation in colonial legacies as the explanation for a known outcome. However, reading history backward opens up the trap of determinism and downplays the potential of human agency to address current development problems. As Abbeloos has argued (Chapter 12), one may seriously question whether Suharto would have survived politically for over 30 years if his program of growth, development, and equity (*Trilogi Pembangunan*) had not been supported by booming oil prices in the 1970s. Similarly, it is questionable whether Mobutu's rule would have become so destructive if copper prices had not collapsed in the 1970s and remained low until the end of the twentieth century. And what if Lumumba had not been murdered and Mobutu had not entered the scene in the first place?

A second trap is specific to the selection of our comparative cases. The Congo offers one of the worst-case scenarios of post-colonial collapse one can imagine. Compared with this disaster, one may evaluate the Indonesian experience as a highly successful example of post-colonial development, whereas in a broader Asian perspective it is perhaps best described as a moderate success. This points to a more general concern not to take these comparative cases as a model by which to assess overall divergence in economic performance between Africa and Asia in the post-1960 era. Although there are good reasons to believe that some aspects concerning the formation of the colonial state, the fiscal system, the education system, and the specific nature of rural–urban inequality reflect a more general pattern of African–Asian variation, we should also emphasize that differences in demographic development, land tenure systems, and industrialization during the colonial era were probably as large *within* Africa and Asia, as they were between the two regions as a whole.

These disclaimers do not undermine the basic rationale for this study, however. There were striking similarities in the exploitative nature of Dutch and Belgian rule in the tropics and notable differences in the post-colonial economic development record. The colonial institutional framework implemented by the Dutch and the Belgians was, from its very inception to its dissolution, primarily designed to facilitate the extraction of valuable tropical crops and mineral resources. These institutions were conducive to colonial investments in local economies that turned out to be extremely profitable for the metropole. During the mid-nineteenth century Dutch taxpayers, suffering unbearable levels of public debt service, were bailed out to a considerable degree by the remittances from the Cultivation System. In Belgium the shareholders of the major mining, industrial, and holding companies particularly grew rich from the exploitation of the Congo's natural resources and indigenous labor force. The concessions handed out by Leopold (and later by the Belgian colonial state) reinforced Belgium's industrial competitiveness with a large range of lucrative monopolies. As Exenberger and Hartmann (Chapter 1) and Thee (Chapter 2) have shown, both the Belgians and the Dutch used large-scale violence to break local resistance and pursue their political and economic interests.

What then distinguished these cases of colonial exploitation? Taking all the 12 chapters together, we identify four major categories of variation on the eve of independence. These four categories can be related to four key differences in the historical evolution of colonial rule. In Figure C.1 we connect the evolutionary characteristics to the initial conditions at independence in order to organize the remainder of our discussion. Of course, one should not take this summary

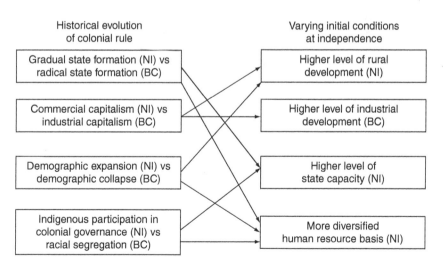

*Figure C.1* Argumentation scheme linking the historical evolution of colonial rule to varying initial conditions for economic development at the eve of independence in the Congo and Indonesia.

scheme as an encompassing explanation, nor do we claim that we cover everything that has been brought forward in this book. We like to think of this scheme as a roadmap showing the main arteries across a vast landscape of causal connections.

Anne Booth (Chapter 3) has argued that the system of colonial exploitation in the Netherlands Indies was more conducive to the commercial development of the rural subsistence sector than in the Belgian Congo. As both Thee (Chapter 2) and Booth (Chapter 3) have shown, the Cultivation System uprooted the traditional organization of land and labor, especially in the Javanese countryside, but it also stimulated investments in the agricultural export sector resulting in diversification of production and the adoption of new technologies in the cash crop and food crop sectors. Exenberger and Hartmann (Chapter 1) have made it clear that such developmental consequences of rural exploitation, whether they were intended or not, were absent under Leopold's system of "Raubwirtschaft," which was an extremely aggressive type of exploitation, characterized by short-term profit maximization objectives under virtually lawless conditions. Clement (Chapter 4) has shown in detail how large-scale land alienation during the Leopoldian era inhibited the development of the rural subsistence sector along the lines witnessed in the Netherlands Indies in the years after 1908.

The demographic collapse in the Congo, whether it was primarily caused by the spread of European diseases or the atrocities committed by the Force Publique in support of the wild rubber scheme, had a devastating impact on the production of food crops. It interrupted traditional divisions of labor, destabilized indigenous trading networks, destroyed entire villages and caused widespread dislocation of people. Although we lack hard evidence, it is very unlikely that the partial depopulation of the Congo basin generated a "Malthusian" effect on productivity in the long term. Yes, in post-plague Western Europe the economic recovery in the late fourteenth century was supported by higher rising land and labor productivity levels, but in the Congo land had never been a scarce resource. As Houben and Seibert (Chapter 8) have pointed out, the colonial response to the potentially strong bargaining position of rural households with regard to their labor allocation was to increase coercion and close the land frontier where possible, rather than to stimulate the development of a free wage labor market. According to Buelens and Cassimon (Chapter 11) basic living conditions probably improved after 1920, especially in the main urban areas, but the colonial state kept treating the rural smallholder sector as a subsidiary to the development of the mining industry and schemes to revolutionize the indigenous peasantry had little effect.

Clarence-Smith (Chapter 9) has offered a powerful example of how the relative neglect of the indigenous subsistence sector played out in the long-term development of the rubber economy. After all, both colonies have been world market leaders in rubber at some point in time. However, whereas in the Netherlands Indies the plantation sector received increasing competition from indigenous smallholders who gained a significant proportion of total rubber production, in the Congo the export of tropical cash crops remained monopolized by foreign-owned plantation companies. The cash crop revolutions that occurred in various parts of West Africa (Ghana, cocoa; Nigeria, palm oil; Senegal, peanuts) and Central Africa (Uganda, cotton) indicate that the lack of smallholder initiative is not a typical Africa–Asia distinction, on the contrary. The suppression of Congolese entrepreneurship in the countryside was a direct result of colonial institutions favoring the exploitation of the Congo's mineral riches and protecting the interests of European plantation firms.

The case of rubber nicely illustrates the notable difference in the nature of capitalist development in the two colonies, two types of capitalism that shaped the colonial legacies in distinctive ways. In the Netherlands Indies the approach of the colonial state was historically rooted in mercantilist trade policies, which were transformed into a more liberal variant of commercial capitalism during the second half of the nineteenth century. Notwithstanding the direct intervention in the production structures of the Indonesian village economy by the introduction of forced cultivation schemes, the system of colonial exploitation was primarily designed to expand and consolidate international trade in tropical cash crops such as sugar, coffee, tobacco, and rubber. This system favored the participation of indigenous entrepreneurs and the use of indigenous technologies as long as it was consistent with the rent-seeking objectives of the colonial power. Rural development strengthened the fiscal backbone of the colonial state, supported the development of financial services, and created linkages to various other service industries which were developed partly by Europeans and partly by Indonesians and Chinese.

Nevertheless, GDP per capita estimates indicate that the Congo in 1960 was, on the whole, richer than Indonesia. The income difference can be fully ascribed to the rapid growth of the Congo's industrial complex, in which mining activities stimulated the emergence of new manufacturing industries and commercial services and a rapid development of the transport infrastructure (railways). The growth of the Congo's industry was impressive. With the exception of South Africa, there exists no comparable case in colonial Africa. Buelens and Cassimon (Chapter 11) have argued that this industrial basis opened up new opportunities for a long-term path of structural economic change and innovation-led growth. However, the fundamental weakness of the system was that the adopted model of industrial capitalist development did not consider indigenous involvement as a crucial factor for long-term sustainability. Belgian industrial capitalism differed from Dutch commercial capitalism in that production factors and investments were almost exclusively controlled by foreign industrial enterprises. Mining operations and complementary manufacturing industries depended crucially on imported technology, and generated few spill-overs toward indigenous rural production techniques. The differences in the organization of colonial extraction, which were amplified by the higher potential of mineral extraction in the Congo, induced a different nature of indigenous stakeholdership. The Congolese were involved in the colonial economy, but first and foremost as a source of raw labor, and only later as a potential source of skilled labor. Labor mobilization policies in the Congo were detrimental to the sustainability of the rural subsistence sector, as they depleted the village economy of the young adult male labor force.

In the Netherlands Indies rapid demographic growth and access to an unlimited supply of indentured Asian migrants released the pressure on rural labor and resulted in less pronounced rural–urban inequalities. Lindblad's contribution (Chapter 10) has suggested that the agrarian-commercial focus of the colonial economy left the potential for an earlier industrial transformation on the basis of foreign capital investment unutilized. Lindblad's case study of Unilever, a British–Dutch company operating in palm oil-related industries in both Indonesia and the Congo, reveals the successes of a soap factory catering for both the domestic and the international market. In general, however, Dutch industrial entrepreneurs were reluctant to invest in the colony and the colonial state never developed a serious industrial policy. Indeed, this stood in sharp contrast to the "development model" applied in the Belgian Congo from the 1920s onwards.

The substantial variation in state capacity levels that have been observed in various chapters underscores the different social and political relationships between Europeans and indigenous peoples in both colonies. As Wahid (Chapter 5) and Gardner (Chapter 6) have demonstrated, the fiscal foundation of the state administration in the Netherlands Indies was more diversified and better resistant to world market shocks, despite the severe blows cast upon the government budgets of both colonies during the 1930s depression. The Dutch managed to engage indigenous elites and Chinese middlemen in their revenue collection effort by the auctioning of tax farms for a wide range of productive and consumer activities. The success of the tax farm system, as discussed in detail by Wahid, by itself testifies to the different degree of commercialization of the indigenous economy. The stronger revenue basis of the Netherlands Indies, in turn, allowed the Dutch to experiment with rudimentary forms of public services in health care – a topic which has not received the attention it deserves in this study – and education, from the mid-nineteenth century onwards.

If anything, it has become clear that the peculiar design of the Congo Free State hampered the long-term development of a solid fiscal basis. As both Clement (Chapter 4) and Gardner (Chapter 6) have argued, the absence of trade taxation implied that the state had to generate revenues in unconventional ways. The effects of land sales have already been discussed. Added to this were the effects of heavy poll taxes in order to enforce wage labor from non-monetarized sectors and increase the spending capacity of the colonial state. The large discrepancy between the weak revenue basis and the enormous administrative challenges flowing from control over such a vast territory resulted in a structural reluctance to government involvement in the provision of basic public services. Not only was education left in the hands of Protestant and Catholic missionaries, key parts of the administration were initially also run by private companies and missionary societies. Gardner has shown that after 1908 the Belgian Congo succeeded in raising its per capita revenue levels, rapidly catching up with and even overtaking neighboring African colonies, but the overreliance on mining receipts made the colonial state, and the independent Congo state for that matter, exceptionally vulnerable to the volatility of world markets for minerals and tropical cash crops, and in particular the international demand for copper.

The longer period of the Dutch physical presence in the East Indies, and the more gradual expansion of their territorial control over the archipelago, created a larger time-frame for both the establishment of a fine-grained fiscal structure and for fundamental reforms of colonial policies. The historical connection of the Dutch republic with the East Indies, dating back to the conception of the Dutch East India Company (VOC), ensured that colonial policy reforms were fueled by stronger feedback mechanisms from public debates in the Netherlands. The Belgian state inherited a territory in 1908 ruled by an amalgam of private companies, missionaries, army officers, and local chiefs without a clear centre of authority. In fact, few Belgians at that time realized that they were in possession of an overseas territory. Indeed, it seems as if in all stages of colonial rule, from outright exploitation under the Cultivation System, through the liberal reforms and the civil emancipation process of the Ethical Policy era, the reform agenda of the Netherlands Indies government was a few steps ahead. In the Netherlands a public – or at least a political elitist – awareness that the welfare of the indigenous population was vital to the sustainability of the colonial project slowly arose in the late nineteenth century; a similar public awareness emerged only after World War II in Belgium. Only after the war did the Belgian government begin to challenge the iron grip of the Catholic church on important social institutions such as the education system, while the colonial state in the Netherlands Indies had already settled this struggle to its advantage by the late nineteenth century.

The unique conception of the Congolese state had thus thrown up barriers of vested interests against the policy reforms necessary for a balanced path of political and socio-economic modernization. However, the biggest obstruction to fundamental reforms of the exploitative system was the deep-seated paternalist mentality which led to the practice of racial segregation. This was only slightly relaxed in the late 1950s, the final years of Belgian rule in the Congo. The encompassing application of the color bar in all spheres of the colonial society implied that the indigenous population had no access to higher political management levels, no access to the top positions in the army, and no access to management positions in international companies operating in the Congo. In the long run this meant a waste of human potential, a neglect of education and training, and an increasingly expensive system of governance, since Europeans demanded salaries each of which would have easily sufficed to employ 10 to 20 Congolese in their place. The color bar also implied that only a strategy of coercion, rather than negotiation or persuasion, was suited to set the course of colonial economic and political affairs. This required huge investments in the maintenance of the Force Publique, the linchpin of the system, money which had so many more productive alternative uses.

Of course the idea of racial superiority and paternalist mentalities long dominated the colonial discourse in the Netherlands Indies as well. But the development of the education system in the Netherlands Indies reveals that the opportunities for social mobility were not constrained to a similar degree as in the Congo. As pointed out by Frankema (Chapter 7), missionaries virtually monopolized the school system in the Congo, while the state took responsibility for education in the Netherlands Indies. Primary school enrollment rates spread faster in the Belgian Congo, but educational expenditure was much higher in the Netherlands Indies. How far this imbalance affected the quality of primary education is hard to say, although it probably only produced a difference in degree. Both education systems were known for their poor quality. Yet the crucial distinction was that the color bar inhibited the development of higher levels of education in the Congo. In the Netherlands Indies the opportunities for social mobility via Western-style primary, secondary, and tertiary education were limited, but they existed nevertheless. These opportunities proved to be essential for the emergence of an indigenous intellectual elite, including later independence leaders, who steered Indonesia through the turmoil of war and economic crises into the era of independence. The earlier and more pronounced rise of indigenous schooling movements with outspoken emancipatory objectives again testifies that the unequal racial power relations in the two colonies were perceived, legitimized, confirmed, and challenged in different ways. In the Congo there were fewer sparks of indigenous political consciousness and where they flared up they were immediately extinguished.

Congolese independence was the outcome of a swift political revolution that very few had anticipated just a few months before it happened. Belgium's overreaction to a small-scale army mutiny set a spiral of revolts and violence in motion which prevented a "normal" transition of power and responsibilities. The hard ceilings blocking indigenous political and civil emancipation left the Congo decapitated at independence. The lack of solidified structures of governance created a major power vacuum. Yes, the Congo possessed a more industrialized and capital-intensive economy than Indonesia in 1960, but the sustainability of its economic power was inextricably connected to foreign capital, foreign know-how, foreign technology, and the blessings of favorable international copper prices. As foreign investors withdrew and copper prices started to tumble, the industrial complex on which the Congolese economy floated was bound to collapse.

The Dutch bequeathed Indonesia a corrupted governance structure, but it was a structure. It was corrupt, but it was tested, tried, and rooted in indigenous customs. Indonesia gained independence after fighting first the Japanese (1942–5) and then the Dutch (1945–9). The Dutch completely misunderstood that for the Indonesians the world had changed so dramatically during the 1930s and 1940s, that it was inconceivable to "restore" previous colonial relations. Yet this prolonged struggle drew the Indonesians together. The fact that Indonesia survived a range of political and economic crises in the post-independence era as a nation-state and was capable of resisting the centrifugal forces of what had emerged from a "forced union of islands," testifies to the governance qualities of its post-independence political leaders. These qualities eventually enabled the Suharto government to tap into a fertile breeding ground for labour-intensive industrialization and rapid welfare growth. Indonesia has now become a self-reliant and assertive world power, making a relatively successful democratic transition, while the Congolese people find themselves trapped in a state of political chaos, endemic violence, and extreme poverty.

# Index

Page numbers in *italics* denote tables, those in **bold** denote figures. Please note that page numbers relating to notes will be denoted by the letter 'n'. The Congo includes the Belgian Congo, Congo Free State, Congo Region, Democratic Republic of the Congo and Zaïre, while Indonesia refers to Indonesia (post-World War II), Indian Archipelago and Netherlands Indies. Indonesia and Netherlands Indies have been grouped together for ease of access.